Thinking Arabic Translation

Thinking Arabic Translation is an indispensable book for linguists who want to develop their Arabic-to-English translation skills. Clear explanations, discussions, examples and exercises enable students to acquire the skills necessary for tackling a broad range of translation problems.

The book has a practical orientation, addressing key issues for translators, such as cultural differences, genre, and revision and editing. It is a book on translation method, drawing on a range of notions from linguistics and translation theory to encourage thoughtful consideration of possible solutions to practical problems.

This new edition includes:

- new material in almost all chapters
- a new chapter on parallelism
- two new chapters on technical translation: botanical and Islamic finance texts
- new and up-to-date examples from all types of translation, covering broad issues that have emerged in the Arab world in recent years
- texts drawn from a wide variety of writing types, including newspapers, prose fiction, poetry, tourist material, scientific texts, financial texts, recipes, academic writing, constitutions and political speeches
- at least three full-length practical translation exercises in each chapter to complement the discussions and consolidate learning.

In addition to the updated *Tutor's Handbook,* a *Supplement*, containing textual material and practical exercises aimed at further developing the translation issues discussed in the main text, and a *Tutor's Handbook to the Supplement*, are available at www.routledge.com/cw/dickins.

Thinking Arabic Translation is key reading for advanced students wishing to perfect their language skills or considering a career in translation.

James Dickins is Professor of Arabic at the University of Leeds, UK.

Ian Higgins, who, with the late **Sándor Hervey**, originated the Thinking Translation series, is Honorary Senior Lecturer in Modern Languages at the University of St Andrews.

Titles of related interest

For a full list of titles in the *Thinking Translation* series, please visit www.routledge.com

Thinking Italian Translation
A Course in Translation Method: Italian to English
Sàndor Hervey, Ian Higgins, Stella Cragie and Patrizia Gambarotta

Russian Translation
Theory and Practice
Edna Andrews and Elena Maksimova

Routledge Course in Japanese Translation
Yoko Hasegawa

Routledge Encyclopedia of Translation Studies
Second Edition
Mona Baker and Gabriela Saldanha

Arabic-English-Arabic Legal Translation
Hanem El-Farahaty

In Other Words
A Coursebook on Translation
Mona Baker

Becoming a Translator
An Accelerated Course
Douglas Robinson

The Scandals of Translation
Lawrence Venuti

Translation Studies
Susan Bassnett

Thinking Arabic Translation

A course in translation method:
Arabic to English

Second edition

**James Dickins, Sándor Hervey
and Ian Higgins**

Routledge
Taylor & Francis Group

LONDON AND NEW YORK

Second edition published 2017
by Routledge
2 Park Square, Milton Park, Abingdon, Oxon OX14 4RN

and by Routledge
711 Third Avenue, New York, NY 10017

Routledge is an imprint of the Taylor & Francis Group, an informa business

First edition published by Routledge 2002

British Library Cataloguing in Publication Data
A catalogue record for this book is available from the British Library

Library of Congress Cataloging-in-Publication Data
Names: Dickins, J. (James), author. | Hervey, Sándor G. J., author. |
    Higgins, Ian, author.
Title: Thinking Arabic translation : a course in translation method :
    Arabic to English / James Dickins, Sándor Hervey and Ian Higgins.
Description: Second edition. | Abingdon, Oxon ; New York :
    Routledge, 2016. | Includes bibliographical references, glossary, and index.
Identifiers: LCCN 2016013513 | ISBN 9780415705622 (hardback : alk. paper) |
    ISBN 9780415705639 (pbk. : alk. paper) | ISBN 9781315471570 (ebk)
Subjects: LCSH: Arabic language—Translating into English.
Classification: LCC PJ6403 .D53 2016 | DDC 428/.02927—dc23
LC record available at http://lccn.loc.gov/2016013513

ISBN: 978-0-415-70562-2 (hbk)
ISBN: 978-0-415-70563-9 (pbk)
ISBN: 978-1-315-47157-0 (ebk)

Typeset in Times New Roman
by Apex CoVantage, LLC

Contents

Acknowledgements

First edition

We owe a debt of gratitude to many people without whose help and advice this book could not have been written. In particular, we would like to thank Muhammad Al-Fuhaid, Hasan Al-Shamahi, John Bery, Lynne Bery, Tony Burns, Tamara Hervey, Hilary Higgins, Roger Keys, Richard Kimber, Tim Mackintosh-Smith, Dinah Manisty, Salah Niazi, Jenny Shouls, Kid Wan Shum, Paul Starkey, John Steinhardt, Jack Wesson and Emma Westney.

Richard Kimber also gave generously of his time and expertise in helping us produce the camera-ready copy of the book; we are particularly grateful to him for that.

James Dickins acknowledges the help of the University of Durham for granting him study leave from October to December 2000 and unpaid leave of absence from January 2001 to September 2001. He also thanks the Yemen Center for Arabic Studies and its director, Sabri Saleem, for giving him membership to the center while he was completing his work on the book during the academic year 2000–2001 and for making his stay in Yemen so uncomplicated and enjoyable.

Finally, we would like to thank the students of Arabic>English translation over the years at the Centre for Middle Eastern and Islamic Studies, University of Durham. Not only have their positive criticisms of previous versions done a great deal to improve this book, but several of them have also contributed more directly: material from their translation projects is a major source of the translation examples used in the book.

Second edition

James Dickins thanks the University of Leeds for giving him extended study leave, which allowed him to complete the second edition of this book. He also thanks the numerous undergraduate and postgraduate students at the universities of Durham, Salford and Leeds whose insights and positive criticisms since 2002 have been vital to the development of this second edition. He thanks for their particular help Ahmed Elgindy, Tajul Islam, Miranda Morris and Mustapha Sheikh, as well as three anonymous reviewers who provided very useful comments on a previous draft.

Introduction

This book is a practical course in translation from Arabic to English. It grew out of a course piloted at the University of Durham in the 1990s and has its origins in *Thinking Translation,* a course in French–English translation by Sándor Hervey and Ian Higgins, first published in 1992. The second edition of *Thinking Arabic Translation* draws on a dozen years' further experience of teaching Arabic>English translation, as well as refinements to the treatment of issues, such as cultural transposition, compensation and genre, in subsequent editions of *Thinking French Translation, Thinking German Translation, Thinking Spanish Translation* and *Thinking Italian Translation.* This book also contains topics not found in the versions for European languages, dealing with various forms of repetition and parallelism in Arabic, as well as a chapter on metaphor, which poses specific challenges in Arabic>English translation.

Can translation be taught? This question is asked surprisingly often – sometimes even by good translators, whom one would expect to know better. Certainly, as teachers of translation know, some people are naturally better at it than others. In this, aptitude for translation is no different from aptitude for any other activity: teaching and practice help anyone, including the most gifted, to perform at a higher level. Even Mozart had music lessons.

Most of us, however, are not geniuses. Here again, anyone who has taught the subject knows that a structured course will help most students to become significantly better at translation – sometimes good enough to earn their living at it. This book offers just such a course. Its progressive exposition of different sorts of translation problems is accompanied by plenty of practice in developing a rationale for solving them. It is a course not in translation theory but in translation method, encouraging thoughtful consideration of possible solutions to practical problems. Theoretical issues do inevitably arise, but the aim of the course is to develop proficiency in the method, not to investigate its theoretical implications. The theoretical notions that we apply are borrowed eclectically from translation theory and linguistics, solely with this practical aim in mind. (If you are interested in translation theory, Munday 2016 provides an extremely clear introduction, while more detailed accounts are given in Gentzler 2001 and Pym 2009.)

If this is not a course in translation theory or linguistics, it is not a language-teaching course, either. The focus is on how to translate. It is assumed that the student already has a good command of Arabic and is familiar with the proper use of dictionaries and, where appropriate, databases. The course is therefore aimed at final-year undergraduates and at postgraduates or others seeking an academic or professional qualification in translation. That said, the analytical attention given to a wide variety of texts means that students do learn a lot of Arabic – and probably a fair bit of English, too.

This last point is important. While our main aim is to improve quality in translation, it must be remembered that this quality requires the translator to have an adequate command of English as well as Arabic. Assuming that this is the case, translator training normally focuses on translation into the mother tongue, because higher quality is achieved in that direction than in translating into a foreign language. Hence the almost exclusive focus on translation into English in this course. By its very nature, however, the course is also useful for Arab students seeking to improve their skills in translation into English: this is a staple part of English studies throughout the Arab world, and *Thinking Arabic Translation* offers a new methodology and plenty of practical work in this area.

The course has a progressive structure, with an overall movement from general genre-independent issues to specific genre-dependent ones. Chapters 1–5 deal with the fundamental issues, options and alternatives of which a translator must be aware: translation as process, translation as product, cultural issues in translation and the nature and crucial importance of compensation in translation, as well as techniques for revising and **editing** that are an integral part of any polished translation. Chapter 6 provides an introduction to genre. Chapters 7–13 deal with translation issues relating to key linguistic notions: semantics (denotative and connotative meaning, and metaphor) and the formal properties of text (considered on six levels of **textual variables** from the phonic/graphic to the intertextual), as well as a consideration of parallelism (Chapter 11), which involves both grammatical and semantic, and sometimes also phonic, considerations. Chapter 14 deals with metaphor. Chapter 15 deals with stylistic issues (register, sociolect, dialect). Chapters 16–19 focus on specific technical areas in which Arabic>English translators might do professional work: medicine, botany, constitutions and Islamic finance. Chapter 20 looks at consumer-oriented translation, with a focus on tourist brochures. Finally, Chapter 21 provides a summary and conclusion, together with information about pursuing a career as a professional translator.

Chapter by chapter, then, the student is progressively trained to ask, and to answer, a series of questions that apply to any text given for translation. Preeminent among these are: What is the purpose of my translation, and what are the salient features of this text? No translation is produced in a vacuum, and we stress throughout the course that the needs of the target audience and the requirements of the person commissioning the translation are primary factors in translation decisions. For this same reason, we always include a translation brief in the assignment. As for the salient features of the text, these are what add up to its specificity as typical or atypical of a particular genre or genres. Once its genre membership, and therefore its purpose, has been pinned down, the translator can decide on a strategy for meeting the translation brief. The student's attention is kept focused on this issue by the wide variety of genres found in the practicals: in addition to scientific, legal and consumer-oriented texts, students are asked to work on various sorts of journalistic, literary and academic texts, political speeches, tourist brochures, etc.

The sorts of questions that need to be asked in determining the salient features of any text are listed in the schema of textual matrices at the end of this Introduction. The schema amounts to a checklist of potentially relevant kinds of textual features. On the whole, the features in the schema of textual matrices are presented in the order in which they arise in the course. However, there are two exceptions. First, metaphor is included within the semantic matrix, where it most coherently belongs (its placing at Chapter 14, after the chapters on the formal properties of text, is motivated by the fact that metaphor is a complex issue, with a bearing on generic issues, discussed in chapters 6 and 13, as well as semantic ones). Second, as a reminder of the prime importance of purpose and genre, the genre matrix is placed at the top of the schema.

Apart from genre, the schema of textual matrices outlines the investigation, in chapters 4, 6–10 and 12–13, of translation issues raised by textual features. Compensation, the subject of Chapter 5, is not a textual feature and so does not figure in the schema. Parallelism, the subject of Chapter 11, is complex, involving both grammatical and semantic, and in some cases also phonic, features and thus belongs to more than one category in the schema. Students are advised to refer to the schema whenever they tackle a practical: it is a progressive reminder of what questions to ask of the text set for translation.

While the course systematically builds up a methodological approach, we are not trying to 'mechanize' translation by offering some inflexible rule or recipe. Very much the opposite: translation is a creative activity, and the translator's personal responsibility is paramount. We therefore emphasize the need to recognize options and alternatives, the need for rational discussion and the need for decision making. Each chapter is intended for class discussion at the start of the corresponding seminar, and many of the practicals are best done by students working in small groups. This is to help students keep in mind that, whatever approach the translator adopts, it should be self-aware and methodical.

The course requires an academic timetable lasting at least twenty weeks over the span of one year, with a minimum of two hours per week of class time. Assuming students have read the chapter before the seminar and done the practical(s) to be completed in the seminar, each chapter needs at least two hours of seminar time – up to thirty minutes to discuss the chapter and one-and-one-half hours to do a standard-length translation practical. For a course in which all practicals are attempted, at least four hours per week of seminar time will be needed. Some of the practical work will be done at home – sometimes individually, sometimes in groups – and handed in for assessment by the tutor. How often this is done will be decided by between the tutors and students.

Further materials relating to this course, including the *Tutor's Handbook* and *Supplement,* can be found at http://routledgetextbooks.com/textbooks/_author/thinkingtranslation/. These materials include additional discussion of

Arabic>English translation issues, additional practical materials and further handouts. The materials are particularly suitable for tutors teaching more intensive Arabic>English translation courses of four or more class hours per week. Any comments on this book are welcome, particularly those relating to possible improvements.

We have used several symbols throughout this book, as follows:

{ }	Indicates key elements in source text and/or target text where these might not otherwise be clear.
ø	Indicates zero elements in translation (translation by omission).
bold	When technical or theoretical terms first occur, they are set out in bold type; they are also listed in the Glossary.

SCHEMA OF TEXTUAL MATRICES

QUESTION TO ASK ABOUT THE TEXT	MATRIX OF FEATURES	EXAMPLES OF TYPICAL FEATURES
What genre(s) does this text belong to:	**GENRE MATRIX** (Chapter 5) Genre types:	
	Literary	Short story, etc.
	Religious	Quranic commentary, etc.
	Philosophical	Essay on good and evil, etc.
	Empirical	Scientific paper, balance sheet, etc.
	Persuasive	Law, advertisement, etc.
	Hybrid	Sermon, parody, job contract, etc.
	Oral versus written	Dialogue, song, subtitles, etc.
Are there significant features presenting a choice between:	**CULTURAL MATRIX** (Chapter 3)	
	Exoticism	Wholesale foreignness
	Calque	Idiom translated literally, etc.
	Cultural borrowing	Name of historical movement, etc.
	Communicative translation	Public notices, proverbs, etc.
	Cultural transplantation	Romeo recast as قيس, etc.
Are there significant instances of:	**SEMANTIC MATRIX** (chapters 6, 7, 13)	
	Denotative meaning	Synonymy, etc.
	Connotative meaning:	
	Attitudinal meaning	Hostile attitude to referent, etc.
	Associative meaning	Gender stereotyping of referent, etc.
	Affective meaning	Offensive attitude to addressee, etc.
	Allusive meaning	Echo of proverb, etc.
	Collocative meaning	Collocative clash, etc.
	Reflective meaning	Play on words, etc.
	Metaphorical meaning	Original metaphor, etc.
Are there significant features on the:	**FORMAL MATRIX** (Chapters 8–9, 11–12)	
	Phonic/graphic level	Alliteration, onomatopoeia, etc.
	Prosodic level	Vocal pitch, rhythm, etc.
	Grammatical level:	
	Lexis	Overtones, etc.
	Morphology	Morphological repetition, etc.
	Syntax	Simple versus complex syntax, etc.
	Sentential level	Intonation, subordination, etc.
	Discourse level	Cohesion markers, etc.
	Intertextual level	Pastiche, Quranic allusion, etc.
Are there significant instances of:	**VARIETAL MATRIX** (Chapter 14)	
	Tonal register	Ingratiating tone, etc.
	Social register	Islamist intellectual, etc.
	Sociolect	Urban working class, etc.
	Dialect	Egyptianisms, etc.
	Temporal variety	Classical (pre-modern) usages, etc.

1　Translation as a process

1.1　Basic definitions

An obvious place to begin a translation course is to examine translation as a
process – what it is that the translator actually does. To do this, we must note at
the outset a few basic terms that will be used throughout the course:

Text Any given stretch of speech or writing assumed to make a **coherent**
whole. A minimal text may consist of a single word – for instance, the road
sign قف 'stop' – provided this is construed as an independent message. A
maximal text may run into thousands of pages. An example of a maximal
text in Arabic would be the many volumes of كتاب تاريخ الرسل والملوك by
the classical Islamic writer محمد بن جرير الطبري, sometimes referred to in
English as Tabari's *Annals.* The notion of 'coherent whole' is inherently
vague. So, while Tabari's *Annals* might be said to make a 'coherent whole'
and thus be a text, so might a chapter within Tabari's *Annals,* or even
a section within a chapter. It is thus possible to have larger texts which
themselves contain numerous shorter texts.

Source text (ST) The text requiring translation.

Target text (TT) The text that is a translation of the ST.

Source language (SL) The language in which the ST is spoken or written.

Target language (TL) The language into which the ST is to be translated.

Strategy The translator's overall 'game plan', consisting of a set of **strategic decisions** taken after an initial reading of the ST but before starting
detailed translation.

Strategic decisions The first set of reasoned decisions taken by the translator.
These are taken before starting the translation in detail, in response to the
following questions: What is the message content of this particular ST?
What are its salient linguistic features? What are its principal effects?
What **genre** does it belong to, and what audience is it aimed at? What
are the functions and intended audience of my translation? What are the
implications of these factors? If a choice has to be made among them,
which ones should be given priority?

Decisions of detail Reasoned decisions concerning the specific problems of grammar, **lexis** (vocabulary), etc., encountered in translating particular expressions in their particular contexts. Decisions of detail can only be made in the light of strategy. Naturally, however, problems of detail may arise during translating that raise unforeseen strategic issues and oblige the translator to refine the original strategy somewhat.

With these notions in mind, the translation process can be broken down into two types of activity: understanding an ST and formulating a TT. These do not occur successively but simultaneously; indeed, one often does not even realize that one has imperfectly understood the ST until coming up against a problem in formulating the TT. When this happens, it may be necessary to go back and reinterpret the ST in the light of one's new understanding of it. This reinterpretation sometimes means that the original strategy has to be revised, this **revision** in turn entailing changes to some of the decisions of detail already taken. Nevertheless, it is useful to discuss ST interpretation and TT formulation as different, separable processes.

The component processes of translation are not different from familiar things that all speakers and listeners do every day. Comprehension and interpretation are processes that we all perform whenever we listen to or read a piece of linguistically imparted information. Understanding even the simplest message potentially involves all of our experiential baggage – the knowledge, beliefs, suppositions, inferences and expectations that are the stuff of personal, social and cultural life. Understanding everyday messages is therefore not all that different from what a translator does when first confronting an ST – and it is certainly no less complicated.

In everyday communication, evidence that a message has been understood may come from appropriate practical responses – for example, if someone has asked you for a spoon, and you give them a spoon and not a fork. Or it may come from an appropriate *linguistic* response – such things as returning a greeting correctly, answering a question satisfactorily or filling in a form. None of these are translation-like processes, but they do show that the comprehension and interpretation stage of translation involves a perfectly ordinary everyday activity that simply requires a standard command of the language used.

1.2   Intersemiotic translation

One everyday activity that does resemble translation proper is what Roman Jakobson calls **intersemiotic translation** (Jakobson 1971: 260–266) – that is, translation between two semiotic systems (a semiotic system being a system for communication). 'The green light means go' is an act of intersemiotic translation, as is 'The big hand's pointing to twelve and the little hand's pointing to four, so it's four o'clock.' In each case, there is translation from a non-linguistic communication system (traffic lights, clock face) to a linguistic one. To this extent, everyone is a translator of a sort.

1.3   Intralingual translation

Still more common are various sorts of linguistic response to linguistic stimuli, which are also very like translation proper, even though they actually take place within a single language. These sorts of processes are what Jakobson (ibid.) calls **intralingual translation**.

To understand its major implications, we will consider the two extremes of intralingual translation. Consider the following scenario. Jill is driving Jack through the narrow streets of a small town. A policeman steps out and stops them. As he leans in to speak to Jill, she can see over his shoulder that, farther on, a lorry has jackknifed and blocked the street. At one extreme of intralingual translation lies the kind of response typified in this exchange:

POLICEMAN: There's been an accident ahead, Madam – I'm afraid you'll have to turn left down St Mary's Lane here; the road's blocked.
JILL: Oh, OK. Thanks.
JACK: What did he say?
JILL: We've got to turn left.

The policeman's essential message is 'Turn left'. But he has been trained in public relations, and he does not want to sound brusque. So he starts by mollifying the driver with a partial explanation, 'There's been an accident,' and then presents his instruction somewhat apologetically, by introducing it with 'I'm afraid'. 'St Mary's Lane' even implies a shared sense of local solidarity with the motorist; but the policeman also adds 'here', in case Jill does not in fact know the town. Finally, he completes his explanation.

When Jack asks what the policeman has said, however, Jill separates the gist of the policeman's message from the circumstantial details and the tonal subtleties and reports it in her own words. This is an example of a type of intralingual translation that we shall call **gist translation**. The example also shows two other features that intralingual translation shares with translation proper. First, Jill's is not the only gist translation possible. For instance, she might have said, 'We've got to go down here.' Amongst other things, this implies that at least one of the people in the car does not know the town: the street name would be of no help in identifying which road is meant. A third possibility is, 'We've got to go down St Mary's Lane'; if Jack and Jill do know the town, the gist of the policeman's message is accurately conveyed.

The other feature shared by intralingual translation and translation proper is that the situation in which a message is expressed crucially affects both how it is expressed and how it is received. By 'situation' here we mean a combination of three elements:

1   Linguistic context (e.g. the policeman's words and Jack's question).
2   Non-linguistic circumstances (such as being stopped in a car and having to take a diversion).

3   The experiential baggage of the participants (knowing or not knowing the town, familiarity or unfamiliarity with conventions for giving and receiving instructions, liking or disliking the police, etc.).

There are so many variables in the message situation that it is impossible to predict what the gist translation will be or how the addressee will take it. For example, Jill might simply have said, 'Turn left', a highly economical way of reporting the gist – no bad thing when she is concentrating on driving. However, depending on how she says it, and how Jack receives it, it could give the impression that the policeman was rude.

Another reason why 'Turn left' could sound rude is that, grammatically, it looks like direct speech – an imperative – whereas all Jill's other gist translations are clearly *in*direct speech (or 'reported speech'). All translation might be regarded as a form of indirect speech, inasmuch as it does not repeat the ST but reformulates it. Yet most TTs, like 'Turn left', mask the fact that they are indirect speech by omitting such markers as 'The author says that . . .' or modulation of point of view (as in substituting 'we' for 'you' or 'he' for 'I'). As a result, it is very easy for reformulation to consciously or unconsciously become distortion, either because the translator misrepresents the ST or because the reader misreads the TT or both.

Gist translation, like any translation, is thus a process of *interpretation*. This is seen still more clearly if we take an example at the opposite extreme of intralingual translation. Jill might easily have interpreted the policeman's words by expanding them. For example, she could build on an initial gist translation as follows:

> We've got to go down St Mary's Lane – some fool's jackknifed and blocked the High Street.

Here, she puts two sorts of gloss on the policeman's message: she adds details that he did not give (the jackknifing, the name of the street) and her own judgement of the driver. We shall use the term **exegetic translation** to denote a translation that explains and elaborates on the ST in this way. The inevitable part played by the translator's experiential baggage becomes obvious in exegetic translation, for any exegesis by definition involves explicitly invoking considerations from outside the text in one's reading of it – here, the jackknifed lorry, Jill's knowledge of the town and her attitude towards other road users.

An exegetic translation can be shorter than the ST, as in this example, but exegesis is usually longer and can easily shade into general observations triggered by the ST but not really explaining it. Knowing the town as she does, Jill might easily have gone on like this:

> That's the second time in a month. The street's just too *narrow* for a thing that size.

The explanation added in the second **sentence** is still about as admissible as exegetic translation, but it does go much farther than the policeman's statement.

As these examples suggest, it is sometimes hard to keep gist translation and exegetic translation apart or to see where translation shades into comment pure and simple. It certainly seems very hard to achieve an ideal **rephrasing**, a halfway point between gist and exegesis that would use terms radically different from those of the ST but add nothing to, and omit nothing from, its message content. Might one say that 'A pulchritudinous neonate' is a rephrasing of 'A beautiful baby'? If it is, it is distinctly inexact: the tone and **connotations** of the two utterances are very different, and 'neonate' and 'baby' can hardly be said to have the same **denotative meaning**.

1.4 Interlingual translation

Just as it is possible to have intralingual gist and exegetic translation, so it is possible to have interlingual translation (i.e. translation proper), which involves gist or exegesis. In Arabic>English translation, translations that involve gisting are most likely to arise where the Arabic ST involves a high degree of repetition of meaning (i.e. **semantic repetition**). Consider the following example (Johnstone 1991: 89–90):

الشعر تعبير وتصوير لمشاعر الشعراء وأفكارهم سواءً كانت التجربة واقعية أو من نسج خيال
الشاعر. وفي كلتا الحالتين فإن التجربة صادقة، لأنه حتى ولو كانت التجربة غير واقعية – أي
خيالية – فإن الشاعر يعيش فيها مدة طويلة قبل أن ينظم شعره يحس فيها نبضات قلبه ويشعرها
تسري في دمائه.

A fairly **literal translation** of this reads as follows (Johnstone 1991: 90):

Poetry is an expression and description of the feelings of poets and their thoughts, whether the experience is real or from the fabric of the poet's imagination. And in both cases, the experience is true, because even if the experience is not real – that is, imaginary – the poet lives in it for a long time before he composes his poetry, sensing it in the pulses of his heart and feeling it flow in his blood. (75 words)

A rather more **idiomatic** translation might read:

Poetry is an expression of the thoughts and feelings of the poet. Whether the experience be real or imaginary, it is true in the sense that the poet has spent a great deal of time experiencing it internally before composing his poetry. (42 words)

Good examples of exegetic translation in various degrees can be found in different English interpretations of the Quran. Consider for example the following three translations of سورة الإخلاص by Rodwell (1909), Al-Hilali and Khan (1997) and Turner (1997) (the translations are presented with corresponding verse numbering to the original; the translation of Al-Hilali and Khan has been slightly amended to omit information that is irrelevant to the current discussion):

بِسم اللَّهِ الرَّحْمَنِ الرَّحِيم
(١) قُلْ هُوَ اللَّهُ أَحَدٌ
(٢) اللَّهُ الصَّمَدُ
(٣) لَمْ يَلِدْ وَلَمْ يُولَدْ
(٤) وَلَمْ يَكُن لَّهُ كُفُوًا أَحَدٌ

Rodwell

In the name of God, the Compassionate, the Merciful

1   SAY: He is God alone:
2   God the eternal!
3   He begetteth not, and He is not begotten
4   And there is none like unto Him.

Al-Hilali and Khan

In the name of Allah, the Most Beneficent, the Most Merciful

1   Say, O Muhammad: He is Allah, (the) One.
2   Allah As-Samad (the Self-Sufficient Master, Whom all creatures need. He neither eats nor drinks).
3   He begets not, nor was He begotten,
4   And there is none co-equal or comparable unto Him.

Turner

In the Name of God, the Compassionate, the Merciful

1   Say: 'My God is One;
2   The cosmos is a manifestation of His eternal names, for He is mirrored in all things in a most subtle manner, and He is free from all wants and needs.
3   He does not beget or produce anything, nor is he begotten or produced by anything
4   And there is nothing in the whole of the cosmos that can be likened to Him.'

Rodwell's translation here can be regarded as having no exegetical elements. Al-Hilali and Khan include an exegetical gloss 'O Muhammad', and another gloss on As-Samad (which they transliterate rather than translate), and they translate كُفُوًا as 'co-equal or comparable', which is arguably an exegetical expansion. Turner's is the most obviously exegetical version, and he refers to his interpretation as an '"exegetically-led" reading' (Turner 1997: xvi).

In general, although translation proper may include elements of gist or exegesis, the dominant mode of translation is one that involves rephrasing between the ST and the TT.

1.5   The tools of the trade

Each student should have the necessary reference books in class and access to them out of class: a comprehensive Arabic-English dictionary (we recommend *A Dictionary of Modern Written Arabic* by Hans Wehr or the *Oxford Arabic Dictionary*, general editor Tressy Arts), a similar-sized English–Arabic dictionary, a monolingual Arabic dictionary (such as المنجد في اللغة والإعلام 2010), a monolingual English dictionary (such as *Collins English Dictionary* or the *Oxford English Dictionary*) and an English thesaurus (such as the *Collins English Thesaurus*). *A Dictionary of Modern Written Arabic* has more Arabic entries than does the *Oxford Arabic Dictionary,* but the latter contains many more modern terms: the *Oxford Arabic Dictionary* was published in 2014, while the fourth and most recent edition of *A Dictionary of Modern Written Arabic* came out in 1979. A particular advantage of *A Dictionary of Modern Written Arabic* for Arabic>English translators is that it includes numerous potential English translations for each Arabic word (far more than the *Oxford Arabic Dictionary*). As such, it can function as a thesaurus, offering different translation possibilities for a particular Arabic word.

Many of these resources are now available online. Some, such as the *Oxford Arabic Dictionary* and the *Oxford English Dictionary Online,* require a paid subscription – though your university may already have one (and, if not, can be requested to buy one). Others are available for free. These include the online version of the *Collins English Dictionary* (http://www.collinsdictionary.com/dictionary/english), the *Collins English Thesaurus* (http://www.collinsdictionary.com/english-thesaurus) and the Oxford online thesaurus (http://www.oxforddictionaries.com/thesaurus/).

The Internet – providing almost instant access to vast amounts of even the most technical material – is a wonderful source for information previously only available in printed books and articles, which were sometimes difficult to locate, particularly if academic in nature, and difficult to work through.

You can also employ the Internet for other translation purposes. One is as a source of information about word frequency, using a search engine – we recommend Google, which covers much more online material than its competitors. For example, assume you want to know which of the terms 'methanal' and 'formaldehyde' is more usual – both refer to the same chemical compound (i.e. they are **synonyms**; Section 7.1.1). To ascertain this, do a Google search for 'methanal' first. This gives 'About 147,000 results' (as of 15 December 2015) – information that appears near the top of the Google page. Then do a separate search for 'formaledehyde'. This gives 'About 15,700,000 results' (as of 15 December 2015). This is enough to make clear that 'formaldehyde' is the standard chemical name for this compound – information that can be confirmed if necessary by consulting reputable academic sources, whether online or printed.

Another use of the Internet for translation purposes is to check the frequency of different **collocations** – that is, words that occur together (cf. Section 8.6). Thus, suppose you are looking for a translation of غابات النخيل, and you have the three possibilities in mind: 'palm woods', 'palm forests' and 'palm groves'. Enter "palm woods" first into Google, using double (not single) inverted commas: these signify that you are looking for the entire phrase, not just the two words separately. This gives 'About 98,200 results' (as of 15 December 2015). Then do a separate search for 'palm forests' – giving 'About 29,300 results', and finally a third search for 'palm groves' – giving 'About 291,000 results' (both as of 15 December 2015). This makes plain that the commonest phrase is 'palm groves'. Assuming this fits the context (i.e. what is intended is a small wood as signified by 'grove') and that there is no other compelling reason to use 'woods' or 'forests', 'groves' is likely to the most natural-sounding translation. For further discussion on the use of the Internet for translation, see Enríquez Raído (2014).

There are more specialized computational tools that can be used for both word frequencies and collocations. Examples include the British National Corpus (http://corpus.byu.edu/bnc/) and Intellitext (http://corpus.leeds.ac.uk/itweb/htdocs/Query.html), both of which are free. Other resources, such as the Corpus of Contemporary American English (http://corpus.byu.edu/), are by paid subscription – though you may find that your institution is already a subscriber.

Computer Assisted Translation (CAT) tools are specifically aimed at professional translators. If you are taking this course as part of a specialist translation degree, you will no doubt be introduced to these in other modules. Whether you are or not, however, you can happily try these tools in this course. The most useful CAT tools are those that involve translation memory. These store details of your previously produced translations and, based on these, suggest solutions to translation problems in your current text. The most popular at the time of this writing are likely SDL Trados and MemoQ, both of which need to be bought – though your university may already have a licence for student use. There are also several free online CAT tools, such as OmegaT. Also useful are online translation dictionaries, such as Glosbe, which automatically identify SL words and phrases and their TL correspondents in STs and their corresponding TTs found on the Internet. (Another popular site, Linguee, does not at the time of this writing include Arabic, while WordReference caters only to English>Arabic, not Arabic>English, translation.)

There is also machine translation (MT) software, which provides an automatic translation of an inputted text. The best known for Arabic>English translation is probably Sakhr (http://www.sakhr.com/index.php/en/solutions/machine-translation). Of the free online software, the best known is Google Translate. The current limitations of Google Translate in translating from Arabic to English are illustrated by the following Google Translate TT of the text discussed in Section 1.4 beginning الشعر تعبير وتصوير لمشاعر الشعراء وأفكارهم:

> Hair and expression to the feelings of poets portray their ideas and experience and whether they are realistic or a figment of the imagination of the poet. In both cases, the experience honest, because even though the experience was unrealistic – that is fictional – where the poet lived for a long time before that regulates hair feels where his heart and Ichaaraa apply in his blood.

As this TT suggests, Google Translate is, at the current time, of very limited use for Arabic>English translators, although it may yield words or phrases that could potentially be incorporated into a TT otherwise produced by a human translator (an example in the previous TT being the fairly elegant phrase 'figment of the imagination').

One area that is currently potentially more useful than machine translation for Arabic>English translation is social media, most obviously the numerous translator forums where translators can ask one another for advice about specific translation difficulties, among other things. These include ProZ and TranslatorsCafé. For further information on computer-based resources for translators see Cragie, Higgins, Hervey and Gambarotta (2016; Chapter 18). We will consider the use of the Internet for technical translation in more detail in Section 16.6.

Practical 1

Practical 1.1 Gist translation: فيما عبر عن تطلعاته

Assignment

Produce a gist translation of the following ST from the online version of the Iraqi المدى newspaper (http://almadapaper.net/sub/03–619/p02.htm, March 2006). Your gist translation is to be based on the ST and the fairly idiomatic TT (364 words in length), which is a complete translation of the ST, following the ST. The gist translation should comprise about 200 words. You are an official employed by the New Zealand embassy in Cairo, and you are doing the translation for the embassy political officer. She is interested in the main characters and events. Identify which elements you decided to remove from your translation, and explain why you did so. Do this by inserting into your TT a superscript note number after each point you intend to discuss, and then discuss these points in order, starting on a fresh sheet of paper. Whenever you annotate your own TTs (normally by adding decisions of detail; cf. Section 1.1), this is the system you should use.

Contextual information

The ST deals with the crisis related to the Iranian nuclear energy programme that the United States claimed was a covert attempt by Iran to develop nuclear weapons.

ST

فيما عبر عن تطلعاته إلى حل دبلوماسي بشأن الطموح النووي للجمهورية الإسلامية، قال الرئيس الأمريكي جورج بوش إن إيران تمثل تهديداً بالغ الخطورة على الأمن القومي.

وتتزامن تصريحات بوش مع وصف حكومة طهران للاتحاد الاوروبي بـ«الدمية لسياسات واشنطن» إثر إشارة التكتل الأوروبي علانية لإمكانية فرض حظر اقتصادي على إيران.

وقال بوش أمام حشد من الصحفيين إن القلق الأمريكي مستمد من رغبة طهران المعلنة في تدمير إسرائيل. وشدد الرئيس الأمريكي على أهمية الاستمرار «في العمل مع الآخرين لحل القضية عبر الدبلوماسية».

وعلى صعيد متصل، طرح منسق الشؤون الخارجية بالاتحاد الاوروبي، خافيير سولانا، فرض حظر على إيران «كضرورة محتملة» مضى المسؤول الأوروبي قائلاً «نحن ما زلنا في طور البداية .. نحن بالتأكيد لا نريد استهداف الشعب الإيراني».

ومن جانبها ردت إيران على تصريحات سولانا وعلى لسان أحمد خاتمي، الذي اتهم الرئيس الأمريكي باستخدام القضية النووية كواجهة لمساع تهدف للإطاحة بالنظام الإيراني قائلاً «بوش يتحدث عن تغيير النظام، أو تغيير منهجه، كلاهما واحد، هذا يعني زوال النظام الإسلامي، والبقية مجرد ذرائع». ومضى قائلاً «اليوم أزمة الطاقة النووية وما أن تُحسم ستبرز مشكلة حقوق الإنسان ومن ثم محاربة الإرهاب».

وإلى ذلك قال قائد الثورة الإسلامية في إيران، آية الله علي خامنئي، إن تركيز الولايات المتحدة على الملف النووي الإيراني ما هو إلا ذريعة لاستمرار الحرب النفسية ضد طهران ونظامها الإسلامي. وقال «إن الشعب الإيراني سيقاوم مثل الفولاذ أي ضغوط أو مؤامرات وسيواصلون نشاطاته في التوصل إلى التكنولوجيا المتطورة بما فيها الطاقة النووية».

وعلى الصعيد الدبلوماسي، تدرس القوى الخمس المالكة لحق النقض في مجلس الأمن الجمعة مقترحات لممارسة ضغوط على إيران حول برنامجها النووي المثير للجدل من بينها مطالبة طهران بوقف برنامج التخصيب وبناء مفاعل نووي الذي تقول أمريكا إنه غطاء لامتلاك اسلحة نووية.

Fairly idiomatic TT

While expressing his wish to find a diplomatic solution to the nuclear ambitions of the Islamic Republic, the American President George Bush said that Iran constitutes a grave threat to national security.

Bush's statement coincides with the description by the government in Tehran of the European Union as "Washington's political puppet", following the public declaration by the European bloc of the possibility of imposing economic sanctions on Iran.

In front of a group of journalists, Bush stated that American concern derives from the stated desire of Iran to destroy Israel. The American President stressed the importance of "working with others to solve the crisis diplomatically".

On a related matter, the EU Foreign Affairs Co-ordinator, Javier Solana, suggested the imposition of sanctions on Iran as "a possible necessity". He continued, "We are still at an early stage. We definitely do not want to target the Iranian people."

Responding to Solana's statements on behalf of Iran, Ahmed Khatami accused the American President of using the nuclear issue as a front for efforts aimed at overthrowing the Iranian regime. He said, "Bush is talking about regime change, or a change in its behaviour. These are the same thing. This means the overthrow of the Islamic regime. All the rest is pretext." He went on, "Today, we have the nuclear energy crisis. No sooner will this be resolved than the issue of human rights will be raised, then the war on terrorism."

Speaking on the same subject, the leader of the Islamic revolution in Iran, Ayatollah Khamanei, claimed that US stress on the nuclear issue is no more than a pretext to pursue the war against Iran and against the Islamic regime. "The Iranian regime will oppose like tigers any forms of pressure or conspiracy. It will continue its activities to develop advanced technology, including nuclear energy."

On the diplomatic front, the five powers which have a veto in the UN Security Council will study proposals for pressuring Iran over its controversial nuclear programme on Friday. These proposals include the demand that Tehran halts its enrichment programme and stops the building of a nuclear reactor which America says is a cover for the acquisition of nuclear weapons.

Practical 1.2 Gist translation: ومما هو جدير بالذكر والملاحظة

Assignment

Produce an approximately fifty-word gist translation of the following extract by the Arabic nationalist writer ساطع الحُصَري (cited in Johnstone 1991: 78–79). If you have already completed Practical 1.1, say whether it is easier to produce the gist translation in Practical 1.1 or this one, and why.

ST

ومما هو جدير بالذكر والملاحظة أن جميع الآراء التي أُبديت والأبحاث التي نُشرت في «فكرة القومية» وفي «مبدأ حقوق القوميات» خلال القرن التاسع عشر كانت تنحصر بالشعوب الأوربية وفروعها ولم تشمل الشعوب الآسيوية والإفريقية. لأن جميع المفكرين الأوربيين كانوا يزعمون أن تلك الشعوب ليست «متأخرة» فحسب بل هي «محرومة من قابلية التقدم والتمدن» أيضا. ولذلك فهي لا تستحق الحقوق التي تستحقها الشعوب الأوربية. حتى الكتاب الذين كانوا التزموا مبدأ «حقوق القوميات» أشد الالتزام، وتحمسوا له أشد التحمس، لم يخرجوا بآرائهم في ذلك خارج نطاق الأوربيين، ولم يسلّموا بمثل تلك الحقوق للشعوب الآسيوية والإفريقية.

Practical 1.3 Gist translation: توقف: عوادم السيارات .. الموت البطيء

Assignment

Produce a gist translation of no more than 120 words of the following ST from the Yemeni newspaper الثورة (21 April 2001). In your gist translation, you should summarize the information in each paragraph, focusing on essential facts and figures relating to environmental questions. You are employed by the BBC Monitoring Service in Caversham, England, and this gist translation is part of your work to monitor and summarize articles from major Arab newspapers.

Contextual information

الثورة is a semi-official newspaper, which generally represents the views of the Yemeni government. The original Arabic text is accompanied by several pictures (not reproduced here) illustrating different aspects of pollution from motor vehicles.

ST

توقف: عوادم السيارات .. الموت البطيء!!..
كتب/ محمد عبد الله السيد

حاجة الإنسان إلى الانتقال وحمل الأثقال كانت تنافس حاجته لمسكن صناعي يأويه، ففي البدء كانت جذوع الأشجار الطافية فوق ماء النهر أو البحر وسيلة للانتقال، وفي البدء أيضا كانت عضلات الإنسان وقوى الطبيعة من رياح وتدفق الأنهار الطاقة المحركة لوسيلة النقل، لتأتي السفينة الشراعية والعربة البدائية بعد ذلك.

ولأن الحاجة أم الاختراع فقد سارت الأمور بأسرع مما نتصور فتعددت وسائل النقل المختلفة وأصبحت شيئًا مهما في حياة الإنسان فقربت البعيد وغيرت نمط الحياة، إلا أنها مع كل ذلك كانت ولا تزال الشر الذي لا بد منه .. حيث أصبحت مصدرا رئيسيا للتلوث البيئي .. تنفث الى الهواء آلاف الأطنان من الغازات والمواد الخطرة كالرصاص وأكاسيد النيتروجين وأول أكسيد الكربون وغيرها، مسببة الأذى والضرر للإنسان والحيوان والنبات.

إن بتدقيق بسيط في الصور التي أمامك تجد ما نعنيه، حيث تشاهد عوادم سامة صادرة من عينة بسيطة ضمن أعداد كبيرة من تلك السيارات القديمة التي تجوب شوارعنا أشبه ما تكون بنفايات متحركة تمثل أعباء كبيرة على البلاد، سواء من الناحية الاقتصادية، من حيث استمرار الصيانة او بيئيا وصحيا.

٭بيئيا تقول الدراسات إن عوادم وسائل النقل تشكل نسبة كبيرة من الملوثات الرئيسية للبيئة، فهي تنفث حوالي ٩٠٪ من العوادم والغازات السامة في الهواء، ٤٠٪ منها ناتجة عن الآليات التي تعمل بالديزل، فيما يأتي نصيب وسائل النقل التي تعمل بالبترول ٥٠٪!!

وبالدخول في التفاصيل فقد قدر معدل ما تنفثه سيارة متوسطة في كل ساعة تشغيل حوالي ٦٠ متر مكعب من غاز العوادم الخطرة.

٭صحيا التقارير الطبية لا تدعو إلى التفاؤل، حيث أكدت خطورة هذه الغازات والعوادم المنبعثة من وسائل النقل على صحة الإنسان! وبلغة الارقام هناك ٩٥٪ من الآليات التي تسير بالبنزين تعد أهم مصدر للرصاص السام الذي يتسبب في الشلل الدماغي والضعف العام، وكذا إنجاب أطفال مشوهين، وتكسير كريات الدم الحمراء أما غازات الهيدروكربونات المنبعثة فهناك تحذيرات من وقوفها خلف حالات تلف الكلى والكبد والتحجر الرئوي والتهاب الجهاز التنفسي.

2 Translation as a product

2.1 Degrees of freedom in translation

As we saw in Chapter 1, translation can be viewed as a process. However, in each of the examples where the driver 'translated' the policeman's words, the evidence we had for the process was a *product* – a gist translation and an exegetic translation. Here, too, it is useful to examine two diametric opposites: in this case, two opposed degrees of freedom of translation, showing extreme SL bias on the one hand and extreme TL bias on the other.

2.1.1 *Interlinear translation*

At the extreme of SL bias is **interlinear translation**, where the TT does not necessarily respect TL grammar but has grammatical units corresponding as closely as possible to every grammatical unit of the ST. Here is an example of an interlinear translation of an Arabic proverb (found, with some variants, in several Arabic **dialects**):

اللي فات مات

The/What passed died

The following is an interlinear translation of the first line of one of the pre-Islamic معلقة poems, معلقة لبيد. (The مُعَلَّقات are seven pre-Islamic 'odes' – قصائد, sg. قصيدة – considered to be the most outstanding examples of pre-Islamic poetry, one of which, مُعَلَّقة لبيد, was written byأبو عقيل العامري لبيد بن ربيعة بن مالك. According to tradition, they were hung on the Ka'ba in Mecca.) In this translation, ~ indicates that the two English words so linked correspond jointly to one Arabic word in the ST; - indicates that the two English words so linked correspond to two linked Arabic forms or words in the ST and // indicates a hemistich (half-line) break in the middle of the line. This is a standard feature of traditional Arabic poetry and is marked in the ST by a space between the words فَمُقامُها and بِمِنَى, which is longer than the spaces between other words in the line:

عَـفَـتِ الـدِّيـارُ مـحـلُّـها فَـمُـقـامُـها،   بِـمِـنَـى تَـأَبَّـدَ غَـوْلـُها فَـرِجـامُـها

Disappeared the-camping~grounds alighting~places-their and-stopping ~places-their // in-Mina became~deserted Ghaul-its and-Rijam-its

As is apparent from the incomprehensibility of the English TT here, interlinear translation is normally only employed where the purpose of the translation is to shed light on the structure of the ST. Mainly used in descriptive linguistics or language teaching, interlinear translation is of no practical use for this course, and we shall not consider it further.

2.1.2   *Literal translation*

Interlinear translation is an extreme form of the much more common literal translation. In literal translation proper, the denotative meaning of words is taken as if straight from the dictionary (i.e. out of context), but TL grammar is respected. Because TL grammar is respected, literal translation very often unavoidably involves **grammatical transposition** – the replacement or reinforcement of given parts of speech in the ST by other parts of speech in the TT. A simple example is translating the colloquially oriented الدنيا شمس as 'It's sunny': the TT has a dummy subject 'it' where the ST has the word الدنيا ('the world') and an adjective 'sunny' where the ST has the noun شمس ('sun').

The following is the first line of معلقة لبيد, with a literal translation:

عَـظَـفَـتِ الـدِّيَـارُ مـحَـلُّـها فَـمُـقـامُـها،   بِـمِـنَـى تَـأَبَّـدَ غَـوْلُـها فَـرِجِـامُـها

The camping grounds have disappeared – their alighting places and their stopping places // at Mina; its Ghaul and its Rijam have become deserted

In this translation, the standard grammar and word order of English are respected; however, everything that might be transferred on a simple word-by-word basis from the Arabic is so transferred. For most purposes, literal translation can be regarded as the practical extreme of SL bias.

2.1.3   *Free translation*

At the opposite extreme, where there is maximum TL bias, there is **free translation**. Here, there is only a global correspondence between the textual units of the ST and those of the TT. A possible free translation of the colloquial Arabic proverb اللي فات مات, discussed earlier, would be 'Let bygones be bygones'. Here, the grammar is completely different, and the **metaphor** of 'dying' is lost. Similarly, a free translation of the proverb يوم لك ويوم عليك might be 'You win some, you lose some'; here, the grammar and vocabulary are completely different.

2.1.4   *Communicative translation*

These examples of free translation are also examples of **communicative translation**. A communicative translation is produced, when, in a given situation, the ST uses an SL expression standard for that situation, and the TT uses a TL expression standard for an equivalent target culture situation. 'Let bygones be bygones' is an obvious translation of اللي فات مات, and, in some situations at least, would be virtually mandatory. This is true of very many culturally conventional formulae that do not invite literal translation. Public notices, proverbs and conversational clichés illustrate this point:

ممنوع التدخين	No smoking	(public notice)
ضرب عصفورين بحجر واحد	To kill two birds with one stone	(Standard Arabic proverb)
لا شكر على واجب	Don't mention it	(conversational cliché)

As these few examples suggest, communicative translation is very common. Communicative translation apart, however, this degree of freedom is no more useful as standard practice than interlinear translation, because potentially important details of message content are bound to be lost.

2.1.5   *From interlinear to free translation*

Between the two extremes of literal translation and free translation, the degrees of freedom are infinitely variable. Whether there is any perfect halfway point between the two is open to question. However, in assessing translation freedom, it is useful to situate the TT on a scale between extreme SL bias and extreme TL bias, with notional intermediate points schematized as shown in Figure 2.1, adapted from Newmark (1981: 39).

By an **idiomizing translation**, we mean one that respects the ST message content but prioritizes TL 'naturalness' over faithfulness to ST detail; it will typically use **idioms** or familiar phonic and rhythmic patterns to give an easy read, even if this means sacrificing nuances of meaning or tone. By 'idiom' we mean a fixed figurative expression whose meaning cannot be deduced from the denotative meanings of the words that make it up, as in 'football's not *my cup of tea*', 'office politics is a *can of worms*', etc. Note that 'idiomizing' is not synonymous with 'idiomatic': throughout this course, we use the term 'idiomatic' to denote what sounds 'natural' and 'normal' to native speakers – a **linguistic expression** that is unexceptional and acceptable in a given language in a given context.

The five points on the scale – as well as the rarely used interlinear translation – can be illustrated by the following translations of the phrase مثل هذه الاشياء عليها إقبال كثير الآن:

[INTERLINEAR	Like these things to them demand much now.]
LITERAL	The likes of these things have much demand now.
FAITHFUL	Things like these are in great demand now.
BALANCED	This kind of things in great demand at the moment.
IDIOMIZING	This type's all the rage.
FREE	This one's dead trendy.

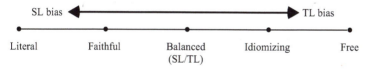

Figure 2.1 Degrees of freedom in translation.

Note that the last four TTs are all idiomatic, but only one of them is an idiomizing translation. It should also be noted that, quite frequently, as translations get more free, they become more informal, as illustrated by these examples. There is, however, no necessary correlation between informality and freeness of translation. The pompous 'Such artifacts are at the absolute pinnacle of their popularity, madam' is just as possible a free translation of مثل هذه الاشياء عليها إقبال كثير الآن as is 'This one's dead trendy'.

2.2   Equivalence and translation loss

In defining communicative translation, we used the term 'equivalent target culture situation'. As a matter of fact, most writers on translation use the terms 'equivalence' and 'equivalent' but in so many different ways that equivalence can be a confusing concept for teachers of translation, let alone for their students. Before going any farther, then, we need to say what we mean, and what we do not mean, by 'equivalence' and 'equivalent'. Because this is not a course in translation theory, we shall not go in detail into the more general philosophical implications of the term 'equivalence'. Nida (1964), Toury (1980 and 1995), Holmes (1988), Snell-Hornby (1988), Koller (1995), Hermans (1999) and Pym (2009) among them provide a useful introduction to the question.

2.2.1   Equivalence

The many different definitions of equivalence in translation fall broadly into one of two categories: they are either descriptive or prescriptive. Descriptively, 'equivalence' denotes the relationship between ST features and TT features that are seen as directly corresponding to one another, regardless of the quality of the TT. Thus, descriptively, the following utterances are equivalents:

ممنوع الدخول	forbidden is the entrance
مع السلامة	with the well-being

Prescriptively, 'equivalence' denotes the relationship between an SL expression and the canonical TL rendering of it as required, for example, by a teacher. So, prescriptively, the following pairs of utterances are equivalents:

ممنوع الدخول	no entry
مع السلامة	goodbye

An influential variant of prescriptive equivalence is the 'dynamic equivalence' of the eminent Bible translator Eugene Nida. This is based on the 'principle of equivalent effect', which states that 'the relationship between receptor and message should be substantially the same as that which existed between the original receptors and the message' (Nida 1964: 159). Nida's view does have real attractions. We shall be suggesting throughout the course that there are all sorts of reasons – reasons of grammar, idiom, context, genre, etc. – why a translator might not want to translate a given expression literally. A case in point is communicative translation, which may be said to be an example of 'dynamic equivalence' (cf. Nida 1964: 166: 'That is just the way we would say it'). However, there is a danger, especially for student translators with exceptional mother-tongue facility, that 'dynamic equivalence' might be seen as giving carte blanche for excessive freedom – that is, freedom to write more or less anything as long as it sounds good and does reflect, however tenuously, something of the ST message content. This danger is a very real one, as any teacher of translation will confirm. It is in fact a symptom of theoretical problems contained in the very notion of 'equivalent effect', most notably the normative ones.

To begin with, who is to know what the relationship between ST message and source-culture receptors is? For that matter, is it plausible to speak of *the* relationship, as if there were only one: are there not as many relationships as there are receptors? And who is to know what such relationships can have been in the past? In any case, few texts have a *single* effect, even in one reading by one person.

A good example of the problematicity of achieving an equivalent effect in Arabic>English translation is the translation of a piece of ancient Arabic poetry, such as مُعَلَّقة لبيد. Even in principle, it seems impossible to achieve in an English translation the effect created by معلقة لبيد on the original audience of the poem – that is, the Arabs of pre-Islamic Arabia. In fact, it seems impossible even to determine what these effects might have been. Equally, it seems almost certain that the effects achieved on a modern Arabic audience will be quite different from those achieved on the original audience. The differences between the two audiences are obviously enormous – pre-Islamic pagan Bedouins versus mainly Muslim town dwellers and villagers; a largely illiterate audience listening to an essentially oral performance in a poetic genre with which it is likely to be intimately acquainted versus an exclusively literate audience, which is likely to be making use of a heavily annotated edition in a school or university and which is used to a modern version of Standard Arabic (even in the poetic domain) significantly different from the Arabic of pre-Islamic poetry.

All this illustrates the dangers in the normative use of the term 'equivalence' to imply 'sameness', as it does in logic, mathematics and sign theory. In mathematics, an equivalent relationship is objective, incontrovertible and, crucially, reversible. In translation, however, such unanimity and reversibility are unthinkable for any but the very simplest of texts – and even then, only in terms of denotative meaning. For example, if هل أعجبتك مصر؟ translates as 'Do you like Egypt?', will **back-translation** (i.e. translating a TT back into the SL) automatically give هل أعجبتك مصر؟, or will it give هل تعجبك مصر؟, or هل تحب مصر؟? The answer depends, as it always does in translation matters, on context – both the context of the ST utterance and the context of the TT utterance. The simplest of contexts is usually enough to inhibit the reversibility that is crucial to equivalence in the mathematical sense. And certainly even something as elementary as the difference in tense gives هل تعجبك مصر؟ and هل أعجبتك مصر؟ potentially quite distinct interpretations.

It would seem that, in so far as the principle of equivalent effect implies 'sameness' or is used normatively, it is more of a hindrance than a help, both theoretically and pedagogically. Consequently, when we spoke of an 'equivalent target culture situation', we were not intending 'equivalent' to have a sense specific to any particular translation theory but were using it in its everyday sense of 'counterpart' – something different, but with points of resemblance in relevant aspects. This is how the term will be used in this book.

We have found it useful, both in translating and in teaching translation, to avoid an absolutist ambition to *maximize sameness* between ST and TT in favour of a relativist ambition to *minimize difference*: to look not for what is to be put into the TT but for what one might save from the ST. There is a vital difference between the two ambitions. The aim of maximizing sameness encourages the belief that, floating somewhere out in the ether, there is the 'right' translation, the TT that is 'equi-valent' to the ST, at some ideal point between SL bias and TL bias. But it is more realistic, and more productive, to start by admitting that, because SL and TL are fundamentally different, the transfer from ST to TT *inevitably* entails difference – that is, loss.

2.2.2   Translation loss

It is helpful here to draw an analogy with 'energy loss' in engineering. The transfer of energy in any machine necessarily involves energy loss. Engineers do not see this as a theoretical anomaly but simply as a practical problem that they confront by striving to design more efficient machines in which energy loss is reduced. We shall give the term **translation loss** to the incomplete replication of the ST in the TT – that is, the inevitable loss of textually and culturally relevant features. This term is intended to suggest that translators should not agonize over the loss but should concentrate on reducing it.

In fact, the analogy with energy loss is imperfect: whereas energy loss is a loss (or rather, a diversion) of energy, translation loss is not a loss *of* translation but a loss *in* the translation process. It is a loss *of* textual effects. Further, because these effects cannot be quantified, neither can the loss. So, when trying to reduce it, the translator never knows how far there is still to go.

Nevertheless, despite the limitations of the analogy, we have found it practical for translators, students and teachers alike. Once one accepts the concept of inevitable translation loss, a TT that is not, even in all important respects, a replica of the ST is not a theoretical anomaly, and the translator can concentrate on the realistic aim of reducing translation loss rather than the unrealistic one of seeking the ultimate TT.

A few very simple examples, at the level of sounds and denotative meanings of individual words, will be enough to show some of the forms translation loss can take and what its implications are for the translator.

There is translation loss even at the most elementary level. True SL–TL *homonymy* rarely occurs (as there is almost always some difference in pronunciation across languages), and rhythm and intonation are usually different as well. For instance, in most contexts, بقرة and 'cow' will be synonyms, and there will be no loss in denotative meaning in translating one with the other. But بقرة and 'cow' clearly sound different: there is significant translation loss on the **phonic** and **prosodic** levels. In a veterinary textbook, this loss is not likely to matter. But if the ST word is part of an alliterative pattern in a literary text, or, worse, if it rhymes, the loss could be crucial.

Even if the ST word has entered the TL as a loan word (e.g. 'intifada'), using it in the TT entails translation loss in at least two different ways. For example, English speakers pronounce 'intifada' differently from the way in which Arabic speakers pronounce انتفاضة (consider, for example, the pronunciation of the ض in Arabic), so using it in an English TT involves loss on the phonic level. In any case, 'intifada' still sounds foreign (cf. Section 4.5) in English, despite the relative frequency of use in newspapers and political writing over the past few years. Accordingly, using 'intifada' in an English TT introduces a foreign element that is not present in an Arabic ST, thereby losing the cultural neutrality of the ST expression.

In the opposite sort of case, where the ST contains a TL expression (e.g. كمبيوتر 'computer', موبايل 'mobile phone'), it is tempting to see the TT as 'correcting' the ST and therefore producing 'gain' rather than 'loss'. In fact, however, there is no less loss. If Arabic موبايل is translated as 'mobile phone' (as it might well be in many contexts), there is palpable phonic and prosodic loss, because the ST expression and the TT expression are pronounced in ways that are clearly different from each other. There is also grammatical translation loss, because the TT is less economical than the ST, and there is **lexical** translation loss, because TT 'mobile phone' loses the foreignness that موبايل has in Arabic. And a translation of Arabic كمبيوتر as English 'computer' involves not only a loss of foreignness but also an addition of a transparent link with 'compute', which is lacking in the SL form.

As these examples suggest, it is important to recognize that, even where the TT is more explicit, precise, economical or vivid than the ST, this difference is still a case of translation loss. Some writers refer to such differences as 'translation gains'. It is certainly true that the following TTs, for example, can be said to be grammatically more economical, sometimes even more elegant and easier to say, than their STs. But these so-called gains are by the same token grammatical, phonic or prosodic failures to replicate the ST structures and are therefore by definition instances of translation loss, as in the following examples:

ST	TT
cross-eyed	أحول
Islamic jurisprudence	فقه
سيارة أجرة	taxi
كلب ماء	otter

Conversely, if we reverse these columns, we have a set of TTs that are clearer, or more vivid, than their STs: these TTs, too, all show translation loss, because the ST structures have been violated:

ST	TT
أحول	cross-eyed
فقه	Islamic jurisprudence
taxi	سيارة أجرة
otter	كلب ماء

If translation loss is inevitable even in translating single words, then it will feature at more complex levels as well – in respect to connotations, for example, or of sentence structure, discourse, language variety and so on. Examples will arise in Practicals 2.1–2.3 and many more later on, chapter by chapter, as we deal with these and other topics.

2.2.2.1   Translation by omission

The most obvious form of translation loss is when something that occurs in the ST is simply omitted from the TT. Such **omission** occurs fairly frequently in Arabic>English translation and is therefore worth specifically identifying. (For helpful further discussion of **translation by omission**, see Baker 2011: 42–43.)

Omission can occur for many legitimate reasons; the following are a few illustrative examples. Quite often, omission reflects the different ways in which Arabic and English link bits of text together (i.e. different patterns of **cohesion**; cf. Section 13.2.1). Arabic radio broadcasts, for example, often make use of the phrase هذا و . . . to introduce a piece of information related to the material that has gone before but takes the broadcast onto a new subtopic. Normally, the best translation of this in English is to simply miss the phrase out. Similarly, one often finds the phrase جدير بالذكر (also associated 'variants' such as ومما يجدر ذكره) at the start of paragraphs in Arabic newspapers; this can be regarded as a signal in Arabic that what comes next is **background information** to the main argument (cf. Hatim 1997: 67–74). Again, one would normally not expect this to be translated in an English TT.

Another occasion for omission is when the information conveyed is not particularly important and adding it would unnecessarily complicate the structure of the TT. Consider, for example, the following extract from an Arabic newspaper وكان الرئيس الامريكي بيل كلينتون قد أكد مساء أول من أمس [. . .]. Given a context in which it is not particularly important that this statement was made in the evening, a reasonable translation of this would be along the lines 'Two days ago, the American President, Bill Clinton, confirmed [. . .]' (Ives 1999: 3); unlike Arabic, English does not afford a particularly elegant or stylistically normal way in this context of expressing the concept 'two days ago in the evening'.

Cultural difference (cf. Chapter 4) provides another area in which simple omission may be a reasonable strategy. For example, when a Christian-oriented Lebanese newspaper refers to the former Phalangist leader as الشيخ بيار جميل, the obvious translation is 'Pierre Gemayel' (Jones 1999: 5); not enough hangs on the associations in respect to الشيخ here to warrant including any equivalent in the TT. Similarly, in most contexts, the phrase بابا الفاتيكان يوحنا بولس الثاني is likely to be most reasonably translated as 'Pope John Paul II' with the omission of any English equivalent of the ST الفاتيكان; most Western readers are likely to be unaware of any popes (such as the Coptic pope) other than the Catholic one, and even if they are aware of these other possibilities, such knowledge will in many contexts be irrelevant, because it is only the Catholic pope in English who is typically referred to as 'the Pope'.

Wherever omission reduces the specificity of the information regarding a particular person, thing, process, etc. that is being referred to, it is also a case of **generalizing translation**; cf. Section 7.1.3.

2.2.2.2   *Translation by addition*

Translation by addition is translation in which something is added to the TT that is not present in the ST. Like omission, addition is a fairly common feature of Arabic>English translation and is therefore worth specifically identifying.

Examples of translation by addition frequently occur where either general considerations of English usage or specific contexts require something to be added. Consider the phrase from a newspaper text about the Kosovo war of 1999 منذ الهيمنة التركية. This is much more acceptably translated as 'ever since the days of Turkish hegemony' (Ives 1999: 13) than as 'ever since Turkish hegemony' ('time of Turkish hegemony' would also be possible). The operative principle here seems to be that English resists regarding 'hegemony' as a concept involving time more strongly than does Arabic with respect to هيمنة. In English, it is therefore necessary to add 'days of' (or something similar).

A similar example, which involves the specific context rather than general considerations of usage, is the following from the novel مدينة البغي by عيسى بشارة:

هو كاتم أنفاسه ومغمض عينيه عما يجري

This has been translated (Brown 1996: 58) as:

He was holding his breath and had closed his eyes to what was going on around him

The context here is fairly personal; the author is interested in the events immediately surrounding the central character of the novel, صابر. The translator has accordingly chosen to add 'around him', as this is an obvious idiomatic means of expressing the personal nature of what is involved. There is, however, no equivalent of 'around him' (e.g. حوله) in the Arabic ST (although it would be perfectly possible to have one); nor is any dictionary likely to list 'to go on around [one]' as an equivalent of جرى. Accordingly, it is justifiable to identify this as a case of translation by addition.

Wherever addition provides further specification regarding a particular person, thing, process, etc. that is being referred to, it is also a case of **particularizing translation**; cf. Section 7.1.3.

2.2.2.3   Controlling translation loss

As we have suggested, translation loss is an inevitable consequence of the fact that languages and cultures are different. Given this, the challenge to the translator is not to eliminate it but to control and channel it by deciding which features, in a given ST, it is most important to respect and which can most legitimately be sacrificed in respecting them. The translator has always to be asking, and answering, such questions as: does it *matter* if 'Do you like Egypt?' does not reflect the distinction between هل أعجبتك مصر؟ and هل تعجبك مصر؟ ? Does it matter if موبايل is foreign in Arabic but 'mobile phone' is not foreign in English and sounds different in each case? If إللي فات مات is phonically, rhythmically, grammatically, lexically and metaphorically different from 'Let bygones be bygones'? As we have already suggested, there is no once-and-for-all answer to questions like these. Everything depends on the purpose of the translation and on the role of the textual feature in its context. Sometimes a given translation loss will matter a lot, sometimes little. Whether the final decision is simple or complicated, it does have to be made, every time, and the translator is the only one who can make it.

Practical 2

Practical 2.1 Literal versus balanced translation: وتميز حكم المحافظين

Assignment

(i) With a view to producing your own balanced TT, consider the following text and the literal TT that follows it. Make a note of any elements in the literal TT that immediately strike you as unidiomatic.
(ii) Discuss the strategic problems confronting the translator of the text, and outline your own strategy for dealing with them in order to produce a balanced TT.
(iii) Translate the text into English.
(iv) Explain the decisions of detail you made in producing your TT.

Contextual information

This text is taken from an unsigned article titled الانتخابات البريطانية, which appeared in May 1997 in the London-based political magazine العالم (from Conduit 1998: 19–21). The article deals with the British general election of that year, which brought the Labour Party into power following more than seventeen years of Conservative rule, first under Margaret Thatcher as Prime Minister and then John Major. The section of the article from which the ST is taken discusses the nature of the Conservative government under Margaret Thatcher. It begins with a comparison between the Thatcher government and the previous Labour administration.

ST

وتميز حكم المحافظين بنزوعه الأكثر وضوحا ومبدئية إلى قيم الرأسمالية الغربية وبتبنيهم برنامجاً تدريجياً شاملاً من أجل الفصل بين الدولة والمجتمع وبدء مشروع التخلي التدريجي للدولة عن مهمة الرعاية الاجتماعية وفسح المجال أمام حركة الاستثمار ورؤوس الأموال عن طريق تقليل الضرائب. وقد انطلقت تاتشر من تصور فلسفي أيديولوجي متصلب حاربت به النقابات وكسرت شوكتها ثم نقلت ملكيات الدولة العامة في الشركات الكبرى وحولتها إلى القطاع الخاص وفتحت الباب أمام المواطنين لاقتناء أسهمها وشملت سياسة التخصيص أكثر من عشرين شركة كبيرة منها شركة الحديد الصلب وشركة الغاز والكهرباء والهاتف والنفط والمطارات. كما أعطت لمستأجري المساكن الحكومية الحق في شراء وتملك مساكنهم وغيرها من الإجراءات التي أجبرت فيها الدولة على التنازل عن ممتلكاتها لصالح المواطنين. فكانت النتيجة هي أن شهدت بريطانيا في الثمانينات حركة اقتصادية وانتعاشا نسبيا وتدفق رؤوس الأموال الأجنبية وتكونت قناعة الناخب البريطاني بالفوائد المباشرة الملموسة لحكم المحافظين.

Literal TT

The rule of the Conservatives was distinguished by its clearer and more principled striving for the values of Western capitalism and by their adoption of a gradual, total programme in order to separate the state and the society; and the start of the project of gradual relinquishing of/by the state of/from the task of social care and the clearing of the way in front of the movement of investment and capital by means of the reduction of taxes. And Thatcher set off from an unyielding philosophical-ideological conception with which she fought the unions and broke their power; then she transferred the public properties of the state in the great companies and converted them to the private sector, and opened the door in front of the citizens to buy their shares; and the policy of privatization covered more than twenty large companies, including the iron–steel company, the gas company, the electricity, the telephone, the oil, and the airports. She also gave the renters of government houses the right to buy and own their houses, and [she undertook] other measures in which she forced the state to give up its properties to the benefit of the citizens. And/So the result was that Britain in the eighties witnessed an economic movement and a relative revival, and the inpouring of foreign capital, and the conviction of the British voter came into being of the tangible, direct benefits of the rule of the Conservatives.

Practical 2.2 Degrees of freedom in translation: ماذا ستقول أمك

Assignment

(i) Discuss the strategic decisions that must be taken before starting detailed translation of the following text, and outline and justify the strategy you adopt. You are to translate the text as part of an anthology of modern Arabic short stories. Your intended readership is educated English speakers with only a general knowledge of the Arab world.

(ii) Translate the text into English.

(iii) Explain the main decisions of detail you made in producing your TT, paying special attention to the question of where on the free–literal continuum the translation is most appropriately placed.

Contextual information

This passage is taken from the short story النار والماء by the Syrian writer زكريا تامر (from St John 1999: 22–24). The main characters, فواز and إلهام, are two young people from a poor part of town who have fallen in love. The two have just met up, as previously agreed, in another part of town. At the start of this extract, إلهام is speaking.

ST

«ــ ماذا ستقول أمك عندما تراني معك؟».

«ــ ستزغرد طبعاً».

«ــ الزغردة في الأعراس».

«ــ طبعا سيكون هناك عرس».

«ــ عرس من؟».

«ــ عرس ولد اسمه فواز».

«ــ ومن العروس؟».

«ــ العروس بنت اسمها إلهام».

ضحكت إلهام بغبطة وحياء.

قال فواز: «سأطلب منك طلباً».

«ـ اطلب».

«ــ أريد أن أرى وجهك».

قالت: «انظر اليه. من يمنعك؟».

قال: «أريد أن أراه دون هذا الحائط الأسود».

وأشار بسبابته الى الحجاب.

قالت إلهام: «لا».

«ــ أنت الآن بعيدة عن الحارة ولا أحد هنا يعرفنا فلماذا الخوف؟».

فرفعت إلهام الحجاب عن وجه أبيض وعينين سوداوين. فهتف بإعجاب ونشوة: «آه».

فقالت إلهام متسائلة بمكر: «هل سمعت أغنية تحبها؟».

«ــ أريد منك شيئا آخر».

«ــ أنت طماع».

«ــ أريد أن أمسك يدك».

«ــ سأصرخ حتى يأتي رجال الشرطة».

«ــ اصرخي».

«ــ سيأتي رجال الشرطة».

«ــ فليأتوا .. سأقول لهم: البنت خطيبتي ولا يحق لكم التدخل في الحياة الخاصة للمواطنين».

«ــ كلام لطيف».

«ــ سيدركون خطأهم ويعتذرون وينسحبون خجلين».

Practical 2.3   *Literal versus free translation*: لغتنا الجميلة

Assignment

(i) Discuss the strategic decisions that you must take before starting detailed translation of the following text, and outline and justify the strategy you adopt. You are to translate the text for an online English-language version of the الحياة newspaper.

(ii) Translate the text into English.

(iii) Explain the decisions of detail you made in producing your TT. For each decision of detail, identify whether the translation is (fairly) literal or fairly non-literal, and why this is.

Contextual information

This text is taken from the الحياة newspaper, 9 February 2009.

ST

«لغتنا الجميلة»

الاستخدام اليومي للّغة العربية يزيد سوءاً يوماً تلو يوم، ولا يبدو أنَّ في الأفق حلاً لهذه المشكلة المستعصية. فقدت اللغة رهبتها فباتت عرضة للانتهاك المفضوح في معظم المرافق العامة، في الإذاعة كما على الشاشات الصغيرة، في رحلات السفر كما على الهاتف، في الندوات والمؤتمرات، يخاطب قائد الطائرة الركاب بالعربية فيرتكب أخطاء جمة، أما بالإنكليزية فلا. يرفع المواطن السماعة فتجيب آلة التسجيل بعربية «مكسرة»، وإذا أجابت بالإنكليزية أو الفرنسية فاللغة سليمة. «تشعل» جهاز التلفزيون فتنهمر عليك الأخطاء من كل حدب وصوب، أخطاء في نشرات الأخبار، أخطاء في الترجمة، أخطاء في الشرائط التي تحتل أسفل الشاشات، ناهيك عن الأخطاء الفادحة التي تُرتكب في الخطب السياسية وغير السياسية التي تبثها الفضائيات. وقد لا تُفاجأ إذا تلقيت بيانات حافلة بالأخطاء، كل أنواع الأخطاء، وكأن كاتبيها أو محرريها لا علاقة لهم بلغتهم. لكنك حتماً تُفاجأ إذا تلقيت بيانا يحمل توقيع أحد اتحادات الكتاب أو الصحفيين العرب، ووجدته مفعماً بالأخطاء. أما الملصقات والإعلانات التي تحتل الجدران والشوارع فلا تحصى أخطاؤها.

هذه الظاهرة لا يمكن تفسيرها لغوياً فقط قد يخطئ المرء أن يخطئ في اللغة مثلما يخطئ في أي أمر. هذا على المستوى الفردي أو الشخصي، أما أن يعمّم الخطأ ويصبح رائجاً مثل أي شائعة، فهذا ما لا يمكن الإغضاء عنه. وهنا يجب الفصل بين ما يُسمّى خطأ شائعاً وخطأ لغوياً، فالخطأ الشائع يظل على هامش القاعدة ولو شذ عنها، أما الخطأ اللغوي فهو خطأ في قلب اللغة وقواعدها.

إنها ظاهرة تتعدّى تخوم الصرف والنحو وتدلّ على حال من الانحطاط الثقافي. فاللغة، كأداة تواصل، يجب ألا تلقى مثل هذه اللامبالاة ومثل هذا الإهمال والتقاعس. قائد الطائرة يلم تمام الإلمام بقواعد القيادة الجوية، ولا يمكنه أن يخل بها، ومثله يلم التقنيون، في الإذاعة والتلفزيون، بأسرار هذين الجهازين الحديثين، وهلمّ جراً. إذاً هناك قواعد لا يمكن تجاهلها أو إهمالها وإلا وقعت الواقعة التي لا تُحمد عقباها.

ليس مسموحاً في الغرب ارتكاب مثل هذه الأخطاء في الحياة العامة وفي الاستخدام «الرسمي» أو «الوظيفي» اليومي للغة. هذا ما يمكن المرء أن يلاحظه بسهولة حيثما حل وهذه الميزة لا ترجع إلى كون الأجانب يكتبون كما يتكلمون. لقد أسقط علماء اللغة، قديماً وحديثاً، هذه الذريعة التي يتمسك بها البعض لتبرير صعوبة اللغة العربية. وقال هؤلاء أن أمر الكتابة يختلف تماماً عن الكلام، وأن اللغة المكتوبة ليست بتاتاً اللغة التي يُحكى بها. وقد يتذرع هذا البعض بصعوبة القواعد العربية وتعقّدها وقدامتها وعدم تحديثها . . . لكنّ ما فات هؤلاء أنّ اللغة العربية الراهنة ليست لغة الماضي. لقد شهدت لغتنا حالاً من التحديث الطبيعي بعيداً عن أي افتعال أو تحدّ.

3   Revising and editing TTs

3.1   Introduction

In Chapter 1, we considered translation as a process and, in Chapter 2, as a product. In this chapter, we turn our attention to the final stages of translation as a process, where the proposed TT is actually examined as a product: revising and editing.

Revising and editing are vital features of any polished translation, and you will need to carry out these activities on your translation work throughout this course. For this reason, we deal with revising and editing in this chapter before turning to the main issues covered by this course, even though successful revising and editing build on the issues discussed in subsequent chapters.

Any form of post-translation process is intrinsically an operation carried out in writing on a pre-existent text. There are two basic kinds of operations to be carried out on a preliminary TT. The first involves checking for accuracy; this we shall refer to as revision. The second involves the 'polishing' of the TT after the revision process; this we shall refer to as editing. It is worth distinguishing between these two operations, as they correspond to the phases that professional translators standardly go through in bringing their work up to an acceptable standard for delivery to a client. However, the two operations overlap to some extent: it may not always be clear whether TT peculiarities are errors or just features of style; in any case, what is theoretically an edit may well occur to the reviser/editor during the revising stage.

As elsewhere in this book, therefore, the guidelines given here are meant to provide a framework that allows the apprentice translator to adopt a coherent approach to the process of translation. They are not meant to be applied in such a way that they hinder the translator by putting obstacles in the way of creative problem solving. (For a detailed introduction to revising and editing for translators, see Mossop 2014.)

3.2   Revision

The main task during the revision stage is checking the TT for adherence to the ST in terms of accuracy: the reviser focuses on errors, omissions, additions, inconsistencies, names and titles, figures and tables, etc. Errors of accuracy can be relatively minor, such as spelling mistakes or punctuation, or lexical and phrasal errors. However, they can also include more complex errors, such as ungrammatical constructions, or obscure, ambiguous or misleading configurations on the **sentential** and **discourse levels**. At the revision or checking stage, greater emphasis is usually placed on accuracy than on terminology. The reviser's objectivity should ensure that any ambiguities or unclear phrasings are dealt with before passing on to the editing stage.

The following extract, which is taken from a bilingual Arabic>English tourist brochure about the island of Socotra off the southern coast of mainland Yemen, is a good example of an English TT that requires basic revision of this type (Republic of Yemen, Ministry of Culture and Tourism n.d.: ٣, 3).

ST

٤- الأودية:

يخترق السهول العديد من الأودية التي يصب بعضها شمال الجزيرة والبعض الآخر جنوبها وأهمها وادي (دي عزرو) الذي يقطع الجزيرة من الشمال الى الجنوب، بالإضافة الى الأودية التي تتبع من جبال (حجهر) المتميزة بمياهها الجارية على مدار العام.

Published TT (unrevised)

4–The Wadis (Valleys):

The plains are intersspersed by many vallies .Some of which pour at the northern part of the Island and some of which pouer at its southern part and the most important of which is Azroo Valley which intersects the Island from north to south in addition to the valleys springing out from the Hajhar Mountainous Range which are characterized for their running water all along the year.

This TT contains three spelling errors ('intersspersed', 'vallies', 'pouer'). There are also errors of capitalization and punctuation ('Island' should be 'island' (two occurrences); 'vallies .Some' should be 'valleys. Some'; 'Valley' in the second sentence should likely be 'valley', 'Mountainous Range' should be 'mountain range'; see also subsequent discussion). There are several basic lexical and phrasal errors: 'interspersed by' would be better as 'interspersed with'; 'pour at' could be 'flow out at' (two occurrences); 'springing out' could be 'leading out'; 'characterized for' could be 'characterized by'; 'all along the year' could be 'throughout the year'. Finally, 'Azroo' should likely be 'the Di Azroo' (or 'the Dee Azroo', etc. depending on what form of **transliteration** is adopted), given that the Arabic has دي عزرو and that there are no standard English forms for Socotran names of a type that might lead to the 'dropping' of elements within names.

Taken together, these proposed changes to the TT would yield the following:

4–The Wadis (Valleys):

The plains are interspersed with many valleys. Some of which flow out at the northern part of the island and some of which flow out at its southern part and the most important of which is the Di Azroo valley which intersects the island from north to south in addition to the valleys leading out from the Hajhar mountain range which are characterized by their running water throughout the year.

Somewhat more difficult to deal with are problems relating to the discourse and sentential levels. The most obvious of these is the element 'Some of which [. . .] and some of which [. . .] and the most important of which [. . .] throughout the year'. Such a sentence would only be plausible in an informal context. The relative formality of the present piece of writing rules this out. This element can be converted easily enough into a contextually acceptable English sentence by replacing the first 'which' with 'these' and the second and third with 'them', giving a second sentence, incorporating also previously discussed changes, as follows:

Some of these flow out at the northern part of the island and some of them flow out at its southern part and the most important of them is the Di Azroo valley which intersects the island from north to south in addition to the valleys leading out from the Hajhar mountain range which are characterized by their running water throughout the year.

However, this still leaves several other problems on the sentential and discourse levels. The most obvious is the lack of commas after 'Di Azroo valley' and 'mountain range': in each case, the relative clause is a describing clause, not a defining one, and thus requires a comma before it. Also notable is the use of 'and' in the phrase 'and the most important of them'. In Arabic, it is perfectly reasonable in this context to use the coordinating conjunction و, following a previous use of the coordinating و in the phrase والبعض الآخر. However, in English, such piling up of coordinated clauses is typically avoided (cf. Section 12.2.5). A common means of dealing with this problem is to start a new sentence in English. With some additional changes to the English wording, this gives a TT for the main part of the text as follows:

Some of these flow out at the northern part of the island and some of them flow out at its southern part. The most important of these is the Di Azroo valley, which intersects the island from north to south in addition to the valleys leading out from the Hajhar mountain range, which are characterized by their running water throughout the year.

The final sentence of this version, however, is still rather odd. The main reason for this is that it involves multiple subordinate elements: the relative clause beginning 'which intersects' followed by the subordinating phrase 'in addition to', followed by a further relative clause, beginning 'which are characterized'. Arabic seems to tolerate such multiple subordination more readily than English (cf. Section 12.2.4). One solution to this problem would be to change the subordinating 'in addition to' to the coordinating 'and', with the concomitant change of 'The most important of these is' to 'The most important of these are' to make the verb agree with the plural subject in the new version. This would give a final sentence in the English TT as follows:

> The most important of these are the Di Azroo valley, which intersects the island from north to south, and the valleys leading out from the Hajhar mountain range, which are characterized by their running water throughout the year.

We shall return to this text later, when we consider the issue of editing.

So far we have considered accuracy in relation to linguistic features of various kinds. However, accuracy also has a factual aspect: it is not only the language of the TT that may be wrong or unsuitable, but the concepts themselves may have been distorted in transmission. The TT is the sum not only of a translator's knowledge of the two linguistic systems concerned and the ability to interface and apply them but also of knowledge of the subject matter in question. Thus, a translator may be linguistically equipped to tackle a text on computer software but lack the expertise necessary to make the right terminological and practical decisions, thereby undermining the TT's **register** and lexis and, ultimately, its quality and authoritativeness.

In this light, consider the following from the same brochure about the island of Socotra used earlier (Republic of Yemen, Ministry of Culture and Tourism n.d.: ٧, 7). This section is discussing caves on Socotra.

ST

تشكلت من عوامل التعرية «الجيومائية» حيث تعمل المياه الجوفية أثناء تحركها على إذابة الكلس من الصخور وترسيبها في سقف المغارة مشكلة أعمدة نازلة كبيرة وفي قاع المغارة أعمدة أخرى صاعدة تلتقي أحيانا فترسم لوحات بديعة الالوان، غاية في الجمال.

TT

They are formed by the erosion factors (Geo-hydro) for the underground water during its movement dissolves the Lime from the rocks and precipitates it on the roof of the grotto forming big perpendicular columns and on the ground of the grotto other climbing columns that meet sometimes and draw wonderful colored pictures of extreme beauty.

Leaving aside the linguistic problems in this TT, the text is marred, and made somewhat obscure, by the fact that the translator has failed to identify the correct technical equivalent for الجيومائية 'hydrogeological'. He or she has also failed to identify the standard English terms 'stalactite[s]' (for أعمدة نازلة) and 'stalagmite[s]' (for أعمدة صاعدة).

3.3   Editing

The second and final stage of the post-translation process, that of editing, focuses on the end user of the TT and attempts to achieve the 'optimum orientation of the translated text to the requirements of the target readership' (Graham 1983: 104).

There are no hard-and-fast rules for editing, though critical factors are certainly appearance, appeal, impact, harmony, taste, register and style. If revision is concerned with the 'bare bones' of the TT, the editing process will perform 'remedial surgery' (Graham 1983: 103), which should consist of 'upgrading the terminology, clarifying obscurities, reinforcing the impact, honing the emotive appeal to suit the target reader'. A final 'cosmetic' stage should be to ensure that the appearance and layout of the TT respect the requirements as stated by the client.

With particularly difficult texts, it is sometimes worth doing the revision process itself in two phases. During the first phase, the editor may focus entirely on the TT, considering it from the point of view of style, terminology, etc. as if it were an original English text. During the second and final stage, the TT may be compared again with the ST to check that concern with style has not led to unacceptable translation loss.

A knotty issue is always that of style, as style and language use vary from one translator to another. Thus, care must be taken that edits are made only to items that are in some way incorrect or unsuitable, not to those that are merely phrased differently from the way the translator/reviser would phrase them. For example, in everyday English, there is little difference between 'shall' and 'will' used in the first person; in a text containing direct speech, there would be little point in changing 'I shall go out later' to 'I will go out later', unless there was a particular contextual reason to do so. In legal English, by contrast, there is an enormous difference between 'will' and 'shall' used in the third person, particularly in the context of contracts and agreements (cf. Section 18.2.2.2). Thus, if the TT of a contract contained the words 'The contractor *will* complete the work by August 10th' instead of '*shall* complete', the reviser would have to intervene: the former TT implies that it is a forgone conclusion that the work will be completed by August 10th, whereas the latter makes it a legal requirement for the contractor to finish the work by the deadline stipulated.

In the light of the forgoing, consider the version of the short text dealing with the valleys of Socotra, which we revised earlier. The revisions that we previously carried out yielded the following, as yet unedited, TT. The edited version should not read like an academic description of Socotra but should be accessible to the average intelligent English-speaking reader. The edited TT should be discussed in class; you may well want to improve it with edits of your own.

Unedited TT

4–The Wadis (Valleys):

The plains are interspersed with many valleys. Some of these flow out at the northern part of the island and some of them flow out at its southern part. The most important of these are the Di Azroo valley, which intersects the island from north to south, and the valleys leading out from the Hajhar mountain range, which are characterized by their running water throughout the year.

Edited TT

4–The Wadis (Valleys):

Running through the plains are many river valleys, some of which flow into the sea in the north, others in the south. The most important of these are the Di Azroo valley, which cuts across the island from north to south, and the valleys leading out from the Hajhar mountain range, the rivers of which run throughout the year.

Some texts are passed on to an editor before publication, and here the translator or reviser will often play no further part: in reality, it is unlikely that they will be consulted about changes to the TT. An editor may wish to prune what are considered to be irrelevancies from the TT or to reduce the length of the text due to typographical or impagination constraints. Revisers and editors use proofreading marks to amend and edit translations, which means marking the TT on the text and in the left-hand margin. Using the standard proofreading marks makes it easier for a secretary, typesetter or editor to understand what is being edited and how.

In effect, the editor is responsible to the translator for any changes made to the TT, whether or not the translator is consulted about them. If readers subsequently judge the TT defective in some way, it is the translator and no one else who will automatically be held responsible. As John Graham wisely points out,

> This is why the translator has to accept that his work ought to be checked and, if need be, revised and edited in the interest of the consumer. There is no need for him to fear the verdict or comments of the checker, reviser or editor unless he knows that he has handed in a poor job and then he deserves to be afraid. The checking, revising and editing functions are a safeguard of quality to the user of the translation and the target reader and, at the same time, a safety net for the translator.
>
> (Graham 1983: 105)

It should be remembered that revision and editing are part of the 'quality control' procedure that all translators should implement on completing their translating (or during and after translating, depending on how the translator works). Revision and editing are not only activities carried out by third parties on TTs, though this is standard practice nowadays on the part of work providers. It is essential that translators have their own systems for self-assessment of the work and that, even when completing a rush job, careful reading and checking is carried out to repair errors and omissions (cf. Anderson and Avery 1995: 26).

Practical 3

Practical 3.1 Revising and editing: سقطرى جزيرة السعادة

Assignment

(i) Taking no more than forty-five minutes, produce a revised TT of the unrevised English TT below. In order to make this process practical, do not attempt to write down any decisions of detail while you are doing the revisions. Instead, simply add superscript numbers for the revision notes at this stage, and write the accompanying notes for (ii) when you have done the revisions themselves.

(ii) Explain the decisions of detail that you made in producing your revised TT.

(iii) Exchange revised TTs with another student and then, taking no more than twenty minutes, produce a final edited version of the other student's revised TT. In order to make this process practical, do not attempt to write down any decisions of detail while you are doing the edits. Instead, simply add superscript numbers for the editing notes at this stage, and write the accompanying notes for (iv) when you have done the edits themselves.

(iv) Explain the decisions of detail that you made in producing your edited TT.

Contextual information

The Yemeni Ministry of Culture and Tourism is developing a programme to attract more Western tourists to the country. As part of this, it has decided to produce new and more appealing versions of its tourist literature. You have been employed by the Ministry to revise and edit some of its existing tourist brochures. These include the bilingual Arabic>English brochure on the island of Socotra, which we looked at in Sections 3.2 and 3.3, which also contains the following text (from Republic of Yemen, Ministry of Culture and Tourism n.d.: ١, 1).

ST

سقطرى جزيرة السعادة

ترجع شهرة سقطرى وأهميتها التاريخية الى بداية ازدهار تجارة السلع المقدسة ونشاط الطريق التجاري القديم (المشهور بطريق اللبان). إذ كانت الجزيرة أحد الأماكن الرئيسية لإنتاج تلك السلع الهامة بالإضافة الى كونها المخزن الخلفي لدعم اقتصاد مملكة حضرموت (ملك بلاد اللبان)، وفي تلك العصور القديمة اشتهرت جزيرة سقطرى بإنتاج (الند) وهو صنف من البخور وبالصبر السوقطري كأجود انواع الصبر. وزادت أهميتها، وتردد ذكرها وذاع صيتها حتى تجاوز حدود المكان الى شعوب حضارات العالم القديم التي كانت تنظر الى السلع المقدسة (البخور، المر، الصبر، اللبان ومختلف الطيوب) نظرة تقديس وكانوا يسمون الأرض التي تنتج هذه السلع (الأرض المقدسة) أو (أرض الآله) ولهذا سميت جزيرة سقطرى عند قدماء اليونان والرومان بـ(جزيرة السعادة) وبسبب صعوبة الوصول اليها في الماضي نُسج حولها عدد من القصص والأساطير.

وهي اليوم مثار اهتمام الباحثين المتخصصين في مناطق المحميات الطبيعية النادرة، فسقطرى واحدة من أهم تلك المحميات الطبيعية الكونية.

Unrevised TT

Socotra the Island of happiness

The fame and historic importance of socotra dates back to the beginning
of holy commodities trade prosperity and the activity of the old trade route
which is much better known as Frankincense, Myrrh and Ladanum Route
for the Island was one of the main producers of such essential commodities
in addition to its being the back reserve for the support of Yemeni ancient
Hadramawt Civilization along the first millennium B.C. when the king of
Hadhramawt was named King of Frankincense, Myrrh & Ladanum. In those
old days Socotra Island became famous for the production of Incense Sticks
(a kind of incense) and Socotra Glue as the best quality glue. The Island
became even more important and was widely known to furthermost places
of ancient civilizations who used to consider those holy commodities e.g.
incense, myrhh, Ladanum, glue and other perfumes as hallowed not only
this but named the land producing them as the Holy Land or The Land of
The Gods. This is why Socotra Island was named by ancient Greeks and
Romans as the Happiness Island. Due to the difficulty to reach it in the past.
Many stories and legends have been woven in respect thereto. Today it is the
focus of specialist researchers in the field of rare protected natural areas for
Socotra Island is considered one of the most important Worldwide Protected
Natural Areas.

Practical 3.2 Revising and editing: الأردن .. على العهد

Assignment

You are working for the *Jordan Weekly Herald,* an English-language newspaper
aimed at English-speaking expatriates in Jordan. Your task is to revise and edit
a draft English version of the Arabic text الأردن .. على العهد into idiomatic English
for a section in your newspaper that provides translations of material from the
Arabic-language Jordanian press. The Arabic text is given first, followed by the
draft English translation that you are to revise and edit. You may find you need
to make significant changes in order to accord your version with typical features
of English newspaper editorials. These changes should not, however, remove any
significant information given in the original Arabic text.

(i) Taking no more than forty minutes, produce a revised TT of the unrevised
   English TT below. In order to make this process practical, do not attempt
   to write down any decisions of detail while you are doing the revisions.
   Instead, simply add superscript numbers for the revision notes at this stage,
   and write the accompanying notes for (ii) when you have done the revisions
   themselves.
(ii) Explain the decisions of detail that you made in producing your revised TT.

(iii) Exchange revised TTs with another student and then, taking no more than twenty-five minutes, produce a final edited version of the other student's revised TT. In order to make this process practical, do not attempt to write down any decisions of detail while you are doing the edits. Instead, simply add superscript numbers for the editing notes at this stage, and write the accompanying notes for (iv) when you have done the edits themselves.

(iv) Explain the decisions of detail you made in producing your edited TT.

Contextual information

This text is the beginning of a main editorial from the Jordanian newspaper الرأي, 12 December 1988.

ST

الأردن .. على العهد

في حديث الحسين، الذي بثته هيئة الإذاعة البريطانية، اخيرا، اكد جلالته على ان العلاقة الاردنية الفلسطينية مميزة وخاصة وان الاردن في جميع الاحوال لم يتخل عن أبناء فلسطين ولن يتخلى عنهم، او عن واجبه نحوهم، الى ان يستعيدوا حقوقهم الكاملة، على ترابهم الوطني. وجاء هذا الحديث تعبيرا عن التأييد المستمر للانتفاضة، وهي تدخل عامها الثاني .. ودفاعا عن مشروعيتها، ودعوة للضمير العالمي، ليترجم تعاطفه معها، الى عمل يعجل عقد المؤتمر الدولي ليتسنى تنفيذ الحل الحقيقي، الذي يعيد السلام والاستقرار الى المنطقة ..

وآثر الحسين، ان ينبه مجددا الى ان الصراع الناشب في المنطقة لا يهددها وحدها .. وانما يهدد السلام العالمي .. وكان جلالته، قد وجه التحذير ذاته، غير مرة، خلال الاحاديث التي افضى بها .. من قبل الى عدد من الصحف والاذاعات العالمية ..

وغني عن القول، ان هذا كله، هو تجسيد للالتزام القومي الذي يتمسك به الاردن .. والذي يأخذ مداه، من خلال تنقية الاجواء العربية، والعمل الجاد على حشد الطاقات العربية .. وقد تبدى هذا العمل اوضح ما يكون في المسعى الذي يقوم به جلالته، لاقامة كيان عربي يضم الدول العربية شرقي البحر المتوسط .. والذي من شأنه ان يبعث الجبهة الشرقية ويتيح للعرب ان يمارسوا الخيارات المناسبة لاستعادة حقوقهم وارساء السلام العادل والشامل في منطقتهم.

Unrevised TT

Jordan .. keeps its promise

In his recent speech broadcast by the BBC, his Majesty King Hussein of Jordan affirmed that Jordanian-Palestinian relations are very special since Jordan has not abandoned and will not abandon the Palestinian people until they are granted their full rights on their own national territory. The king's speech came as an expression of Jordan's continuing support for the uprising which is entering its second year, a defence for its legitimacy and a call to the conscience of the international community to translate its sympathy for the uprising into urgent action to convene an international conference that leads to a genuine solution and the restoration of peace and stability in the region.

King Hussein took the opportunity to repeat his warning once again that the ongoing conflict does not just threaten the region alone but that it threatens the whole world. King Hussein has given the same warning repeatedly on previous occasions to a number of international newspapers, radio stations, and T.V. networks.

Needless to say, all this underlines Jordan's steadfast commitment to the Arab nation, whose goal is to clear the air in the Arab world, and to take serious steps to mobilize Arab resources. This is demonstrated with the utmost clarity by the king's endeavour to establish an Arab entity comprising the East Mediterranean Arab countries with the aim of reviving the eastern front and providing Arabs with the appropriate choices to restore their rights and to establish a just and comprehensive peace in the region.

4 Cultural transposition

4.1 Basic principles

In this chapter, we complete our introduction to the notion of translation loss by looking at some implications of the fact that translating involves not just two languages but also a transfer from *one culture to another*. General cultural differences are sometimes bigger obstacles to successful translation than linguistic differences.

We shall use the term **cultural transposition** for the main types and degrees of departure from literal translation that one may resort to in the process of transferring the contents of an ST from one culture to another. Any degree of cultural transposition involves the choice of features indigenous to the TL and the target culture in preference to features with their roots in the source culture. The result is to reduce foreign (i.e. SL-specific) features in the TT, thereby to some extent naturalizing it into the TL and its cultural setting.

The various degrees of cultural transposition can be visualized as points along a scale between the extremes of **exoticism** and **cultural transplantation**, as shown in Figure 4.1.

Source-culture bias	←	→	Target-culture bias
Exoticism and calque	Cultural borrowing	Communicative translation	Cultural transplantation

Figure 4.1 Degrees of cultural transposition.

4.2 Exoticism

The extreme options in signalling cultural foreignness in a TT fall into the category of exoticism. A TT marked by exoticism is one that constantly uses grammatical and cultural features imported from the ST with minimal adaptation, thereby constantly signalling the exotic source culture and its cultural strangeness. This may indeed be one of the TT's chief attractions, as with some translations of Classical Arabic literature that deliberately trade on exoticism. A TT like this, however, has an impact on the TL public, which the ST could never have had on the SL public, for whom the text has no features of an alien culture.

A sample of exoticism in translation from Arabic would be a more or less literal translation of the following simple conversation (we have given versions of the conversation in both Standard Arabic, as it might appear in a short story or novel, and the contextually more natural colloquial Arabic):

Literal translation	Standard Arabic	Colloquial Arabic (Egyptian)
A Peace be upon you.	A السلام عليكم	A سلامو عليكم
B And upon you be peace.	B وعليكم السلام	B وعليكم سلام
A How is the state?	A كيف الحال؟	A إزي الحال؟
B Praise be to Allah.	B الحمد لله.	B الحمد لله.
How is your state?	كيف حالك انت؟	إزي حالك إنت؟
A Praise be to Allah;	A الحمد لله.	A الحمد لله.
how is the family?	كيف الأهل؟	إزي الأهل؟
If Allah wills, well.	إن شاء الله بخير	إن شاء الله بخير
B Well, praise be to Allah.	B بخير الحمد لله	B بخير الحمد لله
etc.	etc.	etc.

Sometimes the nature of the ST makes it virtually impossible to avoid exoticism in the TT. Consider the following from the Classical Arabic text البخلاء by الجاحظ (from Lane 1994: 48, 56–57) in which formal features, such as **parallelism** (cf. Chapter 11), are extremely important in the ST but are not easily matched by typical formal features of English:

> وليس من أصل الأدب ولا في ترتيب الحكم ولا في عادات القادة ولا في تدبير السادة، أن يستوي في
> نفيس المأكول وغريب المشروب وثمين الملبوس وخطير المركوب، والناعم من كل فن واللباب من
> كل شكل، التابع والمتبوع والسيد والمسود [. . .]

It is not consistent with the principles of etiquette, the hierarchy of authority, the customs of leaders, and the good rule of princes that the follower and the followed, the ruler and the ruled become equals with respect to precious food and marvelous drinks, valuable clothes and noble horses, and the finest and best kinds of things.

4.3 Calque

Sometimes, even where the TT as a whole is not marked by exoticism, a momentary foreignness is introduced. A calque is an expression that consists of TL words and respects TL **syntax** but is unidiomatic in the TL, because it is modelled on the structure of an SL expression. This lack of idiomaticity may be purely lexical and relatively innocuous, or it may be more generally grammatical. The following calques of Arabic proverbs illustrate decreasing degrees of idiomaticity:

اللي فات مات	What is past has died
يوم لك ويوم عليك	A day for you, a day against you
زاد الطين بلة	It increased the clay moistness

For most translation purposes, it can be said that a bad calque (like the third exam-ple) imitates ST features to the point of being ungrammatical in the TL, while a good one (like the first example) compromises between imitating ST features and offending against TL grammar. Any translator will confirm that it is easy, through ignorance, or – more usually – haste, to mar the TT with bad calques. However, it is conceivable that in some TTs the calque – and ensuing exoticism – may actually be necessary, even if its effects need to be palliated by some form of **compensation**.

For example, if the strategy is to produce a TT marked by exoticism, the proverb يوم لك ويوم عليك may well be calqued as 'A day for you, a day against you'. But, because of the prevailing exoticism of the TT, it might not be clear that this is actually a proverb. This would be a significant translation loss if it were important that the reader should realize that the speaker is using a proverb. In that case, the loss could be reduced with an explanatory addition such as 'you know the saying': 'You know the saying: "A day for you, a day against you".'

What was originally a calqued expression sometimes actually becomes a stan-dard TL cultural equivalent of its SL equivalent. A good example of a calque from Arabic into current English is 'Mother of . . . ', from the Arabic أم المـعارك used by Saddam Hussein to describe the 'battle' between Iraqi troops and those of the coalition organized to drive the invading Iraqi army from Kuwait. (In fact, this is often mis-calqued into English as 'Mother of all . . . ', rather than simply 'Mother of . . . '.)

Standardized calques from English into modern Arabic include إعادة تدوير 'recy-cling', لاعنف 'non-violence', لعب دوراً 'play a rôle', among many others. Sometimes calques generate further quasi-calques in the TL. So, in addition to ألقى ضوءًا على for 'to shed/throw light on', forms are encountered such as سلّط الأضواء على. It is, however, normally impossible to say in English 'shed lights on'. In using a calque, it is clearly important to get the form right. A failed calque may sound endearing (as does a lot of 'foreignerese'), or it may jar with speakers of the TL. In either case, it is likely to distract from the intended message.

4.4 Cultural transplantation

At the opposite end of the scale from exoticism is cultural transplantation, whose extreme forms are hardly translations at all but more like adaptations – the whole-sale transplanting of the entire setting of the ST, resulting in the entire text being rewritten in an indigenous target culture setting.

An example of cultural transplantation is the remaking of the Japanese film 'The Seven Samurai' as the Hollywood film 'The Magnificent Seven'. An example involving Arabic would be the retelling of a Juha joke with the replacement of Juha and other typical Middle Eastern characters with characters typical of the TL culture and corresponding changes in background setting. In a British context, one might, for example, begin the 'translation' of the joke 'A man walked into a pub'.

It is not unusual to find examples of cultural transplantation on a small scale in translation. For example, in a scene from the short story النار والماء by the Syrian writer زكريا تامر, some rich adolescent girls are poking fun at a girl and boy from a poor part of town who are wandering around together, obviously in love. One of the rich girls calls out «قيس وليلى», alluding to the story of the semi-legendary doomed love affair between the poet قيس بن المُلَوَّح (also known as مجنون) and a woman called ليلى. This has been translated (St John 1999: 30) as 'Just like Romeo and Juliet'.

By and large, normal translation practice avoids the two extremes of wholesale exoticism and wholesale cultural transplantation. In avoiding the two extremes, the translator will consider the alternatives lying between them on the scale given at the end of Section 4.1 of this chapter.

4.5 Cultural borrowing

The first alternative is to transfer an ST expression verbatim into the TT. This is termed **cultural borrowing**. It introduces a foreign element into the TT. Of course, something foreign is by definition exotic; this is why, when the occasion demands, it can be useful to talk about exotic elements introduced by various translation practices. But cultural borrowing is different from exoticism proper, as just defined: unlike exoticism, cultural borrowing does not involve adaptation of the SL expression into TL forms.

An example of cultural borrowing would be the rendering of a culturally specific term by a transliteration without further explanation. Thus, for example, فوطة, as traditionally used in Iraq, would be rendered by 'futa' rather than, say, by 'wrap' or 'robe' (a فوطة in Iraq being traditionally a sarong-like garment worn by women). A cultural borrowing of this kind might well be signalled by the use of italics.

Sometimes, the nature of the text may make the use of exoticism more or less unavoidable. Consider the following from a fairly academic text about the Academy of Musical Studies in Iraq, which describes a concert given by the Academy (Evans 1994: ١٦٥):

تلخص منهاج الحفلة في (١٥) فقرة .. (٦) منها تمثل الاتجاه العربي المصري كما نعرفه من الراديو والتلفزيون. وهذه الفقرات الست اشتملت على غناء الموشحات وعلى تقاسيم متأثرة بالمدرسة المصرية – للآلات العربية الكلاسيكية كالقانون والعود والناي. أضف الى ذلك تأثير المدرسة المصرية في تكوين الفرق الموسيقية التي تدخل فيها الآن الكمان بأعداد كبيرة.

This has been translated (Evans 1994: 15) as:

The concert programme consisted of fifteen sections, six of which were in the Egyptian style as we know it from radio and television. These six parts comprised *muwashshahat* and solos influenced by the Egyptian School – from classical instruments such as the *qanun*, the *ud* and the *nay*. The structure of the music groups was also influenced by the Egyptian School, as they also contained large numbers of violins.

Here, the word كمان translates easily into English as 'violin', because the same instrument is used in both cultures. However, the other instruments are specific to the Middle East. A قانون is an instrument rather like a dulcimer, whose strings are plucked using metal plectrums attached to the fingers; an عود is a short-necked lute, the strings of which are plucked with a plectrum; and a ناي is a flute without a mouthpiece, made of bamboo or more rarely of wood, which, unlike the European flute, is held in a slanting forward position when blown (cf. Wehr). Translating قانون as 'dulcimer', or ناي as 'flute', would significantly distort what is meant by the Arabic; even translating عود as 'lute' (the word 'lute' is derived from the Arabic العود) would disguise the fact that an عود is recognizably different from a European lute. Similarly, translating موشح as 'strophic poem' or the like would here disguise the precise nature of the material being used as well as the fact that what is being dealt with here is poetry set to music. Cultural borrowing on this scale introduces so many exotic elements into the TT that it almost shades into exoticism proper.

Where precise technical terms are important, one solution is for the translator to add a glossary at the end of the book or to use footnotes or endnotes. Alternatively, where the translator decides that for some reason it is necessary to retain an SL term but also to make it plain to the reader roughly what is meant, it is sometimes possible to insert an explanation, or partial explanation, into the TT alongside the cultural borrowing, normally as unobtrusively as possible. Using this technique, the earlier extract could have been translated along the following lines:

> The concert programme consisted of fifteen sections, six of which were in the Egyptian style as we know it from radio and television. These six parts comprised pieces involving the *muwashshah* verse form and solos influenced by the Egyptian School – from classical instruments such as the plucked dulcimer (the *qanun*) and the Arab lute (the *oud*) and the *nay* flute. The structure of the music groups was also influenced by the Egyptian School, as they also contained large numbers of violins.

This translation sounds somewhat strained, but elsewhere the combination of cultural borrowing plus additional explanatory material can be a useful technique. An example is the following (from Pennington 1999: 4), which deals with the response of American Muslims to the use of the crescent and star as a general symbol of Islam in American public places:

واعترضت قلة منهم بحجة ان الهلال والنجمة في أمريكا «بدعة» تخالف الاسلام [. . .]

> A few of them objected, on the grounds that the American use of the Crescent and Star is *bid'a* ('innovation', which Islam opposes) [. . .]

Here, the English gloss 'innovation' on the Arabic word بدعة has been unobtrusively introduced into the TT. (The translator has also included 'which Islam opposes' inside the brackets, in contrast with تخالف الاسلام in the ST, which is part of the main text.)

Sometimes, a cultural borrowing becomes an established TT expression. Examples from Arabic into English are often religious in nature – for example, 'imam', 'Allah', 'sheikh'. A fairly recent cultural borrowing is 'intifada' (cf.

Section 2.2.2). Cultural borrowings shade into (i) forms that were originally borrowed but are no longer regarded as foreign (e.g. 'algebra' from الجبر), (ii) forms that have been borrowed but have shifted meaning in the course of borrowing (e.g. 'algorithm' ultimately from الخوارزمي, the man who invented them), and (iii) forms that have been borrowed but have a sense in the TL that is not the normal sense in the SL (e.g. 'minaret' from منارة, where the word for 'minaret' in most of the Arab world is مئذنة, and 'alcohol' from الكحل, which means 'antimony' in Arabic). It is possible to include these latter types under cultural borrowings, although they might more reasonably be regarded as simple denotative equivalents (cf. Chapter 7), inasmuch as the words are no longer popularly regarded as 'foreign' in nature.

4.6 Communicative translation

As we have seen (Section 2.1.4), communicative translation is normal in the case of culturally conventional formulae where literal translation would be inappropriate.

Examples of stock phrases in Arabic and English are ممنوع التدخين 'no smoking', ممنوع الدخول 'no entry'. Problems may arise where the TL has no corresponding stock phrase to one used in the SL (e.g. because there is no cultural equivalent). Consider, in this regard, the use of religious formulae in everyday Arabic: عليكم السلام ورحمة الله وبركاته, الحمد لله, إن شاء الله. 'Equivalents' for these can be found in English, but they will often either seem unnatural or will involve considerable rephrasing. إن شاء الله, for example, may often be most naturally rendered by 'I hope', a formula in English that clearly lacks the religious aspect of the original Arabic. Similarly, take the phrase نعيماً, said to someone who has had his or her hair cut, and the reply أنعم الله عليك. Here, نعيماً might be translated as 'Your hair looks nice' ('Congratulations' in this context seems overly enthusiastic in English), to which the most natural reply would be something like 'Thanks very much' or 'Oh, that's kind of you to say so'. These are not, however, stock phrases in the same sense as the Arabic نعيماً and أنعم الله عليك, and it would be wrong to overuse them in a TT.

Regarding proverbial expressions, consider again إللي فات مات. Three possible translations of this might be:

LITERAL	That which has passed has died
BALANCED	What's past is gone
COMMUNICATIVE	Let bygones be bygones/What's done is done

In most contexts, one might expect 'Let bygones be bygones' to be the most reasonable translation. However, in a context in which the word 'past' figures prominently, it might be that the second translation would be appropriate, as it would echo the key word directly. Similarly, one might want to avoid the use of the proverb 'Let bygones be bygones' in a context where it could make the TT more clichéd than the ST.

4.7   **Transliterating names**

The issues involved in cultural transposition are well illustrated in the transliteration of names. In transliterating Arabic names, it is possible to follow either one of several more or less standard transliteration systems or to adopt a more *ad-hoc* approach. A transliteration of the mountainous area of Yemen بعدان using a transliteration system, for example, might be *baʿdân*. Here, the symbol ʿ transliterates the Arabic letter ع, while the symbol *â* transliterates the Arabic combination ا . The advantage of a transliteration system is that it allows the reader to reconvert the English back into Arabic script. However, because this is something that is only normally required in an academic context, the use of transliteration systems is generally limited to academic translations. The use of a transliteration system in other cases may give a stronger sense of the exotic than is appropriate for the context. If you are interested in finding out more about different transliteration systems, the Wikipedia article 'Romanization of Arabic' provides a valuable guide (http://en.wikipedia.org/wiki/Romanization_of_ Arabic). Perhaps the most commonly used systems are the DIN system (often with ḍ for ظ, instead of ẓ) and the Library of Congress system (https://www.loc.gov/catdir/ cpso/romanization/arabic.pdf), which is also used by the British Library.

The use of a more *ad-hoc* approach is illustrated by the transliteration of بعدان as *Ba'dan* or *Badan*. The advantage of this approach is that the transliterated form looks more like an English word; there are no obviously strange symbols involved – although the transliteration may contain elements that are not standard letters in English, an example in this case occurring in the first transliteration of بعدان, *Ba'dan*, which involves the use of the apostrophe. The disadvantage of the *ad-hoc* approach is that the transliteration adopted may suggest a pronunciation of the word in English that is very far from the pronunciation of the Arabic original. The form *Badan,* for example, is supposed to render the Arabic بعدان in this case. However, the same English form could also correspond to Arabic forms, such as بَدَن or بادَن or بدان, etc.

Many Arabic proper names have transliteration-type English equivalents. For instance, عَمّان is standardly 'Amman'. In other cases, the transliteration-type English equivalent is more localized. In many parts of the Middle East, the name حُسين is standardly transcribed as 'Hussein', or 'Hussain'; in North Africa, however, where French is the dominant European language, the standard transcription is 'Hoceine'.

Some Arabic proper names have standard indigenous English equivalents that cannot properly be regarded as transliterations (e.g. 'Cairo' for القاهرة, 'Damascus' for دمشق). Other cases are even more complicated; for example, for الدار البيضاء, English uses 'Casablanca' (i.e. the Spanish name for the city, of which the Arabic is itself a calque).

Where there is a standard indigenous English equivalent, a translator would be expected to use this, except where there is a compelling reason not to do so (e.g. a need to introduce a greater degree of exoticism into the TL text than would be conveyed by the use of the standard English TL equivalent). For further discussion of cultural transposition in Arabic>English translation, see Dickins (2012).

Practical 4

Practical 4.1 Cultural transposition: وقادته خطواته

Assignment

Consider the following translation (St John 1999: 7–8). What different techniques of cultural transposition does the translator use? What motivations might there be for adopting these different approaches at different points in the translation?

Contextual information

This text is taken from the short story حقل البنفسج by the Syrian writer زكريا تامر. In this part of the story, the hero محمد is infatuated with an unknown young woman, whom he briefly glimpsed in a field of violets, and dreams of winning her heart. He is currently walking around in a confused daydream.

ST

وقادته خطواته إلى مسجد كبير، وكان يجلس في داخله شيخ له لحية بيضاء، تحلق حوله عدد من الرجال. وكان الشيخ يتكلم عن الله والشيطان: «الله هو خالق كل الأشياء، وجميع المخلوقات لا تفعل شيئًا إلا بأمره.»

فقال محمد لنفسه: إذن يستطيع الله مساعدتي على تحقيق أمنيتي.

وقال الشيخ : إبليس عدو البشر .. إنه الشر».

وغادر محمد المسجد بينما كانت دماء شرايينه أصواتًا تتوسل بلهفة، وتهتف ضارعة : «يا الله».

TT

His feet led him to a large mosque, and inside it sat a religious teacher with a white beard. Several men were gathered round him and he was talking about God and the Devil.

'Allah is the Creator of all things, and no creature can do anything unless He wills it.'

'So Allah can help me realize my dream,' said Mohammed to himself. The teacher continued.

'Satan is the enemy of Man – he is evil.'

Mohammed left the mosque, and as he did so, the blood in his veins became a mass of imploring voices, calling out woefully: 'Oh God.'

Practical 4.2 Cultural transposition: ويبرز حجم الحضور الخليجي

Assignment

Consider the following text and the incomplete TT following it, which is to appear in the *Peninsular Daily News,* an English-language newspaper aimed at expatriate English speakers in Saudi Arabia and the Gulf. In this TT, several culturally specific, and other culturally related, terms have been left untranslated (and appear in the incomplete TT in Arabic). Produce translations for these terms. For each translation where you use a cultural translation technique, say which cultural transposition technique you have used, and explain why you used this technique.

Contextual information

This text is taken from الشرق الأوسط newspaper, 21 March 2007. It deals with Gulf tourists in the West and was written by إيمان الخطاب.

ST

ويبرز حجم الحضور الخليجي بنحو واضح خلال فصل الصيف، حيث يتوزع السياح في أشهر دول العالم برفقة ثقافتهم المحلية، وأزيائهم اللافتة، سواء لكونها تضم الأشمغة الملونة والعباءات المطرزة، أو التكلف الواضح في هيئتها وأناقتها الباذخة، كما يفضل الشباب والفتيات خاصة، حيث تظهر هذه الفئة لافتة للعيان في حال تحولت إلى متجر خليجي متحرك لعرض أحدث منتجات الدور العالمية.

ولم يعد غريباً أن يرى زائر العاصمة البريطانية، لندن، انتشار المحلات العربية المختصة ببيع «برطمانات» اللبنة بالزعتر والبهارات، والأرز المصري، والكفتة المجمدة، وساندويتشات الفول والطعمية، والتي ترفع لافتات كتبت باللغة العربية كـ«المأكولات اللبنانية»، و«الوادي الأخضر»، و«المصطفى»، و«أسواق الشرق الأوسط» ساعية لجذب السياح الخليجيين عبر واجهات تحمل كلمة «حلال» كناية عن وجود السلع الغذائية المتوافقة مع الشريعة الإسلامية، حيث يبلغ حجم التعامل في الأغذية الحلال داخل السوق البريطاني وحده حوالى أربعة مليارات دولار، نتيجة الطلب المتزايد على الأغذية الحلال في السنوات الأخيرة. وكعادة الكثير من مدن العالم، تختص لندن بوجود شارع للعرب وهو «إدجور رود» الشهير بضمه خليطاً منوعاً من الأجناس العربية، تتكثف نسبة الخليجيين بينها خلال إجازة الصيف من كل سنة، لينتشر كبار السن بثيابهم البيضاء، فيما تتفنن الخليجيات باستعراض الطرح والعباءات والتعطر بدهن العود النافث، المختلط برائحة الأرجيلة والشواء المتطايرة في الشارع الذي يشهد تجمعات لا تغيب عنها المشاكل الأمنية والسرقات، والذي يقع على بعد خطوات من حديقة الـ«هايد بارك» حيث لا يطيب للخليجيين التنزه فيها إلا بعد الرابعة مساءً وحتى مغيب الشمس، لتتحول فيما بعد إلى رقعة خليجية بالكامل. ويستغرب الزائر مشاهدة صور «المباسط» النسائية الموزعة، ظناً بأنه يقف في أحد منتزهات عسير أو روابي الباحة، وليس في قلب العاصمة البريطانية لندن!

TT

الخليجي tourists are most numerous in the summer. They gather in tourist areas throughout the world, bringing with them their المحلية culture and distinctive dress – brightly coloured الاشمغة, embroidered عباءات, and the chic and expensive clothing and accessories favoured by the young, whose display of the latest international designer goods gives them something of the air of mobile boutiques.

It is not unusual for a visitor to لندن العاصمة البريطانية، to see Arab المحلات selling jars of لبنة flavoured with الزعتر والبهارات, Egyptian rice, frozen كفتة, طعمية sandwiches and الفول لافتات كتبت باللغة العربية ترفع – Many shops 'المأكولات اللبنانية', 'الوادي الأخضر', 'المصطفى','اسواق الشرق الاوسط', and, in an attempt to attract tourists from the Gulf, the word حلال is prominently displayed, الاغذية الحلال are كناية عن وجود السلع الغذائية المتوافقة مع الشريعة الاسلامية، In fact, now worth about two billion pounds annually in Britain alone, and demand for الاغذية الحلال has increased exponentially in recent years.

Like many مدن العالم, London has شارع للعرب – إدجور رود – frequented by خليطاً are particularly in evidence in the summer منوعاً من الأجناس العربية. الخليجيين holidays – old men بثيابهم البيضاء, and الجليجيات sporting الطرح and العباءات. In this crowded and rather unsafe street where theft is commonplace, the smell of رائحة الأرجيلة mixes with الشواء المتطايرة. التعطر بدهن العود النافث of «إدجور رود» is only a few hundred yards from حديقة الـهايد بارك, where many الخليجيين like to stroll between late afternoon and sunset, turning the whole area into رقعة خليجية بالكامل. Seeing النسائية «المباسط», the visitor might imagine that he is in عسير or العاصمة البريطانية لندن rather than in the heart of الباحة!

Practical 4.3 Cultural transposition: وحين كان يسترد أنفاسه

Assignment

(i) Discuss the strategic decisions that you must take before starting detailed translation of the following text, and outline and justify the strategy you adopt. You are to translate the text as part of a collection of translations of short stories by يوسف إدريس, which you are producing. The intended reader-ship consists of educated native English speakers with general knowledge of the Arab world but no specific expertise in Arabic or Islamic culture. Accordingly, the translation is expected to be readily understandable to the target audience. However, it should attempt to avoid extreme deviations from the source culture (cultural transplantation).

(ii) Translate the text into English.

(iii) Explain the main decisions of detail you made in producing your TT.

Contextual information

The text is taken from مشوار, a short story by the Egyptian writer يوسف إدريس (1954: 140) about a village policeman, الشبراوي, who is detailed to take a deranged woman, زبيدة, from her home in the Delta to a mental hospital in Cairo. الشبراوي has become detained in Cairo, and it is now evening. الشبراوي has been thinking about what he can do with زبيدة overnight. At this point in the story, the two characters find themselves caught up in the popular Sufi ceremonies that regularly take place by the mosque of السيدة زينب (who was a granddaughter of the Prophet) in central Cairo.

This text contains several features that are taken from Egyptian Arabic. In this regard, you may find the following information useful:

حُرْمه   This means 'woman' as well as 'sanctity', 'inviolability' in both Standard Arabic and colloquial Egyptian. However, it is more commonly used to mean 'woman' in Egyptian. As the double meaning 'inviolability/woman' suggests, the word carries strong cultural associations on

the status of women in Egyptian society. The rendering of the feminine
suffix as ـﺔ here, rather than ـﺔ, indicates the colloquialism.

ﺣِﺴْﺒﺔ   In Standard Arabic, ﺣِﺴْﺒﺔ means 'arithmetical problem, sum' (Wehr),
but in Egyptian colloquial, it has the sense of 'calculation'. Here, what
is meant is the cost of the hotel.

ﺑﺎﻟﺮﺍﺣﺔ   In Standard Arabic, this means 'leisurely, gently, slowly, at one's ease'
(Wehr). Here, the author has used the phrase in the more colloquial
sense of 'at least'.

ﻋﻠﻰ ﺍﷲ   The phrase ﻋﻠﻰ ﺍﷲ is used in Egyptian Arabic 'to imply misgiving about
an outcome' (Badawi and Hinds 1986). ﺣﻜﺎﻳﺔ in Egyptian Arabic can
mean 'matter', 'affair' (as well as 'story'). Here, what seems to be
meant is that ﺍﻟﺸﺒﺮﺍﻭﻱ can't afford the hotel.

ST

وحين كان يسترد أنفاسه لاحت له فكرة اللوكاندة، ولكنه نبذها في الحال فهما اثنان، وزبيدة حرمه
وخطرة، والحسبة فيها بالراحة خمسون ستون قرشا، والحكاية على الله.
ولم يبتعد الشبراوي كثيرا فقد تربع أمام جامع السيدة وجذبها حتى تهاوت بجانبه، الحياء يمنعه من
البكاء فلم يكن يعتقد أن انسانا آخر في العالم له مثل تعاسته .. وبؤسه، وكان مجاذيب السيدة حولهما
كالنمل، وحين زغردت زبيدة ضاع صوتها في تمتمة الشيوخ وبسملتهم وزقزقة النساء ودوامات
الذكر ..

Practical 4.4 Cultural transposition: وليس هناك إخصائي

Assignment

(i) Discuss the strategic decisions that you must take before starting detailed
translation of the following text, and outline and justify the strategy you
adopt. You are to translate the text as part of a brochure for a British museum
exhibition on folk customs in Sudan. The intended readership of the brochure
will be museum visitors who do not necessarily know anything about Sudan.

(ii) Translate the text into English.

(iii) Explain the decisions of detail you made in producing your translation.

(iv) Underline any words and phrases that raised cultural issues in your
translation. Now, produce a translation of this first paragraph aimed not
at the general museum-going public but for an academic journal whose
readership is expected to have specialist existing knowledge of Sudanese
culture.

Contextual information

The text is taken from a book titled الشلوخ by the Sudanese academic يوسف فضل حسن
(1986: 51–52). This book is a study of the origins and social significance of the
traditional custom of 'scarification' (التشليخ) in northern Sudan: that is, the making
of long cuts (normally either vertical or horizontal) into people's cheeks with a

sharp blade or razor in order to produce a lasting scar on the face. A scar produced in this way is called a شَلْخ or شَلْخة (plural شلوخ). The action of producing the scar is referred to in this book as فصادة (cf. Wehr for general senses of فصد).

Boys typically underwent scarification around the age of five, and girls around the age of ten. The custom of scarification has in effect died out in the last few decades (although it may still persist in some very isolated rural communities).

The second paragraph of this extract begins with a recapitulation of some ideas that have been discussed just prior to the extract itself (hence the opening phrase نخلص من هذا كله).

You may also find the following information useful:

الدامر	'Ed Damer': town on the Nile, north of Khartoum.
الجعليين	'the Ja'aliyyin': large tribal grouping in northern Sudan (sg. جعلي).
عَبَّاسي	– refers to the tracing of ancestry to the paternal uncle of the Prophet العباس بن عبد المطلب.
الشايقية	'the Shaygiyya': tribe in northern Sudan. The Shaygiyya are some-times classified as part of the Ja'aliyyin.
حساب الجمل	– a system of numerical representation that predates the introduc-tion of Arabic numerals (الأرقام الهندية) in the Arab world. Each letter represents a particular number. Accordingly, by adding together the numerical values of each of the letters that make up a particular word, it is possible to calculate a numerical value for the entire word.
طريقة	'religious brotherhood, dervish order' (Wehr).

ST

وليس هناك اخصائي معلوم ينفرد بإجراء عمليات الفصادة. إذ الغالب أن يقوم بها الحجّام أو المزين أو البصير (الطبيب البلدي) أو القابلة وأمثالهم. وهناك من اشتهروا بإجراء هذه العملية لحسن أدائهم لها، مثل بنت المزين التي كانت تعيش في الدامر في أواسط هذا القرن وكانت قبلة لكثير من الراغبات في الشلوخ من سائر المناطق المجاورة.

نخلص من هذا كله الى أن المجموعات الجعلية العباسية، عدا الشايقية قد اقتبست الشلوخ العمودية الثلاثة من تقليد قديم كان سائدا في تلك المناطق وان هذه الشلوخ من علامات التمييز. ويقول بعض الجعليين ان الثلاثة خطوط العمودية أي III – مائة واحدى عشر تعني كلمة كافي، احد أسماء الله الحسنى، اذا اسقطت بحساب الجمل. وعلى ضوء ما توصلنا اليه من قدم هذه الشلوخ الثلاثة خطوط العمودية في تلك المنطقة فإن هذا التفسير غير منطقي.

ومع أن كلمتي (مشلخ جعلي) تشيران اساساً الى الثلاثة خطوط العمودية، فإن الجعليين قد عرفوا علامات تمييز أخرى. ومن أشهر هذه العلامات (السلم) ذو الدرجة الواحدة وهو كالحرف أتش H بالحروف اللاتينية [...] ويسمي البعض هذا الشلخ بسُلّم الشيخ الطيب البشير الجموعي (١٨٢٤-١٨٧٤) منشئ الطريقة السمانية في السودان.

5 Compensation

5.1 Basic principles

In Section 4.3, we referred to the need on some occasions to palliate the effects of the use of calque by some form of compensation. The example we gave was the insertion of 'You know the saying' before 'A day for you, a day against you' to make it clear that this is a proverb and not an original formulation. This example is the tip of the iceberg. Compensation, in one or another of its many forms, is absolutely crucial to successful translation. In this chapter, we shall look more closely at what compensation is and is not and at a few of the forms it can take.

To introduce the question, we shall take examples from the last sentence of the ST in Practical 4.3 from the short story مشوار (إدريس 1954: 127):

[...] كان مجاذيب السيدة حولهما كالنمل، وحين زغردت زبيدة ضاع صوتها في تمتمة الشيوخ وبسملتهم وزقزقة النساء ودوامات الذكر ..

A possible translation of زغردت in this extract is 'let out a ululation'. This would maintain a certain foreignness, the assumption being that even a reader who did not know what a ululation was in the context of women's behaviour in social gatherings in Egypt would be able to guess that it was some sort of culture-specific vocal sound. However, in a different context, or with a different readership, this assumption might not be justified – 'ululation' could sound facetious or comic. These effects would be a betrayal of the ST effects and therefore count as a serious translation loss. The loss could be palliated by adding an exegetic element (cf. Section 1.3) along the lines 'let out a ululation as women do at times of great joy'. This does not make the idea of ululation any less unfamiliar in itself, but it does make the unfamiliarity less likely to have a misleading effect. This exegetic translation is a simple example of compensation: that is, mitigating the loss of important ST features by approximating their effects in the TT through means other than those used in the ST. In other words, one type of translation loss is palliated by the deliberate introduction of another that is considered less unacceptable by the translator. So, in our example, adding 'as women do at times of great joy' incurs great translation loss in terms of economy, denotative meaning (cf. Chapter 7) and cultural presupposition, but this is accepted because it significantly reduces an even greater loss in terms of message content. It is important to note the *ad-hoc,* one-off element in compensation: this is what distinguishes it from constraint, as we shall see in a moment.

Translators make this sort of compromise all the time, balancing loss against loss in order to do most justice to what, in a given ST, they think is most important. Our main aim in this book is to encourage student translators to make these compromises as a result of deliberate decisions taken in the light of such factors as the nature and purpose of the ST, the purpose of the TT, the nature and needs of the target public and so on. In making these decisions, it is vital to remember that compensation is not a matter of inserting any elegant-sounding phrase into a TT to counterbalance any weaknesses that may have crept in but of countering a specific, clearly defined, serious loss with a specific, clearly defined less serious one.

To discern the parameters of compensation a bit more clearly, we can begin by looking at another expression in the extract from مشوار cited earlier, the final two words دوامات الذكر. There is a double difficulty here.

The first difficulty is the word ذكر. In a Sufi context, ذكر involves chanting a religious phrase, typically الله or one of the other names of God. In this context, this would be a communal practice. A transliteration of ذكر as a cultural borrowing – for example, 'dhikr' – would be incomprehensible to any but a specialist reader. An exegetic translation would be clearer – for example, 'communal invocations of the name of God'. This rendering is like a dictionary entry, a paraphrase that defines the term ذكر, for which there is no conventional lexical equivalent in English (cf. the definition in Wehr of ذكر in Sufism as 'incessant repetition of certain words or formulas in praise of God, often accompanied by music and dancing'). Such a translation incurs notable translation loss in that it is less economical and semantically less precise than the ST ذكر, but this loss is not as serious as the obscurity of English 'dhikr' would be.

We can use this case to explore the boundary between compensation and constraint. This is a less straightforward example of compensation than was the exegetic translation of زغرد. 'Ululate' is a fairly common lexical equivalent for زغرد – although we may note that even this involves semantic distortion. *Collins English Dictionary* defines 'ululate' as 'to howl or wail, as with grief', and the word is derived from the Latin *ulula* 'screech owl', which suggests a sound rather different from the 'ululation' of women in the Middle East. Nonetheless, given that 'ululate' is commonly used to translate زغرد, the translator can freely choose whether to use it on its own and accept the slight obscurity and the misleading connotations or to minimize these by introducing a different loss in terms of denotative meaning and economy. ذكر is different. To the extent that 'dhikr' is not feasible, the translator has no choice but to paraphrase. In principle, where there is no choice, there is constraint, not compensation. In our example, of course, there is still an element of choice in that it is the translator who decides what the paraphrase will be; to this extent, there is an element of compensation in the translation. This would change if the paraphrase became the conventional TL rendering of ذكر. Once a rendering has entered the bilingual dictionary as a conventional lexical equivalent, using it is not a case of compensation. Thus, if the dictionary gave the meaning of ذكر as 'communal invocation of the name of God', and if this were standardly used as this equivalent in English, using this rendering in a TT would not be an instance of compensation but of constraint – there would be little option but to adopt the conventional rendering.

The boundary between compensation and constraint is more clearly seen in communicative translations. For example, if we can imagine the very first time زاد الطين بلة was translated as 'it made matters worse', this was a case of compensation: the calque 'it increased the clay moistness' is, effectively, ungrammatical and meaningless. The first translator was prepared to incur major semantic and grammatical loss in order to avoid meaninglessness, an even greater loss. This was a resourceful piece of compensation. Since then, however, in so far as the communicative translation is mandatory, the translator is not exercising true choice but simply identifying the conventionally correct translation.

Of course, the translator may decide that, in a given context, adopting the conventional dictionary translation would incur unacceptable translation loss. If the conventional translation is modified in order to palliate the loss, this may well be a case of compensation. To return to our earlier example from مشوار, two key elements in the sentence as a whole are كان [مجاذيب السيدة حولهما] كالنمل 'teemed like ants' (the implication of 'communal') and the clashing noise of many voices (زغردت '[let out a] ululation', تمتمة 'murmuring', زقزقة 'chirping' and ذكر 'invocations'). Supposing the dictionary gives 'communal invocations of the name of God' as the conventional translation of ذكر. It may be felt, in this particular context, that 'invocations' would be too abstract, denoting a particular mode of relationship with God and losing the stress on 'voice' that is conveyed in the ST implication of 'chanting'. The translator might then decide on a new rendering of ذكر. One possibility is 'communal chanting(s) of the name of God', which keeps both elements but loses that of 'throng of people'. A third possibility is to keep all three elements, as in 'communal chanted invocations' or 'chanted communal invocations', but these collocations (cf. Section 8.6) sound odd in English, more like technical definitions than expressive descriptions. This loss in idiomaticity might be avoided by conflating 'communal' and 'chanting' into a single verb, as in 'chorusing invocations of the name of God'; the loss here is that the element of musicality that is typically present in ذكر is at best only implicit: a chorus of voices does not necessarily sing – it can just as easily be speaking or shouting.

All of these alternatives therefore incur significant loss. But to the extent that each is a one-off, unpredictable translation, created to meet the demands of a specific context, they are all instances of compensation rather than of constraint. Whichever one is chosen, the translator is balancing loss against loss in an attempt to preserve in the TT the textual effects that are deemed most important in this particular ST, even though they are produced there by different means.

The second difficulty posed by دوامات الذكر is the use of دوامات 'whirlpools' as the first part of this genitive structure. The metaphor is clear, vivid and appropriate, fitting in well with the imagery of throng (especially the teeming ants) and noise of many voices. But a literal translation, such as 'whirlpool of communal invocations', is inelegant (where the ST is not) and perhaps somewhat obscure. It could even be positively misleading, with a connotation of 'fast and short', via **collocative meanings** (Section 8.6) of 'whirlwind' – cf. 'whirlwind campaign/romance/tour', etc. The temptation is strong to drop the image, accept the loss, operate a grammatical transposition and use an adjective like 'ceaseless' or 'unceasing'. 'Eddying' would be closer than these in terms of denotative meaning, but 'eddying of communal invocations' is almost as obscure as 'whirlpool of communal invocations'; any sense it does make is too gentle and decorative. Yet the whirlpool image is too important in this text to be surrendered without a fight. Can it be preserved through compensation? In such cases, it is always worth looking to see where else in the clause, sentence or paragraph the image might be fitted in, without loss of coherence or idiomaticity and without too great a loss of ST textual effect. The essential point is that Zubaida's voice is lost in a whirlpool of other voices. One possibility is therefore to combine grammatical transposition and a change of place in the sentence. Here are two alternatives for discussion:

> . . . her voice was whirled away among the pious murmurings . . .
> . . . her voice was whirled away, lost among the pious murmurings . . .

Another possibility is to keep the noun 'whirlpool', but to apply it to all the voices:

> . . . when Zubaida let out a ululation, it was lost in a whirlpool of voices, the pious murmurings, . . .

In all three versions, the specific application of دوامات to ذكر is lost, and the grammar is changed. But at least the strategic connection between teeming people and whirling voices is kept. In any case, the adjective 'ceaseless' can still be applied to whatever rendering is chosen for ذكر: if this is done, the ST emphasis on the insistent presence of the invocations/chants is kept, as they are marked apart from the murmurings and cries/chirpings. There is thus, in the sentence as a whole, grammatical loss and a loss in semantic precision; but there would have been a far greater loss if 'whirlpool' had been applied to 'invocations' or if it had been dropped altogether. Each of these three alternatives is a good example of compensation: although the ST effects are not preserved completely, far less of them is lost than would have been the case if the translator had not introduced the specific, anodyne losses we have outlined.

5.2 Categories of compensation

In discussing TTs, it is sometimes helpful to distinguish between different categories of compensation. We shall suggest three. Remember, however, that most cases of compensation belong to more than one category. The most important thing is not to agonize over what label to give to an instance of compensation but to be clear what loss it compensates for and how it does so. Remember, too, that the question of how to compensate can never be considered in and of itself in isolation from other crucial factors: context, style, genre, the purpose of the ST and the TT.

Compensation is needed whenever consideration of these factors confronts the translator with inevitable, but unwelcome, compromise. Simply put, it is a less unwelcome compromise. It usually entails a difference in kind between the ST textual effect and the TT textual effect. We shall call this **compensation in kind**, which can take many forms. For instance, it may involve making explicit what is implicit in the ST or making implicit what is explicit. Denotative meaning may have to replace **connotative meaning** and vice versa. Compensation may involve substituting concrete for abstract or abstract for concrete. It nearly always involves different parts of speech and **syntactic** structures from those indicated by literal translation. In some texts, compensation in kind might involve replacing a piece of Classical Arabic poetry by an analogous piece of English poetry. An ST pun may have to be replaced with a different form of word play. All of these sorts of substitutions may be confined to single words, but they more usually extend to whole phrases, sentences or even paragraphs. Sometimes, a whole text is affected. For instance, quite apart from lexical or grammatical considerations, if a poem is heavily marked by **rhyme** and **assonance**, and the translator decides that for some reason rhyme and assonance would lead to unacceptable translation loss, compensation might consist of heavily marking the TT with rhythm and **alliteration** instead.

The compensation examples we have discussed so far are various sorts of compensation in kind. Here is another, taken from a translation of the opening two paragraphs of the short story نخلة على الجدول by the Sudanese writer الطيب صالح. This section consists of an exchange between Sheikh Mahjoub and Hussein the Merchant, who wants to buy the produce of his date palm. What is striking about Hussein the Merchant's speech is that it uses Standard Arabic (and a rather formal version of Standard Arabic at that), whereas almost all the other dialogue in the story uses Sudanese colloquial. The use of Standard Arabic here is intended to emphasize the haughtiness of Hussein the Merchant, clearly distinguishing his character from others within the short story. The original Arabic reads:

«يفتح الله»

«عشرون جنيها يا رجل، تحل منها ما عليك من دين، وتصلح بها حالك. وغدًا العيد، وانت لم تشتر بعد كبش الضحية! واقسم لولا انني اريد مساعدتك، فان هذه النخلة لا تساوي عشرة جنيهات».

This has been translated (Montgomery 1994: 21) as:

'No deal!'
'Look here my man, with twenty pounds you could settle your debts and make your life a lot easier. The Eid festival is tomorrow and you haven't even bought a sacrificial lamb yet. As I would not ordinarily pay more than ten pounds for a date palm like this, I would like to think that I am being of some assistance to you.'

The style of this translation is somewhat formal and stilted and is hardly typical of everyday spoken English – take for instance 'my man' (for يا رجل), 'ordinarily' (where 'normally' might be expected) and 'I am being of some assistance to you' (for اريد مساعدتك). This is deliberate compensation in kind; whereas Hussein the Merchant's haughtiness is conveyed in the Arabic by the use of Standard Arabic, in English it is conveyed by the use of a rather stuffy register.

Compensation also usually entails change of place, the TT textual effect occurring at a different place, relative to the other features in the TT, from the corresponding textual effect in the ST. We shall call this **compensation in place**. Moving 'whirlpool' so that it qualifies 'murmurings' and 'cries' as well as 'invocations' is a good example. And, as in the same example, compensation very often involves both change in kind and change in place. Here is another example, from the story البسيها وتعالي خوّفي اخوتي الصغار فهم النار والماء by زكريا تامر. The ST phrase كالعفاريت has been translated as 'You can put it on and frighten my naughty little brothers' (St John 1999: 29). Here, the prepositional phrase كالعفاريت is not translated literally, 'like devils': grammatically, 'my little brothers for they are like devils' would not fit in idiomatically; and semantically, it would give a sense of evil not intended in the ST. So the translator has made use of compensation in kind, replacing the Arabic clause فهم كالعفاريت by an appropriate English adjective 'naughty'. This compensation in kind, however, also involves compensation in place: the clause فهم كالعفاريت of the ST is lost from its position after the noun in the ST, to be rendered by an adjective before the noun in the TT. That is, while a literal translation ('for they are like devils') would entail unacceptable grammatical and semantic loss, omitting the idea altogether would be just as unacceptable; the TT introduces grammatical and semantic changes (and therefore losses), but these are compensated for because the changes preserve the idiomaticity and the essential message content.

Another example of compensation in place occurs in السيد ومراته في مصر by بيرم التونسي. This is a play, written in the 1930s in Egyptian colloquial Arabic, about the return to Egypt of an Egyptian couple who have spent the last few years in Paris. This example occurs where the wife is complaining about the treatment she receives from a female Egyptian customs official. The wife says: ياما انا منكادة من المرة الخنزيرة اللي في الجمرك دي. This is translated as: 'Really, it's just that woman at the customs got my goat by being piggish to me' (Foreman 1996: 35). Here, the translator has chosen not to translate the phrase المرة الخنزيرة as 'piggish woman', or even 'pig of a woman', but has opted for compensation in place 'by being piggish to me' (as well as introducing a pun of his own – that is, a further element of compensation in kind – through the use of 'has got my goat').

Another example of compensation in place and kind in السيد ومراته في مصر by بيرم التونسي occurs when the wife adopts a pseudo-French style of broken Arabic as she is discussing how a French woman might view Egypt:

أيوه بقت تقول له مصر كله ناس وسخين كتير .. ياكل زي واخد خمار .. وينام زي واخد طور .. والدنيا هنا كله كناسة كتير كتير .. الستات هنا كله يرمي الكناسة في عربيات مخصوصة .

The ST here includes pseudo-Frenchisms on both the phonic level and the **grammatical level**. Phonically, we find خ for ح (واخد for واحد) twice; خمار for حمار) and also ط for ت (طور for تور). Grammatically, we find other features felt to be typical of native French speakers (e.g. lack of proper gender agreement). These effects cannot be copied exactly in English, because English is too different from Arabic phonically and grammatically. But to lose them from the TT would be unacceptable – the text would be pointless without them. Accordingly, the translator (Foreman 1996: 35) renders this speech as:

> – Yes, she'd say to me that Egypt is full of extremely feelthy people zey eat and zey sleep like zee peeg and zat everywhere round here is covered in garbage. In France all zee garbage is throuwn on zee dust cart.

The translator has mimicked the pronunciation of English by French speakers (or at least this pronunciation as it is popularly presented); so 'feelthy' for 'filthy', 'zey' for 'they', 'zee' for 'the', 'peeg' for 'pig', etc. He has also introduced some grammatical errors typically made in English by French speakers – for example, 'zey eat and zey sleep like zee peeg' instead of 'they eat and sleep like pigs'. The pseudo-French forms of the TT, however, do not precisely mirror those of the ST. There is thus a touch of cultural transplantation (Section 4.4), and it amounts to compensation in kind and in place: ST phonic and grammatical features are lost, but the textual effects are largely restored by other means and in other places in the TT.

Compensation also often involves a change in 'economy', ST features being spread over a longer length of TT. We shall call this **compensation by splitting**. Compensation by splitting very often also involves compensation in kind. Examples are the earlier renderings of زغردت and ذكر. Here is an example of compensation by splitting that involves minimal change in kind. It is from the novel مدينة البغي by the Palestinian writer عيسى بشارة. The ST concerns the relations among the workers at a newspaper:

لم يكن ثمة ود واحترام متبادلان على الصعيد الشخصي يمكن أن يشكلا خطوة في الاتجاه الصحيح لتحقيق الانسجام في العمل على الأقل. ولهذا بقي الجميع يتعاملون بحرص وحذر شديدين ..

This has been translated (Brown 1996: 43) as:

> There was neither mutual friendship nor respect on a personal level, which would make possible a step in the right direction towards achieving harmony at work at least. Owing to this, their dealings with each other continued to be motivated by overwhelming greed and extreme caution.

In the ST, the Arabic dual adjective شديدين applies to both حرص 'greed' and حذر 'caution'. However, rather than go for a translation such as 'extreme greed and caution', the translator has opted to split the Arabic adjective شديدين into the two English adjectives 'overwhelming' and 'extreme'. She has done this on the grounds that these two forms collocate more happily with each of their respective nouns than would any single adjective applied to both nouns. In other words, a small loss of accuracy in denotative meaning is compensated for by a greater degree of collocational acceptability than would be possible in literal translation.

A similar rationale applies to the following example, from a book titled العسكر :والحكم في البلدان العربية

ومن التناقض الواضح أن ترى الفريق، العسكر الحاكم، الذي يتبنى سياسة التنمية والإنماء والمشاريع الضخمة والمضخمة [. . .]

This has been translated (Humphrys 1999: 12) as:

> It is clearly contradictory that the ruling military, who adopt a policy of development and promote huge state projects [. . .]

Here, the single word يتبنى in Arabic has been split in the TT, being translated first as 'adopt', as this is a word that typically goes with 'development', and second as 'promote', as this is a word that typically goes with '[state] projects'.

We have labelled the last two examples compensation rather than constraint, because the translation decisions are unpredictable, depending entirely on context: neither splitting is likely to be prescribed in the dictionary. However, translation by expansion is often the conventional, more or less mandatory, solution. In such cases, compensation does not come into the reckoning. For example, فراش in Arabic includes both 'moths' and 'butterflies' in English (that is to say, it is a **hyperonym** of 'moth' and 'butterfly'; cf. Section 7.1.2). Accordingly, one would expect an Arabic entomological book title الفراش to be translated into English as 'Moths and Butterflies' or as 'Butterflies and Moths'. In either case, there is no question of compensation being involved here.

Similarly, expansion is sometimes dictated by the grammatical or stylistic norms of the TL. For example, subject phrases beginning with أن in Arabic are very typically translated by the initial phrase 'the fact that' in English. Thus, the Arabic أن يكون التوظيف في الجيش [. . .] will in many contexts almost inevitably be translated as 'The fact that employment in the army is [. . .]' (Humphrys 1999: 5).

The distinction between compensation in kind, compensation in place and compensation by splitting is a rough-and-ready categorization. One could even argue for a fourth general category, that of 'compensation by merging', as in this description:

تململ صابر في سريره دون أن يستبدّ به النعاس وجعل يطوف بناظريه في أرجاء الحجرة: طاولة مخلعة صغيرة، وكتب متناثرة على حصيرة من القش والقصب، وإبريق من الفخار مملوء بالماء، وبعض الملابس الرثة على أحد الجدران.

This has been translated (Brown 1996: 38) as:

> Saber fidgeted in his bed without feeling sleepy. Instead he let his eyes roam about the room: a small broken table, books scattered on a straw mat, a clay pitcher full of water and some old clothes hanging on one of the walls.

Here, حصيرة من القش والقصب has been translated as 'a straw mat' rather than the literal 'straw and cane mat', on the grounds that this is overly descriptive in English, the Western target audience caring little for the distinction between 'straw' and 'cane'. Perhaps, then, the semantic loss is compensated for by avoidance of the greater loss in idiomaticity that literal translation would have entailed.

This kind of instance aside, it is certainly true that translation by compression or omission is, like translation by expansion, often virtually mandatory. Consider, for example, . . . (وهذا) when used in an Arabic radio broadcast to introduce a new subtopic or جدير بالذكر at the start of a paragraph in an Arabic newspaper. Given the mandatory nature of the omission, the notion of compensation is not applicable here.

However many categories of compensation it may be theoretically possible to define, our aim here is not to elaborate a taxonomy but simply to alert students to the possibilities and mechanisms of compensation, both in producing and in analyzing and explaining TTs. In fact, in the case of compensation in kind and in place, it is not usually even necessary to label them as such, because virtually all compensation entails difference in kind and in place. It cannot be stressed enough that the point of this course is to enable students to produce good translations and to give them an apparatus and a terminology that will help them to say why they are good. The aim is not to show off the terminology for its own sake but to put it to use where it is helpful.

The most important lesson to be learned from the discussion is that compensation is a matter of choice and decision. It is the reduction of an unacceptable translation loss through the calculated introduction of a less unacceptable one. Or, to put it differently, a deliberately introduced translation loss is a small price to pay if it is used to avoid the more serious loss that would be entailed by literal translation. So where there is no real choice open to the translator, the element of active compensation is minimal. The clearest illustrations of this, as we have seen, are communicative translation and the myriad cases where the generally accepted literal translation involves grammatical transposition and/or expansion or contraction.

Compensation, then, is a matter of conscious choice, and it is unlikely to be successful if left purely to inspiration (although a touch of inspiration never comes amiss!). Before deciding on how to compensate for a translation loss, translators are therefore best advised to assess as precisely as possible what the loss is and why it matters, both in its immediate context and in the ST as a whole. Only then can they be reasonably sure of not inadvertently introducing, somewhere in the TT, more serious translation losses than the ones they are trying to reduce.

Practical 5

Practical 5.1 Compensation: أن ترى واحدا يجري

Assignment

(i) Discuss the strategic decisions that you must take before starting detailed translation of the following text, and outline and justify the strategy you

adopt. You are to translate the text for inclusion in an anthology of modern Arabic short stories. The intended readership is educated English speakers with no specific knowledge of the Arab world.

(ii) Translate the text into English, paying particular attention to issues of compensation.

(iii) Explain the decisions of detail you made in producing your TT, paying special attention to whether your rendering is an instance of compensation or of constraint. For each decision of detail, identify (a) whether there is compensation or not and where there is compensation, (b) what is lost in the TT, (c) what compensates for this loss in the TT and (d) how it does so.

Contextual information

This text is taken from a short story by يوسف إدريس titled طبلية من السماء in the collection حادثة شرف (n.d.*b*: 40–1) and concerns an incident in the village of Munyat El Nasr.

ST

أن ترى واحدا يجري في منية النصر فذلك حادث .. وكأنه صوت السرينة في عربة بوليس النجدة فلا بد أن وراء جريه أمراً مثيراً . وما أجمل أن يحدث في البلدة الهادئة البطيئة أمر مثير !
وفي يوم الجمعة ذاك لم يكن واحد فقط هو الذي يجري في منية النصر، الواقع أنه كانت هناك حركة جري واسعة النطاق. ولم يكن أحد يعرف السبب . فالشوارع والأزقة تسبح في هدوئها الأبدي وينتابها ذلك الركود الذي يستتب في العادة بعد صلاة الجمعة، حيث ترش أرضها بماء الغسيل المختلط بالرغوة والزهرة ورائحة الصابون الرخيص، وحيث النسوة في الداخل مشغولات بإعداد الغداء والرجال في الخارج يتسكعون ويتصعلكون الى أن ينتهي اعداد الغداء .. واذا بهذا الهدوء كله يتعكر بسيقان ضخمة غليظة تجري وتهز البيوت، ويمر الجاري بجماعة جالسة أمام بيت فلا ينسى وهو يجري أن يلقي السلام، ويرد الجالسون سلامه ويحاولون سؤاله عن سبب الجري ولكنه يكون قد نفذ . حينئذ يقفون ويحاولون معرفة السبب وطبعا لا يستطيعون، وحينئذ يدفعهم حب الاستطلاع الى المشي ثم يقترح أحدهم الإسراع فيسرعون ويجدون أنفسهم آخر الأمر يجرون، ولا ينسون أن يلقوا السلام على جماعات الجالسين فتقف الجماعات ولا تلبث أن تجد نفسها تجري هي الأخرى.

Practical 5.2 Compensation: قد يمر وقت طويل

Assignment

(i) Discuss the strategic decisions that you must take before starting detailed translation of the following text, and outline and justify the strategy you adopt. Pay particular attention to issues of compensation. You are to translate this text for the general reader with no specialist knowledge about Lebanon for a book titled *The Lebanese Civil War: Arab Perspectives.*

(ii) Translate the text into English.

(iii) Explain the decisions of detail you made in producing your TT, paying special attention to whether your rendering is an instance of compensation or of constraint. For each decision of detail, identify (a) whether there is compensation or not and where there is compensation, (b) what is lost in the TT, (c) what compensates for this loss in the TT and (d) how it does so.

Contextual information

This text is taken from the start of a book titled سقوط الإمبراطورية اللبنانية by فؤاد مطر (1984, vol. 1: 7). The book deals with the breakdown of the political consensus in Lebanon in the mid-1970s and the ensuing civil war.

ST

قد يمر وقت طويل قبل أن يصبح في وسعنا فهم حقائق الحرب اللبنانية التي عصفت بهذا الوطن الصغير فدمّرته كما لم تدمّر حرب من قبل، ومن هذا النوع، وطنا من الأوطان في العالم.

وهذه الحرب التي بدأت في ١٣ نيسان (أبريل) ١٩٧٥ واستمرّت قرابة سنتين، لها خلفيّات يمكن القول إنها تكوّنت مع ولادة لبنان المستقل في العام ١٩٤٣ واستمرت تنمو على الخطأ، ثم نشأت ظروف موضوعية، ساعدت على تكريس الخطأ، إلى أن كانت لحظة الانفجار، فإذا بها لحظة قاسية جدا حوّلت الوطن الصغير إلى ساحة حرب لم يسجّل التاريخ الحديث، على الأقل، مثيلاً لها.

إن الحرب اللبنانية من النوع الذي يصعب تحديد هويته، فلا هي طائفية فقط، ولا هي لبنانية – فلسطينية فقط، ولا هي إصلاحية فقط. إنها كل هذه الأمور وغيرها مجتمعة.

Practical 5.3 Compensation: نشأت في أسرة مصرية صميمة

Assignment

(i) Before starting detailed translation of the following text, outline and justify the strategy you adopt. Pay particular attention to issues of compensation. Your translation should be aimed at an educated, but non-specialist, readership and will be included in a book to be published in Britain titled *Other Lives*, which will consist of extracts from autobiographies of figures from around the world.

(ii) Translate the text into English.

(iii) Explain the decisions of detail you made in producing your TT, paying special attention to whether your rendering is an instance of compensation or of constraint. For each decision of detail, identify (a) whether there is compensation or not and where there is compensation, (b) what is lost in the TT, (c) what compensates for this loss in the TT and (d) how it does so.

Contextual information

The text is taken from قصة حياتي, the autobiography of أحمد لطفي السيد, an Egyptian politician and literary figure in the early twentieth century.

ST

نشأت في أسرة مصرية صميمة لا تعرف لها إلا الوطن المصري، ولا تعتز إلا بالمصرية، ولا تنتمي إلا إلى مصر .. ذلك البلد الطيب الذي نشأ التمدن فيه منذ أقدم العصور .. وله من الثروة الطبيعية والشرف القديم ما يكفل له الرقي والمجد.

وقد ولدت في ١٥ يناير سنة ١٨٧٢ م. بقرية «برقين» من أعمال مركز السنبلاوين بمديرية الدقهلية. وهي قرية صغيرة كان تعدادها في ذلك الحين يبلغ مائة نفس. ويشاع بين أهل الريف أن

اسمها «النزلة» وربما سميت باسم «برقين» الفلسطينية. وقد تضاعف سكانها، فأصبح عددهم الآن نحو ألفي نفس. وهم زراع ماهرون، مشهورون بالجد والنشاط والاستقامة، وقد اعتادوا أن ينطقوا القاف «جافا»، والجيم جيما معطشة كسائر أهالي مركز السنبلاوين، وما زالت هذه اللهجة تغلب علي في حديثي.

وكان والدي «السيد باشا أبو علي» عمدة هذه القرية، كوالده «علي أبو سيد أحمد». وقد كان يجيد حفظ القرآن الكريم كله. وعرف بشخصيته المهيبة، وقوة شكيمته، وعدالته في معاملته، وعطفه على أهل قريته وغيرهم. وأذكر أنه ما قسا يوما علي، ولا وجه اليَّ كلمة نابية أو عبارة تؤلم نفسي، بل كان – طيب الله ثراه – عطوفا حكيما في تربية أبنائه، يعني بالقدوة الحسنة، وحسن التوجيه والارشاد.

ولما بلغت الرابعة من عمري، أدخلني كتاب القرية، وكانت صاحبته سيدة تدعى «الشيخة فاطمة»، فمكثت فيه ست سنوات تعلمت فيها القراءة والكتابة، وحفظت القرآن كله. وكنت أجلس مع زملائي على الحصير، ونصنع الحبر بأيدينا. وإلى هذه السيدة يرجع فضل تنشئتي الأولى في تلك السنين.

6 Genre

6.1 Introduction

Different STs require different strategic priorities. In deciding which **textual variables** to prioritize, the translator has always to ask: What is the purpose of the ST, and what is the purpose of the TT? These questions imply two others: What kind of text is the ST, and what kind of text should the TT be?

At issue here is a fundamental consideration in translation: all texts are defined in terms of genre. By genre we mean what Hymes calls a 'type of communicative event' (quoted in Hervey 1992: 199) – that is, a category to which, in a given culture, a given text is seen to belong and within which the text is seen to share a type of communicative purpose and effect with other texts. In this definition, the term also covers the traditionally identified genres of literature, as well as genres bearing what Baker calls 'institutionalized labels', such as 'journal article,' 'science textbook', 'newspaper editorial' or 'travel brochure' (Baker 2011: 123).

The term **text type** is often used in a similar sense to 'genre'. (In fact, different scholars use the terms 'text type' and 'genre' in a bewildering variety of ways. For a brief discussion of the various uses of these terms, see Lee 2001.) The best-known classification of text types has been that of Katharina Reiss, who distinguishes three, each characterized by a different function of language – artistic and creative self-expression, conveying information and persuading somebody to do something (Reiss [1977] 1989: 105–115). Snell-Hornby (1988) sees this classification as too limited and suggests a much more complex 'prototypology' – certainly too complex for our purposes. Neubert and Shreve (1992: 125–135) also try to get round the problem with a concept of 'prototype'. Yet another classification is proposed by Hatim and Mason (1990: 153–158), who distinguish among the argumentative, expository and instructional text types found functioning alongside one another as what amount to multiple texts within texts. (For a refined analysis of the argumentative text type, with useful examples of conventional differences between Arabic and English argumentation, see Hatim and Mason 1997: 127–142.)

In all of these taxonomies, a decisive factor in distinguishing text type is the author's intention. This is something they have in common with genre as we have defined it. However, in foregrounding intention rather than event, these writers may be laying less stress than we do on the text as outcome, perhaps implying that the author's purpose and the actual effect of the text coincide, or that, in respects where they do not, this does not matter. From the translation point of view, this in turn may imply a normative assumption that there are certain archetypal invariants that can and should be transferred without loss from ST to TL. However legitimate or illegitimate these possible inferences may be, the term 'text type' is used so variously that we shall stick to 'genre', because the element of 'event' in its definition ensures that the definable qualities of a text are seen as together constituting the outcome of an attempt to realize a particular communicative purpose.

Most texts belong to a genre or genres. Some innovative texts arguably do not, when they first appear: but even these are defined by contrast with genres to which they do not belong. Innovative texts aside, one can say that any ST shares some of its properties with other texts of the same genre and is perceived by an SL audience as being what it is on account of some genre-defining properties. Therefore, in order to assess the nature and purpose of the ST, the translator must have some sort of overview of genre types in the source culture and be familiar with the characteristics of relevant genres within those types.

What is true of SL texts is true of TL texts. Because the nature and purpose of a given text imply each other, the translator has to be as familiar with target-culture genre types as with those of the source culture. Paying due attention to the nature and purpose of the TT guarantees a degree of TL bias that helps to prevent the excessive SL bias, or literalness, that so often defeats the stated or implied purpose of the TT.

Consider the following ST, which is taken from a 'personal opinion' column by مصطفى أمين from الشرق الاوسط, 21 September 1982, and the two TTs that follow it:

ST

في استطاعة أي حزب أن ينجح إذا دافع عن قضية الحرية وحقوق الإنسان، إذا احتضن كل مظلوم،
إذا قاوم الفساد، إذا ضرب الأمثلة في القدوة الصالحة، إذا حوّل الكلمات إلى افعال والوعود إلى
حقائق. كل حزب يقف إلى جانب الشعب يقف الشعب إلى جانبه يحيط به عندما تُوجَّه إلى ظهره
الخناجر وإلى صدره المدافع والسيوف.

TT (a)

It is possible for any political party to succeed if it defends the issue of freedom and human rights, if it embraces every unjustly treated person, if it opposes corruption, if it sets the highest standards in upright behaviour, if it changes words into deeds and promises into facts. Every party which stands by the people will find that the people stand by it, surrounding it when daggers are aimed at its back and guns and swords at its front.

TT (b)

For any political party to succeed, it must be prepared to stand up for freedom of expression and human rights, to protect the weak, to oppose corruption, to set itself the highest standards, and to act according to these standards. Any

party which supports and defends the people will find that it is supported and
defended by the people.

Some of the ways in which TT (a) reads strangely have to do with features of
meaning that correlate with formal differences (chapters 9–10 and 12–13) between
English and Arabic. Others, however, simply reflect the fact that the formal features of English in certain kinds of writing tend to be different from the formal
features of Arabic, notably in respect to parallelism (cf. Chapter 11) and metaphor
(cf. Chapter 14). There is nothing in the linguistic structure of English that requires
that the use of parallelism and metaphor in 'personal opinion' columns in English
to be different from their use in Arabic. It is simply conventional that writing of
this kind in English does not make as dense use of these features as is normal in
Arabic. In other kinds of writing – particularly in poetry – it would be much more
normal for English to make wider use of them.

In translating a 'personal opinion' text of this kind, the translator has to bear in
mind that the conventions of English for this kind of writing are rather different
from those for Arabic. Assuming that the intention is to produce an idiomatic TT,
the translator must attempt at least to modify the TT in the direction of more typical English-language forms, as in TT (b). Of course, it may not always be possible
to achieve a TT that reads entirely like an original English text. For example, an
attempt to produce an entirely natural-sounding English text might result in unacceptable loss of message content.

Because translators need to consider these genre-related questions before translating a text, it is useful for them to have a framework of broad genre types. This
will help them to identify salient generic characteristics of the ST and to check the
generic characteristics of the TT they are producing. We are not going to attempt
an exhaustive typology of genres; that would be too elaborate for our purposes. In
determining the genre of a text, the essential factor is the author's attitude to the
treatment of the subject matter of the text. (We use 'author' to denote the originator
of the text, whether it is oral or written.)

6.2   Treatment of subject matter

Subject matter in itself is not a useful criterion for describing genres, because the
same subject matter can figure in very different genres. What is at issue is the
author's attitude, implicit or explicit, to treatment of the subject matter. This attitude also includes the *intention* that the text should have a particular sort of effect
on the reader or listener and an *acceptance* of the probability or improbability of
this intention being completely achieved. On this basis, we shall distinguish five
broad categories of genre, each corresponding to a traditional Western categorization, and illustrate these with Arabic examples. We will then consider how these
relate more broadly to traditional Arabic genres and then to modern Arabic genres.

The first category is that of literary genres. Literary genres have subdivided and
diversified very greatly over the centuries. There are innumerable subgenres of
poetry, fiction and drama, each with its own characteristic style. However, all texts

in this category have two essential features. First, they concern a world created autonomously in and through the texts themselves and not controlled by the physical world outside. However close a literary text is to history or autobiography, it still approaches its subject matter by recreating experience in terms of a subjective internal world, which is fundamentally perceived as fictive, for all its similarities to the world outside the text. Second, whatever other characteristics they have, and whatever their subject matter, literary texts contain features of *expression,* on any level of textual variables, that emphasize, modify or actually create features of *content*.

In this respect, consider the use of **onomatopoeia** and sound symbolism in the following (discussed in Section 5.1): ودوامات الذكر . . . تمتمة الشيوخ وبسملتهم وزقزقة النساء. Here, the words زقزقة, تمتمة and even بسملة are intrinsically onomatopoeic, while دوامات is not. However, placed in a parallelistic context involving تمتمة, بسملة and زقزقة, the word دوامات acquires a quasi-onomatopoeic, or secondary onomatopoeic (Section 9.1.2), status; the reader is led to interpret the دوامات not just in the sense of the whirlpool movement of the Sufis but also in the sense of whirlpools of sound.

With their reliance on suggestion – for example, **polysemy**, connotation, analogy – literary genres illustrate very clearly the potential for discrepancy between intention and outcome: however carefully the author tries to control the reactions of the reader or listener, it is less possible than with most other genre types to predict what effects the text will have. An acceptance of this is part of the literary author's attitude to treatment of subject matter.

The second category comprises religious genres. In terms of the author's attitude, the subject matter of religious texts implies the existence of a spiritual world that is not fictive but has its own external realities and truths. The author is understood not to be free to create the world that animates the subject matter but to be merely instrumental in exploring it. This category has perhaps diversified less than any of the others, but, certainly in the field of Christianity, it still has a wide range of styles, from Authorized Version to 'happy-clappy'.

In an Arabic and Islamic context, there is less diversity still, because of the dominance of فصحى التراث – that is, classically oriented Standard Arabic (cf. Section 15.5.1) – in a religious context. However, even here, there will be linguistic differences between a religious text aimed at scholars and one aimed at the general public. And in the case of a sermon (خطبة) in a mosque, with a perhaps partially illiterate congregation, the preacher often makes some use of colloquial Arabic.

The third category comprises philosophical genres. These have as their subject matter a 'world' of ideas. Pure mathematics is the best example of the kind of subject matter that defines philosophical genres. Even in the field of metaphysics, however original the text, the author is understood not to be free to develop theoretical structures at will but to be constrained by some standard of rationality. Philosophical genres have not proliferated as much as literary ones, but they are strikingly diverse nonetheless.

The fourth category is that of empirical genres. Genres in this category purport to deal with the real world as it is experienced by observers. An empirical text is more or less informative, and it is understood to take an objective view of observable phenomena. Scientific, technological and many scholarly texts fall into this category. It thus goes on diversifying into new genres and subgenres as new scientific and academic disciplines are created.

Finally, there is the category of persuasive genres. The essence of these genres is that they aim at getting listeners or readers to behave in prescribed or suggested ways. This aim can be pursued through various means: we are classifying in a single category the entire gamut of texts from instruction manuals, through laws, rules and regulations, to propaganda leaflets, newspaper opinion columns and editorials and advertisements. The indefinite number of genres and subgenres in this category has a common purpose, that of getting an audience to take a certain course of action and perhaps explaining how to take it.

Some of the categories established for pre-modern Western writing apply happily to Classical Arabic writing. Thus, we can identify Classical Arabic texts that are empirical in nature, for example, كتاب الجامع لمفردات الأدوية والأغذية (*Compendium on Simple Medicaments and Foods*) by ابن البيطر, which is a pharmacopoeia (pharmaceutical encyclopedia) listing 1,400 plants, foods and drugs and their uses. We can similarly identify Classical Arabic philosophical texts, such as آراء اهل المدينة الفاضلة (*The Opinions of People of the Perfect State*) by الفارابي, in which الفارابي theorized an ideal state along the lines of Plato's *Republic*. Religious texts are an obvious feature of Classical Arabic, not only authoritative texts – the Quran and Hadith – but also a wide variety of other religious writing. We can also, no doubt, find persuasive texts – a lot of Islamic religious writing, for example, has a strongly persuasive aspect to it; writing of this kind can be regarded as both religious and persuasive in genre.

The most problematic element in the classification of pre-modern Western writing from the point of view of Classical Arabic writing is the distinction between fiction and non-fiction. Van Gelder argues of fictionality that:

> its role in traditional Arabic literature has been a rather minor one. Almost anybody, it was argued, is able to concoct fantastic stories, parables, or fairy-tales [. . .]. What really counts are matters of poetic and rhetorical style, and the invention of clever conceits.
>
> (van Gelder 2000: 25–26)

This relative marginality of the fiction versus non-fiction distinction in Classical Arabic writing is underlined by Allen (2000), who classifies the major genres of Classical Arabic, alongside the Quran and literary criticism, as:

> Poetry – with subtypes: panegyric, lampoon, elegy, wine poetry, hunt poetry, ascetic poetry, love poetry.
>   Belle-lettristic prose and narrative (أَدَب) – with subtypes including journeys of the imagination and the مقامة.

In all of these types of writing, even those that might be classified as prose fiction, such as the مقامة, the form of the writing is normally as important or more important than its content: 'The individual *maqamas* should not be read as short stories, as they are insufficiently and inconsistently plotted. Language and the display of language skills take precedence over story-telling in each of the episodes' (Irwin 1999: 179). For further discussion of the مقامة, see Section 13.3.1.

Modern Western writing has, of course, heavily influenced modern Arabic, adopting forms from the West such as the novel, short story and serious drama, which did not exist in Classical Arabic. However, in many cases, even these new genres show a greater tendency towards a 'display of language skills' in Arabic than their counterparts do in English. Section 13.3.1 provides further discussion of this.

6.3 Oral and written texts

Another factor in determining genre is the question of whether the text is oral or written. Each of the five traditional Western genre categories discussed in the previous section includes both oral and written texts. In practice, however, it is almost impossible not to distinguish an oral text as belonging to a discrete oral genre and a written text as belonging to a discrete written genre, even where the texts share the same subject matter. The difference in medium generally entails a difference in attitude to treatment of the subject matter. A spoken خطبة about social problems in Egypt, a talk on the history of Arab nationalism, a tutorial explanation on quarks – each is a different genre from any kind of written reflection on the topic. A complicating factor is that many oral genres also involve written texts: songs, plays, sermons, lectures, a salesman's patter – all may be performed on the basis of a written text that is either read out, or spoken from memory or used as the basis for improvisation. To get an idea of the significance of these factors for translation, it is helpful first to look at some of the specific characteristics of oral texts as distinct from written ones.

An oral text is in essence a fleeting and unrepeatable event. This has important implications. First, vocal utterance is usually accompanied by visual cues, such as gestures or facial expressions, that are secondary to it but do form part of the overall text and can play a role in creating its meaning. Second, on every level of textual variable, effective oral texts avoid information overload, elaborate cross-referencing, excessive speed and so on, because these can make the text hard to follow. Naturally, in these respects, what is true for oral STs is true for oral TTs as well.

A third implication of orality is the appearance of spontaneity that often characterizes oral texts. This goes not only for impromptu conversation or narrative but also for prepared texts, such as memorized lines in a play. An oral text is always very different in nature and impact from even the most closely corresponding written version.

An awareness of these properties of oral texts is a necessary starting point for translating an oral ST into an oral TT. Spoken communication has characteristics that are very much language specific. Oral translation is not simply a matter of verbal transposition: the genre-related techniques of the target culture must be respected as well, including gestures, facial expressions and so on. Translating a joke, for instance, will generally involve different genres from conference interpreting. Both, however, make it clear that an oral text in any genre is not only an utterance but also a dramatic performance.

Except in most forms of interpreting (which is a specialized skill and is not part of this course), translators actually do a great deal of their work in a written medium, even if it involves an oral text or texts. Inevitably, metamorphoses result from the crossover from written to oral and vice versa. These metamorphoses are essentially due to the fact that writing is such a pale copy of speech in terms of expressive force. Crossover in the process of translation may take several forms. We shall mention four.

In the first type of crossover, the translator starts with an oral ST and then uses a written transcript to compose a TT that is on paper but suitable for oral performance. Song lyrics are typically translated in this way. In the second type of crossover, the translator starts with a written ST, considers how it might be performed orally and then composes a TT that is on paper but suitable for oral performance. This is generally how plays are translated. Third, the translator may start with a written script, try out the ST orally and then produce a TT suitable either for silent reading or for oral performance, or for both. Poetry is usually translated like this. In the fourth type, a translator starts with an oral ST and its transcript and produces a TT for silent reading. This is how film subtitles are generally produced.

Consideration of the two factors we mentioned at the outset – the author's attitude to treatment of the subject matter and whether the text is an oral or a written one – concentrates the translator's mind on four groups of vital strategic questions. (1) What are the salient features of the ST? What do these features imply about its purpose? What genre or genres do the features and purpose suggest it belongs to? (2) Does the ST have recognizable genre-specific characteristics that require special attention? If so, which of them should be retained in translation? (3) What TL genre(s) provide a match for the ST genre? What do existing specimens of these TL genres suggest regarding formulation of the TT? (4) What genre(s) should the TT ultimately be couched in, and what genre-specific features should it have?

Two words of caution are needed here. First, it is easy for student translators to begin their strategic considerations something like this: 'This text belongs to genre A; therefore, it has characteristics x, y and z.' This is putting the cart before the horse. It is much more useful to identify the text's characteristics first, and then, on that basis, to assign it to a genre. This results in a more sensitive appraisal of the true purpose of the text, which in turn makes it easier to be flexible and to recognize cases where, as very often happens, the ST actually has a blend of features – it may be predominantly typical of one genre but also have features from other genres or even other genre categories. So, for example, instruction manuals may vary in character between the empirical and the persuasive categories. Advertising commonly shares features with literary texts, as do religious and philosophical texts. The same is true of some empirical texts, such as Goethe's scientific work in verse or the ألفية of ابن مالك (d. 1273), which is a pedagogical text on Arabic grammar arranged in the form of one thousand poetic verses. Religious texts often share features with persuasive texts. Many legal or administrative texts – contracts or memoranda of agreement, for instance – combine empirical and persuasive genre features. Texts often contain quotations from texts that belong to other genres.

Such 'hybridization' in genre is common in journalism, as well as in parody and satire, which can make wholesale use of a mixture of features from various genre categories. Such blends may theoretically constitute subgenres, but that is not our concern: our aim here is to encourage and enable students to isolate the salient features and the purpose of an ST so that they can relate these to the purpose of the TT and thus be in a position to develop an appropriate translation strategy on the basis of these things.

The second word of caution is that it is absolutely essential for translators to be familiar with the characteristic features of the TL genre or genres that they decide correspond most closely to the ST genre(s). If in doubt, examine sample texts from the chosen TL genre before starting the translation. Professional translators tend to specialize in particular fields, and one of the first things they do is acquire an awareness of relevant TL genre characteristics.

Practical 6

Practical 6.1 Genre: خريف صلالة

Assignment

(i) Consider the following (as discussed in Section 6.3): (1) What are the salient features of the ST? What do these features imply about its purpose? What genre or genres do the features and purpose suggest it belongs to? (2) Does the ST have recognizable genre-specific characteristics that require special attention? If so, which of them should be retained in translation? (3) What TL genre(s) provide a match for the ST genre? What do existing specimens of these TL genres suggest regarding formulation of the TT? (4) What genre(s) should the TT ultimately be couched in, and what genre-specific features should it have?

(ii) Discuss the strategic decisions that you must take before starting detailed translation of the following text, and outline and justify the strategy you adopt.

(iii) Translate the text into English.

(iv) Explain the decisions of detail you made in producing your translation, paying particular attention to generic issues.

Contextual information

This text is taken from the website http://om.mohe.gov.sa/ar/studyaboard/living/Pages/attraction.aspx. This is run by the Omani government and is intended to attract tourists to Oman. Large numbers of Arab tourists already visit certain parts of Oman, such as Salalah in the south, attracted by the cool (and rainy) weather of the region during the summer. However, the Omani government wants to attract more Western tourists and has accordingly commissioned an English-language version of this ST, which is to appear on an English counterpart web page to the Arabic one.

ST

خريف صلالة

يعتبر أبرز المناطق السياحية في السلطنة، إذ تتحول خلال فصل الخريف من كل عام (يونيو الى سبتمبر) الى مصيف بالغ الجمال والروعة، والمناخ اللطيف الذي يتخلله الرذاذ بينما تكون حرارة الصيف الشديدة على امتداد المناطق الأخرى. ومن ثم لم يكن غريباً أن تجتذب محافظة ظفار أعدادا متزايدة من السائحين العمانيين والخليجيين والعرب والأجانب عاماً بعد عام.

Practical 6.2 Genre: قاس علماء الفلك العرب

Assignment

(i) Consider the following (as discussed in Section 6.3): (1) What are the salient features of the ST? What do these features imply about its purpose? What genre or genres do the features and purpose suggest it belongs to? (2) Does the ST have recognizable genre-specific characteristics that require special attention? If so, which of them should be retained in translation? (3) What TL genre(s) provide a match for the ST genre? What do existing specimens of these TL genres suggest regarding formulation of the TT? (4) What genre(s) should the TT ultimately be couched in, and what genre-specific features should it have?

(ii) Discuss the strategic decisions that you must take before starting detailed translation of the following text, and outline and justify the strategy you adopt.

(iii) Translate the text into English.

(iv) Explain the decisions of detail you made in producing your translation, paying particular attention to generic issues.

Contextual information

The ST is from the start of text titled الإبداع العربي في علم الفلك, which appears on a Syrian government website dedicated to the Arab scientific heritage (http://ar-csq.com/vb/archive/index.php/t-366.html). You are to translate it as part of a book commissioned by the Syrian government titled *Traditional Arab Science*. To find appropriate English translations of some of the words and phrases used here, you may find it useful to look at the Wikipedia page 'History of geodesy' (https://en.wikipedia.org/wiki/History_of_geodesy).

ST

قاس علماء الفلك العرب نصف قطر كوكب الأرض. ويعود الفضل في ذلك إلى العالم الموسوعي أبي الريحان البيروني، الذي توصّل إلى وضع معادلة يمكن بها قياس نصف قطر الكرة الأرضية على الشكل التالي:

ر=ٮ تجب ٮ/ٮ/ 1- تجب ٮ

حيث /رٌ/ تمثّل نصف قطر الكرة الأرضية، و /فٌ/ ارتفاع الجبل الذي صعد عليه البيروني عند إجرائه القياس، و/يه/ الزاوية الحادثة بين أفق الراصد وممّاسّ الأرض.

Practical 6.3 Genre: يا ابن آدم

Assignment

(i) Consider the following (as discussed in Section 6.3): (1) What are the salient features of the ST? What do these features imply about its purpose? What genre or genres do the features and purpose suggest it belongs to? (2) Does the ST have recognizable genre-specific characteristics that require special attention? If so, which of them should be retained in translation? (3) What TL genre(s) provide a match for the ST genre? What do existing specimens of these TL genres suggest regarding formulation of the TT? (4) What genre(s) should the TT ultimately be couched in, and what genre-specific features should it have?

(ii) Discuss the strategic decisions that you must take before starting detailed translation of the following text, and outline and justify the strategy you adopt.

(iii) Translate the text into English.

(iv) Explain the decisions of detail you made in producing your translation, paying particular attention to generic issues.

Contextual information

The ST is from the start of a خُطْبة by الحسن بن أبي الحسن البصري (known as الحسن البصري), who lived AD 642–728. You are to translate this text as part of an anthology of speeches from different cultures titled *An Anthology of Historical Speeches*. The TT readers are not expected to have any significant knowledge of Arab or Islamic culture. You have also been told by the editor of the anthology to avoid cultural borrowing (Section 4.5) and, if possible, exoticism (Section 4.2).

ST

يا ابن آدم، بع دنياك بآخرتك تربحهما جميعا، ولا تبع آخرتك بدنياك فتخسرهما جميعا. يا ابن آدم إذا رأيت الناس في الخير فنافسهم فيه، وإذا رأيتهم في الشر فلا تغبطهم عليه. الثواء ها هنا قليل والبقاء هناك طويل. أمتكم آخر الأمم، وأنتم آخر أمتكم، وقد أسرع بخياركم فماذا تنتظرون؟ [. . .] أما إنه والله لا أمة بعد أمتكم ولا نبي بعد نبيكم، ولا كتاب بعد كتابكم، أنتم تسوقون الناس والساعة تسوقكم؛ وإنما ينتظر بأولكم أن يلحقه آخركم. من رأى محمدا فقد رآه غاديا ورائحا، لم يضع لبنة على لبنة، ولا قصبة على قصبة، رُفع له علم فشمر إليه فالوحاء الوحاء، والنجاء النجاء. علام تعرجون؟! أتيتم ورب الكعبة، قد أسرع بخياركم وأنتم كل يوم ترذلون، فماذا تنتظرون؟!

Practical 6.4 Genre: مقرونة في الكوشة

Assignment

(i) Consider the following (as discussed in Section 6.3): (1) What are the salient features of the ST? What do these features imply about its purpose? What genre or genres do the features and purpose suggest it belongs to? (2) Does the ST have recognizable genre-specific characteristics that require special attention? If so, which of them should be retained in translation? (3) What TL genre(s) provide a match for the ST genre? What do existing specimens of these TL genres suggest regarding formulation of the TT? (4) What genre(s) should the TT ultimately be couched in, and what genre-specific features should it have?

(ii) Discuss the strategic decisions that you must take before starting detailed translation of the following text, and outline and justify the strategy you adopt.

(iii) Translate the text into English.

(iv) Explain the decisions of detail you made in producing your translation, paying particular attention to generic issues.

Contextual information

This recipe is one of a set of recipe cards produced in Tunisia and titled أكلات تونسية. The recipe is on one side of the card, and the picture and list of ingredients on the other (the picture is not reproduced here, and the list of ingredients has been placed above the recipe in conformity with the normal presentation in British recipe books). Your brief is to translate the recipe as part of an English-language version of this set of recipe cards, which is intended to sell mainly to English-speaking tourists visiting Tunisia on holiday.

If you are a regular user of cookery books, it should be fairly easy to find appropriate TT equivalents for the ST terms, weights and measures used here. If you are not, you will need to consult some English-language cookery books in order to try and work out appropriate TT equivalents.

The text contains several terms that are specific to Tunisia. Some of these present challenges that are likely solvable in context; we have left these for you to try and work out for yourself. Others may be more difficult. These are glossed as follows:

د ق	Abbreviation for دقيقة
فل	This usage is obscure. Native Arabic speakers whom we have asked suggested either that it is a brand name or that it is فُل meaning 'Arabian jasmine'. In the latter case, one might translate مقرونة فل as 'jasmine-scented macaroni'. It is probably safer to omit it in the TT.
م.أ.	Abbreviation for ملعقة أكل (i.e. what is known in English as a dessert spoon).
هريسة	Harissa is 'a very strong, peppery preserve [. . .] It should be added with caution' (Roden 1970: 159).
دسل	Abbreviation for دسيلتر (from French *décilitre*).
رفس	This means 'mix' in Tunisian Arabic (rather than 'kick', as is normal for Standard Arabic).

ST

مقرونة في الكوشة

مدة التهيئة: 20 ق د
مدة الاعداد: ساعة ونصف
مقومات لاربعة اشخاص

500 غ مقرونة فل
500 غ لحم عجل هبرة
4 بيض
4 بطاط
1 بصل حجم متوسط
1/2 فص ثوم
3 م.أ. معجون طماطم
1/2 م.أ. هريسة
1/2 م.أ. فلفل احمر مرحي
قطعة جبن قريار
1 دسل زيت زيتون

الاعداد :
يحمى الزيت ويوضع فيه البصل مقطعا والثوم مهروسا واللحم متبلا بالملح والفلفل الاسود. ينضج قليلا، نضيف الفلفل الاحمر والطماطم والهريسة محلولا في مقدار كأس من الماء.
يترك للطهي على نار متوسطة حتى الغليان والى ان تخمشر (تخثر) الصلصة. يستخرج من فوق النار ويترك ليبرد.
نضيف جبن القرويار مقطوعا قطعا صغيرة والجبن المرحي وقطع بيضتين مسلوقتين والبطاطة المسلوقة وبيضتين طازجتين ونرفس الخليط.
نطهي المقرونة في الماء والملح مدة 10 دقائق ونتركها تنضب من مائها.
في طيف صالح للفرن نسوي طبقات من المقرونة تتخللها طبقات من الخليط وندخل في الفرن ذي نار متوسطة مدة 15 دقيقة.

Practical 6.5 *Genre:* الشيخ شيخة

Assignment

(i) Consider the following (as discussed in Section 6.3): (1) What are the salient features of the ST? What do these features imply about its purpose? What genre or genres do the features and purpose suggest it belongs to? (2) Does the ST have recognizable genre-specific characteristics that require special attention? If so, which of them should be retained in translation? (3) What TL genre(s) provide a match for the ST genre? What do existing specimens of these TL genres suggest regarding formulation of the TT? (4) What genre(s) should the TT ultimately be couched in, and what genre-specific features should it have? You are to translate the text as a piece of literary writing for inclusion in an anthology of Modern Arabic short stories aimed at an educated English-speaking audience with only a general knowledge of the Arab world.

 (ii) Translate the text into English.

(iii) Explain the decisions of detail you made in producing your translation, paying particular attention to generic issues.

Contextual information

This is the beginning of a short story titled الشيخ شيخة (إدريس n.d.*a*: 15) from the collection آخر الدنيا by يوسف إدريس.

ST

الشيخ شيخة

بلاد الله واسعة وكثيرة، وكل بلدة فيها ما يكفيها .. كبار وصغار، وصبيان وإناث، أناس وعائلات، ومسلمون وأقباط، وملك واسع تنظمه قوانين وتقض مضاجعه قوانين، وأحيانا يخرج للقاعدة شاذ، كالحال في بلدنا الذي ينفرد دون بلاد الله بهذا الكائن الحي الذي يحيا فيه، والذي لا يمكن وضعه مع أناس بلدنا وخلقها، ولا يمكن وضعه كذلك مع حيواناتها . وأيضا ليس هو الحلقة المفقودة بينهما .. كائن قائم بذاته لا اسم له، أحيانا ينادونه بالشيخ محمد وأحيانا بالشيخة فاطمة، ولكنها أحيان وللسهولة ليس إلا، فالحقيقة أنه ظل بلا اسم ولا أب ولا أم، ولا أحد يعرف من أين جاء ولا من أورثه ذلك الجسد المتين البنيان .. أما أن له ملامح بشرية فقد كانت له ملامح، كانت له عينان وأذنان وأنف ويمشي على ساقين .. ولكن المشكلة أن ملامحه تلك كانت تتخذ أوضاعا غير بشرية بالمرة، فرقبته مثلا تميل على أحد كتفيه في وضع أفقي كالنبات حين تدوسه القدم في صغره فينمو زاحفا على الأرض يحاذيها، وعيناه دائما عين منهما نصف مغلقة، وعين مطبقة. ولم يحدث مرة أن ضيق هذه أو وسع تلك. وذراعاه تسقطان من كتفيه بطريقة تحس معها أنهما لا علاقة لها ببقية جسده، كأنهما ذراعا جلباب مغسول ومعلق ليجف.

7 Denotative meaning and translation issues

↗ Literal Meaning

7.1 Denotative meaning

In this chapter and the next one, we shall consider the two basic aspects of the semantic matrix of language: denotative meaning and connotative meaning.

Translation is concerned with meaning. But, as has already become very clear, the term 'meaning' is elastic and indeterminate, especially when applied to a whole text. This is true even of denotative meaning (also known as **cognitive**, **propositional** or **literal** meaning). Denotative meaning is that kind of meaning that relates directly to the range of 'things' (whether physical, emotional or more abstract) that are conventionally referred to by a word or phrase in a particular sense. Thus, the fact that 'window' by convention refers to a particular kind of aperture in a wall or roof is a matter of denotative meaning.

In the case of words, it is denotative meanings that are the central feature of dictionary definitions. In fact, words may, and typically do, have more than one denotative meaning. The situation in which a word has more than one different and distinct denotative meaning – or, more technically, more than one *sense* – is known as polysemy. Polysemy can be illustrated by the word *plain*, which means (i) 'clear' (as in 'a plain sky'), (ii) 'unadorned' (as in 'a plain paper bag') and (iii) 'obvious' (as in 'it's a plain case of forgery'). There are sometimes problems in deciding between cases where two uses of a word represent more than one sense – that is, cases of polysemy – and where the two uses in question are merely 'variants' of a single overall sense. These need not, however, concern us here, as they are not typically of great importance for translation. There are also problems in deciding between what constitutes two senses of a single word and cases where two words happen to sound the same. This latter situation is known as *homonymy*. An example of homonymy that is fairly frequently quoted is *bank* = 'side of a river' versus *bank* = 'institution for the investment and borrowing of money'. Again, these are not of great importance for translation and need not concern us here. (For further discussion of polysemy and homonymy, see Cruse 1986 and Ravin and Leacock 2001.)

A large proportion of a language's vocabulary is traditionally regarded as polysemous (or polysemic). Typically, dictionaries list polysemous words under single heads, separating what they regard as the distinct senses of a word by a semicolon and what are regarded as merely variants of a single sense by a comma (the Hans Wehr *Dictionary of Modern Written Arabic* and the *Oxford Arabic Dictionary,* for example, both do this).

Unfortunately, even dictionary definitions are not without their problems. This is because they impose, by abstraction and crystallization of one core sense (in the case of non-polysemous, or *monosemous,* words) or a series of core senses (in the case of polysemous words), a rigidity of meaning that words do not often show in reality. In addition, once words are put into a context, their denotative meanings become even more flexible. These two facts make it difficult to pin down the precise denotative meanings in any text of any complexity. The more literary the text, the more this is so; but it is true even of the most soberly informative texts. In this chapter, we shall discuss three degrees of semantic equivalence – that is, how close given expressions are to having identical denotative meanings.

7.1.1   Synonymy

Denotative meaning is a matter of categories into which a language divides the totality of communicable experience. So, for example, the denotative meaning of the word 'pencil' (in the relevant sense) consists of the fact that all over the world one may find similar objects that are included in the category of 'pencil' – and of course all sorts of other objects that are excluded from it. To define a denotative meaning is to specify a 'range' covered by a word or phrase (in the relevant sense) in such a way that one knows what items are included in that range or category and what items are excluded. It is helpful to visualize denotative meanings as rectangles, because rectangles can represent intersections between categories. (Circles are more traditionally used, but rectangles are easier to manipulate, especially to show particular kinds of overlap; e.g. Figure 7.4.)

In exploring correspondence between denotative meanings, it is these intersections that are most significant, because they provide a kind of measure of semantic equivalence. So, for instance, the expressions 'my mother's father' and 'my maternal grandfather' may be represented as two separate rectangles. The two ranges of denotative meaning, however, coincide perfectly: that is, in every specific instance of use, 'my mother's father' and 'my maternal grandfather' include and exclude exactly the same referents. This can be visualized as sliding the two rectangles on top of each other and finding that they are the same size and cover each other exactly, as in Figure 7.1.

This exemplifies the strongest form of semantic equivalence – full **synonymy**: the two expressions are synonyms of each other.

Comparison of denotative meanings can also be made among expressions from two or more different languages. For example, 'maternal uncle' and خال (in one sense of the word خال) cover exactly the same range of meanings and are therefore fully synonymous, as is seen in Figure 7.2.

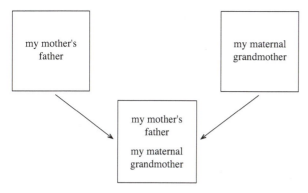

Figure 7.1 Synonymy in English.

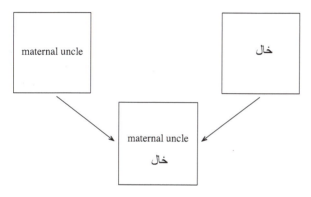

Figure 7.2 Synonymy across English and Arabic.

7.1.2 Hyperonymy-hyponymy

Unfortunately, full synonymy is exceptional, both intralingually and interlingually. Even the nearest semantic equivalent for translating the denotative meaning of an ST expression usually falls short of being a full TL synonym. A simple example of this kind of failure is provided by a comparison between 'uncle' in English and عم and خال in Arabic. Here, the English term 'uncle' might be a typical translation equivalent of the Arabic عم or خال; 'uncle' in English lacks the 'technical' associations of 'paternal uncle' and 'maternal uncle' and would therefore be preferred in many contexts in translating عم or خال, regardless of the translation loss involved. From the point of view of denotative meaning, however, 'uncle' has a greater range of meanings than عم or خال, as 'uncle' includes both paternal uncle and maternal uncle. We can represent the relationship between 'uncle' in English and عم and خال in Arabic as in Figure 7.3.

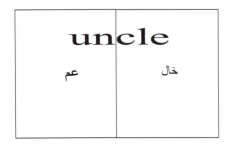

Figure 7.3 Hyperonymy-hyponymy across English and Arabic.

The relationship between 'uncle' and عم and between 'uncle' and خال is known as **hyperonymy-hyponymy**. An expression with a wider, less specific range of denotative meaning is a hyperonym (or **superordinate**) of one with a narrower and more specific meaning. Conversely, an expression with a narrower, more specific range of denotative meaning is a **hyponym** of one with a wider meaning. Thus عم and خال are both hyponyms of 'uncle'.

Hyperonymy-hyponymy is so widespread in all languages that one can say that the entire fabric of linguistic reference is built on such relationships. The same external reality can be described and rephrased in an indefinite number of ways, depending on how precise or vague one wants to be – compare 'I bought a Hans Wehr' with these increasingly general rephrasings: 'I bought an Arabic dictionary', 'I bought a dictionary', 'I bought a book', 'I bought something'. Each of these rephrasings is a hyperonym of the ones before it.

By its very nature, translation is concerned with rephrasing in such a way as to lose as little as possible of the integrity of an ST message. All other things being equal, this includes its degree of precision or vagueness. Therefore, the fact that both a hyperonym and a hyponym can serve for conveying a given message is of great importance to translation practice. It means that when there is no full TL synonym for a given ST expression (e.g. 'uncle'), the translator must look for an appropriate TL hyperonym or hyponym. In fact, translators do this automatically.

This is obvious from the translation of pronouns between Arabic and English. English has one second-person pronoun 'you', which serves to address one, two or more people or animals (and occasionally also plants, inanimate objects and even abstract ideas). English 'you' also makes no distinction between the sex of the person or animal being addressed (or the presumed sex of the plant, etc.). Arabic has five second-person pronouns: أنتم ,أنتما ,أنتِ ,أنتَ and أنتنّ, involving distinctions between singular, dual and plural, as well as masculine and feminine (notions that subsume, but also go beyond, maleness and femaleness). Whenever any one of ST أنتم ,أنتما ,أنتِ ,أنتَ or أنتنّ is translated as TT 'you', the English TT has employed a hyperonym; and whenever ST 'you' is translated as Arabic TT أنتما, أنتم, أنتِ ,أنتَ or أنتنّ, the Arabic TT has employed a hyponym. There is nothing remarkable about this, and it is only occasionally that a translator opts, or is forced, to do something that deviates from this pattern.

7.1.3   *Particularizing translation and generalizing translation*

Translating by a hyponym implies that the TT expression has a narrower and more specific denotative meaning than the ST expression. TT خال is more specific than ST 'uncle', adding particulars not present in the ST expression. We shall call this 'particularizing translation', or **particularization** for short. Another example of particularizing translation is the translation صندوق, which could be used for either a 'box' or a 'bin' (amongst other things). Clearly, in the case of a street sweeper putting his rubbish into a صندوق, the more plausible translation would be 'bin', while in the case of someone packing their books up to move them, the more plausible translation would be 'box'. In either case, however, the English particularizes.

For another example of particularizing translation, consider the word صهر, which means 'husband of one's daughter, son-in-law; husband of one's sister, brother-in-law' (Wehr); these different possibilities can be taken as 'variants' of a single sense (i.e. this is not a case of polysemy). Translating صهر as 'son-in-law' in a particular case would be an example of particularizing translation, as it would explicitly rule out a part of what can be meant by صهر (i.e. 'brother-in-law').

Translating by a hyperonym implies that the TT expression has a wider and less specific denotative meaning than the ST expression. In translating from Arabic to English, TT 'uncle' is more general than ST عم (or خال), omitting particulars given by the ST. We shall call this 'generalizing translation', or **generalization** for short. Translating جلابية as 'garment' or مزمار as 'pipe' are other examples of generalization.

In their semantic near-equivalence, particularization and generalization both entail a degree of translation loss: detail is either added to, or omitted from, the ST text. However, in the absence of plausible synonyms, translating by a hyponym or hyperonym is standard practice and entirely unremarkable. Only when a TL hyponym or hyperonym is unnecessary, contextually inappropriate or misleading can a TT be criticized in this respect.

Particularizing translation is acceptable if the TL offers no suitable alternative and if the added detail does not clash with the overall context of the ST or the TT. Thus, بلد in Arabic means 'country, town, city, place, community, village' (Wehr). There is no single word in English that covers all of these possibilities; therefore, in a particular context, the translator is likely to have to choose the one that he or she feels is most appropriate. Other situations in which particularization is acceptable include the following:

(i) where the context implies something that is typically referred to in more specific terms in the TL than in the SL; thus, an إنذار issued by a military commander is likely to be an 'ultimatum' rather than simply a 'warning'; a بيان in a similar context is likely to be a 'proclamation' or a 'communique' rather than a 'statement'; غارات in the context of NATO raids on Kosovo is likely to be 'strikes' or 'air strikes' rather than 'attacks';

(ii) where the TL typically makes use of a specific collocation (cf. Section 8.6) that happens to involve a hyponym of the TL form; for example, كنز ثمين is likely to be translated as 'priceless treasure' rather than as 'valuable treasure', as 'priceless treasure' is the more common collocation in English.

Particularizing translation may also be used for other reasons. For example, كنيسة قديمة might be translated as 'ancient church' in a particular context where this was appropriate to avoid the ambiguity of 'old church', as this latter could be interpreted to mean 'former church' instead of the intended 'old [= not new] church'. That is to say, 'old' in English is polysemous between the two senses of 'not new' and 'former', and in this context, it would not necessarily be clear to the reader which of the two senses was intended.

Particularizing translation is not acceptable if the TL does in fact offer a suitable alternative to the additional detail or if the added detail clashes with the overall context of ST or TT.

As these examples suggest, similar considerations apply to generalizing translation as to particularizing translation. Generalization is acceptable if the TL offers no suitable alternative and the omitted detail is either unimportant in the ST or is implied in the TT context. For instance, Arabic مُحزِن refers only to something, such as a film or story, that makes one feel sad. In this it contrasts with حزين, which may refer to a person (or even to some non-human entity, such as an animal), who is sad (i.e. who feels sad), or it may refer to something, such as a story or film, that makes one feel sad. In English, the word 'sad' covers both possibilities: 'a sad person', 'a sad story'. Typically, there is unlikely to be any confusion in translating محزن as 'sad', and this is likely to be the most natural-sounding translation in most cases. As the examples 'a sad person' and 'a sad story' suggest, normally the context makes immediately plain in English whether what is intended is a 'feeling sad' or a 'making sad' interpretation.

Other situations in which generalization is acceptable include:

(i) where the context implies something that is typically referred to in more specific terms in the SL than in the TL. For instance, it is common to refer to a room as ضيق in Arabic to mean not just that it is small but that it is rather too small. In many contexts in English, however, a suitable translation of حجرة ضيقة would be the generalizing 'small room', a particularizing translation, such as 'cramped room', being reserved for contexts in which it was important to stress that the room was too small. Similarly, عصفور in Arabic is regularly used to refer to any small bird. In translating the phrase عصفور صغير, it is likely to be sufficient to say 'small bird', although properly speaking what is being meant is a specific small member of the class of small birds (i.e. a bird that is small even among small birds);

(ii) where the TL typically makes use of a specific collocation (cf. Section 8.6) that involves a hyperonym of the SL form. For instance, للوهلة الأولى denotatively means 'for the first moment'. However, in English, the normal phrase is 'for the first time'. Similarly, رثّ means 'old and worn out' clothes. However, in many contexts, ملابس رثة would be happily translatable by the standard collocation 'old clothes'.

Generalizing translation can also be used for many other reasons. Consider the following:

ومهما تكون المشاكل القانونية المترتبة على تدخل حلف الناتو والتي كنت نفسي قد أشرت إليها منذ أيام قليلة [. . .]

This has been translated (Ives 1999:11) as:

> Whatever the legal problems linked to NATO intervention, to which I myself have recently referred [. . .]

Here, the generalizing form 'recently' is preferred to the denotative equivalent 'a few days ago' mainly because it results in a less wordy overall phrase. 'Recently' also allows the translator to use the present perfect 'have . . . referred', which adds a sense of immediacy and relevance to the statement; 'a few days ago' would require the use of the simple past 'referred', which suggests more detachment.

Generalizing translation is *not* acceptable if the TL does offer suitable alternatives or if the omitted details are important in the ST but not implied or compensated for in the TT context. Thus, in a context where it is important that the reader identifies the referent of 'you' as a particular individual (i.e. singular 'you'), and not, for example, as a group of people (i.e. plural 'you'), it may be appropriate to compensate for the fact that English 'you' subsumes both singular and plural by adding a noun that specifically identifies the person referred to. One example of this would seem to be Al-Hilali and Khan's translation of the initial word قُلْ in سورة الإخلاص, where they have 'Say, O Muhammad' (cited in Section 1.4). Here, 'O Muhammad' goes beyond relaying the fact that this is the equivalent of the Arabic masculine singular to identifying precisely to whom it is that قُلْ refers. This seems to be motivated by the translators' perceptions that it is not acceptable in this context to present the possibility that 'you' here refers to people (or even one person) other than the Prophet Muhammad.

Generalization is acceptable if the TL offers no suitable alternative and the omitted detail is either unimportant in the ST or is implied in the TT context. For instance, قِدر and قِدْرة in Sudanese Arabic are both words for 'cooking pot', the difference being that قدر refers to something bigger than قدرة. For most translation purposes into English, however, the distinction could probably be ignored, and 'cooking pot' would be a sufficient translation.

Generalizing translation is *not* acceptable if the TL offers suitable alternatives or if the omitted details are important in the ST but not implied or compensated for in the TT context.

7.1.4 Semantic overlap and overlapping translation

There is a third degree of semantic equivalence. Consider the following:

لقد وصف الكاتب البريطاني المرموق روبرت فيسك حفلة غناء في بلغراد [. . .]

This has been translated (Ives 1999: 10) as:

> The distinguished British writer Robert Fisk recently described a concert in Belgrade.

Here, the meaning of حفلة غناء overlaps with that of 'concert'. Some concerts are examples of حفلة غناء; those in which there are singing. Similarly, some cases of حفلة غناء are examples of concerts; those that are organized in a formal way with musical players and audience. However, some concerts are not examples of حفلة غناء; those in which there is no singing. Similarly, some cases of حفلة غناء are not examples of concerts; those, for example, in which the حفلة is not organized in a formal way with musical players and audience. That is, 'concert' as a translation of حفلة غناء generalizes by going beyond the idea of singing to include the possibility of music without song; but at the same time it particularizes by excluding the non-organized form of 'party', which is a possible interpretation of حفلة.

Taking the example of English 'concert' and Arabic حفلة غناء, this kind of situation can be visualized as two partially overlapping rectangles, as shown in Figure 7.4.

Here, the area where the rectangles overlap (the top left-hand 'cell') represents the material the ST and the TT have in common. The cell on the top right where the rectangles do not overlap represents what is omitted from the TT (i.e. singing), and the cell on the bottom left where the rectangles do not overlap represents what is added to the TT (i.e. organized). This is another category of degree in the translation of denotative meaning. We shall call it **partially overlapping translation**, or **partial overlap** for short. Partial overlap is common and often unavoidable. It can apply to single words as well as to phrases or whole sentences. If, in a given context, استاذة is translated as 'lecturer', not 'teacher', the TT certainly keeps the reference to someone who instructs. But it also particularizes, because it adds the specific detail that she works in a university and not in a school; and at the same time it generalizes, because it omits detail of her gender.

When the TL offers no suitable alternatives, partial overlap is acceptable if the *omitted* detail is unimportant or is implied in the overall TT context and if the *added* detail does not clash with the overall ST or TT contexts. Translating أستاذة as 'lecturer' or 'teacher', for example, will – depending on context – normally be as harmless as it is unavoidable.

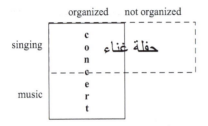

Figure 7.4 Semantic overlap across English and Arabic.

The typical uses of partially overlapping translation parallel those of particularizing translation and generalizing translation. Thus, partially overlapping translation may be used where the context implies something that is typically referred to by a term in the TL whose denotative meaning overlaps with the denotative meaning of the SL term. For example, a poem by the Syrian poet نزار قباني contains the line طاردوها كعصفور ربيعي إلى أن قتلوها. This has been translated (Rolph 1995: 23) as 'They attacked her like a young sparrow until they killed her'. ربيعي here overlaps in meaning with 'young'. Some but not all 'spring sparrows' are young, and some but not all young sparrows are 'spring sparrows' (one could have a sparrow that was, abnormally, born in summer). 'Spring sparrow', however, is a problematic phrase in English; it does not have a clear meaning, and there is nothing in this overall context to make the intended meaning clearer in the English. 'Sparrow' also yields an unfortunate collocative clash with 'spring chicken', meaning most basically 'young chicken for eating (originally available only in spring)' but most commonly found in phrases such as 'he's no spring chicken', where 'spring chicken' is an idiom essentially meaning 'young'; cf. Section 8.6. Accordingly, the translator has chosen a more contextually acceptable overlapping expression.

Partially overlapping translation may also be used where the TL typically makes use of a specific collocation (Section 8.6) that happens to overlap in meaning with the meaning of the SL term. An example of this is وخير شاهد على ذلك, which is typically translated as 'the clearest evidence of this' ('clearest evidence' being a more standard collocation in English than the literal 'best evidence'). 'Clear/clearest' and خير overlap with each other in meaning; some but not all good things are clear, and some but not all clear things are good. Another example is 'coup perpetrators' for رجال الانقلابات, which might typically be translated as 'coup perpetrators' or '[the] perpetrators of coups' ('coup men' or 'men of coups' being quite abnormal in English). 'Perpetrators' and رجال overlap with each other; some but not all perpetrators are men (other perpetrators, even of coups, might be women), and some but not all men are perpetrators (there are, or could no doubt be, men who have never perpetrated anything in their lives).

Partial overlap is unacceptable if the omitted detail is important in the ST but is not implied in the overall context of the TT or if the added detail clashes with the overall ST or TT contexts. If the TL does not offer suitable alternatives, then only compensation can counteract the omission or addition. Thus, in a particular context, it may be necessary to make plain that someone referred to as a 'teacher', as a translation of Arabic استاذة, is in fact female. In this case, the teacher's gender can be made plain through the introduction of the pronoun 'she' at an appropriate point in the TT.

7.1.5 Near-synonymy and translation

In Section 7.1, we considered synonymy and translation, in sections 7.1.2 and 7.1.3 hyperonymy-hyponymy and the related translation techniques of particularizing translation and generalizing translation and in section 7.1.4 semantic overlap and overlapping translation. In this section, we will briefly consider the notion of

near-synonymy and near-synonyms, as these are referred to on several subsequent occasions in this book.

Near-synonymy is a case not of synonymy but of hyperonymy-hyponymy or semantic overlap, which comes near to being synonymy. Thus, in the situation of near-synonymy involving hyperonymy-hyponymy, typically entities (things, etc.) that can be referred to by a particular hyperonym can also be referred to by the hyponym. An example from English is 'thin' versus 'skinny' – assuming the reasonableness of a statement such as 'She's thin but not skinny' but not the reasonableness of a statement 'She's skinny but not thin'. All skinny people are accordingly thin, but not all thin people are skinny. 'Thin' is a hyperonym of 'skinny'. However, there is a very significant overlap between 'thin' and 'skinny' such that thin people are typically also skinny. 'Thin' and 'skinny' can accordingly be regarded as near-synonyms in English.

As the example of 'thin' versus 'skinny' shows, near-synonymy is a rather vague concept. It does not seem possible to say exactly how great the overlap between a hyperonym-hyponym pair has to be for them to qualify as near-synonyms (or how great the non-overlap has to be for them not to qualify as near-synonyms). Near-synonym remains, however, a useful concept in translation analysis.

An example of near-synonymy involving a hyperonym-hyponym pair in English>Arabic translation is translating Arabic زعلان as English 'angry'. زعلان, as understood in Egypt and Sudan at least (where the definition of the Standard Arabic usage of زعلان reflects the definition of the colloquial usage of زعلان), means not just angry but angry with a degree of sadness (i.e. 'sadly angry'). Arabic زعلان is thus technically a hyponym of English 'angry' (as it excludes those cases of anger that do not also involve sadness). زعلان is, however, close enough to the meaning of 'angry' to be considered a near-synonym of 'angry'.

An example of near-synonymy involving semantic overlap in English is 'wood' (in the sense 'collection of trees growing more or less thickly together'; *Oxford English Dictionary Online*) versus 'forest' (in the sense 'extensive tract of land covered with trees and undergrowth'; *Oxford English Dictionary Online*) – assuming the reasonableness of the following statements 'That's a wood, not a forest', 'That's a forest, not a wood', 'You could call that either a forest or a wood' – that is, that some but not all woods are also forests, and some but not all forests are also woods.

As with cases of near-synonyms involving hyperonymy-hyponymy, what is and is not near-synonymy involving semantic overlap is rather vague. We cannot be sure how much semantic overlap is required for two words (in a particular sense) to qualify as near-synonyms or how much semantic non-overlap there would need to be for them to qualify as not near-synonyms. Nonetheless, the notion of near-synonymy is, as already stated, a useful one in practice.

7.2   Semantic repetition in Arabic

Semantic repetition is repetition of meaning. Most basically, this involves the use of two (or more) synonyms or near-synonyms (Section 7.2.1). But it can also be extended to include hyperonym-hyponym pairs (Section 7.2.2) and words and phrases standing in an 'associative' relationship (Section 7.2.3).

7.2.1   *Synonym and near-synonym repetition*

Arabic frequently makes use of repetition of synonyms or near-synonyms in a way that is not normally found in English. This kind of repetition is sometimes referred to as semantic repetition (cf. Dickins and Watson 1999: 541–553). Here, we will refer to it as **(near-)synonym repetition**. (Near-)synonym repetition is of two basic kinds: (i) where the two words or phrases used have closely related but distinguishable meanings – that is, they are near-synonyms; an example of this is الاستقصاء والتحليل 'investigation and analysis'; (ii) where the words or phrases used are fully synonymous or, at least in the context in which they are being used, there is no clear difference in meaning; an example of this is the doublet مستمرة متواصلة in the phrase بصورة مستمرة متواصلة, literally, 'in a continuing continuous manner'.

(Near-)synonym repetition may involve any of the major parts of speech: nouns, as in الاستقصاء والتحليل; adjectives, as in مستمرة متواصلة; verbs, for instance, يدهشه ويذهله 'surprise and baffle' in the phrase كان منظرها يدهشه ويذهله (literally, 'her look surprised and baffled him'); and adverbs, for instance, واجمةً مكتئبةً 'silently and dispiritedly' in the phrase أبصر المرأة نفسها تمشي واجمةً مكتئبةً (literally, 'he saw the same woman walking silently and dispiritedly'; cf. St John 1999: 4–5).

(Near-)synonym repetition may be syndetic (i.e. it may involve the use of a **connective**, typically و) or – in the case of adjectives in particular, but also occasionally in the case of nouns and verbs – it may be asyndetic (i.e. it may occur without the use of a connective). An example of syndetic (near-)synonym repetition is الهمجي والبربري in the phrase السلوك الهمجي والبربري 'savage and barbaric behaviour'. An example of asyndetic (near-)synonym repetition is جميلات انيقات in the phrase فتيات جميلات انيقات, literally, 'pretty, elegant girls' (for more details of syndetic versus asyndetic connection in Arabic, see Dickins and Watson 1999: 47–49).

Several techniques can be used to translate (near-)synonym repetition into English. The first of these is to merge the two Arabic words into one English word. This is particularly likely to be an appropriate strategy where there is no clear difference in meaning between the two Arabic words. So تدابير صارمة وقاسية may be translated as 'severe measures' – (near-)synonym repetition of صارمة and قاسية; قدرة العسكر على تحديث [. . .] والمجتمع وعصرنته [. . .] may be translated as '[. . .] the military's ability to modernize society [. . .]' – (near-)synonym repetition of تحديث and عصرنة; بصورة مستمرة متواصلة is likely to be translated as 'continually'. In this last example, the asyndetic coordination between مستمرة and متواصلة makes a single-word translation still more likely; asyndetic doublets are typically used to represent a single concept.

A second fairly common technique, and one that is used where the two words in the (near-)synonym repetition have clearly different meanings, is to employ at least partial grammatical transposition. So the phrase تحلل القيم والأخلاقيات might be translated as 'the collapse of all moral values'. Here, the noun doublet of the Arabic has been replaced by an adjective–noun phrase in English.

The following are examples of grammatical transposition: وشعر الرجل بالضيق والحرج 'the man began to feel slightly claustrophobic', where the adverb–adjective phrase 'slightly claustrophobic' transposes the Arabic noun doublet الضيق والحرج; similarly, لقد أكدت البحوث الجامعية هذه الظاهرة المخلّة وتناولتها بالاستقصاء والتحليل 'Academic research has confirmed and carefully analyzed this disgraceful phenomenon', where the adverb–participial phrase 'carefully analyzed' transposes the Arabic الاستقصاء والتحليل.

The final two translation techniques that we will consider take account of a feature of (near-)synonym repetition that we have not yet looked at: namely, that it tends to provide a sense of emphasis. This is both because two words give two sets of meanings (even if it is only the same meaning repeated) and because they are longer and therefore 'heavier' in the sentence than only a single word would be.

The first technique that takes into account the potentially emphatic aspect of (near-)synonym repetition is what we shall call **semantic distancing**. This involves relaying both elements of the Arabic doublet by different words in English but choosing English words whose meanings are more obviously distinct than those of their Arabic counterparts. For example, in وكان منظرها يدهشه ويذهله, the two words يدهش and يذهل are quite close in meaning (and according to Wehr's dictionary even share the English translation equivalents 'baffle' and 'startle'). The phrase has been translated (St John 1999: 5), however, as 'Her appearance had both astonished and alarmed him'; the semantic difference between 'aston-ish' and 'alarm' is greater than that between أدهش and أذهل. This semantic distanc-ing ensures that the English translation does not involve what would otherwise be the stylistic oddity in English of having two words with virtually the same meaning conjoined with each other.

It is also possible to combine semantic distancing with grammatical transposi-tion. An example of this is أنا مستمر ومتمسك أكثر من أي وقت مضى بمشروع التوحيد والتجديد. This was said by a Lebanese Phalangist politician about his attitude to the Party. It has been translated (Jones 1999: 7) as: 'I remain committed more than ever to the project of unification and reform'. Here, the adjectival (active participle) doublet مستمر ومتمسك has been grammatically transposed to a verb–adjective (past participle) doublet 'remain committed'. In addition, however, the senses of مستمر and متمسك have been distanced more in the English version.

One final technique for translating (near-)synonym repetition into English is to maintain the same form of repetition. An example of this is السلوك الهمجي والبربري, translatable as 'this savage and barbaric behaviour' (cf. Ives 1999: 15). Here, the repetition in English carries the same emphatic – and more specifically emotive – force as it does in Arabic. The convention that operates otherwise in English that words having much the same meaning are not conjoined is overridden.

Something similar happens with respect to formulaic language, especially where this is of a religious or legal nature. The following is from an oath made by mem-bers of the Muslim Brotherhood to their first leader حسن البنا:

[. . .] «إن من حقك علينا الطاعة والثقة الكاملة والطمأنينة الشاملة وعلى هذا بايعنا وعاهدنا» [. . .]

This might be translated as:

[. . .] 'You have the right to our unquestioning obedience, complete trust and total confidence. This is the oath which we have taken and the pledge which we have made'.

Here, the (near-)synonym repetition of بايعنا and عاهدنا is retained in the English and even expanded as 'the oath we have taken', 'the pledge we have made'.

Just as Arabic has (near-)synonym repetition involving individual words (lexical items), so it may have (near-)synonym repetition involving whole phrases. Here are some examples.[. . .] بين الشكل والجوهر، بين الاسلوب والمضمون، بين التكتيك والاستراتيجية. can be translated as '[. . .] between form and substance, and between tactic and strategy' (Flacke 1999: 7); here, the virtually synonymous Arabic phrases الشكل والجوهر and الاسلوب والمضمون are reduced to the single phrase 'between form and substance' in English. [. . .] الاجراءات التي تقعد حركة التنمية وتقزّم الإنماء can be translated with semantic distancing as '[. . .] the very measures that hinder development and stunt economic growth' (Humphrys 1999: 12). Here, the translator has distanced the meaning of تقعد حركة التنمية from that of تقزّم الإنماء, particularly by translating التنمية as the general term 'development' and الإنماء by the more specific 'economic growth'.

As with (near-)synonym repetition involving individual lexical items, some of the best examples of maintenance of phrasal (near-)synonym repetition occur in formulaic language. Consider again الطاعة والثقة الكاملة والطمأنينة الشاملة from the oath made by members of the Muslim Brotherhood to حسن البنا (cited earlier). This phrase has been translated as 'unquestioning obedience, complete trust and total confidence'. Here, the repetition of the Arabic has not only been maintained but in fact increased by the addition of 'unquestioning' before 'obedience' in the English.

7.2.2 *Hyperonym–hyponym repetition*

Not only are synonyms and near-synonyms in Arabic repeated in ways that are unusual in English, but it is also fairly common in Arabic for a hyperonym to be followed by its hyponym in a way that appears to an English speaker to result in a semantic anomaly. Consider the following from the short story حفنـة تـراب by انيس منصور (1964: 47–49; also discussed in Dickins and Watson 1999: 550):

وهم لا يتحدثون إلى أحد من الناس .. ولكنهم يداعبون {الباعة} و {المتجولين}

This might be translated fairly literally as:

They don't talk to anyone, but they joke with the sellers and the barrow-men.

Here, الباعة 'the sellers' is a hyperonym of المتجولين 'barrow-men' (literally, 'travelling [people]' but normally used to describe people who sell goods from a barrow or handcart); all barrow-men are sellers but not all sellers are barrow-men.

In cases such as this, the meaning of the first word in the particular context has to be taken as excluding that of the second word. In this context, therefore, باعة has to be interpreted as meaning not sellers in general but that group of sellers who are not المتجولين 'the barrow–men'. Accordingly, باعة here means the 'non-barrow-men sellers' and could be translated idiomatically as something like 'shopkeepers', giving an overall idiomatic translation along the lines:

> They don't talk to anyone, but they joke with the shopkeepers and the barrow-men.

The following examples are also to be understood along the same lines (the examples are also discussed in Dickins and Watson 1999: 550–551; the full original text is found in Dickins and Watson 1999: 444–445). Comments are provided after each example.

[. . .] أن سياسة تصدير الثورة [. . .] اوقعت ايران في العديد من {المشاكل} و{الازمات} [. . .]

This might be translated fairly literally as:

> [. . .] that the policy of exporting the revolution [. . .] led Iran into a series of problems and crises [. . .]

Here, المشاكل is a hyperonym (or virtual hyperonym) of الازمات. It is not possible (or hardly so) to have a crisis that is not a problem, but it is possible to have a problem that is not a crisis. (All crises are problems, but not all problems are crises.) Here, the best solution from a translation point of view might be to go for the more dramatic 'crises' and to abandon the notion المشاكل, giving:

> [. . .] that the policy of exporting the revolution [. . .] led Iran into a series of crises [. . .]

Alternatively, given that semantic repetition in Arabic is often used for emphasis, one might use an emphatic adjective such as 'grave' or 'serious' in combination with 'crises', giving an idiomatic translation along the lines:

> [. . .] that the policy of exporting the revolution [. . .] led Iran into a series of grave crises [. . .]

Another example of hyperonym-hyponym repetition is the following:

[. . .] الحرب مع العراق التي كلفت البلاد اكثر من مليوني قتيل ومئات الآلاف من {الجرحى}
و{المعاقين} [. . .]

This might be translated fairly literally as:

> [. . .] the war with Iraq, which cost more than two million dead and hundreds of thousands of wounded and disabled [. . .]

Here, الجرحى 'wounded' is a virtual hyperonym of المعاقين 'disabled' (although it is in fact possible for someone to be disabled from birth, the disabled people referred to here are those who have become disabled by virtue of the wounds they received in the war with Iraq). A more idiomatic translation might take this into account by rearranging the information, perhaps along the lines:

> [. . .] the war with Iraq, which cost more than two million dead and hundreds of thousands of disabled and other wounded [. . .]

Alternatively, if it were felt that the writer's major intention was to stress the seriousness of the wounds by this use of a form of semantic repetition, one might, in an English translation, sacrifice a certain amount of accuracy for a greater degree of idiomaticness and go for a translation along the lines:

> [. . .] the war with Iraq, which cost more than two million dead and hundreds of thousands of seriously wounded . . .

The following example is taken from the Quran (Chapter 2, Verse 238):

حافظوا على الصلوات والصلاة الوسطى [. . .]

This could be translated literally as:

> Keep your prayers and the middle prayer [. . .}

A more idiomatic translation (Yusuf Ali 1938) reads:

> Guard strictly your (habit of) prayers, especially the Middle Prayer [. . .]

Here, الصلاة الوسطى is a hyponym of صلاة (appearing in the plural form صلوات). A literal translation 'prayers and the middle prayer' would seem to suggest that the 'middle prayer' is somehow not a 'prayer'. Ali's translation 'prayers, especially the Middle Prayer' avoids this with the introduction of 'especially'.

The previous examples of hyperonym-hyponym pairs have been cases in which the hyperonym occurs first. It is, however, possible to find cases in which the hyponym comes first, as in the following (also discussed in Dickins and Watson 1999: 551; original text in Dickins and Watson 1999: 444–445):

[. . .] هوية ايران السياسية الجديدة وطبيعة علاقاتها مع {جيرانه}ـا و{دول العالم}

Literal TT

> [. . .] the identity of Iran and the nature of its relations with its neighbours and the states of the world.

In this context, جيران is effectively a hyponym and دول العالم a hyperonym. That is to say, what is meant by جيران 'neighbours' in this context is the neighbouring states; and because all neighbouring states are states of the world (but not vice versa), this looks like a hyponym-hyperonym relationship. In fact, دول العالم should be interpreted here as referring to the other non-neighbouring states only, and an adequate idiomatic translation can be achieved by adding the word 'other', resulting in an idiomatic translation along the lines:

> [. . .] the identity of Iran and the nature of its relations with its neighbours and other states of the world.

An alternative might be to eliminate the word 'states' altogether on the basis that it is clear from the context that what is being talked about are states, giving an idiomatic translation along the lines:

> [. . .] the identity of Iran and the nature of its relations with its neighbours and the rest of the world.

7.2.3   *Associative repetition*

A third form of semantic repetition that is frequently found in Arabic but does not normally occur in English is what can be termed **associative repetition**. Associative repetition involves at least two or more elements, one of which is a basic element and the other, or others, of which are associated with that element. An example is 'ship' and 'crew of a ship'. 'Crew of a ship' is not a type of 'ship' (i.e. this is not a hyperonym-hyponym relationship); nor is it a part of a ship (as is a ship's mast, for example); this would be meronymic – that is, part–whole – relationship (thus, 'windscreen', 'bonnet', 'headlight', 'tyre' and 'wheel' are linked to 'car' by a meronymic – part–whole – relationship). An associative relationship does, however, bear some similarity to the figure of speech of metonymy (not to be confused with 'meronymy'!). This is '(A figure of speech characterized by) the action of substituting for a word or phrase denoting an object, action, institution, etc., a word or phrase denoting a property or something associated with it; an instance of this' (*Oxford English Dictionary Online*). An example of meronymy is 'Table 5' in 'Table 5 wants to pay his bill' (said in a restaurant), where 'Table 5' means the person sitting at Table 5 (i.e. the person associated with Table 5). In associative repetition, however, no figure of speech is involved; all the words are used in standard non-figurative senses.

We will now look at several examples that involve associative relations. The following is from an article titled الإبداع العربي في علم الفلك in the online academic journal مجلة التراث العربي (http://www.hiramagazine.com/المنحى-الفكري-العام):

استطاع علماء العرب المسلمين الجمع بين قطبي المعرفة وهما الفلسفة والعلم، فاستعملوا الامتحان – أي التجربة النظرية والعلمية – وعرفوا {المنهج التجريبي ومزاياه وقوانينه} بينما كان الإغريق أصحاب المنهج التجريدي.

This could be translated fairly literally as:

> Muslim Arab scholars were able to combine the two poles of knowledge, philosophy and science. They used testing, i.e. experimentation and scientific theorising. They knew {the experimental method, and its features and rules}, while the Greeks were the masters of the abstract method.

A more idiomatic translation reads:

> Muslim Arab scholars were able to combine the two poles of knowledge, philosophy and science. They used testing, i.e. experimentation and scientific theorising. While the Greeks had been the masters of the abstract method, the Muslims understood {the rules and features of the experimental method}.

In this example, مزاياه (i.e. مزايا المنهج التجريبي 'the features of the experimental method') and قوانينه (i.e. قوانين المنهج التجريبي 'the rules of the experimental method') are not meronyms of المنهج التجريبي ('the experimental method'); that is, they are not parts of the experimental method. However, there are features very closely associated with it.

A similar situation is found in the following from the same text:

فالنجوم ومجموعاتها وأفلاكها وأبعادها، والشمس وحركتها، والقمر وأطواره ومنازله والسماء وما حوت، وتعاقب الليل والنهار، والشروق والغروب، كل ذلك يرى فيه المؤمن الخاشع دلائل صدق وشواهد حق على وجود الخالق وقدرته العظيمة وعلمه الذي لا يخفى عليه شيء في السموات أو في الأرض، أو فيما بينهما.

This could be translated fairly literally as:

> The stars and their groups, orbits, and distances, the sun and its movements, the moon and its phases and mansions, the sky and what it contained, the succession of night and day, and the rising and setting of the sun were all matters in which the humble believer saw the proofs of the veracity and the evidence of the truth of the existence of the Creator, and His overwhelming power and knowledge, from Whom nothing is hidden in the heavens or earth or what is between them.

Here, the first relevant elements, مجموعاتها (i.e. مجموعات النجوم 'the groups of stars'), أفلاكها (i.e. أفلاك النجوم 'the orbits of the stars') and أبعادها (i.e. أبعاد النجوم 'the distances/ dimensions of the stars') stand in an associative relationship to the stars themselves: they are features associated with the stars.

A more idiomatic translation of فالنجوم ومجموعاتها وأفلاكها وأبعادها would be 'The orbits and positions of the stars and constellations'. This eliminates this associative repetition. It does this by taking the two first elements النجوم مجموعاتها and re-expressing them as simple coordinated nouns ('the stars and constellations') rather than as the more literal 'the stars and their constellations'. The idiomatic TT then takes مجموعاتها (i.e. the last two elements of the ST associative triplet أفلاكها وأبعادها وأفلاكها وأبعادها,) and links these as a coordinated phrase ('the orbits and positions') to which the phrase 'the stars and constellations' is subordinated via 'of', giving the complete TT phrase 'The orbits and positions of the stars and constellations'. Other parts of this extract, which form part of Practical 7.3, can be analyzed in the same way.

7.3   List restructuring

One particularly striking feature in Arabic is a tendency to use fairly long lists of terms belonging to the same **semantic field** – a semantic field being a general, normally rather impressionistically defined, area of meaning (e.g. the semantic field of farm machinery, or the semantic field of emotions or the semantic field of types of movement. For a useful discussion of semantic fields, see Baker 2011: 16–18.) The following examples, ST (a) and ST (b), are both taken from a political article in the Egyptian magazine روز اليوسف (no. 3521, 4 December 1995), which criticizes the use of political violence in the Middle East. They compare the behaviour of the Prophet Adam with that of extremist political groups and individuals in the modern Middle East (from Hetherington 1996: 19, 20):

ST (a)

لقد اختار آدم العقل فكسب الدين والحياء .. منتهى الحكمة والذكاء .. لكن أحفاده في الشرق الأوسط نسوا خبرته. وتجاهلوا اختياره .. فأغلقوا العقل وفتحوا النيران .. وغاصوا في الكتب المقدسة لكنهم لم ينتبهوا فيها إلا لـ{العنف والغضب، والتعصب، والاستعلاء، والرفض، والتمرد، والألم، والفتنة} [. . .]

ST (b)

إن هؤلاء {يقتلون باسم الله .. ويسلحون، يفجرون، ويذبحون، ويغسلون العقول، يكسرون العظام، ويحرمون الإبداع} أيضا باسم الله!

In the case of these extracts, a translation of the list in ST (a) in curly brackets along the lines 'violence, anger, fanaticism, false superiority, bigotry, insurrection, pain and infighting' would clearly be possible, as would a translation along the lines 'kill, take up arms, detonate bombs, massacre, brainwash, break bones and forbid originality' in the case of the ST (b). In both cases, however, such a translation seems a little strained in English, reflecting the tendency of English to avoid such long lists.

In some contexts, an appropriate strategy in translating long lists into English is simply to reduce the listed elements. Thus, 'ties of blood and marriage' would in many contexts be a sufficient translation of علاقات القربى والنسب والمصاهرة (cf. Humphrys 1999: 7); similarly, 'based upon kinship, marriage, and ethnic and tribal origin' would be a sufficient translation of على اساس القرابة والزواج والأصل الإثني والعائلي والقبلي (cf. Humphrys 1999: 7).

One function of listing in Arabic seems to be to suggest an overall scene or situation by extensive exemplification of aspects of that scene or situation. In several contexts, an appropriate strategy in translating into English is to reduce the listed elements and to substitute other information that provides a summary account of the overall scene or situation. Consider the following, which describes the behaviour of senior military figures in the Arab world:

فهم، كالسياسيين، يصرون على ممارسة الوجاهة بجميع فروعها: {البيوت المفتوحة، القصور، الحرس الخاص، الزلم، البذخ، واقتناء ما عز من الألبسة والحلي والحلل}.

This might be translated (cf. Humphrys 1999: 7–8) as:

> Like politicians, they insist upon all the outward trappings of privilege: mansions, palaces, bodyguards, and all the finery that money can buy.

This translation omits specific translation of the later listed elements in the Arabic الزلم، البذخ، واقتناء ما عز من الألبسة والحلي والحلل, utilizing instead the phrase 'all the finery which money can buy' (i.e. the English summarizes while the Arabic exemplifies).

The following is a fairly similar example from the same book:

«كنا نخافه، يدخل إلى قاعة الاجتماعات {يحاضر ويتوعد، يهدد ويحذر}».

This has been translated (Humphrys 1999: 3) as:

> "We fear the officer forcing his way into civilian life, {imposing his will and laying the law down}."

Here again, the English provides a summary account of the officer's behaviour, using the two parallel composite phrases 'imposing his will' and 'laying the law down', while the Arabic exemplifies the kind of things he does through the four verbs يحاضر ويتوعد، يهدد ويحذر.

Because English does not so readily use exemplification through listing to suggest an overall scene or situation as does Arabic, it is sometimes appropriate when translating into English to insert a summary phrase, even when it seems reasonable to retain all or most of the elements of the original Arabic list. Consider the following, which is taken from an account of the internal leadership elections of the Phalange (الكتائب) party in Lebanon in 1999:

شبح ١٩٩٢ كان حاضرا بقوة مع كل {الاجتماعات والتحالفات واللقاءات الجانبية} {على الشرفات وفي المكاتب الجانبية وعلى السلم الخارجي}.

This has been translated (Jones 1999: 8) as follows:

> The ghost of 1992 was present in force, with {countless meetings} taking place in any available space: {on the balconies, in side offices, and even on the outside stairs}.

The Arabic ST here has two lists: على [كل] الاجتماعات والتحالفات واللقاءات الجانبية and الشرفات وفي المكاتب الجانبية وعلى السلم الخارجي. The first of these is summarized in English as 'countless meetings', while the second is retained in full (and in fact strengthened by the addition of 'even' before 'on the balconies'). However, before the second list in the English, the translator inserted the additional summarizing phrase 'in every available space'. (The translation also contains a somewhat unfortunate mixed metaphor 'ghost [. . .] present in force'; cf. Section 14.4.) For further discussion of list restructuring in Arabic>English translation, see Dickins (2010a).

Practical 7

Practical 7.1 Denotative meaning: تقف البشرية اليوم

Assignment

(i) Discuss the strategic decisions that you must take before starting detailed translation of the following text, and outline and justify the strategy you adopt. You are to translate it as part of an anthology of political writing from the Middle East. The readership is expected to have general knowledge of the Arab world but no specific expertise in Islamic thought.

(ii) Translate the text into English.

(iii) Explain the main decisions of detail you made in producing your TT.

Contextual information

The text is from معالم في الطريق (قطب 1990: 5) by the leading Egyptian Islamist سيد قطب (1906–1966). The text was written around 1962, while سيد قطب was a political prisoner in Egypt. The text reflects the global political situation of the time, in which the world was seen as becoming increasingly polarized between the communism of Eastern Europe, led by the Soviet Union, and the capitalism of the West, led by the United States.

ST

تقف البشرية اليوم على حافة الهاوية .. لا بسبب التهديد بالفناء المعلق على رأسها .. فهذا عَرَضٌ للمرض وليس هو المرض .. ولكن بسبب إفلاسها في عالم «القيم» التي يمكن أن تنمو الحياة الإنسانية في ظلالها نموّاً سليماً وتترقى ترقياً صحيحاً . وهذا واضح كل الوضوح في العالم الغربي، الذي لم يعد لديه ما يعطيه للبشرية من «القيم» بل الذي لم يعد لديه ما يُقنع ضميره باستحقاقه للوجود، بعدما انتهت «الديمقراطية» فيه الى ما يشبه الإفلاس، حيث بدأت تستعير – ببطء – وتقتبس من أنظمة المعسكر الشرقي وبالخاصة في الانظمة الاقتصادية! تحت اسم الاشتراكية !

كذلك الحال في المعسكر الشرقي نفسه .. فالنظريات الجماعية وفي مقدمتها الماركسية التي اجتذبت في أول عهدها عدداً كبيراً في الشرق – وفي الغرب نفسه – باعتبار ها مذهباً يحمل طابع العقيدة، قد تراجعت هي الأخرى تراجعاً واضحاً من ناحية «الفكرة» حتى لتكاد تنحصر الآن في «الدولة» وأنظمتها والتي تبعد بعداً كبيراً عن أصول المذهب .. وهي على العموم تناهض طبيعة الفطرة البشرية ومقتضياتها، و لا تنمو إلا في بيئة محطمة ! أو بيئة قد ألفت النظام الدكتاتوري فترات طويلة !

Practical 7.2 Denotative meaning: عندما يستمع المرء

Assignment

(i) Before starting detailed translation of the following text, outline and justify the strategy you adopt. You are to translate this text for a book titled *Musical Traditions in the Global Age*.

(ii) Translate the text into English.

(iii) Explain the decisions of detail you made in producing your translation.

Contextual information

This text is taken from a book titled دراسات في الموسيقى العراقية by قاسم حسين (n.d.).

ST

عندما يستمع المرء إلى الموسيقى الشائعة التي تبثها أجهزة الإعلام عندنا، وإلى ما يقدم في حفلات الهواة من أهل المدينة، ينسى أنه وموسيقاه سليلان لواحدة من أعظم حضارات العالم التي أنتجت فنونا وآدابا أصيلة اسهمت في إغناء الحياة الروحية للبشريه عبر أكثر من ٥٢ قرنا. ولولا تلك النفحات النادرة ─ رغم كونها تمثل موسيقى الأغلبية العامة للشعب ─ من المقام العراقي من غناء البادية والسهول التي ترجع الثقة بوجود المميز والأصيل في موسيقانا، لانجرفنا جملة إلى الاعتقاد بأن اللجوء إلى المتنوعات وإلى الأنواع السهلة في الموسيقى إنما يعود إلى نقص في الحيوية الداخلية لموسيقانا وفي قدرتها على العطاء.

إن الوعي بوجود موسيقى أصيلة تمتلك الخصوصية، والوعي بضرورة الانطلاق منها لكي يكون ما نقدمه إبداعاً وإغناء للموسيقى العربية والعالمية، مسألة جديده لم تهضم بكل أبعادها عند المثقف العراقي كما هي جديدة على مخططي الثقافة عندنا. فالموسيقى العراقية الجيدة ما زالت حبيسة في مواقعها تنتظر أن يطلق عنانها، والمدينة بمركزيتها الثقافيه تتشبث وتنشر السهل الذي لا يتماس والأعماق إلا تماسًا سطحاً، وتلجأ إلى الاقتباس الذي لا يجتاز إلا أسهل العناصر من كل الحضارات. كما أنها تدعم الاتجاه الغربي البحت، الذي وإن كان جديداً عندنا فإنه في واقع الحال إعادة أداء وتمرين لموسيقى عمرها الزمني قديم.

إن الوضع الراهن للموسيقى يعكس حالة حضارية عامة مرجعها الالتباس في فهم الهوية المحلية عند المتعلم وعدم اطلاعه على تاريخه بصورة عميقة مما يضيع عليه توازنه في مجابهة العالم المعاصر. أما الموسيقي فإنه كثير التشكك في إمكانية موسيقاه وإمكانية الاستفادة منها، تتجاذبه تيارات مختلفة مختلطة هزت جذوره بحيث لم يعد يستطيع التمييز بين ما هو أصيل وبين ما هو قشرة مستعارة، حتى أن طبيعة الاستعارة مهما كانت مفتعلة وبعيدة عن ملاءمة الأصل لا تثير عنده أي إزعاج او قلق. والمثقف كالموسيقي كلاهما يمر بأزمة الانبهار بكل ما يأتي من الخارج حتى وإن جاء من بلد عربي شقيق، فيأخذ به محاولاً تقليده سطحياً أو نقله حرفياً والاستفادة منه فيما يسميه بـ«تطوير الموسيقى العراقية». وغالباً ما يأتي ذلك على حساب الخصوصية المحلية.

Practical 7.3 List restructuring and associative repetition:
كانت متطلبات الدين الإسلامي

Assignment

(i) Discuss the strategic problems confronting the translator of the following text, and outline your strategy for dealing with them. You are to translate the text for an online English-language magazine dealing with traditional Islamic science.

(ii) Translate the text into English.

(iii) Explain the decisions of detail you made in producing your translation.

Contextual information

This text is an article from an online Arabic journal, مجلة التراث العربي (http://www. hiramagazine.com/المنحى-الفكري-العام), which is devoted to traditional Islamic science.

ST

كانت متطلبات الدين الإسلامي ذات ضرورة لرصد دائم لقبة السماء الزرقاء، لأن الرسول (ص) وضع قوانين ثابتة بفروض العبادة كما أن نزول عدد من الآيات في سور عديدة تحدثت عن السماء والأفلاك والبروج والنجوم والأجرام السماوية والشمس والقمر، جعلت المسلم المؤمن يفكر بشأنها، ويحترم هذه القوانين ويحاول تطبيقها. لذلك كان للمسلمين حاجة ماسة إلى علم النجوم لتعيين أوقات الصلاة وإثبات موعدي العيدين الأضحى والفطر، وتحديد سير القوافل في الصحارى، وفي الملاحة البحرية في البحار والمحيطات، وكذلك معرفة أحوال الشفق وهلال رمضان – شهر الصوم – فكان يتطلب من المسلم الذي يريد إقامة الصلاة الاتجاه إلى القبلة في الكعبة بمدينة مكة المكرمة، وذلك يقتضي معرفة سمت القبلة، لأن زمن الصلاة يختلف حسب الموقع الجغرافي وحركة سير الشمس في دائرة البروج، وكذلك معرفة أحوال الشفق والتماس هلال شهر رمضان كل ذلك تطلب حل مسألة من مسائل علم الهيئة الكروي المبني على حساب المثلثات، وكذلك شروط رؤية هلال رمضان وأحوال الشفق للصوم والإمساك والإفطار، وكذلك صلاتا الكسوف والخسوف اللذين تتطلب معرفتهما استعمال الجداول الفلكية (الأزياج)، لذلك كله كان لعلم النجوم معنى ديني عميق، فالنجوم ومجموعاتها وأفلاكها وأبعادها، والشمس وحركتها، والقمر وأطواره ومنازله، والسماء وما حوت، وتعاقب الليل والنهار، والشروق الغروب، كل ذلك يرى فيه المؤمن الخاشع دلائل صدق وشواهد حق على وجود الخالق وقدرته العظيمة وعلمه الذي لا يخفى عليه شيء في السموات أو في الأرض، أو فيما بينهما. وهنا ما دعا أكبر فلكي عربي عرفه التاريخ وهو محمد القباني (ت 317هـ / 929م)، إلى القول: «إن علم النجوم يتوجب على كل إنسان أن يعلمه، كما يجب على المؤمن أن يلم بأمور الدين وقوانينه، لأن علم النجوم يوصل إلى برهان وحدة الله، ومعرفة عظمته الفائقة وحكمته السامية، وقدرته العظيمة وكمال خلقه».

8 Connotative meaning and translation issues

8.1 Basic principles

Denotative meaning as discussed in Chapter 7 is only one aspect of verbal meaning. The meaning of a text comprises several different layers: referential content, emotional colouring, cultural associations, social and personal connotations and so on. The many-layered nature of meaning is something translators must never forget.

Even within a single language, synonyms are usually different in their overall semantic effects – compare 'clergyman' and 'sky pilot', 'adder' and 'viper', 'go away' and 'piss off', etc. Each of these expressions has overtones that differentiate it from its synonym. We shall call such overtones 'connotative meanings' – that is, associations that, over and above the denotative meaning of an expression, form part of its overall meaning. In fact, of course, connotative meanings are many and varied, and it is common for a single piece of text, or even a single expression, to combine more than one kind into a single overall effect. However, it is useful at this stage to distinguish six major types of connotative meaning, because learning to identify them sharpens students' awareness of the presence and significance of connotations in STs and TTs alike. Note that, by definition, we are only concerned here with socially widespread connotations, not personal ones. Only in exceptional circumstances do translators allow personal connotations to influence a TT.

8.2 Attitudinal meaning

Attitudinal meaning is that part of the overall meaning of an expression that consists of some widespread *attitude to the referent*. The expression does not merely denote the referent in a neutral way but also hints at some attitude to it.

So, for instance, in appropriate contexts, 'the police', 'the filth' and 'the boys in blue' are synonyms in terms of denotative content, but they have different overall meanings. 'The police' is a neutral expression, but 'the filth' has pejorative overtones and 'the boys in blue' affectionate ones. These attitudes to the police are not part of the denotative meaning of the expressions, but it is impossible to ignore them in responding to the expressions. It is therefore important not to overlook them when translating. Normally, words that have attitudinal meaning also have denotative meaning. Expletives such as 'damn (it)!', however, are arguably an exception, having only attitudinal meaning (cf. Baker 2011: 12).

It is relatively difficult to find examples of attitudinal meaning in Standard Arabic that are intrinsic features of the word itself. This is at least in part because of the formal nature of Standard Arabic. As can be seen from the example 'the boys in blue' versus 'the police', there is typically a close relation between attitudinal meaning and informality. Formal terms show a markedly smaller tendency to display attitudinal meaning than do informal terms. The inherent formality of Standard Arabic therefore correlates with the relative infrequency of words having strong attitudinal connotations.

This does not mean, however, that attitudinal meaning is unimportant in translating Standard Arabic into English, as an attitudinal meaning can sometimes emerge from the context of usage of a word in an Arabic ST. In such cases, it is sometimes appropriate to use a word with a different denotative meaning in English. Consider the following:

باختصار، توفر الانقلابات العسكرية الفرص لتحويل قادتها من مناصب عسكرية الى زعامات سياسية [. . .]

This has been translated (Humphrys 1999: 9) as:

In short, military coups provide their perpetrators with the opportunity to move from military posts to political leadership [. . .]

This is taken from a book that deals with the relationship between the military and political power in the Arab world and that is very critical of military involvement in Arab politics. Accordingly, قادة 'leaders' in this context acquires rather negative overtones. In the TT, the translator reflects this by using the word 'perpetrators'. The negative aspect of 'perpetrators' is part of its denotative meaning, not its connotative meaning: it is by definition not possible to perpetrate a good deed.

It is also important to remember that, because English makes widespread use of attitudinal meaning, such meaning is likely to figure in idiomizing translations in particular. In such cases, the translator must ensure that the TT attitudinal meaning does not clash with the context. Consider the following from a poem by نزار قباني:

آه يا بيروت.. يا أنثايَ من بين ملايين النساءْ

This has been translated (Rolph 1995: 23) as:

Ah Beirut . . . my lady amongst millions of women

In Arabic, أنثى 'female' and امرأة 'woman' (plural نساء) have clearly differentiated meanings; أنثى is a hyperonym of امرأة. In the TT, however, the translator has used 'lady' and 'women'. 'Lady' and 'woman' are synonyms in English, the difference between them being that 'lady' has overtones of respect.

Another example of the use of attitudinal connotation in translation is provided by this extract concerning the behaviour of Serbian troops towards Kosovo

Albanians, taken from an article on the subject that is very sympathetic to the Albanian side:

ولقد راحوا يقتحمون البيوت بيتاً بيتاً [. . .]

This has been translated (Ives 1999: 9) as follows:

> They have raided homes one by one.

Here, 'homes' can be contrasted with its near-synonym 'houses'. 'Houses' is a neutral word in English, whereas 'home' has warm emotional connotations.

8.3 Associative meaning

Associative meaning is that part of the overall meaning of an expression that consists of expectations that are – rightly or wrongly – *associated with the referent* of the expression. The word 'nurse' is a good example. Most people automatically associate 'nurse' with the idea of female gender, as if 'nurse' were synonymous with 'female who looks after the sick'. This unconscious association is so wide-spread that the term 'male nurse' has had to be coined to counteract its effect: 'he is a nurse' still sounds semantically odd, even today.

Any area of reference in which prejudices and stereotypes, however innocuous, operate is likely to give examples of associative meaning. Consider in this respect the associations of 'Crusade' in English, which continue to be positive (regardless of recent Western scholarly reassessments in this area), and contrast this with the strongly negative associations of حملة صليبية in Arabic. Conversely, the word جهاد in Arabic traditionally has highly positive associations, but in English the cultural borrowing 'jihad' is chiefly associated with organizations such as Islamic Jihad, which are widely regarded in the West as extremist and anti-democratic. (For the same reasons, the word جهاد has also acquired negative associations among some Arabic speakers.)

It is important here not to confuse associative meaning with polysemy (Section 7.1). The word 'crusade' is polysemous, having amongst its senses (1) 'A military expedition undertaken by the Christians of Europe in the 11th, 12th, and 13th centuries to recover the Holy Land from the Muslims, and by extension any war instigated and blessed by the Church for alleged religious ends, a 'holy war'; applied esp. to expeditions undertaken under papal sanction against infidels or heretics' and (2) 'An aggressive movement or enterprise against some public evil, or some institution or class of persons considered as evil' (definitions from *Oxford English Dictionary Online*). Sense 2 of 'crusade' ('An aggressive movement or enterprise against some public evil [. . .]') is not an associative meaning of sense 1. ('A military expedition undertaken by the Christians of Europe in the 11th, 12th, and 13th centuries to recover the Holy Land [. . .]'). Rather, this is a case of polysemy: 'crusade' is polysemous, having – amongst other senses – senses 1 and 2 given here. This example is further discussed under **reflected meaning** (Section 8.7).

A good example of associative meaning is provided by 'Ramadan' in English (and رمضان in Arabic). Westerners who know something about Islam might regard Ramadan as a time of self-denial and fasting, which it is. However, in Muslim countries, Ramadan is also a time of celebration, in which children are allowed to stay up late, when there is a lot going on in the streets into the middle of the night, when families who have been separated come together again, etc. These associations are likely to be missed, even by an informed Western readership of a text in which Ramadan figures, unless they have some personal experience of the Middle East.

Given the relative cultural distance between the Arab world and the English-speaking world, associative meanings are likely to be a problem. Consider the potential difficulty of translating مقهى into English; a denotative near-equivalent might be 'tea house', 'tea garden', 'coffee house' or possibly 'cafe'. However, in terms of the cultural status of the مقهى as the centre of informal male social life, the nearest equivalent in British culture might be the pub. Given the Islamic prohibition on the drinking of alcohol, however, such a translation would in most cases be ruled out.

Another example of how associative meaning may motivate a shift in denotative meaning between the ST and the TT is provided by the following, which describes a young man tending his dying mother: ثم شد الغطاء على جسمها الهرم. This is translated (Brown 1996: 32) as: 'then pulling the covers over her frail body'. Here, the translator has not translated هرم by a TL term that is roughly synonymous with it, such as 'old' or 'aged'. ('Aged' here is perhaps relatively acceptable, although it provides information that is already well known to the reader and therefore seems irrelevant in this context. For further discussion of the odder translation 'then pulling the covers over her old body', see Section 8.7.) Rather than using the terms 'old' or 'aged', the translator has taken the association of هرم 'old' with frailty (old people tend to be frail, particularly if they are very ill) and has accordingly used the denotative meaning 'frail' to render this associative meaning of هرم.

The associative meanings that we have examined so far are extralinguistically motivated. Thus, the associations of مقهى ('tea house', 'tea garden', 'coffee house', etc.) are a function of the status that a مقهى enjoys in the Arab world, not of features intrinsic to the word itself. There are, however, associative meanings that are linguistically determined. These can be seen in cases of what is sometimes termed imperfect synonymy. An example is the verbs *vernietigen* and *vernielen* in nineteenth-century Dutch, where these two words appear to have referred to exactly the same range of situations, even in the writings of one and the same author. However, differences become apparent when the frequencies of different senses are compared, *vernietigen* being used typically in an abstract sense, *vernielen* typically referring to an act of physical destruction. Nineteenth-century handbooks of good usage in Dutch also pointed to a difference in the 'conceptual centres' of the two words (cf. Geeraerts 1988; Taylor 1989: 56).

Vernietigen and *vernielen* here have the same denotative meanings – that is, they cover the same range of referents and are thus synonyms (Section 7.1.1). However, there is a tendency for *vernietigen* to refer to abstract destruction and *vernielen* to physical destruction. We may say that *vernietigen* has an associative meaning of 'abstract destruction', while *vernielen* has an associative meaning of 'physical destruction'.

Pairs of the *vernietigen/vernielen* type seem fairly common in different languages. An example in English may be 'bucket' and 'pail'. According to *Collins English Dictionary,* a bucket is an 'open-topped, roughly cylindrical container; pail', while a pail is a 'bucket; esp. one made of wood or metal'. The denotative range of 'bucket' and 'pail' appears to be the same – anything that one can call a bucket one can call a pail and vice versa. They are therefore synonyms (as defined in Section 7.1.1). However, 'pail' apparently tends to refer to something made of wood or metal (rather than, for instance, to something made of plastic). We may says that 'pail' has an associative meaning of 'bucket/pail made of wood or metal', while 'bucket' lacks this associative meaning.

An example of linguistically motivated associative meaning difference in Classical Arabic is that between إثم and ذنب (Elewa 2004). These words both mean 'sin, wrong, offence', and both seem to have had the same range of meaning: anything that could be called an إثم could also be called a ذنب and vice versa. They were thus synonyms (i.e. they had the same denotative meaning). On the basis of a survey of the usages of these two words in a corpus (group) of Classical Arabic texts, however, Elewa concludes that the two words tended to be associated with different types of activity. إثم was typically used for sins that are personal or do not entail a punishment in this world (such as failing to perform obligatory acts of worship, or doing a bad deed whose effects are liable to have a bad effect on oneself, such as drinking or gambling). ذنب, on the other hand, was typically used for sins that involve punishment in this world or the next, such as killing, theft or adultery (Elewa 2004: 123–124).

There may, of course, be cases where an associative meaning seems to be partly extralinguistically motivated and partly linguistically determined or where it is not clear which of the two factors is operative – or more important, if both seem to be operative. (For further discussion of these issues from a more technical linguistic perspective, see Dickins 2014.)

8.4 Affective meaning

Affective meaning is an *emotive effect worked on the addressee* by the choice of expression and that forms part of its overall meaning. The expression does not merely denote its referent but also hints at some attitude of the speaker or writer to the addressee.

Features of linguistic politeness, flattery, rudeness or insult are typical examples of expressions carrying affective meanings. Compare, for example, 'Silence please' and 'Shut up', or الرجاء الصمت and أسكت in Arabic. These expressions share the same core denotative meaning of 'Be quiet', but the speaker's implied attitude to the listener produces a different affective impact in each case: polite in the first, rude in the second.

Not only imperative forms, but also statements and questions, can have alternative forms identical in basic denotative meaning yet totally different in affective meaning. An example is 'I want the bog', which carries affective overtones of disrespect or at least extreme familiarity, versus 'I need to go to the lavatory', whose formality and politeness suggest respect for the addressee.

Clearly, translators must be able to recognize affective meanings in the ST. But they must also be careful not to introduce unwanted affective meanings into the TT. To take an example from colloquial Arabic (Sudanese), a customer in a general store says أَدِّيني كيلو رز 'Give me a kilo of rice'. In accordance with the standard conventions in Arabic for requests that can be easily complied, no politeness formula is included here. It would of course be possible to translate this sentence into English as 'Give me a kilo of rice'. However, this might sound rude, as the normal convention in English in shops is to use terms such as 'Please' and 'Thank you' (often repeatedly throughout the exchange). A safer option might be to cushion the TT by translating the ST as something like 'A kilo of rice, please', or 'May I have a kilo of rice, please?'.

The most important, though not perhaps the most obvious, area in which affective meaning operates is formality versus informality. Formality and informality are features of words and phrases – or, more precisely, they are features of words and phrases used in particular senses. Thus, 'chair' in the sense of 'object for sitting on' is a standard word with no particular formality. 'Chair' in the sense of 'professorship', by contrast, has somewhat formal and even technical associations, perhaps rather more so than its synonym 'professorship'.

Formality and informality can be thought of as being on a cline (continuum) from very informal to very formal, as shown in Figure 8.1.

Formality is thus not an all-or-nothing matter. We may reasonably describe a word or phrase as being relatively informal, slightly formal, etc.

Although it is words and phrases (in particular senses) that are formal or informal, formality and informality imply affective meaning. This is because they connote a relationship between the speaker/writer on the one hand and the listener/reader on the other. In informal writing/speech, this connoted relationship is one of emotional closeness and normally also rough equality of status, at least in the context in which the utterance is made. In formal writing/speech, the relationship is one of emotional distance and normally also of non-equality of status.

It is fairly easy to confuse attitudinal meaning with affective meaning. The difference is that attitudinal meaning involves attitude to the referent (i.e. the person or thing referred to), whereas affective meaning involves attitude to the addressee (i.e. the person spoken to). Where the referent is also the addressee, affective meaning and attitudinal meaning will coincide.

Both attitudinal meaning and affective meaning are 'emotional' in nature (they convey how the speaker/writer feels about the referent or the addressee). Associative meaning, by contrast, has to do with a tendency to refer (e.g. the tendency of إِثْم to refer to a sin that is personal or does not involve a punishment in this world or the tendency of ذَنب to refer to a sin that does involve punishment in this world or the next). Associative meaning is thus focused on the referent.

(very) informal   (very) formal

Figure 8.1 Formality and informality.

8.5 Allusive meaning

Allusive meaning is an intertextual feature (cf. Section 13.3.2). It occurs when an expression evokes an associated saying or quotation in such a way that the meaning of that saying or quotation becomes part of the overall meaning of the expression.

Although allusion is most typically a feature of literary texts, it also fairly frequently found outside literature. A book on the fall of Soviet Communism written in 1993, for example, is titled *The Future that Failed.* This title involves an allusion to the name of the series in which the book was published: 'Social Futures'. It also contains at least two further allusions, however. The first is to a line 'I've seen the future and it works', found on the title page of a book titled *Red Virtue* by the American writer – and communist – Ella Winter (though also attributed to her husband, the journalist Lincoln Steffens). The final allusion is to a book written by a group of disillusioned ex-communists in 1949 titled *The God that Failed* (the 'God' in the title being communism itself, which the authors had come to recognize as a religion substitute rather than as a political philosophy in the more normal sense).

An example of allusion in Arabic occurs in the novel مدينة البغي *The City of Oppression* by the Palestinian novelist عيسى بشارة; the city in question is clearly Jerusalem (or a fictional equivalent). The term مدينة البغي, which is used as the name of the city, alludes to the fact that Jerusalem is sometimes referred to as مدينة السلام 'City of Peace'. It also perhaps recalls St Augustine's 'City of God' (عيسى بشارة is a Christian and makes widespread use of Christian symbolism in this work). For Arabic readers, a further possible allusive meaning is مدينة النبي – that is, the term from which is derived the name for the city 'Medina' المدينة (in pre-Islamic times known as يثرب). For English-speaking readers, particularly those of a Protestant background, the TT 'City of Oppression' might also carry echoes of John Bunyan's 'City of Destruction' in *A Pilgrim's Progress,* although it is extremely doubtful that these would have been intended in the ST.

Another example of allusive meaning is from the oath that members of the Muslim Brotherhood swore to حسن البنا and that reads «الالتزام التام بالإخلاص والثقة والسمع والطاعة في العسر واليسر والمنشط والمكره». This perhaps contains an allusion to the Quran, سورة الشرح, verse 5 فَإِنَّ مَعَ الْعُسْرِ يُسْرًا and verse 6 إِنَّ مَعَ الْعُسْرِ يُسْرًا.

8.6 Collocation and collocative meaning

The term 'to collocate' means 'to typically occur in close proximity with'; hence, a **collocation** is an occurrence of one word in close proximity to another. 'Pretty' and 'handsome', for example, have a shared sense of 'good looking' in English. However, 'pretty' collocates readily with 'girl', 'boy', 'woman', 'flower', 'garden', 'colour', 'village', while 'handsome' collocates with 'boy', 'man', 'car', 'vessel', 'overcoat', 'airliner', 'typewriter' (cf. Leech 1981: 17; also, for translation implications of collocation, see Baker 2011: 52–67).

The importance of finding appropriate collocations in translation can be illustrated by the following examples: التعاون الوثيق 'close cooperation' (not, for example, 'firm cooperation'), الذكاء التجاري 'commercial acumen' (cf. the slight oddity of 'commercial intelligence'), ابتسامة مصطنعة 'forced smile' (cf. the oddity of 'artificial smile').

An important area for collocation is the use of conjoined phrases on the pattern 'X and Y'. Thus, English tends to say 'knives and forks' rather than 'forks and knives' and 'pots and pans' rather than 'pans and pots'; for أصحاب النفوذ وأهل الود, one would expect 'the rich and powerful' (rather than 'the powerful and rich'); for ١٤، الف جندي وضابط عراقي, one would expect '14,000 Iraqi officers and men' (rather than '14,000 Iraqi men and officers'). Some collocations of this kind have become established idioms. Thus, من ثمه ولحمه has to be translated as 'his own flesh and blood', rather than the reverse 'his own blood and flesh', or some alternative phrasing such as 'his own blood and body'. (For a reader of Christian background, 'His own blood and body' would have the disadvantage of an allusive meaning of 'Last Supper' and an associative meaning of 'Eucharist'.)

Deriving from the notion of collocation is the notion of collocative meaning. This is the meaning given to an expression over and above its denotative meaning by the meaning of some other expression with which it collocates to form a commonly used phrase. An example is the word 'intercourse'. This has largely dropped out of usage in modern English, because of its purely connotative sexual associations, derived from the common collocation 'sexual intercourse'.

Clearly, the translator must be able to recognize and render ST collocative meanings. But it is just as important to avoid unwanted collocative clashes in the TT. Consider the following: [. . .] الايام الماضية بكل دفقها الدموي الشديد الحرارة [. . .]. A fairly literal translation of this would be 'the past with all its extremely hot bloodshed'. This does not work in English, and although a factor in this failure may be that the phrase sounds overly dramatic, a toned-down version works no better (e.g. 'The past with all its hot bloodshed'). The failure of these proposed translations has to do partly with the fact that 'hot bloodshed' is not a standard collocation in English. However, collocational failure is made worse by the existence of the phrase 'hot-blooded' meaning 'short-tempered', 'easily angered' (i.e. 'hot bloodshed' involves a collocational clash with 'hot-blooded'). A more plausible translation of this phrase is something like: '[. . .] the past with all its terrible bloodshed [. . .]' (cf. Ives 1999: 14). We shall consider this example further from the perspective of metaphor (Section 14.3.4).

Collocative meaning can also be an aid to the translator, allowing him or her to make use of collocations in the TT that are appropriate to the denotative meaning of the ST but that might otherwise seem odd on the TL. An example from the Syrian poet نزار قباني is the following:

أحمل الزمن المحترق في عيني

This has been translated (Rolph 1995: 10) as:

I carry this scorched era in my eyes

Here, 'scorched era' sounds more acceptable than other more literal alternatives because of the existence of the phrase 'scorched earth'. The denotative meaning of 'scorched earth' gives 'scorched era' a collocative meaning that is strongly suggestive of the devastation wrought by war. We shall return to this example in Section 10.2.1.

8.7 Reflected meaning

Reflected meaning is the meaning given to an expression over and above the denotative meaning that it has in that context by the fact that it also calls to mind another meaning of the same word or phrase. Thus, if someone says, 'Richard Nixon was a rat', using 'rat' in the sense of 'a person who deserts his friends or associates' (*Collins English Dictionary*), the word 'rat' not only carries this particular denotative meaning, but it also conjures up the more basic denotative meaning of the animal 'rat'. (Note also the standard collocation 'dirty rat'.)

Reflected meaning is normally a function of polysemy – that is, the existence of two or more denotative meanings for a single word (Section 7.1). The simplest forms of reflected meaning are when a single word has two or more senses, and its use in a particular context in one of its senses conjures up at least one of its other senses, as in the earlier example 'rat'. A similar example in Arabic is calling someone حمار. In colloquial Arabic, حمار applied to a person means 'stupid'. However, this metaphorical meaning also very strongly calls to mind the more basic sense of حمار 'donkey'.

An example of reflected meaning that has already been partly considered involves 'crusade' (cf. Section 8.3) when used in the secondary sense 'An aggressive movement or enterprise against some public evil [. . .]'. This sense calls to mind – that is, carries the reflected meaning of – the primary sense of 'crusade' as 'A military expedition undertaken by the Christians of Europe in the 11th, 12th, and 13th centuries to recover the Holy Land from the Muslims, and by extension any war instigated and blessed by the Church for alleged religious ends, a "holy war"; applied esp. to expeditions undertaken under papal sanction against infidels or heretics'.

More complex cases of reflected meaning also occur, where parts of phrases are involved in a form of polysemy. One frequently quoted example compares the connotative difference between the two synonyms 'Holy Ghost' and 'Holy Spirit' (Leech 1981: 19). Through polysemous association, the 'Ghost' part of 'Holy Ghost' is reminiscent of the reflected meaning of 'ghost' ('spook' or 'spectre'). Although such an association is not part of the denotative meaning of 'Holy Ghost', it has a tendency to form part of the overall meaning of the expression and therefore often actually interferes with its denotative meaning. By another polysemous association, the 'Spirit' part of 'Holy Spirit' may call to mind the reflected meaning of 'spirits' ('alcoholic drinks'); here again, the association tends to interfere with the denotative meaning. Clearly, then, while 'Holy Spirit' and 'Holy Ghost' are referential synonyms, their total semantic effects cannot be called identical in so far as they evoke different images through different reflected meanings.

Reflected meanings do not usually occur spontaneously to the listener or reader. When an expression is taken in isolation, its reflected meaning or meanings are usually merely latent. It is the textual context that triggers these latent reflected meanings. A good example of context triggering reflected meaning is the possible translation (discussed first in Section 8.3 under associative meaning) of ثم شد الغطاء على جسمها الهرم as 'then pulling the covers over her old body'. The reader has, in fact, learnt earlier in the book that the mother of the central character صابر is old. The statement that her body is old, therefore, does not provide any information in this context. In order to extract some meaning, or, more technically, to find some relevance (cf. Sperber and Wilson 1986) for this comment, the reader therefore looks for another interpretation of 'old' in this context. One possible interpretation that presents itself is that based on another sense of 'old', namely, 'former'. That is to say, 'old' is polysemous, having senses 'not new' and 'former', amongst other senses (cf. Section 7.1.3). Thus, the interpretation 'former body' (i.e. not the one in which the lady is now incarnated) momentarily presents itself as a possibility. This is, of course, rejected in the context. However, this reflected meaning of 'old' has enough of an influence here, in combination with the oddity of 'old' in the sense of 'not new' (discussed earlier), to make the reader feel that 'old' is odd in this context.

Although the six types of connotative meaning that we have just discussed are distinct from one another, it often happens that two or more occur together and nourish each other, as illustrated by the examples of هرم and 'blood and body'. In acquiring a translation method, it is useful to learn to distinguish exactly which sorts of connotative meaning are in play. It is also important to remember that, as with denotative meaning, being receptive to connotative meaning is a matter of considering words and phrases within the particular context in which they occur. It is not the same as looking up every possible use of a word in the dictionary and assuming that they are all relevant in the particular context in question.

8.8   Other types of connotative meaning

The six types of connotative meaning that we have discussed in this chapter are the most important forms of connotative meaning. However, strictly speaking, one may regard any form of meaning that is not denotative as connotative. In this book, we consider three major additional types of connotative meaning. These are emphasis, presentation of information as predictable or unpredictable and presentation of information as foregrounded or backgrounded. Predictability and unpredictability are typically a function of the formal properties of **theme** and **rheme**, while **foregrounding** and **backgrounding** are typically a function of the formal features of mainness and subordination; all of these features will be dealt with in Chapter 12.

Emphasis may be a function of several formal features in Arabic, including (near-)synonym repetition (Section 7.2.1), parallelism (Chapter 11), alliteration, assonance and rhyme (Section 9.1.1), **morphological** repetition of all kinds (Section 10.2.3), the use of emphatic intonation in speech or an exclamation mark in writing (Section 12.2.1), emphatic preposing (Section 12.2.2.2), **rhetorical anaphora** (Section 13.2.1) and metaphor (Chapter 14). Emphasis may also be conveyed by the use of emphatic particles. An example in English is 'so' (as in 'That was so amusing!'). In Arabic, independent pronouns (أنا, أنتَ, هو, هي, etc.) may also convey emphasis (cf. the example of أنتم in Section 13.2.1).

One could go on adding indefinitely to the forms of connotative meaning. For example, an utterance 'Do you want to do the washing up?' made in a context where this was clearly a request to do the washing up could be said to have the connotative meaning 'Do the washing up'. An ironic utterance 'What beautiful weather!' made in the context of foul driving rain could be said to have the connotative meaning 'What horrible weather!', etc. The types of connotative meanings we have picked out in Sections 8.2–8.7 and in the previous paragraphs of this section are, however, the most important for translation purposes. These are therefore the ones on which students should concentrate.

Practical 8

Practical 8.1 Collocation: (a) وتشمل هذه النظم *(b)* تقوم العديد

Assignment

Translate the following extracts, paying particular attention to the English collocational equivalents of the forms in curly brackets.

(a) From العسكر والحكم في البلدان العربية, a book about the role of the military in Arab societies (Humphrys 1999: 6). (Translate the initial النظم as 'societies' here.)

وتشمل هذه النظم التمييز الحاد بين المراتب الاجتماعية، كما تشمل {الهوة الساحقة} التي تفصل بين النخبة العسكرية والجماهير، وعزل النخبة أنفسهم عن مواقع العامة من الناس.

(b) From العربي تعريب التعليم في نهايات القرن العشرين, an article in العربي magazine (Stabler 1999: 16).

تقوم العديد من المراكز التعريبية والتعليمية المنتشرة في جميع الدول العربية، بجهد مشكور في سبيل استعادة اللغة العربية {لمكانتها الطبيعية} كلغة العلم والتعليم [. . .].

Practical 8.2 Collocation: (a) أن الحرب دائما *(b)* خسرت الرئاسة

Assignment

Complete the following translations by filling in the blanks.

(a) From لعبة الضفادع والعقارب في عواصم الشرق الاوسط, an article in the Egyptian magazine روز اليوسف (Hetherington 1996: 28).

[. . .] أن الحرب دائما هي إعلان بالحديد والنار عن الموت والميلاد.

[. . .] that war is always a declaration by means of _____ of both _____.

(b) From الحاج رئيسا للكتـائبيين بـفارق ٧ أصوات, an article in the Lebanese newspaper الـنهار (Jones 1999: 7) (the Kataeb, also known as the Phalange, are a
Lebanese political party).

خسرت الرئاسة ولكنني ربحت ضمير الكتائب ووجدانهم.

I may have lost the election, but I have won the _____ of the
Kataeb.

Practical 8.3 Connotative meaning: الرحلة

Assignment

(i) Discuss the strategic decisions that you must take before starting detailed
translation of the following text, and outline and justify the strategy you
adopt. You are to translate the text as part of an anthology of modern Arabic
short stories. Your intended readership is educated English speakers with
only a general knowledge of the Arab world.
(ii) Translate the text into English, paying particular attention to connotative
translation issues.
(iii) Explain the decisions of detail you made in producing your translation.

Contextual information

This passage is from the beginning of a short story by يوسف إدريس called الرحلة
(إدريس 1971: 66). This story was written shortly before the death of Nasser
(جمال عبد الناصر). يوسف إدريس had originally been an enthusiastic supporter of
Nasser and had written numerous newspaper articles in support of him in the
1950s and early 1960s. However, like many others, he subsequently became
disenchanted with Nasser, particularly following Egypt's defeat in the 1967
war against Israel. الرحلة was published in يوسف إدريس's short-story collection
بيت من لحم. The story concerns a journey undertaken by a younger man and his
father. The relationship between the two men is close, perhaps almost sexual.
As the story progresses, it gradually becomes apparent that the father is dead.
The story is regarded as a direct criticism of Nasser's regime, and even as a
prophetic work predicting Nasser's fast-approaching death.

ST

الـــــرحـــلة

أنت وأنا ومن بعدنا الطوفان. لا تخف ! سنرحل حالا سنرحل الى بعيد بعيد . الى حيث لا ينالك ولا
ينالني احد . الى حيث نكون أحرارا تماما نحيا بمطلق قوتنا وإرادتنا وبلا خوف . لا تخف . لقد اتخذت
الاحتياطات كلها . لا تخف ! كل شيء سيتم على ما يرام . أعرف أنك تفضل اللون الكحلي . ها هو
البنطلون اذن . ها هي السترة . بالتأكيد ربطة العنق المحمرة فأنا أعرف طبعك .. لست بالغ الاناقة
نعم ولكنك ترتدي دائما ما يجب، ما يليق . سأساعدك في تصفيف شعرك . أنت لا تعرف اني أحب

شعرك . خفيف هو متناثر وكأنما صنع خصيصا ليخفي صلعتك ولكنه أبيض كله سهل التمشيط . بيدي سأمشطه . بعدها وبالفرشاة نفسها أسوي شاربك . حتى هذا النوع من الشوارب أحبه . هكذا رأيتك مئات المرات تفعل، وهكذا أحببت كل ما تفعل، كل ما أصبح لك عادة، حتى كل ما يصدر كنزوة . أتعرف أني فرحان فرحة لا حد لها . فرحة الإقدام على أمر لن يعرفه سوانا . لست مريضا هذه المرة وأستصحبك كالعادة الى طبيب، ولسنا في طريقنا لزيارة أقارب مملين . فليظل الأمر اذن سرا بيني وبينك.

Practical 8.4 Connotative meaning: القرصنة الصهيونية

Assignment

  (i) Discuss the strategic decisions that you must take before starting detailed translation of the following text, and outline and justify the strategy you adopt. Pay particular attention to issues of compensation. You are to translate this text for *Al-Ahram Weekly,* which is published in English in Egypt.
 (ii) Translate the text into English.
(iii) Explain the decisions of detail you made in producing your TT, noting in particular where there are connotative features in the ST and/or the TT.

Contextual information

This text is taken from the Egyptian الشعب newspaper of 1 June 2010. It follows the storming by Israeli troops of a Turkish ship, the *Mavi Marmara,* which was attempting to take aid to Gaza. During the raid, the Israelis shot and killed nine Turkish activists on board the ship.

ST

القرصنة الصهيونية جريمة صغرى متكررة
والحصار هو الجريمة الكبرى
بقلم:
خالد يوسف

أعلم سيدي القارئ أن الحديث اليوم بعقل متدبر في شأن الجريمة الصهيونية الجديدة.. القديمة، والقرصنة التي مارسها الكيان الصهيوني على قافلة الحرية هو أمر شاق، كما أعلم أن ضوضاء الشجب والإدانة الفارغة من أي مضمون عملي سوف تسيطر على الخطاب الإعلامي العربي والعالمي، تماشيا مع النهج الصهيوني الدائم في التعامل مع جرائم الكيان الغاصب «ليكن لنا الفعل على الارض، ولهم خطابات الاستنكار» وفي هذه المقالة محاولة متواضعة لفهم الحدث وتحليله والاستفادة من إيجابياته .... وهي كثيرة.

الجريمة الصغرى والجريمة الكبرى!!

بداية أعلن وبملء الفم وبمنتهى القناعة، أن ما ارتكبه الكيان الصهيوني من جريمة قرصنة في عرض البحر، وفي مياه دولية محمية بمقتضى القانون الدولي، هو جريمة صغرى معتادة ومتكررة في تاريخ هذا الكيان العنصري، وهي صغرى رغم بشاعتها إذا ما قورنت بجرائمه الكبرى مثل الحصار وتجويع شعب بأكمله [. . .]

Introduction to the formal properties of texts

We have suggested that translation is most usefully taken not as a matter of replicating an ST in the TL but as a challenge to reduce translation loss. The threat of loss is most obvious when the translator confronts general issues of cultural transfer like those discussed in Chapter 4. However, many issues of cultural transfer arise not from extralinguistic cultural sources but from intralinguistic sources, specifically the demonstrable formal properties of the ST. These properties actually present a threat of greater translation loss than the more obvious one posed by the general question of cultural transfer.

We have already seen an aspect of this in respect of (near-)synonym repetition (Section 7.2.1). Repetition in Arabic of words with similar meaning in close proximity can be used for emphasis or semantic precision. Frequently, however, it has no more than a marginally decorative purpose. Other forms of repetition, such as **pattern repetition**, **root repetition** and **lexical item repetition** (Chapter 10), are similarly sometimes used for only marginal decorative effect. These various formal features result in a general cultural tendency, in some kinds of texts at least, for Arabic to be more wordy than English.

The traditional قصيدة type of poem provides another example where demonstrable formal linguistic features can give rise to problems of cultural transfer. The قصيدة is a feature of Arabic culture and one that in many ways has no correspondence to any form of poetry in English. However, it is at least partially defined by features of versification (i.e. formal features on the prosodic level) that are quite different from features of versification in English poetry.

There are doubtless technical philosophical problems in establishing what the demonstrable properties of texts are, but these problems are not our concern in this course. What matters for us is the fact that meanings and effects triggered by a text must originate from features objectively present in it. This is why the translator has to look at the text as a linguistic object.

In assessing the formal properties of texts, it is helpful to borrow some fundamental notions from linguistics. Linguistics offers a hierarchically ordered series of discrete levels on which the formal properties of texts can be discussed in a systematic way. These levels complement one another, of course. That is, although it is essential to distinguish among them when analyzing texts, they do not actually function separately from one another: textual features on a given level always have their effect in terms of features on all other levels.

It is obvious that in any text there are many points at which it could have been different. Where there is one sound there could have been another (compare 'road tolls' and 'toad rolls'). Or where there is a question mark there might have been an exclamation mark (compare 'What rubbish?' with 'What rubbish!'). Or where there is an allusion to the Bible there might have been an allusion to Shakespeare. All of these points of detail where a text could have been different – that is, where it could have been another text – are what we shall call 'textual variables'. These textual variables are what the series of levels defined in linguistics make it possible to identify.

Taking the levels one at a time has two main advantages. First, looking at textual variables on a series of isolated levels makes it possible to see which are important in the ST and which are less important. As we have seen, all ST features inevitably fall prey to translation loss in some respect or other. For example, even if the TT conveys the denotative meaning (Chapter 7) exactly, there will at the very least be phonic loss (Chapter 9) and very likely also loss in terms of connotations (Chapter 8), register (Chapter 15) and so on. It is therefore excellent translation strategy to decide in broad terms which category or categories of textual variable are indispensable in a given ST and which can be ignored. To show what we mean by 'broad terms', we can take a simple example on the sentential level of textual variables. If a particular text contains complex sentences, the translator can scan on the sentential level and decide whether this stylistic feature has a significant function. If it does not, then the strategic decision will probably be that keeping the complexity in the TT is less important than producing a clear, idiomatic TT in the kind of style expected of TL texts of that particular type. In a literary ST, on the other hand, complex sentence structure may be crucial to textual effects: in that case, the strategic decision on the sentential level might well be to create similar effects through complex sentences in the TT and to be prepared to sacrifice details on other levels that, in this ST, have lower priority.

The other advantage in scanning the text level by level is that a TT can be assessed by isolating and comparing the formal variables of ST and TT. The translator or editor is thus able to see precisely what textual variables of the ST are absent from the TT and vice versa. This makes the assessment of translation loss less impressionistic, which in turn permits a more self-aware and methodical way of reducing it.

We suggest six levels of textual variables, hierarchically arranged, in the sense that each level is built on top of the preceding one. Thus, we can think of the **phonic/graphic level** as being at the bottom of the hierarchy, followed further up by the prosodic level, the **grammatical level**, the sentential level, the discourse level and, at the very top, the **intertextual level**. These features constitute the formal matrix, which is part of the overall schema of textual matrices, represented at the end of the Introduction to this book. Note that the representation there places the elements of the formal matrix in the reverse order to the hierarchy as we have just outlined it: thus, the phonic/graphic level is represented at the top and the intertextual level at the bottom, etc. This is because the representation of the schema of textual matrices in the Introduction typically presents elements in the order in which they occur in the book (as discussed in the Introduction itself), not according to any more abstractly conceived overall hierarchy.

Using the term 'hierarchy' here is not meant to imply that features on a 'higher' level are by definition more important than those on a 'lower' level: the variables only have their effect in terms of one another, and their relative importance varies from text to text or even utterance to utterance. Other categories and hierarchies could have been adopted: we have chosen this hierarchy because of its practicability, not for its coherence in abstract linguistic terms. We shall progress 'bottom up', from phonic detail to intertextual considerations. We have chosen this order simply because we have found that students are more comfortable with this than with a 'top-down' approach. In Chapters 9–10 and 12–13, we shall work our way up through the levels, showing what kinds of textual variables can be found on each and how they may function in a text. Chapter 11 deals with parallelism, which may involve phonic/graphic features (Chapter 9) as well as grammatical features (Chapter 10) and denotative features (Chapter 7). The method adopted here does not imply a plodding or piecemeal approach to translation: applying the matrix analysis quickly becomes automatic and very effective.

9 Phonic/graphic and prosodic issues

9.1 The phonic/graphic level

Although they are the 'lowest' in the hierarchy, the phonic/graphic and prosodic levels of textual variables demand as much attention as any other – even if the considered decision proves to be that they are not important enough in a given ST to be allowed to influence translation choice.

Taking a text on the phonic/graphic level means looking at it as a sequence of sound segments (or *phonemes*), or as a sequence of letters (or *graphemes*), or as both. Oral texts are normally only looked at in phonic terms. Written texts are always first encountered on the graphic level, but they may need to be looked at in phonic terms as well – in fact, from a translation point of view, they are more often considered phonically than graphically. Although phonemes and graphemes are different things, we shall normally refer to the 'phonic/graphic level', whether the text in question is an oral one or a written one.

Language is nothing without the sounds of the utterances we hear or the shape on the page of those we read: every text is a phonic/graphic configuration. These configurations are restricted by the conventions of the language in which the text is couched. This is why, the occasional coincidence apart, no TT can reproduce exactly the same sequence of sound segments/letters as any ST. This always and automatically constitutes a source of translation loss. The real question for the translator, however, is whether this loss matters at all. The answer, as usual, is that it all depends.

Generally, we take little or no notice of the sounds or shapes of what we hear and read, paying attention primarily to the message of the utterance. We do tend to notice sounds that are accidentally repeated, but even then we attach little importance to them in most texts, especially in written ones. Often, however, repetition of sounds is a significant factor, so it is useful to have precise terms in which to analyze them.

9.1.1 *Alliteration, assonance and rhyme*

Repetition of sounds can generally be classified either as alliteration or as assonance. There are various current definitions of these terms. For this course, we shall define alliteration as the recurrence of the same sound or sound cluster at the beginning of words, as in *'two tired toads'* or *'all awful ornithologists'*. We define assonance as the recurrence, within words, of the same sound or sound cluster, as in *'a great day's painting'* or *'a swift lift afterwards'*. The two often occur together, of course, as in *'French influence also explains Frederick II's splendid castles in the South of Italy and Sicily'*. Terminal sounds that are not rhymes are best defined as assonance; the five [z] sounds in the following are most simply described as assonance: *'jazzy photos of animals in zoos'*. A vital point to remember is that, as all of these examples show, it is the sound, not the spelling, that counts in discussing alliteration and assonance. Even in Arabic, where the correspondence between graphemes and phonemes is much closer than in English and is therefore not generally such an issue, the translator has to be aware whether a letter such as ة is to be pronounced as 'a' or as 'at' in a particular context.

In general, the more technical or purely informative the text, the less account translators take of sound patterns, because they hardly ever seem to have any thematic or expressive function. That is true of the sentence about Frederick's castles, and it is true of the following sentence from a text on coal mining: 'Testwork has been carried out on screenbowl centrifuges dewatering froth-floated coal.' The alliteration and assonance in these two examples are incidental to the message.

However, many texts are marked by the deliberate use of phonic patterns for expressive purposes. The less purely factual the text, the more this tends to be the case. The most obvious example is poetry, where various types and degrees of rhyme are found, as well as alliteration and assonance. We shall say that two words rhyme where the last stressed vowel, and all the sounds that follow it, are identical and occur in the same order, as in 'br*eam* / s*eem*', 'W*arwick* / euph*oric*', 'incid*entally* / m*entally*'. So, in the mining example, 'screenbowl' and 'coal' are at best imperfect rhymes, because 'coal' is stressed but 'bowl' is not. However, as regards phonic effects, the only difference between poetry and many other genres is one of degree: alliteration, assonance and even rhyme are often exploited in fiction, drama, journalism, polemic and so on.

What are the implications of these observations for translators? As always, the translator must be guided by the purpose of the text, the needs of the target public and, above all, the function of the phonic feature in its context. In general, the sorts of features we have been looking at will not have expressive function in a scientific, technical or other purely informative text, so the translator can happily ignore them. Even in the mining example, the considerable loss on the phonic/graphic level will simply not matter.

Sometimes, of course, even if the ST contains no marked phonic features, a draft TT will inadvertently contain a distracting concentration of sounds. In general, the translator will want to avoid *introducing* tongue-twisters or other phonic effects that impair the TT's communicative function.

In this light, consider the following:

كان يستقصي الحقائق من نقائضها في مجتمع مدينة البغي التي ترعرع فيها [. . .]

Brown (1996: 13) translates this as:

> He used to study the reality behind the contradictions of the City of Oppression where he grew up.

مجتمع 'society' has not been translated; including 'society' would have resulted in something like 'He used to study the reality behind the contradictions of the society of the City of Oppression where he grew up'. Here, the phrase 'contradictions of the society of the City of Oppression', with its multiple alliterations and assonances, is particularly difficult to pronounce.

The use of phonic echoes and affinities for thematic and expressive purposes is sometimes called 'sound symbolism'. It takes two main forms. In the context, the sounds of given words may evoke other words that are not present in the text. Or the sound of a given word occurs in one or more others and sets up a link among the words, conferring on each of them connotations of the other(s). The first two lines of Keats's 'To Autumn' offer simple examples of both:

> Season of mists and mellow fruitfulness, Close bosom-friend of the maturing sun; [. . .]

> (Keats 1958: 273)

The context is crucial. Given the title of the poem and the reference to fruitfulness, 'mellow' is almost certain to evoke 'yellow', a colour of fruit and autumn leaves. In its turn, the 'sun' is likely to be a rich yellow, glowing like a ripe fruit through the autumn haze. These two effects ensure that the 'mists' are received positively by the reader/listener and not as cold, damp and grey. The alliteration in 'mists . . . mellow . . . maturing' reinforces the effect and also gives 'maturing' an intransitive sense as well as its transitive one: the sun itself is growing mature as the year advances. Further, if the sun is maturing (whether in the year or in the day), it may well be low in the sky; if so, it looks extra big when seen through the mist, like a swelling fruit. The [m] in 'bosom' links this word, too, with the other three; so the mellow fruits are perhaps reminiscent of milk-filled breasts, as if season, sun and earth are affectionately uniting in maternal bountifulness. This suggestion is itself reinforced by the alliteration and assonance in 'fruitfulness . . . friend' and by the alliteration and assonance on [s] throughout the two lines, which associates all of these key words still more closely with one another.

Not many translators earn their livings translating poetry, of course. But in respect to sound symbolism – as of many other things – poetry offers extremely clear examples of vital factors that all translators do need to bear in mind. The Keats example is useful for this very reason. Practically none of the images and associations we saw in those two lines derive from denotative meaning alone – that is why perceiving and reacting to sound symbolism is bound to be subjective. All of them are reinforced, and some are actually created, by phonic features. Yet those phonic features are objectively present in the text. This points to the first factor that must be remembered: unlike many other sorts of symbols, those in sound symbolism do not have a single unchanging meaning. In fact, none of the phonic features in the lines from Keats has any *intrinsic* meaning or expressive power at all. Such expressiveness as they have derives from the context – and that is the second vital factor. In a different context, the same features would almost certainly have a different effect. The *sounds* of the words have their effect in terms of the denotative and connotative *meanings* of the words. So, without the title, 'mellow' might very well not evoke 'yellow'. Neither is there anything intrinsically mellow, maternal or mature about the sound [m]: the smell in a pig-yard might be described as 'the mingling miasmata from the slime and muck'. And, in [fr], there is as much frightful frumpishness as there is fruitfulness and friendship.

In other words, translators confronted with sound symbolism must decide what its function is before they start translating. The aim will be to convey as much of the ST message as possible. If it is essential to this message that the TT convey sound symbolism, it is almost certain that the TL sounds involved will be *different* from the ST ones: trying to reproduce phonic effects and affiliations in the TT usually entails far too great a loss in respect to denotative and connotative meaning. The translator's question therefore has to be: Is what matters the *specific sounds* in the ST's alliteration, assonance, etc., or is it rather *the fact that there is* alliteration, assonance, etc.? Fortunately, the latter is usually the case, and it is usually possible to compensate for the loss of given ST phonic details by replacing them with TL ones that have a comparable effect. Consider the following:

كان الحوار حوار جرحى أمضهم الجرح وأعياهم التعب [. . .]

This has been translated (Brown 1996: 21) as:

> Their conversation was that of the wounded, who were tormented by their wounds and worn out by exhaustion.

Here, the Arabic makes use of various kinds of repetition (cf. Chapter 10) to achieve a sense of emphasis, stressing the degree to which the people concerned were ground down by their afflictions. The English translation compensates in kind and in place by the use of alliteration ('*w*ounded', '*w*ounds' and '*w*orn') and assonance ('w*ou*nded', '*tor*men*ted*', 'w*ou*nds', 'w*or*n', 'o*u*t' and 'exh*au*stion') to give a similar sense of emphasis.

Similar remarks apply to rhyme. There can be no hard-and-fast rule regarding rhyme in translation. Each TT requires its own strategy. Often, producing a rhyming TT means an unacceptable sacrifice of denotative and connotative meaning. With some sorts of ST (especially comic or sarcastic ones), where the precise nuances of meaning are less important than the phonic mockery, it is often easier, and even desirable, to stock the TT with rhymes and echoes that are different from those of the ST but just as obtrusive and to similar effect. Some genres of writing in Arabic also make use of rhyme, and particularly of سَجْع, or 'rhymed prose' (cf. Section 13.3.1), in contexts where rhyme would be highly inappropriate in English. Consider the following:

ولم يكن بوسعه ان يطفي نار العين بالإغضاء او يخفي تكشيرة الناب بالإصغاء [. . .]

This has been translated (Brown 1996: 13) as:

> It was not in his power to smother the fire in his heart with indifference or, by listening, to disguise his grimace.

The Arabic contains a double rhyme, يخفي – يطفي and بالإصغاء – بالإغضاء (it also involves parallelism, Chapter 11, and pattern repetition, Section 10.2.3.1). The rhyme here is obviously deliberate in the Arabic; in fact, the writer employs rhyme at various points in the book, particularly in 'poetic' contexts that reflect the inner life of the central character صابر. In the context of an English novel, however, such rhyme would seem highly inappropriate and probably comic. The translator has accordingly ignored the rhyme in her translation.

9.1.2 Onomatopoeia

The only time when a translator is likely to want to try replicating ST sounds is when they are onomatopoeic. **Onomatopoeia** must not be confused with alliteration and assonance. An onomatopoeia is a word whose phonic form imitates a sound – 'splosh', 'bang', 'cuckoo', etc.

Standard Arabic has a fair number of words that can be regarded as onomatopoeic; colloquial dialects probably have more. Perhaps the most obvious cases in Standard Arabic are doubled and reduplicative verbs (reduplicative verbs being quadriliteral verbs in which the third and fourth radical repeat the first and second radical). Examples of doubled verbs are طَقَّ 'to crack, pop; to clack, smack, flap'; صَرَّ 'to chirp; to creak (door); to squeak, screech; to grate, scratch; to gnash, chatter (teeth)'; دَقَّ 'to knock, rap, bang (on the door)'. Examples of onomatopoeic reduplicative verbs are طَقْطَقَ 'to crack, snap, rattle, clatter, chug, pop, crash'; صَرْصَرَ 'to let out a piercing cry, scream shrilly'; دَنْدَنَ 'to buzz, hum; to drone; to hum softly, croon (a song); to murmur'; هَمْهَمَ 'to say "hmm"; to mumble, mutter; to grumble; to growl, snarl; to hum, buzz, drone' (all definitions from Wehr).

There are often marked linguistic discrepancies in onomatopoeia as between different languages. Thus, the fact that a word in one language is imitative of a particular sound does not necessarily mean that a word in another language that imitates the same sound will be particularly similar phonically to the word in the first language. Thus, although دَنَّ sounds rather like 'drone', it does not sound anything like its most normal translation equivalents 'hum' and 'buzz'. Similarly, the fact that an onomatopoeic word exists in one language to describe a particular sound does not necessarily mean that a similarly onomatopoeic word will exist in another language. Thus, 'snore' is hardly onomatopoeic in English, whereas خَرْخَرَ is obviously so in Arabic. Finally, while onomatopoeic words in different languages are often in some sense similar in terms of meaning, the range of meaning they have will very often differ significantly (e.g. هَمْهَمَ 'to say "hmm"; to mumble, mutter; to grumble; to growl, snarl; to hum, buzz, drone').

Beyond basic onomatopoeia, in which a word sounds like the sound it denotes, there are various kinds of secondary onomatopoeia. Most obvious are cases in children's language, such as 'bow wow' for 'dog' (as in the old song, 'Daddy wouldn't buy me a bow wow'). Here, 'bow wow' denotes dog but is imitative of the barking sound that a dog makes rather than of the dog itself (a dog, being an animal, is not a sound, though it can of course make various sounds): the onomatopoeia is thus indirect. Secondary onomatopoeia of this kind might also be termed 'metonymic onomatopoeia', metonymy (see also Chapter 14) being, as noted in Section 7.2.3 '(A figure of speech characterized by) the action of substituting for a word or phrase denoting an object, action, institution, etc., a word or phrase denoting a property or something associated with it' (*Oxford English Dictionary Online*). An example of metonymy is 'Table three wants to pay his bill', where 'table three' refers to the person sitting at table three rather than to the table itself. Similarly, in the case of 'bow wow' meaning 'dog', 'bow wow' refers to the dog rather than to the sound made by the dog.

Metonymic secondary onomatopoeia is fairly easy to find in children's language in English – as well as 'a bow wow' for a dog, 'a miaow' for a cat, 'a moo moo' for a cow, etc. It is not, however, so easy to find in standard (adult) English. A possible example, however, is the word 'cow', which is fairly imitative of the sound a cow makes. As this example suggests, however, what is and is not to be regarded as secondary onomatopoeia is not always clear.

Possible examples of metonymic onomatopoeia involving birds in Arabic are عَقْعَق 'magpie' and هُدهُد 'hoopoe' on the basis that these are imitative of the calls of these birds (cf. Versteegh 2009: 283). A clearer example of metonymic onomatopoeia in Arabic is found in the title of a short story لغة الآي آي by the Egyptian writer يوسف ادريس, where آي آي is an Egyptian Arabic form denoting pain on the basis that, when people are in pain, they make a sound that is rather like آي آي.

Because of the differences in onomatopoeia between languages, care may be needed in translating an ST onomatopoeia, particularly when it has a thematic or expressive function. Frequently, the safest approach may be to translate the ST onomatopoeia with something other than a TT onomatopoeia, with or without some form of compensation. A case in point is the short story لغة الآي آي, mentioned earlier, that deals with the nature of extreme pain, both physical and psychological. آي آي is a metonymic onomatopoeic expression in Egyptian Arabic, rather similar to 'ouch' in English; both express the sense of pain by mimicking with the use of standard phonic elements of the language the kinds of vocal sounds that people naturally make when they are in pain. However, 'The Language of Ouch' sounds rather too difficult to interpret in English to be a viable story title, perhaps because 'ouch' in English is typically used as an interjection. It is also too weak for this context. A stronger alternative, such as 'Aargh', is also unviable, because it is even less like a standard English word than 'ouch'. Given this, it seems better to translate لغة الآي آي by something fairly bland, but comprehensible, such as 'The Language of Pain', albeit that there is fairly significant translation loss in terms of expressiveness.

9.2 The prosodic level

On the prosodic level, utterances count as 'metrically' structured stretches. 'Metric' here covers three sorts of things. First, in a given utterance, some syllables will conventionally always be accented more than others; on top of their standard accentuation, voice stress and emphasis will be used for greater clarity and expressiveness. Second, clarity and expressiveness also depend on variations in vowel pitch and voice modulation. And third, the speed of vocal delivery also varies, for similar reasons. On the prosodic level, therefore, groups of syllables may form *contrastive* patterns (e.g. short, fast, staccato sections alternating with long, slow, smooth ones), or *recurrent* ones or both.

For the translator, there are four factors to bear in mind when considering the prosodic level. The first factor is that Arabic and English are quite different from each another on the prosodic level, having very different tempi, rhythms and melodic undulations. It is virtually impossible to produce a TT that both sounds natural and reproduces the prosodic characteristics of the ST. Just occasionally, it is worth aiming for similar rhythms in the TT to those of the ST. For instance, if part of the ST's expressive effect stems from imitative rhythms – galloping horses, breaking waves, dripping water, etc. – there would be significant translation loss on the prosodic level if the TT failed to use similar rhythms to similar effect.

However, prosodic translation loss far more commonly arises from a failure to heed one or more of the other three factors. The first of these – that is, the second factor overall – is the nature and function of intonation and stress. This is relatively straightforward in the case of oral texts. Even in written texts, either the grammatical structure or the context will usually show what the intonation should be when the text is read out loud and what its communicative purpose is. Consider the following from the short story الخيول by the Iraqi writer عبد الرحمن مجيد الربيعي. A young man has just met a young woman in a hotel:

ST

سألته:
- أحجزت؟
وهز رأسه وقال:
- على وشك.
- أطلبت غرفة بحمام؟
- نعم.
- حسنا. أخبرني عن رقمها. فغرفتي بلا حمام.
وأضافت:
- الوسخ يضايقني.

TT (adapted from Tunnicliffe 1994: 12)

'Have you checked in?', she asked.
He shook his head and said, 'Almost'.
'Did you ask for a room with a bathroom?'

'Yes.'

'Good. Give me the number; my room hasn't got one'.

And then she added: 'I get fed up with the dirt'.

As a spoken text, this dialogue displays quite subtle variations in intonation and stress; it is worth reading the TT out loud to appreciate these. Consider, in particular, the likely intonation of 'Almost' and the young woman's rather suggestive 'I get fed up with the dirt'. Subtle as these issues of intonation and stress are, however, they are fairly naturally 'read in' by competent speakers and therefore do not normally present grave translation problems. The translator's job – and this is the third factor – is to select a written form that suggests an intonation and a stress pattern that ensure that the TT sentence has the same communicative purpose as its ST counterpart. In this text by الربيعي, for example, one might perhaps choose to translate the young woman's final statement الوسخ يضايقني, not as 'I get fed up with the dirt', but as 'You see, I get fed up with the dirt'. The addition of 'You see' explains the relationship between the statement 'I get fed up with the dirt' and the previous statements 'Give me the number; my room hasn't got one' (etc.) and ensures that the intonation pattern that is read in is likely to be appropriate.

The fourth factor is that even where the TL expression does not seem grammatically or prosodically problematic, the translator must be sure not to introduce prosodic features that are inappropriate to the message content. Perhaps the commonest cases of translation loss on the prosodic level arise when a grammatical choice in the TT implies a stress pattern and an intonation that lead the reader/listener to expect a different sort of message from the one that actually materializes. This often happens when the translator chooses an inappropriate connective.

A good example of this is the following, from the Egyptian magazine *Petroleum* (Egyptian General Petroleum Corporation 1999: ١٧, 7), which is the final sentence of an article lauding the achievements of the Egyptian oil industry over the past eighteen years:

ST

ومما لا شك فيه أن حصاد وإنجازات العمل البترولي خلال الـ ١٨ عاماً الماضية هو بمثابة وسام للعاملين بالبترول ومحصلة للسياسات والمجهودات التي تمت خلال تلك الفترة.

TT (adapted)

No doubt, the achievements of the petroleum sector during the past 18 years represent a triumph for the workers in this sector, and reflect the policies and efforts which have been pursued during this period.

In the Arabic ST, the phrase مما لا شك فيه signals that the final sentence of the article is intended to summarize the information previously given in the article. This is why there is no doubt about what is to follow in this sentence. In English, however, sentences beginning 'no doubt' often have an intonation pattern that rises at the end of the sentence. This typically signals that the following sentence will contain a contrast or contradiction to the information given in the sentence in question. The effect of this in the TT is to signal that the lack of doubt about the achievements (etc.) of the petroleum sector is likely to be contrasted in the subsequent sentence, this subsequent sentence perhaps beginning with a contrastive conjunctive element, such as 'however'. Thus, one might imagine the English TT carrying on along the following lines:

> No doubt, the achievements of the petroleum sector during the past 18 years represent a triumph for the workers in this sector, and reflect the policies and efforts which have been pursued during this period. However, this does not obviate the need for future rationalization within the industry.

This sense of subsequent contrast is certainly not intended in the Arabic ST.

The English TT could be improved by replacing the negative 'no doubt' with something more positive and less open to a contrastive interpretation. Thus (with some additional changes):

> When we consider the achievements of the petroleum sector during the past 18 years, it is clear that they represent a triumph for the workers in this sector, and reflect the policies and efforts which have been pursued during this period.

9.2.1 *Rudiments of English and Arabic versification*

A special set of features on the prosodic level are those found in verse, which present specific translation challenges. What follows is a short introduction to the rudiments of English and Arabic versification. Our aim is to give students a foundation for discerning and interpreting the conventional patterns in English and Arabic verse and for making an informed decision between English metres if the strategic decision is to produce a verse TT. We shall focus on the metrical side of versification – that is, the distribution of stressed and unstressed syllables. This ignores tempi and melodic pitch, which are vital prosodic textual variables and that do, of course, require as much attention in preparing to translate verse as they do for prose. We shall not consider other aspects of verse, such as types of stanza or the phonic questions of rhyme. For fuller information on these and on metrical questions, see Hollander (1981) and Stoetzer (1998) (vol. 2: 619–21).

9.2.1.1 *English*

English metre is syllable-and-stress metre. The line is defined in terms of feet. A foot is a conventional group of stressed and/or unstressed syllables in a particular order. A line of traditional verse consists of a fixed number of particular feet. For example:

> The *cur*/few *tolls*/ the *knell*/ of *par*/ting *day*/

This line has five feet; that is, it is a pentameter. In this particular case, the feet have one unstressed followed by one stressed syllable. This is known as an *iamb,* or iambic foot. A line consisting of five iambs is an iambic pentameter. It is the most common English line, found in the work of great playwrights and poets. The commonest other feet are:

trochee (adj. *trochaic*):	***When*** the/ ***pie*** was/ *o*pened/
dactyl (adj. *dactylic*):	***Me***rrily/ ***chat***ting and/ ***clat***tering/
anapest (adj. *anapestic*):	And made *ci*/der in***side***/ her in***side***/

Most poems do not have a regular beat throughout. This would be intolerably dreary. Even limericks are very rarely exclusively anapestic. The opening lines of Keats's 'To Autumn' (Section 9.1.1) are examples of typical variations on the basic iambic pentameter. These lines still count as iambic pentameters, because they do have five feet and are predominantly iambic, and the rest of the poem has these qualities.

One other sort of English metre is worth mentioning: strong-stress metre. This is different from syllable-and-stress metre in that only the stresses count in describing the line, the number of weak syllables being variable. Although very old, being found in Anglo-Saxon poetry, this metre is also used in quite a lot of modern verse, often in combination with syllable-and-stress metre. It is also a feature of nursery rhymes. An example from a nursery rhyme is:

> **One, two,** / **buck**le my **shoe**/
> [...]
> **Nine**teen, **twenty,** / my **plate's em**pty/

Here, in different feet, the distribution of stressed and unstressed syllables is different, and there are a variable number of unstressed syllables but always two stressed syllables.

9.2.1.2   Arabic

Like the English metrical line, the line in Arabic is defined in terms of feet. However, while English metre involves both syllable and stress, Arabic metre is based entirely around syllable type. The basic distinction is between short syllables (consonant + short vowel) and long syllables (consonant + long vowel *or* consonant + short vowel + consonant). All Arabic syllables are treated as beginning with a consonant. Accordingly, there is no ambiguity about where one syllable ends and another begins. Thus, in the word دَمُن, the first syllable is *da* and the second syllable is *mun*. Vowels at the end of the hemistich or line are always scanned long, irrespective of their quantity in prose.

Feet consist of varying numbers of syllables (most commonly three or four syllables), combinations of these feet making up a particular metre. A large number of metres are recognized in Classical Arabic poetry. Compositions are normally in a single metre. However, the fact that metres permit a degree of variation in the syllable types used to constitute their feet means that there is normally a degree of rhythmic variation within an individual composition. In some metres, double short syllables within one line typically alternate with one long syllable in other lines, while in others a long syllable in one line alternates with a short syllable in another.

Most classical poems are of the قصيدة form, a قصيدة having a variable number of lines (بيت, pl. أبيات), normally not more than one hundred. Lines can have up to thirty syllables divided into two hemistichs (مِصْرَع or شَطْر). The first half of the line is called the صدر 'chest' (also الشطر الاول 'the first half') and the second the عجز 'rump' (also الشطر الثاني 'the second half'). These are separated by a gap in the text that is somewhat longer than what standardly occurs between words. The number of syllables per line is variable in some metres and fixed in others. A single rhyme, sometimes termed a 'monorhyme', occurs at the end of every line. First lines (مَطْلَع, pl. مطالع) often have rhyming hemistichs.

As an illustration of the operation of traditional Arabic prosody, we shall take the first two lines from a poem by الإمام الشافعي, the founder of the شافعية School of Law (مذهب):

دَعِ الأَيَّامَ تَــفْــعَــلُ مَـا تَــشَــاءُ   وَطِبْ نَفْسـاً إِذَا حَكَمَ القَضَاءُ
وَلاَ تَــجْــزَعْ لِــحَادِثَــةِ اللــيَالِـي   فَـمَـا لِحَــوَادِثِ الـدُّنـيَـا بَــقَـاءُ

This can be translated fairly literally as follows:

Let the days do what they will,   and be of good cheer when fate judges.
Do not be concerned at the night's event;   for the world's events have no permanence.

The metre is a variation of the وافر metre form, termed by Stoetzer (1998: 621) *wafir-1*. Using U to represent a short syllable, — to represent a long syllable, UU to represent either one long or two short syllables, / to represent a foot division and // to represent a hemistich division, the basic pattern of this variant of وافر can be represented as follows (reading from right to left, i.e. the same direction as the Arabic script).

$$// — \quad — \quad U/ — \quad \underline{U\,U} \quad — \quad U/ — \quad \underline{U\,U} \quad — \quad U/$$

The second hemistich in this metre has exactly the same pattern of feet as the first hemistich and so has not been repeated here.

The first two lines of this poem can be scanned as follows. We have split up the Arabic words into syllable units for ease of presentation and added foot and hemistich divisions in the Arabic as well as in the metrical analysis on the line following this:

//	ءُ	شَا	مَا /تَ	عَ لُ	تَفْ	/مَ	يَا	أَيْ	ع ال	/دَ
//	—	—	U/ —	U U	—	U/	—	—	—	U/

/	ءُ	ضَا	قَ مَ ال /قَ	حَ كَ	ذَا	إِ /	سَأ	نَفْ	طِبْ	/وَ
/	—	—	U/ —	U U	—	U/	—	—	—	U/

// لِي //	يَا	الْ/الَ ةٍ	ثَ دِ	حَا	لِ/	زَعْ	تَجْ	لَا	/وَ
// —	—	U/ —	U U	—	U/	—	—	—	U/

/ ءُ	قَا	/بَ يَا	دُنْ	ثِ ال/	وَا /دِ	حَ	مَا لِ	/فَ
/ —	—	U/ —	—	—	U/ —	U U —	U/	

Since the second half of the twentieth century, many Arab poets have used free verse, abandoning the fixed patterns of the classical verse forms. The basic unit of free verse is the single foot (تَفْعِيلة), this being either a type of foot used in older poetry or a close derivative.

9.2.2   Translating Arabic verse

The translator of a verse text always has to ask what the function of the ST verse is. Is it decorative? Does it have thematic and/or expressive effect? What is the effect of its regularity or irregularity? And, of course, similar questions have to be asked on the phonic/graphic level.

In terms of the choice of an overall TT form for verse translation, issues of appropriateness and practicability are extremely important. In terms of appropriateness, we will consider the issues of rhyme and stanza form, as these are fairly clear-cut. The monorhyme of the traditional Arabic قصيدة, for example, is quite alien to the traditional rhyming patterns of English. Translators of an Arabic قصيدة who decide to use rhyme in their translation are therefore faced with a choice. Either they use an Arabic-type monorhyme, and thereby produce a rather exotic-sounding translation, or they use a rhyming pattern that is more typical of English but involves significant translation loss on the phonic level.

The same is true of the division of the poem into stanzas. As we have seen, the Arabic قصيدة is written as a single block, without any stanza divisions (although there are also traditional Arabic verse forms, such as the مُوَشَّح, which make use of stanzas). Some English poems are written in continuous blocks of many lines, but this is by no means a predominant form. Again, the translator is faced with a choice: either to retain the overall single-block form of the ST or to substitute a perhaps more natural-looking TT stanza form.

Appropriateness often has to be balanced against practicality. A translator might, for example, consider that the ideal translation of a particular Arabic قصيدة would be into an English TT utilizing rhyming iambic pentameters in four-line stanzas. But these constraints are bound to result in significant translation loss. For example, it may not be possible under such circumstances to relay in the TT features on the phonic level of the ST (e.g. alliteration, assonance), which may be just as important as features of metre and rhyme. It may also prove necessary to make dramatic changes to denotative meaning in order to make the TT fit the desired verse form. Under such circumstances, it may be preferable to translate the قصيدة into free verse or into a form of prose that maintains at least some prosodic and phonic features typical of poetry. It may also be possible to compensate for some of the loss of metrical and rhyming features by careful use of vocabulary that belongs to an obviously poetic register or that has particularly appropriate connotations in the context in which it is used.

Practical 9

Practical 9.1 The phonic/graphic and prosodic levels:
دع الايام تفعل ما تشاء

Assignment

(i) Consider the two TT versions of the first three lines of the poem: TT (a), and TT (b). What different strategic decisions do TT (a) and TT (b) embody? What are the advantages and disadvantages of each approach? Think particularly about metrical features and the stanza form of TT (b).

(ii) Produce a translation of the entire poem which is a completion of TT (a) and is modelled on the translation patterns established in TT (a). If you feel particularly strongly that there are elements in TT (a) which you can improve on, you should do so. However, do not attempt to change any features which are the result of identifiable strategic decisions.

(iii) Produce a translation of the entire poem which is a completion of TT (b) and is modelled on the translation patterns established in TT (b). If you feel particularly strongly that there are elements in TT (b) which you can improve on, you should do so. However, do not attempt to change any features which are the result of identifiable strategic decisions.

(iv) Write notes explaining where and why you used four-line stanzas in the completion of TT (b), and where and why you used two-line stanzas.

(v) You have been approached by the International Poetry Society to contribute a translation of this poem in an anthology of Islamic verse, to be published in the English-speaking world. This anthology is aimed at a readership which is likely to include the following: (i) people with an existing interest in English-language poetry, (ii) people with an existing interest in religious literature; (iii) English-speaking Muslims. Which of your two TT versions of this ST would you propose that the publisher uses for the anthology, and why?

Contextual information

This ST is a piece of Islamic religious poetry by محمد بن إدريس الشافعي (AD 767–820), the founder of the Sunni شافعية School of Law (مذهب). The poem's metre has already been discussed in Section 9.2.1.2. The ST is popular at least partly because of the accessibility of its language, and posters of it can be found on the walls of shops and restaurants in Yemen (and possibly other Arab countries). It can be regarded as reflecting a 'stoical' attitude to life, which is typical of mainstream Sunni Islam.

ST

وَطِبْ نَفْساً إِذَا حَكَمَ القَضَاءُ	دَعِ الأيَّامَ تَفْعَلُ مَا تَشَاءُ
فَمَا لِحَوَادِثِ الدُّنيَا بَقَاءُ	وَلاَ تَجْزَعْ لِحَادِثَةِ اللَّيَالِي
وَشِيمَتُكَ السَّمَاحَةُ وَالوَفَاءُ	وَكُنْ رَجُلاً عَلَى الأهْوَالِ جَلْداً
وَسَرَّكَ أن يَكُونَ لَهَا غِطَاءُ	وَإِنْ كَثُرَتْ عُيُوبُكَ فِي البَرَايَا

يُغَطِّيهِ كَمَا قِيلَ السَخَاءُ	تَسَتَّرْ بِالسَخَاءِ فَكُلُّ عَيْبٍ
فَإِنَّ شَمَاتَةَ الأَعْدَا بَلاَءُ	وَلاَ تُرِ لِلأَعَادِي قَطُّ ذُلاًّ
فَمَا فِي النَارِ لِلظَّمْآنِ مَاءُ	وَلاَ تَرْجُ السَمَاحَةَ مِنْ بَخِيلٍ
وَلَيْسَ يَزِيدُ فِي الرِّزْقِ العَنَاءُ	وَرِزْقُكَ لَيْسَ يُنْقِصُهُ التَّأَنِّي
وَلاَ بُوسٌ عَلَيْكَ وَلاَ رَخَاءُ	وَلاَ حُزْنٌ يَدُومُ وَلاَ سُرُورٌ
فَأَنْتَ وَمَالِكُ الدُّنْيَا سَوَاءُ	إِذَا مَا كُنْتَ ذَا قَلْبٍ قَنُوعٍ
فَلاَ أَرْضٌ تَقِيهِ وَلاَ سَمَاءُ	وَمَنْ نَزَلَتْ بِسَاحَتِهِ المَنَايَا
إِذَا نَزَلَ القَضَا ضَاقَ الفَضَاءُ	وَأَرْضُ اللهِ وَاسِعَةٌ وَلكِنْ
فَمَا يُغْنِي عَنِ المَوْتِ الدَّوَاءُ	دَعِ الأَيَّامَ تَغْدُرُ كُلَّ حِينٍ

TT (a)

Let the days do what they will, and be of good cheer when fate utters its decree.
Nor be troubled by the night's event; the events of this world have no permanence.
Be steadfast in the face of terrors; let your mark be generosity and trust.

TT (b)

Let the days do what they will,
And with good cheer face fate's decree.
Let night's events cause no concern;
The world's events will cease to be.

Brave all dreads with firm decision
Loyal and generous of disposition.

Practical 9.2 The phonic/graphic and prosodic levels: آهِ .. كم كُنَّا قَبِيحينَ

Assignment

(i) Discuss the strategic decisions that you must take before starting detailed translation of the following text, and outline and justify the strategy you adopt. You have been asked to translate these poems for an anthology of poems titled *War's Words: Poetry of Conflict from Around the Globe*.

(ii) Translate the poems into an appropriate poetic English form.

(iii) Explain the decisions of detail you made in producing your TTs, especially those involving compensation.

Contextual information

These poems (from قباني 1981: 344, 346–347) are the second and fourth in a series of poems by نزار قباني dealing with the Lebanese civil war and collectively titled إلى بيروت الأنثى مع حبي. They are simply numbered '2' and '4' in the original collection (as they are here). Beirut is addressed in the second person (feminine singular) throughout.

قباني was Syrian by origin but lived in Lebanon for many years, attracted there by the greater freedom of expression than in his own country. قباني was a leading exponent of modern Arabic free verse. His writing typically combines simplicity with elegance. Much of his poetry deals with romantic love, but he is also known for his political and social themes.

ST

٢

آه .. كم كُنَّا قبيحينَ، وكُنَّا جُبَنَاءُ
عندما بعناكِ، يا بيروتُ، في سُوق الإماءْ
وحجزنا الشقَقَ الفخمةَ في حيِّ (الأليزيه) وفي (مايْفير) لندنْ ..
وغسَلنا الحزنَ بالخمرةِ، والجنسِ، وقاعاتِ القَمارْ
وتذكَّرنا – على مائدة الروليتِ، أخبارَ الديارْ
وافتقدنا زمنَ الدِفْلى بلبنانَ ..
وعصرَ الجُلَّنارْ ..
وبكيْنا مثلما تبكي النساءُ . . . .

٤

طمئنيني عنكِ
يا صاحبةَ الوجه الحزينْ
كيفَ حالُ البحرِ؟
هل هُمْ قتلوهُ برصاص القنص مثل الآخرينْ؟
كيفَ حالُ الحبّ؟
هل أصبح أيضاً لاجئاً . . . .
بين ألوف اللاجئينْ . . . .
كيفَ حالُ الشِّعْرِ؟
هل بَعْدَكِ – يا بيروتُ – من شِعرٍ يُغَنَّى؟
ذَبَحْتَنا هذه الحربُ التي من غير مَعنى ..
أفرغْتَنا من معانينا تماماً ..
بَعْثَرْتَنا في أقاصي الأرضِ
منبوذينَ ..
مسحوقينَ ..
مَرْضَى . . . .
مُتْعَبينْ
جَعَلَتْ مِنَّا – خلافاً للنُبُوءاتِ ..
يهوداً تائهينْ. . . . .

***Practical 9.3 The phonic/graphic level:* تتابعت الاعوام**

Assignment

(i) Discuss the strategic decisions that you must take before starting detailed translation of the following text, and outline and justify the strategy you

adopt. Consider in particular any points at which assonance or alliteration might figure in your translation. The text is to be translated as a piece of literary writing for an educated English-speaking audience with no specific knowledge of the Arab world.

(ii) Translate the text into English.

(iii) Explain the main decisions of detail you made in producing your TT.

Contextual information

The text is from صالح (عرس الزين, n.d.: 33), a well-known novel by the contemporary Sudanese writer الطيب صالح. الزين himself is a kind of wise fool whose character has religious overtones. Several passages in the book, like this one, are largely descriptive. This text is part of a two-page descriptive 'mini-chapter' (unnumbered and untitled) within the book. The 'overriding' tense of the book's narrative is the perfect. The طنبور (pl. طنابير) is a traditional Sudanese stringed instrument that has almost ceased to be used in Sudan following the introduction of the *oud* (عود).

ST

تتابعت الاعوام، عام يتلو عاماً، ينتفخ صدر النيل، كما يمتلئ صدر الرجل بالغيظ . ويسيل الماء على الضفتين، فيغطي الأرض المزروعة حتى يصل إلى حافة الصحراء عند أسفل البيوت. تنق الضفادع بالليل، وتهب من الشمال ريح رطبة مغمسة بالندى تحمل رائحة هي مزيج من اريج زهر الطلح ورائحة الحطب المبتل ورائحة الأرض الخصبة الظمأى حين ترتوي بالماء ورائحة الأسماك الميتة التي يلقيها الموج على الرمل . وفي الليالي المقمرة حين يستدير وجه القمر، يتحول الماء إلى مرآة ضخمة مضيئة تتحرك فوق صفحتها ظلال النخل واغصان الشجر . والماء يحمل الأصوات إلى أبعاد كبيرة، فإذا اقيم حفل عرس على بعد ميلين تسمع زغاريده ودق طبوله وعزف طنابيره ومزاميره كأنه إلى يمين دارك.

10 Grammatical issues

10.1 Introduction

We have seen in Chapter 9 that the alliteration and assonance of 'Season of mists and mellow fruitfulness' trigger effects over and above the denotative meaning of this phrase. We were considering the alliteration and assonance as features on the phonic/graphic level. But, like all utterances, this one can also be considered on the other five levels of textual variables. The extra meanings, for instance, are the semantic correlates of features on the *grammatical* level, while part of the effect of Keats's phrase derives from features on the *sentential* level. We will consider the grammatical level in the present chapter and the sentential level in Chapter 12.

10.2 The grammatical level

On the grammatical level are considered two things: (1) **morphology** (adj. morphological): that is, words and their formation by affixation, inflection, derivation and compounding; (2) syntax (adj. syntactic): that is, the arrangement of words into phrases and sentences. It is the grammatical level where translation loss is generally most immediately obvious. This is very clear in the examples we have seen in previous chapters, many of which show the need for some degree of grammatical transposition. Because loss on this level is so common, we shall only give a few examples here. As ever, the question is not whether there is translation loss (there always is) but what it consists of and whether it matters.

10.2.1 Words

We are all familiar with dictionaries. They are indispensable for anyone concerned with language, because they list the practical totality of the words in a given language. This totality is known as the lexis of a language (adj. lexical). But it is vital to remember that meanings are not found exclusively in the words listed individually in the dictionary. Any text shows that the combination of words creates meanings that they do not have in isolation, and even meanings that are not wholly predictable from the senses of the words combined.

In translation, lexical loss is very common, but it is just one kind of translation loss among many. It can occur for all sorts of reasons. It very often arises from the fact that exact synonymy between ST words and TL words is relatively rare. The word لحم, for example, might be considered an exact synonym of English 'meat'. For many Arabs, however, chicken may not count as لحم, and fish almost certainly will not. This phenomenon is even clearer in some dialects than it is in Standard Arabic. In Sudan, for example, لغة is only used in speaking to refer to a language that is regularly used in writing. English and Arabic, therefore, both qualify as لغة. Languages that are not normally written, by contrast, are typically referred to as لهجة. This means that Sudanese colloquial Arabic and a language such as Dinka (spoken by perhaps three million people in South Sudan) are both classified as لهجة. (Another term used in Sudan specifically for unwritten languages other than Arabic is رُطانة.) Thus, لغة in Sudanese Arabic is not a synonym of 'language' in English; nor is لهجة a synonym of English 'dialect' (as might be thought if one only considered لهجة in relation to Sudanese colloquial Arabic).

Another common source of lexical translation loss is the fact that, in any text, words acquire associative overtones on top of their denotative meanings. We have seen a good example in the lines from Keats, where alliteration and assonance were extremely important for the effects of the text. Another example is a line from the Syrian poet نزار قباني, which reads أحمل الزمن المحترق في عيني (cf. Section 8.6). This has been translated (Rolph 1995: 10) as 'I carry this scorched era in my eyes'. Here, a more literal translation of محترق (e.g. 'burnt', 'burnt up', 'flaming', 'fiery') would sound odd. 'Scorched', however, sounds much more acceptable in this context, mainly because the phrase 'scorched era' echoes the military phrase 'scorched earth'.

10.2.2 *Grammatical arrangement*

Lexical issues are a particular category of grammatical issue, so it is not surprising that some of them are most conveniently examined under the heading of grammatical arrangement. Under this heading, we subsume two types of grammatical structure: (1) morphological patterns affecting individual words – affixation/inflection, compounding and derivation; (2) syntactic patterns, whereby words are linked to form more or less complex phrases and clauses.

The essentials of morphology are not difficult to understand. Words in both English and Arabic are made up of 'bits', these 'bits' being known in linguistics as 'morphemes'. Thus, in English, the word 'unluckily' can be regarded as being made up of four morphemes: 'un-', 'luck', '-i' (or '-y', as in 'lucky') and '-ly'. Traditionally, the morphemes that make up English words are classified as stems and affixes. The stem is the central bit of the word; in the case of 'unfortunately', the stem is 'fortune'. Affixes are the non-central bits of the word, which come either before or after the stem. Affixes that come before the stem are known as prefixes; in the case of 'unfortunately', 'un-' is a prefix. Affixes that come after the stem are known as suffixes; in the case of 'unluckily', '-i' (or '-y') and '-ly' are suffixes.

Like English, Arabic has both prefixes and suffixes. Thus, in the word يذهبون 'they go', ﻳ is a prefix (indicating third person), while ون is a suffix (indicating masculine plural). More strikingly for an English learner, Arabic does not really have stems along the lines of English. Rather, it operates with a system of root morphemes and pattern morphemes. Consider the word حَظِيظ 'fortunate'. Here, the basic notion of luck or fortune is conveyed by the consonants ح ظ ظ, this element being traditionally known in English as the root (Arabic جذر). The fact that this is an adjective is conveyed by the arrangement of vowels that are interpolated between these letters. This arrangement of vowels is known in English as the pattern (Arabic وَزْن 'weight', 'poetic measure') and is traditionally represented using the dummy verb فعل as a convenient 'peg'. Thus, the word حَظِيظ is said to be on the فَعِيل pattern. While English 'lucky' consists of a stem morpheme 'luck' and a suffix morpheme '-y' (or '-i'), the root morpheme ح ظ ظ and the pattern morpheme فَعِيل that make the Arabic word حَظِيظ are completely interlinked with each another. This situation is sometimes referred to as 'transfixing' (cf. Bauer 2003: 30–31). We shall consider various issues in relation to Arabic morphology in particular later in this chapter.

Morphology yields words of various classes; traditionally in English, words are said to belong to one of eight word classes or what are traditionally known as parts of speech: noun, pronoun, adjective, verb, preposition, conjunction, adverb and interjection. And although this division is not traditionally used for Arabic, it does work fairly well for Arabic, particularly when viewed from the perspective of English. The combination of words into phrases does not pose particular theoretical problems, although we may note in passing that the use of the word 'phrase' in linguistics tends to be much more closely defined than is typically appropriate for translation purposes.

In respect to both morphology and syntax, what concerns the translator is the fact that the structural patterns differ from language to language. Even where apparent cross-linguistic similarities occur, they can be misleading. For example, although the accusative suffix ـا is a recognized means of forming adverbs in Arabic, English more readily adds -*ly* to form adverbs than Arabic does ـا.

Thus, one fairly commonly finds certain adverbs in Arabic that translate simply as adverbs into English, such as كثيراً 'much', 'often' (etc.), قليلاً 'little', 'infrequently', قريباً 'soon', سريعاً 'quickly'. It is more common, however, to find complex forms of various kinds in Arabic translated as English adverbs. Amongst other things, these may be prepositional phrases في الآونة الأخيرة 'recently', على نحو ملح 'persistently', بخطى سريعة 'quickly' (of walking), بخطى وئيدة 'slowly' (of walking), بلهجة مرحة 'cheerfully' (of speaking). They may also be cognate accusatives (absolute accusatives) بكى بكاءً مرًّا 'he wept bitterly'; and they may also be circumstantial clauses (حال-clauses) وكانت عيناها تبتسمان فرحتين 'her eyes twinkled happily', فاستأنف السير مشدود القامة سريع الخطى 'he walked on stiffly and quickly'. Of course, there are also occasions where an Arabic adverbial form is translated by something other than an English adverb. Consider, for instance, the Arabic adverbial أمريكياً in the following newspaper headline (from القدس العربي, 6 September 1999): صدام .وعدي وبرزان ووطبان وعزيز متهمون بجرائم حرب حسب منظمة مدعومة أمريكيا This might be translated into English as 'Saddam, Uday, Barzan, Watban and Aziz branded war-crimes suspects by American-backed organization'. Such cases, however, are the exception rather than the rule.

Compounding, too, differs from language to language. German is famously capable of long compounds, English somewhat less so. Arabic, like French and other Romance languages, is a more analytical language, and compounds are typically formed by the use of the genitive structure – for example, غرفة نوم 'bedroom' or by noun–adjective pairs such as الشرق الاوسط 'the Middle East'. Both of these structures can yield complications when combined with other elements.

Thus, in the complex genitive structure ستائر غرفة النوم الجديدة, it is not clear (in the absence of case-ending markers in the text) whether the phrase means 'the new curtains of the bedroom' or 'the curtains of the new bedroom'. Arabic therefore frequently resorts to more complex phrases in order to avoid such ambiguities – for instance, through the use of لـ; thus, الستائر الجديدة لغرفة النوم 'the new curtains of the bedroom' or 'the new bedroom curtains'. These periphrastic structures in Arabic provide the Arabic>English translator with opportunities to find conciser, more tightly structured TT equivalents.

Compound phrases using the genitive in Arabic can also be problematic when a corresponding adjective is required. Thus, علم البشر is a calqued term for 'anthropology', alongside the cultural borrowing أنثروبولوجيا. However, one cannot use بشري to mean 'anthropological' in Arabic in the same way as one can use أحيائي to mean 'biological' (from علم الأحياء 'biology'). This is because بشري already has an existing meaning of 'human' (as an adjective). Accordingly, in order to say 'anthropological' in Arabic, one either has to use the compound genitive noun علم البشر as itself part of some periphrastic phrase, or one has to use the adjective from the cultural borrowing أنثروبولوجيا (i.e. أنثروبولوجي.). In the second case, there are few difficulties for the translator into English; in the first, there may be an opportunity for the translator to find conciser, more tightly structured equivalents.

Noun–adjective compounds, such as الشرق الأوسط, offer up similar issues to genitive compounds. In English, it is possible to make adjectives from compound nouns of this type; thus, 'Middle Eastern' from 'Middle East'. In Arabic, it is not traditionally possible to do this. Accordingly, the name of an academic institution, such as 'The Centre for Middle Eastern Studies', would have to be translated into Arabic as the complex genitive مركز دراسات الشرق الأوسط. As in the case of the phrase ستائر غرفة النوم الجديدة, discussed earlier, this means that a phrase such as مركز دراسات الشرق الأوسط الجديد is ambiguous between 'The New Centre for Middle Eastern Studies' and 'The Centre for the Studies of the New Middle East' (or more idiomatically 'The Centre for the Study of the New Middle East'). Again, this is likely to generate periphrastic structures in Arabic, utilizing لـ and other forms, providing opportunities for translators into English to find conciser, more tightly structured translation equivalents.

More recently, Arabic has begun to develop adjectival compounds based on noun–adjective compound nouns. So, from الشرق الأوسط 'the Middle East' one now comes across شرق أوسطي 'Middle Eastern'. Accordingly, 'American Middle East policy' might now be translated into Arabic as سياسة أمريكا الشرق أوسطية (note the use

of only a single ‏الـ‎ in the definite phrase ‏الشرق أوسطية‎). However, given that forms
of the type ‏شرق أوسطي‎ are met with extreme disapproval by linguistic purists in
the Middle East, one is relatively unlikely to encounter them outside the realm of
politics and related matters. Thus, 'The Centre for Middle Eastern and Islamic
Studies' is better translated into Arabic as ‏مركز دراسات الشرق الاوسط والدراسات الإسلامية‎
rather than as the more concise ‏مركز الدراسات الشرق أوسطية والإسلامية‎, even though
the former involves a repetition of ‏دراسات‎, which is slightly inelegant because it
uses the word in the first instance without the definite article ‏الـ‎ and in the second
instance with it. The translator from Arabic to English, faced with a form such as
‏مركز دراسات الشرق الاوسط والدراسات الإسلامية‎, will likely need to find the original name
in an English source in order to work out the correct English form.

Grammatical differences are especially clear in differences in verb systems. The
Arabic system of tenses is quite different from English; ‏يشتري‎, for example, can
standardly mean both 'buys' and 'is buying'. In some contexts, it might mean 'will
buy' (although one would more commonly expect ‏سيشتري‎ in this sense); in other
contexts, ‏يشتري‎ might be most naturally translated as 'bought' or 'was buying'
(e.g. in certain subordinate clauses or in a story where a general past-tense setting
has already been established for a particular part of the text). English has a system
of verb tenses in the proper sense; that is to say, particular tenses relate fairly
consistently to natural time. Arabic, on the other hand, operates with a system that
combines tense and aspect. Thus, the perfect can indicate completion of the action
as well as occurrence in the past (as in ‏اشترى‎ 'he bought'), while the imperfect may
indicate non-completion of the action regardless of whether it occurs in the past
or present (e.g. in contexts where ‏يشتري‎ translates as 'is/was buying'). The actual
time significance of the imperfect in particular is very often context dependent.
This is most clearly seen in subordinate clauses. In cases where the main clause
has a perfect verb, dependent subordinate clauses will typically have imperfect
verbs, the fact that the overall time reference is the past being signalled solely by
the use of the perfect in the main clause (cf. Dickins and Watson 1999: 130–131).

The use of the imperfect to express past time goes beyond subordinate clauses.
It is possible to find the imperfect used in almost any situation in which the general
time reference has already been established. Thus, in fictional writing in particular,
an author may establish a general past reference by an initial use of a perfect verb
and then shift to the imperfect throughout the rest of the episode in question, only
returning to the perfect in order to mark the start of a new episode in the story.
This usage has something in common with the so-called vivid present in English,
which is sometimes used in storytelling contexts ('A man comes into a pub. He
goes up to the bar, and he says to the landlord [. . .]'). However, while the English
vivid present is typically confined to informal or dramatic contexts, this use of the
Arabic imperfect to relay narrative events in the past is common in formal writing.

The flexibility of Arabic tense usage may sometimes raise difficulties particularly in translating from Arabic to English. A good example is provided by the start
of the text from ‏عرس الزين‎ beginning ‏تتابعت الأعوام‎ (Practical 9.3).

As the discussion so far has suggested, translators give priority to the *mot juste*
and to constructing idiomatic TL sentences, even where this entails translation

loss in terms of grammatical structure or economy. Exceptions may be made where, for whatever reason, exoticism is required in the TT. More often, the ST may have salient textual properties manifestly resulting from the manipulation of grammatical structure. The marked manipulation of grammatical structure is a common feature in literary texts. The translator of such texts must always decide how distinctive the grammatical structures are, what their function is and what the aim of the ST is. Only then can a decision be taken about how distinctive the TT's grammar should be. A common Arabic feature that poses this problem is morphological repetition.

10.2.3 Morphological repetition

The three forms of morphological repetition that are of most importance for translation, and that therefore concern us here, are pattern repetition, root repetition and **suffix repetition**.

10.2.3.1 Pattern repetition

Pattern repetition involves repetition of the same pattern (فَعَلَ, فاعِل, مَفْعُول, فِعْل, مَفْعَلة, etc.) in two or more words in close proximity, while root repetition involves repetition of the same root in two or more words in close proximity. Both pattern repetition and root repetition can be used to provide textual cohesion. However, more often they fulfil stylistic and other purposes.

Pattern repetition is an extremely common feature of Arabic and quite frequently occurs without having any particular stylistic significance; thus, البيتُ القديم الكبير would be a reasonable translation of 'the big old house' in many contexts, the repetition of the فعيل pattern in قديم and كبير not necessarily having any particular significance.

More important from a stylistic point of view is where pattern repetition is combined with some kind of semantic relationship. Here, the general effect of pattern repetition is normally to give some additional emphasis. We can usefully distinguish three relevant types of semantic relationship: (i) semantically related words; (ii) synonyms or near-synonyms; (iii) antonyms (i.e. semantic opposites, such as 'black' and 'white').

Semantically related words are words whose meanings fall within the same general semantic field but that are clearly distinct in meaning. An example is أفكار and أحلام 'thoughts and dreams' and صدمة and دهشة 'amazement' and 'shock'. These do not generally pose translation problems and can often be translated fairly literally; thus, معظم أفكاره وأحلامه 'most of his thoughts and dreams' (Brown 1996: 23); أصيب صابر بالدهشة والصدمة 'Saber had been amazed and shocked' (Brown 1996: 45).

The translation of synonyms and near-synonyms with pattern repetition typically involves the same techniques as are used with repetition of (near-)synonyms generally (Section 7.2.1) – that is, merging, grammatical transposition, semantic distancing and maintenance.

An example of merging is أربع فتيات جميلات أنيقات 'four pretty young women'. Another example is وكان لا بد له من التأدب والتعلم translated as '[. . .] so he had no alternative left to him but education' (Brown 1996: 19).

An example of grammatical transposition is:

هذا وقد حققت جماعة الإخوان المسلمين هذا النمو الصاروخي دون أي عناء في {التنظير} و {التحليل} أو في الدعاية والعمل الجماهيري أو في التجنيد التنظيمي حيث كانت العضوية تبدأ بمجرد أن يتعاطف الفرد معها [. . .]

This has been translated (Calderbank 1990: 20) as:

This phenomenal success was achieved without any {systematic analysis} of issues, without extensive propaganda, or working with the masses and without any organized recruitment: to be reckoned a member it was simply enough for an individual to sympathize with the Society's aim [. . .]

Here, the noun doublet التنظير والتحليل has been transposed grammatically into the English adjective–noun phrase 'systematic analysis'.

Semantic distancing is illustrated by a translation of خوفاً عليها من الفزع والهلع 'for fear of alarming and upsetting her' (Brown 1996: 38). Wehr gives فزع as meaning 'fear, fright, terror, alarm, dismay, anxiety, consternation, panic' and هلع as meaning 'impatience, restlessness, uneasiness; burning anxiety; alarm, dismay'. The translator has chosen here to distance the meaning of هلع slightly further from فزع than is indicated by the dictionary definitions by interpreting هلع to mean 'upset'. She thus loses something in terms of denotative meaning. However, the resulting phrase 'alarming and upsetting' is idiomatic and stylistically acceptable.

An example of maintenance is the translation of a chapter title from a book about the role of the military in political life in the Arab world. The chapter is titled دور العسكر التغييري: تقويم وتحليل. This has been translated as 'The transformational role of the military: evaluation and analysis' (Humphrys 1999: 1). Here, the meanings of the fairly standard English translations of تقويم 'evaluation' and تحليل 'analysis' are felt to be sufficiently distinct from each other for it to be acceptable to maintain the ST structure in the TT.

Semantic repetition with antonyms is also fairly common. Consider the following:

ولما كان التاريخ الحقيقي هو تاريخ الجماهير ولما كانت علاقة السلطة المصرية بالجماهير هي في الأغلب الأعم علاقة شك متبادل فإن التقييم الموضوعي لجماعة الإخوان المسلمين يفرض علينا التقاط البدايات التاريخية لمواقفها وبالتالي لموقعها بين قضايا الجماهير من جهة وتوجهات السلطة من الجهة المقابلة ثم تتبع هذه الجماعة عبر كافة المنحنيات التي تعرجت داخلها {هبوطاً} و {صعوداً} لاستجلاء الغموض الذي يحيط بحلقاتها المتتالية بدءًا بالحلقة الأولى التي [. . .]

This has been translated (Calderbank 1990: 9) as:

Given that true history is the history of the masses, and that the relationship between the Egyptian ruling class and the masses has, in the vast majority

of cases, been one of mutual suspicion, then an objective evaluation of the
Society of the Muslim Brothers obliges us to trace the historical beginnings
of the group's policies and consequently its position vis-a-vis popular issues
on the one hand and the particular objectives of the ruling classes on the other.
Such an evaluation would also oblige us to follow {the changing fortunes} of
the Society in order to elucidate the mystery which surrounds the successive
episodes in its history, beginning with episode one, which [. . .]

Here, the translator has chosen an adjective–noun phrase 'changing fortunes' to
relay the Arabic antonyms هبوطاً وصعوداً (or, more accurately, to relay the entire
phrase المنحنيات التي تعرجت داخلها {هبوطًا} و{صعوًدا}). The obvious alternative to this
would have been the phrase 'ups and downs'; this, however, sounds rather too
informal for the context.

Pattern repetition may also occur with a combination of synonyms and antonyms. An example is the following:

[. . .] وعليه فقد كان الإمام حسن البنا يجعل مجمل حركة الإخوان المسلمين في جيبه حيث استمد من
الفاشية الطاعة الدكتاتورية وحصرها في نفسه فالإخوان يبايعونه على «الالتزام التام بالإخلاص والثقة
والسمع والطاعة في {العسر} و{اليسر} و{المنشط} و{المكره}» دون أدنى التزام مقابل منه تجاههم

This could be translated (cf. Calderbank 1990: 9) as:

Thus, Hassan El Banna came to assume total control over the Muslim Brotherhood, adopting from Fascism the principle of absolute obedience to the leader,
and thereby concentrating all power in himself. The oath which members of
the Brotherhood swore to El Banna, pledged 'total commitment, loyalty, trust
and unswerving obedience, {in comfort and adversity, suffering and joy}'.
This pledge was not, however, matched by any corresponding commitment
on El Banna's part.

Here, the parallelism of the Arabic has been retained in the English, as one might
expect with formulaic religious language (cf. also Section 13.3.2).

Pattern repetition by definition involves assonance (Section 9.1.1); the more
frequently the pattern is repeated, the greater the assonance will be, as well as the
greater the degree of emphasis conveyed. Consider the following:

وبشكل عام فإن هذه الاتجاهات الجديدة على كافة الأصعدة الاقتصادية والاجتماعية والسياسية
والفكرية أخذت {تتسارع} و{تتصارع} و{تتكالب} جميعها بما تحتويه من إيجابيات وسلبيات على
رأس المجتمع المصري الذي كانت أغلبيته الساحقة تحيا على فطرتها البسيطة . . . .

This has been translated (Calderbank 1990: 16) as:

In short, these various currents began to exercise an unprecedented influence –
whether positive or negative – on all aspects of economic, social, political

and intellectual life. {They thus became locked in a desperate struggle} for the intellectual leadership of an Egyptian society, the great majority of whose members were still living a simple, traditional life . . .

Here, the translator has transposed the ST three-verb structure ({تتسارع} و {تتصارع} و {تتكالب}) grammatically, as a composite verb-prepositional-object phrase 'became locked in a desperate struggle'. He has also made use of alliteration and assonance ('d/t', 's', 'l'), giving the English an added sense of emphasis.

Finally, pattern repetition may give rise to rhymes where the roots involved have radicals with the same final one or two letters. Sometimes such rhymes – like some examples of rhyme elsewhere – will be best ignored in the English translation. An example of this is مشروع التوحيد والتجديد translated as 'the project of unification and reform' (from a Lebanese newspaper article dealing with changes in the Lebanese Phalange Party). Elsewhere, something more striking may be called for in the English TT, such as alliteration, assonance or rhyme, or possibly an appropriate English cliché, as in the case of the formulaic في السراء والضراء, which might be translated as 'in good times or bad'.

10.2.3.2 *Root repetition*

Root repetition involves repetition of the same morphological root in close proximity within a text (thus, درسنا هذا الدرس 'we studied this lesson' involves repetition of the root د ر س). Root repetition may be divided into three kinds: (i) system-intrinsic, (ii) absolute accusative and (iii) 'other' (cf. Dickens and Watson 1999: 514–518).

System-intrinsic root repetition simply reflects the fact that words in Arabic are typically made up of roots along with patterns, etc. and that general semantic considerations will sometimes cause a writer or speaker to use two words having the same root in close proximity. An example of this is كتب كتابا 'he wrote a book'. English generally avoids this kind of repetition. In practice, it is not normally difficult to find forms in translating into English that avoid it; in fact, even where English has similar forms, such as 'he drank a drink', there are often more common alternatives such as 'he had a drink'.

Root repetition with the absolute accusative is used to form adverbials. This typically poses no serious translation problems in English. Thus, the phrase لقد تطورت ظاهرة التطرف الديني تطورا سريعا happily translates as 'The phenomenon of religious extremism has developed rapidly'. Sometimes, however, a more complex structure, such as a prepositional phrase, may be required. Here is an example:

. . . ولكن هذه المدارس السلفية الاربع كانت عاجزة عن {رفض} التغييرات التي شهدها المجتمع {رفضا واعيا مبرمجا} مرتبطا ببدائل محددة كما كانت عاجزة عن مواجهة هذه التغييرات والتصدي لها في نفس الوقت الذي كانت فيه عاجزة عن تبرير هذه التغييرات أو الدفاع عنها [. . .]

This could be translated as follows (adapted from Calderbank 1990: 8):

> These four Salafiya schools were, however, incapable of {refuting} the changes taking place in society {in any rational or systematic way}, or of offering well-defined alternatives. They were unable to confront and resist these changes, or to justify and defend them.

Finally, it may sometimes be necessary to make more radical changes. Consider the following:

وكانت الموقعة الثالثة بين المرشد والإخوان أثناء حرب فلسطين عام ١٩٤٨ عندما تكتلت مجموعة كبيرة من الإخوان المؤسسين بقيادة الأخ أحمد رفعت ضد الممارسات السياسية لحسن البنا متهمين إياه بمجاملة السلطات وبضعف تأييده للشعب الفلسطيني وانحصاره في العمل الدعائي فقط ومطالبين باتخاذ مواقف محددة في مواجهة السلطات وبـ{مساندة} الشعب الفلسطيني {مساندة} جهادية حقيقية [...]

This has been translated (Calderbank 1990: 27) as:

> The third confrontation between the Guide and the Brothers occurred during the Palestine War of 1948. A large number of Brothers, many of them founder members, banded together under the leadership of Ahmed Rifaat against the political dealings of Hassan El Banna, accusing him of courting the favour of the Palace and of weakness in his support for the Palestinian people, restricting himself essentially to propagandizing. They demanded the adoption of well-defined policies both to challenge the government and to {provide real military assistance} to the Palestinians.

Here, the Arabic مساندة (first occurrence) has been transposed grammatically into 'provide . . . assistance', while the phrase مساندة جهادية حقيقية is relayed by the adjectives 'real, military' used attributively with 'assistance'.

The use of the absolute accusative in Arabic potentially gives a sense of emphasis (although there is no clear dividing line between the use of the absolute accusative simply to form an adverbial and its use to form an emphatic adverbial). Consider the following:

إن البورجوازية التي {نمت} {نموا} متسارعا في مصر في بداية القرن الحالي انقسمت الى اتجاهات فكرية متناقضة الاول هو الاتجاه الليبرالي الذي رفع لواءه محمد حسين هيكل وأحمد لطفي السيد، والثاني [...]

This has been translated (Calderbank 1990: 10) as:

> The bourgeoisie, which {grew} {so rapidly} in Egypt at the beginning of this century, soon split into two conflicting intellectual trends, the first being the liberal trend led by Mohamed Hussein Haikal and Ahmad Lutfi El Sayyid and the second [. . .]

Here, the English translation has included an emphatic particle 'so', which seems to reflect the emphasis that is a function of the root repetition (note also, however, the use of متسارعاً in the Arabic, implying ever-increasing speed, as contrasted with the more basic سريعاً, merely meaning 'quickly').

Elsewhere, other translation techniques may be used to give some degree of emphasis in the TT. Thus, in the translation of the phrase ليودّع أمه الوداع الأخير 'in order to bid his mother a final farewell' (Brown 1996: 55), the emphasis of the original root repetition has been relayed by the use of alliteration and assonance in the English 'final farewell' (cf. the less successful 'final adieu/goodbye').

Uses of root repetition that fall under the category of 'other' in general have a more obviously emphatic function. They occur in an unlimited range of grammatical structures. The following are a few examples: (i) subject + verb, as in ثار ثائرُهُ 'to fly into a rage'; (ii) verb + object, as in طلب طلباً 'to make a request'; (iii) verb + prepositional phrase, as in صبغ بصبغة (أخرى) 'to transform'; (iv) conjoined nouns, as in عزة واعتزاز 'honour and self-esteem'; (v) noun + adjective, as in الظل الظليل literally, 'shady shade'; (vi) genitives, as in أطماع الطامعين 'the ambitions of the covetous'; and (vii) conjoined adjectives, as in الضعفاء والمستضعفون 'the weak and oppressed'.

It is also possible to find root repetition in larger stretches of text. Sometimes, this has a rhetorical function rather like that of rhetorical anaphora with respect to lexical items; we shall consider this in Chapter 13. More often, root repetition over larger stretches of text functions not only as a stylistic feature but also as a text-building device (i.e. it contributes to the cohesion of the text). As such, it could be discussed in Chapter 13. For ease of exposition, however, we shall deal with it here, just as we shall deal with lexical item repetition and **phrase repetition** as text-building devices later in this chapter.

The following provides a simple example of root repetition as a text-building device (the entities being spoken to here are أشجار حمراء 'red trees'):

وكلما يحاورها بصوته المذبوح تأخذ بالنشيج. كان الحوار حوار جرحى امضهم الجرح وأعياهم التعب.

This has been translated (Brown 1996: 21) as:

> and whenever he spoke to them in an anguished voice, they started to sob. The conversation was that of the wounded who were tormented by their wounds and worn out by exhaustion.

Here, the Arabic has يحاور in the first sentence (only partially quoted) and حوار in the second sentence. The English TT translates these as 'spoke to' and 'conversation', respectively. The tendency for Arabic to repeat but English to vary parallels that which occurs with lexical item repetition and phrase repetition, as we shall see later. This text-building use of root repetition is also similar to the text-building use of lexical repetition in that the meanings involved are very similar: in this case يحاور and حوار express the same core meaning, يحاور in a verbal form and حوار in a nominal form.

Quite a few cases of root repetition in Arabic involve stock phrases. In such instances, the English translation is likely to involve either an English stock phrase or, if no such stock phrase is available, another phrase that sounds natural in the context. Examples where stock phrases are translated as stock phrases are واضح كل الوضوح 'clearly visible' and بادئ ذي بدء 'from the outset'. Where the Arabic root-repetition phrase involves a subject + verb, this is very likely to be an idiom and is also likely to have a strong poetic/emphatic function. An example, involving ثائرة + ثارت, is the following:

ولا تثور له ثائرة.

This has been translated (Brown 1996: 50) as:

nor had it flared up in rage.

Here, the English TT uses a common stock phrase but one that also involves a fairly strong 'fire' metaphor to relay the emphasis of the Arabic ST.

The emphasis, which, as already noted is a typical feature of 'other' forms of root repetition in Arabic, can also be conveyed in other ways. The following provides an example, involving the idiom صبغ . . . بصبغة:

يعمل المجتمع بدوره على صبغ هذا التنظيم بصبغته الخاصة [. . .]

This has been translated (Humphrys 1999: 5) as:

the more this society in turn makes its mark upon this establishment.

Here, the English idiom 'make its mark' achieves a sense of emphasis through the use of alliteration and assonance.

Even where the Arabic root repetition does not involve a stock phrase, the emphatic nature of such repetition will often make an English emphatic usage appropriate. The following is an example of root repetition plus parallelism (Chapter 11), where the translator has maintained the parallelism in English for the sake of emotional emphasis and has also made use of assonance (root-repetition elements have been noted in curly brackets):

وذلك ليس بغرض البحث الأكاديمي وحسب أو تصفية الحسابات أو التكفير عن الذنوب أمام حائط مبكى فقط ولكن استشرافًا للمستقبل السياسي للوطن حيث تتقلص هذه الأغراض كثيرًا أمام المهام التي يفرضها المجتمع على الباحثين الذين {يعانون} {معاناته} و{يطمحون} {طموحاته}.

This has been translated (Calderbank 1990: 36) as:

not simply for the purposes of academic research or to settle old accounts, or even to atone for our sins before a wailing wall, but to look ahead to Egypt's political future: all other considerations fade into insignificance when compared with the task society sets those writers who {suffer} {its afflictions} and {share} {its aspirations}.

In this example, the assonance in the TT provides the same sort of emotive emphasis as is provided by the complex root repetition and parallelism in the ST.

Metaphor (Chapter 14) is also a fairly frequent translation technique where the Arabic does not involve a stock phrase, just as it is when it does. Consider the following (in which the root repetition elements have been noted in curly brackets):

. . . فرفض البنا الاستجابة لهذا التكتل و}اشتبك} في عدة }اشتباكات} كلامية مع رفعت كانت تنتهي دومًا بالمزيد من المؤيدين لأحمد رفعت وإزاء سيطرة رفعت الكاملة على المركز العام للإخوان [. . .]

This has been translated (Calderbank 1990: 27) as:

El Banna refused to listen to the group and {crossed words} several times with Rifaat. These exchanges always ended up with more support for Rifaat and eventually, faced with Rifaat's complete control of the General Headquarters [. . .]

Here, the translator has attempted to reproduce the striking nature of the Arabic by using a novel English metaphorical phrase 'cross words', which echoes the existing English phrase 'cross swords'.

Of course, there will be occasions where the root repetition in Arabic serves an obviously emphatic function but where it seems better not to try to relay this in English. An example is the following:

وبغض النظر عن أصله الاجتماعي، يكتسب الضابط في الجيش }عزة واعتزازا} بالنفس حتى الادعاء.

This has been translated (Humphrys 1999: 2–3) as:

Regardless of his social class, the army officer acquires a sense of {honour and self-esteem} that border on arrogance.

10.2.3.3 *Suffix repetition*

Somewhat less important than pattern and root repetition, but still significant, is suffix repetition – that is, repetition of the same suffix at the end of words in close proximity. The following extract, from an article in the Egyptian magazine روز اليوسف (Hetherington 1996: 10), which deals with political extremism in the Middle East, provides a simple example of suffix repetition:

أرض النبوءات والرسالات والخرافات والمخابرات.

This might be translated as:

> the land of prophecies and divine messages, superstitions – and secret services.

As this example shows, suffix repetition, like pattern repetition and root repetition, emerges from the grammatical structure of Arabic, in this case from the use of the suffix ات as one of the means of forming the plural. Nonetheless, it still represents a deliberate choice on the part of the writer. Here, the writer has chosen to string together four plurals ending in ات. Typically, suffix repetition would seem to be an emphatic device used in more or less 'poetic' contexts. Very often, it is better ignored in translating. Sometimes, other means of emphasis may be adopted in the translation. In this extract, the four list elements (Section 7.3.) displaying suffix repetition in the ST have been split into groups in the TT, the first positive ('prophecies and divine messages') and the second negative ('superstitions – and secret services'). The two elements in the second group ('superstitions' and 'secret services') have then been further separated by a dash (allowing 'secret services' to function as what one might term the 'punch phrase').

This extract also displays another means of relaying suffix repetition in the TT: the use of alliteration and assonance. In this case, there is alliteration and assonance particularly of [s] in the TT. (For further discussion of suffix repetition, see Dickins and Watson 1999: 520–521.)

10.2.4   *Lexical repetition*

Another common form of repetition in Arabic is the repetition of the same word or even of a whole phrase in a particular sense (cf. Dickins and Watson 1999: 510–514). Repetition of a single word is termed 'word repetition' or 'lexical item repetition', while repetition of a whole phrase is termed 'phrase repetition'.

10.2.4.1   *Lexical item repetition*

Here, for analysis and discussion in class, is an example of lexical item repetition in Arabic, typically translated with lexical variation in English. (In analyzing lexical item repetition, Arabic plurals are to be regarded as the same lexical items as their corresponding singulars):

فالخطاب العام لسياسة الإعلام في تلك الدول يؤكد دوما أن المشكلة السكانية عائق من أهم عوائق التنمية، زاعما أن التنمية الاقتصادية لن تتحقق ما لم تحل هذه المشكلة.

This is translated (El-Serafi 1994: 15) as:

> General media propaganda in these countries constantly emphasizes that the population problem is one of the most important impediments to development, claiming that economic progress will not be realized until the difficulty is resolved.

This example of lexical item repetition occurs within a single sentence. However, it is also possible to have cases of lexical item repetition in Arabic extending over larger stretches of text, often where one lexical item in particular relates closely to the general topic of that particular section of text. In this case, lexical item repetition functions not just as a stylistic feature but also as a text-building device contributing to the cohesion of the text (as may root repetition under similar circumstances). As such, it could be discussed in Chapter 13. However, for ease of exposition, we shall deal with it here. Here, for analysis and discussion in class, is an example followed by a draft English TT. This extract consists of one complete paragraph followed by the first few words of a second paragraph. This is significant, because the Arabic paragraph here, like typical English paragraphs, deals with a fairly self-contained subtopic within the larger text. In this extract, the word اتجاه/اتجاهات runs almost like a theme through the Arabic text. Note, as well, other forms of lexical item repetition involving ظهور. and نمو and أدى (إلى). The text is taken from المهدوي (1986; discussed in Calderbank 1990: 14–15):

وعلى الصعيد الفكري فقد دخلت مصر عام ١٩٢٤ وهي تحمل شبكة جديدة من الاتجاهات الفكرية
المتداخلة والمتناقضة فقد أدت الثورة الشيوعية الروسية عام ١٩١٧ إلى نمو الاتجاهات الاشتراكية
كما أدت الثورة الوطنية المصرية عام ١٩١٩ إلى نمو الاتجاهات الانعزالية الفرعونية المصرية وأدى
قيام كمال أتاتورك بإلغاء الخلافة الاسلامية وتأسيس الدولة العلمانية في تركيا عام ١٩٢٢ إلى نمو
الاتجاهات العلمانية يضاف إلى ذلك أن الجامعة المصرية التي تم إنشاؤها عام ١٩٠٩ لتقوم بتعليم
«جميع سكان مصر على اختلاف جنسياتهم وأديانهم وأجناسهم» والتي قادت التطور الثقافي والعلمي
في البلاد أدت إلى ظهور ونمو الاتجاهات العقلانية على حساب الاتجاهات الغيبية في تحليل مشاكل
الحياة والمجتمع، وعلى النقيض من ذلك فقد أدى استيعاب رأس المال الأجنبي المدعوم بسلطات
الاحتلال لبعض الفئات الاجتماعية إلى ظهور اتجاهات فكرية تدعو إلى إلحاق مصر فكرياً بالحضارة
الغربية أو الحضارة البحر أوسطية تلك التي كان المواطن العادي لا يرى فيها سوى تحلل القيم
والأخلاقيات كما شجع الاحتلال البريطاني لمصر البعثات التبشيرية على اختراق المجتمع المصري
ومحاولة تحويل مسلميه إلى المسيحية بالمحبة حيناً وبالتحايل وباستغلال فقر الغالبية العظمى من
المصريين أحياناً وقادت هذه البعثات التبشيرية اتجاهاً فكرياً يدعو إلى المسيحية، ورغم انحصار هذا
الاتجاه فإنه شكل بالنسبة للأصوليين المسلمين ناقوساً لخطر شديد.
وبشكل عام فإن هذه الاتجاهات الجديدة [. . .]

This might be translated into English as follows:

Intellectually, too, Egypt at the start of 1924 was subject to a series of inter-related but opposing currents. The Russian revolution of 1917 had promoted socialist thinking, while the Egyptian revolution of 1919 had encouraged ideas of pharaonic isolationism. Kemal Atatürk's abolition of the Caliphate and establishment of a secular state in Turkey in 1922 had similarly encouraged the growth of secularism. In addition the Egyptian University, which had been founded in 1909 with the purpose of educating 'all the Egyptian people, regardless of nationality, creed or ethnic group', and played a leading role in the cultural and scientific development of the country, led to the appearance and growth of rationalist as opposed to religious interpretations of human and social problems. On the other hand, calls for the incorporation of Egypt into western or Mediterranean culture, which followed the absorption of foreign capital by various social groups (a phenomenon supported by the occupation authorities), were viewed by the average Egyptian as tantamount to the abandonment of all moral values. Similar results ensued from the encouragement given by the occupation authorities to Christian missionary groups in their efforts to break into Egyptian society and to convert Muslim Egyptians to Christianity, whether through sincere concern, or through deception and the exploitation of the poverty of the great majority of the population. These missionaries were at the forefront of a pro-Christian intellectual current; and though they were few in number, in the eyes of fundamentalist Muslims, they constituted a source of untold danger.

In short, these various currents began to [. . .]

Stylistic lexical item repetition and 'text-building' lexical item repetition of the types discussed in this section shade into each other. There is, however, also another function of lexical item repetition that is important in both English and Arabic. This is known as rhetorical anaphora. We shall deal with this in Chapter 13.

10.2.4.2 *Phrase repetition*

The previous text illustrates not only repetition of individual lexical items but also of whole phrases. This can be termed 'phrase repetition'. Thus, we find أدت/أدى . . . . إلى نمو four times (with other intervening elements).

The following text, which is taken from an article in the Egyptian magazine روز اليوسف (no. 3521, 4 December 1995) about political extremism in the Middle East, provides a good example of phrase repetition. In this extract, the phrase وبعد أيام is repeated four times. Just like اتجاه/اتجاهات in the previous text, وبعد أيام can here be regarded as a text-building device that contributes to the overall cohesion of the text. We have placed وبعد أيام in curly brackets in each case to highlight it.

.. في مالطا قُتل فتحي الشقاقي قائد ثاني اكبر حركة اصولية، فلسطينية، معارضة، بعد «حماس» برصاص الموساد .. {وبعد أيام} قتل إسحق رابين رئيس وزراء إسرائيل بثلاث رصاصات اطلقها متطرف يهودي في عمر احفاده هو إيجال عامير .. {وبعد أيام} انفجرت شحنة ناسفة لا تقل عن ١٠٠ كيلوجرام في مقر الحرس السعودي في الرياض، وكان الضحايا امريكيين وهنودا .. {وبعد أيام} اغتيل في جنيف الملحق التجاري المصري في سويسرا .. {وبعد ايام} فجرت منظمة الجهاد مبنى السفارة المصرية في إسلام أباد عاصمة باكستان في عملية انتحارية.

This has been translated (Hetherington 1996: 23) as follows (we have added curly brackets to highlight correspondences between occurrences of وبعد ايام in the ST and its translation equivalents here):

Fathi al-Shaqaqi, the leader of the second largest Palestinian fundamentalist organization after Hamas, was killed in Malta by Mossad bullets. {A couple of days later} the Israeli Prime Minister Yitzhak Rabin was killed by three bullets fired by Yigal Amir, a Jewish extremist his grandchildren's age.

{Mere days after this}, a charge of dynamite of at least 100 kilograms exploded in the Saudi National Guard barracks in Riyadh claiming both American and Indian victims. {Days later} the Egyptian trade attaché to Switzerland was assassinated in Geneva, and {this was followed by} a suicide bomb planted by the Jihad organization in the Egyptian embassy building in the Pakistani capital, Islamabad.

As with lexical item repetition, it will be seen that English tends to go for variation in phrases, while Arabic frequently prefers repetition. For more on the translation of lexical item and phrase repetition from Arabic to English, see Jawad (2009).

Practical 10

Practical 10.1 Lexical item and root repetition: إن التمييز الطبقي

Assignment

(i) Paying particular attention to lexical item repetition in the ST, discuss the strategic decisions that you must take before starting detailed translation of the following text, and outline and justify the strategy you adopt. Your translation should be aimed at an educated, but non-specialist, readership and will be published as a book.

(ii) Translate the text into English.

(iii) Explain the decisions of detail you made in producing your translation.

Contextual information

The ST is from a book titled العسكر والحكم في البلدان العربية by فؤاد اسحاق الخوري (Hum- phrys 1999: 10). It deals with the relationship between political power and the military in the Arab world and is aimed at the interested non-specialist reader.

ST

إن التمييز الطبقي بين الضباط والعسكر يتأثر إلى حد كبير بمستوى التكنولوجيا للجيش. خُذ مثلاً على ذلك نسبة الجنود إلى الضباط. إن نسبة الجنود للضباط في الجيوش المتخلفة تكنولوجياً تفوق بكثير (حوالي ١٥ جندياً لكل ضابط) النسبة الموجودة في الجيوش الأخرى والتي تتراوح بين ٤ أو ٥ جنود لكل ضابط. كلما ارتفعت نسبة الجنود إلى الضباط، انخفض مستوى التكنولوجيا، والعكس صحيح.

Practical 10.2 Lexical item and root repetition:
وعلى الرغم من عبقرية تشرشل

Assignment

(i) Paying particular attention to lexical item and root repetition in the ST, discuss the strategic decisions that you must take before starting detailed translation of the following text, and outline and justify the strategy you adopt. The ST is a semi-academic book. The TT is also intended to be published as a book. You should take it that the TT audience will also be people with an interest in the subject (and therefore some specialist knowledge).

(ii) Translate the text into English.

(iii) Explain the decisions of detail you made in producing your translation.

Contextual information

This extract is taken from a book titled العبقرية والزعامة السياسية by محمد علي الغتيت (1974: 368–369).

ST

وعلى الرغم من عبقرية تشرشل التي تجلت في أقوى وأروع الصور خلال الحرب العالمية الثانية التي انتهت بهزيمة هتلر وانتصار بريطانيا خذل الشعب الحزب الذي ينتمي إليه تشرشل في الانتخابات فتخلى تشرشل عن الحكم، نزولاً على حكم الدستور. وقد علق أحد كبار الساسة على موقف الشعب البريطاني من تشرشل فقال إنه موقف يؤكد موقف الشعوب العظيمة التي تقدر أعمال الحاكم لا شخصه. على أن عظمة حكام هذه الشعوب تتجسد في أنهم لا ينتظرون من شعوبهم تقديرها لأشخاصهم حال حياتهم، ولأن هذه الشعوب تزن الأشخاص وتقيم أعمالهم وتصدر حكمها عليهم بعد غيابهم عن الحياة، ثم أنها تمجد منهم من يستحق التمجيد فتخلد ذكراه بعمل نافع.

امتثل تشرشل لإرادة الشعب وتخلى عن الحكم ليصبح عضواً عادياً بمجلس العموم واختفى كل ذكر له في دنيا السياسة وعاش هو وأفراد أسرته كما كان يعيش قبل أن يتزعم بلاده في الحرب ويحقق لها النصر. اعتزل الحكم ولكنه ظل علماً من أعلام السياسة ومرجعاً يسترشد القادة بآرائه ويفيدون حكمته وتجاربه. ولما مات كرمه الشعب التكريم الذي يتفق وما قدم له من جلائل الخدمات.

Practical 10.3 Lexical item repetition and other forms of repetition: حوار الثقافات

Assignment

(i) Paying particular attention to lexical item repetition and other forms of repetition in the ST, discuss the strategic decisions that you must take before starting detailed translation of the following text, and outline and justify the strategy you adopt. The ST is an academic book. The TT is also intended to be published as a book. You should take it that the TT audience will also be people with an academic interest in the subject (and therefore some specialist knowledge).

(ii) Translate the text into English.

(iii) Explain the decisions of detail you made in producing your translation.

Contextual information

This extract is taken from the back cover blurb to نحن والآخر by ناصر الدين الأسد (1997). The book deals with relations between the Arab and Islamic worlds and the West.

ST

حوار الثقافات، أو حوار الحضارات، أو حوار الأديان، أو الحوار الإسلامي المسيحي، أو حوار الشمال والجنوب، أو حوار الإسلام والغرب، أو الحوار العربي الأوربي، كلها عناوين لموضوع واحد، أو لموضوعات متقاربة متداخلة، لا تكاد تتمايز إلا بشيء من التعميم أو التخصيص . وهي موضوعات كثر تناولها في عدد من الكتب والمقالات والمحاضرات والندوات والمؤتمرات . وقد سبق لكاتب هذه الدراسة أن تناولها، أو تناول جوانب منها، في مناسبات واجتماعات مختلفة، وعرض حينئذ جوهر الأفكار الواردة هنا في صور متعددة . ومع ذلك فالموضوع جدير بإعادة القول فيه، والصبر عليه، ومداورته، لتوسيع نطاق المتفهمين والمقتنعين به من الجانبين، عسى أن ينتقل الأمر من مرحلة الفهم والاقتناع إلى مرحلة التعاون على العمل المشترك بين جميع المؤمنين بالسلام والعدل واقتلاع بذور الأحقاد بين الشعوب .

11 Parallelism

11.1 Introduction

This is an appropriate point to discuss parallelism, as it involves many of the notions discussed in previous chapters: denotative meaning (Chapter 7), the phonic/graphic level (Chapter 9) and the grammatical level (Chapter 10).

11.2 Definition of parallelism

The term 'parallelism' is used in different ways. For current purposes, parallelism is taken to involve at least two phrases whose denotative meaning (Chapter 7), grammar (Chapter 10) and possibly phonic features (Chapter 9) are closely related to one another.

More precisely, parallelism is defined here as the occurrence in close proximity in a text of two or more phrases having:

(i) Denotative relationship – normally similarity (especially synonymy or near-synonymy; Section 7.1.1), membership of the same semantic field (Section 7.3) or contrast (especially antonymy or near-antonymy; Section 10.2.3.1);

(ii) Grammatical similarity or identity – in respect to their morphology (Section 10.2; also sections 10.2.3.1–10.2.3.3), and/or their lexis (Section 10.2.1; also sections 10.2.4–10.2.4.2) and/or their syntax (Section 10.2) – and possibly also:

(iii) Phonic similarity (in that the phrases contain in relation to one another alliteration/assonance and possibly rhyme; Section 9.1.1).

According to Beeston, parallelism was a pervasive feature of Arabic in the early Islamic period and 'became practically *de rigeur* for all subsequent prose writing down to (and even in some instances into) the present age, whenever the author wishes to raise his writing to the level of solemn or elevated diction' (Beeston 1974: 141).

11.3 Simple cases of parallelism

Consider the following from a text about the dangers of fundamentalism (Hetherington 1996: 16):

والعقل يضيء ظلام الليل، والجهل يطفي نور النهار

This could be translated as:

rationality lights the darkness of night, and ignorance extinguishes the light of day

The two phrases, phrase 1 والعقل يضيء ظلام الليل and phrase 2 والجهل يطفي نور النهار, exhibit significant parallelism, as follows.

Denotatively, عقل 'rationality' in phrase 1 and جهل 'ignorance' in phrase 2 are virtual antonyms (in fact, they are not quite antonyms; عقل and جهل have some semantic overlap: it is possible to be rational but also ignorant). يضيء 'lights' and يطفي 'extinguishes' are antonyms. ظلام 'darkness' and نور 'light' are antonyms. ليل 'night' and نهار 'day' are antonyms.

In relation to grammar, we will consider lexis (words), then morphology and then syntax. In terms of lexis, و and و in phrases 1 and 2 are the same word, while الجهل and العقل are both definite singular nouns. In terms of morphology, عقل (phrase 1) and جهل (phrase 2) are both on the فَعْل pattern. يضيء (phrase 1) and يطفي (phrase 2) are both form IV (أَفْعَل pattern), imperfect indicative, active, third-person masculine singular verbs. نهار (phrase 1) and ظلام (phrase 2) are both on the فَعَال pattern (but note that while ظلام is the penultimate element of phrase 1 والعقل يضيء ظلام الليل, نهار is the final element of phrase 2 والجهل يطفي نور النهار).

Syntactically, both phrase 1 والعقل يضيء ظلام الليل and phrase 2 نور والجهل يطفي النهار consist of و followed by a subject (*mubtada'*) (العقل and الجهل, respectively), followed by a predicate (*xabar*) (يضيء ظلام الليل and يطفي نور النهار, respectively), consisting of a verb (يضيء and يطفي, respectively), followed by an object (ظلام الليل and نور النهار, respectively), consisting of a genitive structure (ظلام plus الليل, and نور plus النهار, respectively).

Phonically, there is similarity (alliteration/assonance) between the two phrases والعقل يضيء ظلام الليل and والجهل يطفي النهار, most obviously between the two وs (starting both phrases), the two لs in العقل and the two لs in الجهل and the two يs in يضيء and the two يs in يطفي. In addition, there is internal phonic similarity (alliteration/ assonance) within both phrase 1 والعقل يضيء ظلام الليل and phrase 2 والجهل يطفي نور النهار. In phrase 1, this is (in addition to elements already discussed, such as the two يs in يضيء) most obviously between the ل in ظلام and the لs in الليل. In phrase 2, there is phonic similarity (assonance/alliteration) in addition to that already discussed between ن in نور and ن in نهار, and ر in نور and ر in نهار. However, because the ل repetition in ظلام and الليل occurs in the two final words in phrase 1 والعقل يضيء

ظلام الليل, and because the ن and ر repetition in نور and نهار occurs in the two final words in phrase 2 والجهل يطفي نور النهار, there is a further correspondence between these two patterns of repetition, creating additional indirect phonic parallelism between the two phrases.

Another example of parallelism is provided by the following from an Arabic advertisement (example from Gully 1996) for an epilator (hair remover) called Feminin:

جودة لا تُقَارَن .. سعر لا يُنافَس

This might be translated as:

incomparable quality . . . unbeatable price

(A more literal translation would be 'a quality which is / cannot be compared, a price which is not / cannot be competed with'.)

The two phrases, phrase 1 جودة لا تُقَارَن and phrase 2 سعر لا يُنافَس, exhibit significant parallelism, as follows.

Denotatively, جودة in phrase 1 and سعر in phrase 2 belong to the same semantic field of desirability (of the product) if good or undesirability if poor. جودة and سعر are also both indefinite singular nouns (though جودة is feminine and سعر is masculine). لا in phrase 1 and لا in phrase 2 are synonyms (as the same word is used in both phrases in the same sense). تُقَارَن in phrase 1 and يُنافَس and in phrase 2 belong to the same semantic field of comparative assessment (competition involves comparison in which one entity is deemed better, etc. than another).

In relation to lexis, لا in phrase 1 and لا in phrase 2 are the same word. Morphologically, تُقَارَن in phrase 1 and يُنافَس in phrase 2 are Form III (فاعَل pattern), imperfect indicative, passive, third-person singular (though يُنافَس is masculine and تُقَارَن is feminine). Syntactically, phrase 1 جودة لا تُقَارَن, and phrase 2 سعر لا يُنافَس both involve a noun followed by a relative clause (consisting of لا followed by a verb).

Phonically, while there is a certain amount of assonance and alliteration across the phrases جودة لا تُقَارَن .. سعر لا يُنافَس, (e.g. of ر and ن), this does not specifically involve parallelism between the two phrases.

11.4 Complex cases of parallelism

The examples in the previous section involved fairly simple cases of parallelism. It is possible, however, for parallelism to be much more complex than this. Consider the following from the start of an article by the Egyptian journalist مصطفى أمين from الشرق الاوسط, 21 September 1982 (previously discussed in Section 6.1; reproduced in transcription in Al-Jabouri 1984, on whose account the following analysis is partly based):

في استطاعة أي حزب أن ينجح إذا دافع عن قضية الحرية وحقوق الإنسان، إذا احتضن كل مظلوم،
إذا قاوم الفساد، إذا ضرب الأمثلة في القدوة الصالحة، إذا حوّل الكلمات إلى أفعال والوعود إلى حقائق.

كل حزب يقف إلى جانب الشعب يقف الشعب إلى جانبه يحيط به عندما تُوجَّه إلى ظهره الخناجر وإلى صدره المدافع والسيوف.

A fairly literal translation of this reads:

> It is possible for any party to succeed if it defends the cause of freedom and the rights of man, if it embraces every oppressed [person], if it combats corruption, if it sets standards in good behaviour, if it changes words into deeds and promises into facts. Every party which stands beside the people, the people stand beside it, surrounding it when daggers are directed at its back and guns and swords at its front.

There are three separate major elements displaying parallelism in this short extract:

element 1	إذا دافع عن قضية الحرية وحقوق الإنسان، إذا احتضن كل مظلوم، إذا قاوم الفساد، إذا ضرب الأمثلة في القدوة الصالحة، إذا حوّل الكلمات إلى أفعال والوعود إلى حقائق
element 2	and يقف إلى جانب الشعب يقف الشعب إلى جانبه
element 3	إلى ظهره الخناجر وإلى صدره المدافع والسيوف.

Each of these elements contains parallel phrases, and some of these phrases themselves contain parallel subphrases. These can be tabulated as follows, and will be discussed in detail next:

element 1:	إذا دافع عن قضية الحرية وحقوق الإنسان، إذا احتضن كل مظلوم، إذا قاوم الفساد، إذا ضربالأمثلة في القدوة الصالحة، إذا حوّل الكلمات إلى أفعال والوعود إلى حقائق
element 1, phrase 1:	إذا دافع عن قضية الحرية وحقوق الإنسان
element 1, phrase 1, subphrase 1.1:	قضية الحرية
element 1, phrase 1, subphrase 1.2:	حقوق الإنسان
element 1, phrase 2:	إذا احتضن كل مظلوم
element 1, phrase 3:	إذا قاوم الفساد
element 1, phrase 4:	إذا ضرب الأمثلة في القدوة الصالحة
element 1, phrase 5:	إذا حوّل الكلمات إلى أفعال والوعود إلى حقائق
element 1, phrase 5, subphrase 5.1:	الكلمات إلى أفعال
element 1, phrase 5, subphrase 5.2:	الوعود إلى حقائق
element 2:	يقف إلى جانب الشعب يقف الشعب إلى جانبه
element 2, phrase 1:	يقف إلى جانب الشعب
element 2, phrase 2:	يقف الشعب إلى جانبه
element 3:	تُوجَّه إلى ظهره الخناجر وإلى صدره المدافع والسيوف
element 3, phrase 1:	إلى ظهره الخناجر
element 3, phrase 2:	إلى صدره المدافع والسيوف

We will consider element 1 first. Element 1 contains the following parallel phrase and subphrases: phrase 1 قضية الحرية وحقوق الإنسان – with the subphrases 1.1 قضية الحرية and 1.2 حقوق الإنسان; phrase 2 إذا احتضن كل مظلوم; phrase 3 إذا قاوم الفساد; phrase 4 إذا ضرب الأمثلة في القدوة الصالحة; and phrase 5 إذا حوّل الكلمات إلى أفعال والوعود إلى حقائق – with the subphrases 5.1 الكلمات إلى أفعال and 5.2 الوعود إلى حقائق. Within element 1, we will take phrases 1, 2, 3, 4 and 5 first, then look at subphrases 1.1 and 1.2 and finally subphrases 5.1 and 5.2.

The most prominent features giving rise to parallelism in element 1 phrases 1–5 are the following. Denotatively, دافع in phrase 1, احتضن in phrase 2 and قاوم in phrase 3 all belong to the general semantic field of defending/protecting. ضرب in phrase 4 and حوّل in phrase 5 do not really fit into this or any similar field and thus do not display this aspect of parallelism.

الحرية وحقوق الإنسان in phrase 1, مظلوم in phrase 2 and الفساد in phrase 3 all belong to the general semantic field of justice/rights. Again, الأمثلة في القدوة الصالحة in phrase 4 and الكلمات إلى أفعال والوعود إلى حقائق in phrase 5 do not fit into this semantic field, but they do belong to another, rather vague, semantic field, along the lines of 'virtue' (or 'virtuous thought and action').

In terms of lexis, the word إذا is repeated five times – at the beginning of each of phrases 1–5. Morphologically, all five verbs in phrases 1–5 دافع, احتضن, قاوم, ضرب and حوّل are perfect, active, third-person masculine singular. Two of the verbs, قاوم and دافع, are Form III verbs (فَاعَلَ pattern). Both حقوق (phrase 1) and وعود (phrase 5) are on the فُعُول pattern – though this is not a very prominent aspect of this extract.

Syntactically, phrases 2–5 إذا احتضن كل مظلوم, إذا قاوم الفساد, إذا ضرب الأمثلة في القدوة الصالحة, إذا حوّل الكلمات إلى أفعال والوعود إلى حقائق, also consist of a conditional particle إذا, followed by a verb followed by an object. Phrase 1 إذا دافع عن قضية الحرية وحقوق الإنسان is very similar, consisting of a verb دافع followed by a preposition عن followed by a 'prepositional object' قضية الحرية وحقوق الإنسان.

Phonically, alliteration/assonance is not particularly prominent in phrases 1–5. However, there is some alliteration and assonance – for example, in the repetition of ق in قضية (phrase 1), قاوم (phrase 3), القدوة (phrase 4) and حقوق and حقائق (phrase 5).

We will turn now to subphrase 1.1 قضية الحرية and subphrase 1.2 حقوق الإنسان. The elements of parallelism in these can be analyzed as follows. Denotatively, الحرية (subphrase 1.1) and حقوق الإنسان (subphrase 1.2) can both be regarded as belonging to the specific semantic field of human rights. Syntactically, the phrases قضية الحرية (subphrase 1.1) and حقوق الإنسان (subphrase 1.2) both involve a genitive structure, in which the second element is made definite by an initial ال (which also, in fact, makes the first element definite). Phonically, there is similarity (alliteration/assonance) between the phrases قضية الحرية and حقوق الإنسان in the repetition of the حs in الحرية (subphrase 1.1) and حقوق (subphrase 1.2) and of the قs in قضية (subphrase 1) and حقوق (subphrase 2). These involve a reversal of the order of the sounds involved between the two words concerned; in subphrase 1.1 قضية الحرية, the ق comes before the ح, while in subphrase 1.2 حقوق الإنسان, the ح comes before the ق. (there is also internal assonance within subphrase 1.2 in the يـ element of قضية and الحرية).

Turning now to subphrases 5.1 الكلمات إلى أفعال and 5.2 الوعود إلى حقائق, the parallelism between these two elements can be analyzed as follows.

Denotatively, الكلمات and الوعود both belong to the general semantic field of 'speaking' (although وعود is obviously much more specific than كلمات). أفعال and حقائق belong to the same semantic field of 'states of affairs'. They are also both indefinite plural. Similarly, إلى in the two phrases is used in the same sense.

Grammatically, there are very clear similarities between the phrases الكلمات إلى أفعال (subphrase 5.1) and الوعود إلى حقائق (subphrase 5.2). Lexically, both الكلمات إلى أفعال (subphrase 5.1) and الوعود إلى حقائق (subphrase 5.2) contain the word إلى as their second element. Syntactically, الكلمات إلى أفعال (subphrase 5.1) and الوعود إلى حقائق (subphrase 5.2) have the same structure: a noun (definite, plural) followed by a preposition (إلى in both cases) followed by another noun (indefinite, plural), which is the object of the preposition.

Phonically, subphrase 5.1 الكلمات إلى أفعال and subphrase 5.2 الوعود إلى حقائق both begin with ا ('a') followed by ل. There is also phonic identity between the two phases in the repetition of the word إلى. While other sounds are repeated (e.g. ع in both الوعود and أفعال), these do not contribute to parallelism, as they do not occur in corresponding (i.e. roughly the same) places in the two phrases.

We will now turn to element 2: يقف إلى جانب الشعب يقف الشعب إلى جانبه. Here, there is very significant parallelism between phrase 1 يقف إلى جانب الشعب and phrase 2 يقف الشعب إلى جانبه, as follows.

Considering denotative and lexical relationships first, the words يقف 'stands', إلى 'to', جانب 'side' and الشعب 'the people' are used in the two phrases in the same abstract sense in all cases. (The only difference between the two phrases in terms of the words and the morphemes they contain is that the second phrase has the suffix ه on the end of جانب.)

Syntactically, the phrases يقف إلى جانب الشعب and يقف الشعب إلى جانبه have a similar structure (though the words in this structure are somewhat differently ordered in the two phrases): a verb (يقف in both cases) with a dependent following prepositional phrase (إلى جانب الشعب in the case of phrase 1 and إلى جانبه in the case of phrase 2). In both cases, this prepositional phrase has, following the preposition إلى, a genitive-type structure (noun + noun in the case of جانب الشعب in phrase 1 and noun + pronoun in the case of إلى جانبه in phrase 2).

One obvious difference between phrase 1 يقف إلى جانب الشعب and phrase 2 يقف الشعب إلى جانبه is in the order of the words. Both phrase 1 and phrase 2 begin with يقف. However, phrase 1 has إلى جانب immediately following يقف and الشعب at the end, while phrase 2 has الشعب immediately following يقف and إلى جانبه at the end. In these respects, the word order in phrase 2 is a 'mirror image' of the word order in phrase 1 – an extension of parallelism, as defined at the start of this section, but constituting a clear form of linkage between phrase 1 and phrase 2. Phonically, the similarity between phrase 1 and phrase 2 is obvious, given that they consist almost entirely of the same words.

Turning finally to element 3 إلى ظهره الخناجر وإلى صدره المدافع والسيوف, phrase 1 إلى صدره المدافع والسيوف and phrase 2 إلى ظهره الخناجر, we find the following aspects of parallelism. Denotatively, إلى in phrases 1 and 2 are used in the same sense (they are synonymous). ظهر in phrase 1 is the antonym of صدر in phrase 2 – and although both are used here metaphorically (Chapter 14) rather than literally, they remain antonyms in their metaphorical senses here, just as they are in the literal senses of '(physical) back' and '(physical) chest/front'. The suffix ه in ظهره (phrase 1) and صدره (phrase 2) is used in the same sense (as well as referring to the 'abstract person'). الخناجر in phrase 1 and المدافع والسيوف in phrase 2 belong to the same semantic field of 'weapons'.

Lexically, phrases 1 and 2 both begin with إلى. Both ظهره and صدره are singular nouns made definite by the suffixing of ه. Both الخناجر in phrase 1 and المدافع and السيوف in phrase 2 are plural nouns made definite by the prefixing of the definite article الـ.

Morphologically, there is significant pattern identity/similarity between phrase 1 and phrase 2. ظهر in Phrase 1 and صدر in. إلى صدره المدافع والسيوف and phrase 2 إلى ظهره الخناجر in phrase 2 are both on the فَعْل pattern, and الخناجر in phrase 1 and المدافع in phrase 2 are both on similar patterns (فَعَالِل in the case of خناجر and مَفَاعِل in the case of مدافع).

Syntactically, both phrase 1 إلى ظهره الخناجر and phrase 2 إلى صدره المدافع والسيوف have the same overall syntactic structure: preposition (إلى in both cases) followed by a prepositional object noun (ظهره and صدره) followed by a subject–noun phrase (الخناجر in phrase 1 and المدافع والسيوف in phrase 2). The noun phrases are, of course, slightly different in that الخناجر consists only of the noun خناجر made definite by the article الـ, while the noun phrase المدافع والسيوف consists of two coordinated definite nouns, المدافع and السيوف.

There are significant phonic similarities between phrase 1 إلى ظهره الخناجر and phrase 2 إلى صدره المدافع والسيوف. These include the obvious repetition of إلى and of the third-person masculine singular suffix ه. Other cases of assonance/alliteration relevant to parallelism, in that they occur at corresponding points in the two phrases, are that between the ر in صدره (phrase 1) and that in ظهره, the initial الـ and the identical pattern of vowels in الخناجر and المدافع (phrase 2). (There are also cases of assonance/alliteration that are not relevant to considerations of parallelism in that they do not occur at corresponding points in the two phrases, e.g. that between the ر in ظهره and the ر in الخناجر in phrase 1 or the ف in المدافع and the ف in السيوف in phrase 2.)

11.5 Translating Arabic parallelism

The translation of Arabic parallelism into English is problematic, principally because English does not typically make use of parallelism to the same extent that Arabic does. It is possible to find cases of parallelism in English. The following are some examples:

> The mistakes of the fool are known to the world, but not to himself. The mistakes of the wise man are known to himself, but not to the world.
>
> (Charles Caleb Colton, 1780–1832)

> He has plundered our seas, ravaged our coasts, burnt our towns, and destroyed the lives of our people.
>
> (Thomas Jefferson, 1743–1826,
> American Declaration of Independence)

> Let that which stood in front go behind,
> Let that which was behind advance to the front.
>
> (from 'Poem of the Propositions of Nakedness',
> by Walt Whitman, 1819–1892)

Sweet is the rose, but grows upon a briar;
Sweet is the juniper, but sharp his bough;
Sweet is the eglantine, but pricketh near;
Sweet is the fir bloom, but his branches rough

(from 'Sonnet 26', by Edmund Spenser,
?1522–1599)

All of these examples have a strongly rhetorical – and even contrived or 'unnatural' – feel to them. The second example 'He has plundered our seas, ravaged our coasts, burnt our towns, and destroyed the lives of our people' is an attack on the English King George III, from whom the American colonists were seeking independence, while the last two examples are from poetry. It is also noteworthy that all the examples are from before the twentieth century, underlining that parallelism is apparently even less common in modern English writing than it was at earlier times.

This makes the translation of Arabic parallelism into English problematic. One could, of course, translate Arabic parallelism fairly literally. This may be most appropriate for literary texts – and particularly Classical Arabic texts where it seems appropriate to convey some of the exotic nature of the ST in the TT. The following example, previously discussed in Section 4.2, from the Classical Arabic text البخلاء by الجاحظ, is a case in point:

وليس من أصل الأدب ولا في ترتيب الحكم ولا في عادات القادة ولا في تدبير السادة، أن يستوي في نفيس المأكول وغريب المشروب وثمين الملبوس وخطير المركوب، والناعم من كل فن واللباب من كل شكل، التابع والمتبوع والسيد والمسود [. . .]

It is not consistent with the principles of etiquette, the hierarchy of authority, the customs of leaders, and the good rule of princes that the follower and the followed, the ruler and the ruled become equals with respect to precious food and marvelous drinks, valuable clothes and noble horses, and the finest and best kinds of things

(Lane 1994: 48, 56–57).

Consider, however, the earlier extract that has been the focus of discussion in this section (reproduced here for convenience):

في استطاعة أي حزب أن ينجح إذا دافع عن قضية الحرية وحقوق الإنسان، إذا احتضن كل مظلوم، إذا قاوم الفساد، إذا ضرب الأمثلة في القدوة الصالحة، إذا حوّل الكلمات إلى أفعال والوعود إلى حقائق. كل حزب يقف إلى جانب الشعب يقف الشعب إلى جانبه يحيط به عندما تُوجَّه إلى ظهره الخناجر وإلى صدره المدافع والسيوف.

The fact that this is a modern ST, talking about modern political notions that are shared by both Arab and Western cultures, suggests that it would be inappropriate to translate the parallelism literally and thus produce an unidiomatic TT. Indeed, by producing such an unidiomatic TT, the translator might convey the impression that not only is the form of the Arabic exotic (i.e. different from English forms) but so is the content – that the message itself is culturally (or otherwise) incompatible with notions in Western culture. For TT readers, this might well undermine the message itself, something that is unlikely to have been intended by the ST writer.

In such cases, therefore, reduction and recasting of at least some of the parallelism is likely to be essential to produce an idiomatic and perhaps also properly comprehensible TT. The following is an attempted idiomatic translation of this text:

> For any political party to succeed it must be prepared to stand up for freedom of expression and human rights, to protect the weak, to oppose corruption, to set itself the highest standards, and to act according to these standards. Any party which supports and defends the people will find that it is supported and defended by the people.

The English TT retains some of the parallelism of the Arabic ST. Thus, several parallel elements belonging to the same semantic field have been retained; in sentence 1, 'stand up for' and 'protect' (corresponding to the ST دافع عن and قاوم); 'freedom of expression' and 'human rights' (corresponding to the ST قضية الحرية and حقوق الانسان). The example of converse meaning is also effectively retained in sentence 2: 'Any party which supports and defends the people' and 'it is supported and defended by the people' (corresponding to the ST كل حزب يقف إلى جانب الشعب and يقف الشعب إلى جانبه).

However, the English TT also removes or modifies significant elements of the parallelism of the Arabic ST. In sentence 1, the complex ST parallelism of الكلمات إلى افعال and الوعود إلى حقائق is reduced to the phrase 'act according to these standards', albeit with some compensatory repetition in the TT with the previous phrase 'set itself the highest standards'. In sentence 2, there is, as already noted, a double aspect of parallelism in the ST phrase ظهر – إلى ظهره الخناجر وإلى صدره المدافع والسيوف with صدر and ظهر being antonyms and سيوف and خناجر, مدافع belonging to the same semantic field. But this double parallelism is subsumed into the English TT 'supports and defends' and 'supported and defended', which more obviously translate the Arabic يقف الشعب إلى جانبه and كل حزب يقف إلى جانب الشعب. The double repetition of the TT 'supports and defends' and 'supported and defended' is an attempt to relay some of the rhetorical force of the complex repetition of the ST without compromising TL idiomaticity. (For more on the translation of parallelism from Arabic to English, see Jawad 2007.)

Practical 11

Practical 11.1 Parallelism: ومما هو جدير بالذكر والملاحظة

Assignment

Using the approach discussed and illustrated in sections 11.2 and 11.3, identify and analyze cases of parallelism in the following text (originally used for Practical 1.2).

Contextual information

This text was written by the Arab nationalist writer ساطع الحُصَري (cited in Johnstone 1991: 78–79).

ST

ومما هو جدير بالذكر والملاحظة أن جميع الآراء التي أُبديت والأبحاث التي نُشرت في «فكرة القومية» وفي «مبدأ حقوق القوميات» خلال القرن التاسع عشر كانت تنحصر بالشعوب الأوربية وفروعها ولم تشمل الشعوب الآسيوية والإفريقية. لأن جميع المفكرين الأوربيين كانوا يزعمون أن تلك الشعوب ليست «متأخرة» فحسب بل هي «محرومة من قابلية التقدم والتمدن» أيضا. ولذلك فهي لا تستحق الحقوق التي تستحقها الشعوب الأوربية. حتى الكتاب الذين كانوا التزموا مبدأ «حقوق القوميات» أشد الالتزام، وتحمسوا له أشد التحمس، لم يخرجوا بآرائهم في ذلك خارج نطاق الأوربيين، ولم يسلّموا بمثل تلك الحقوق للشعوب الآسيوية والإفريقية.

Fairly literal TT

Amongst what is worthy of mention and noting is that all the opinions which were expressed and the studies which were published about 'the idea of Arab nationalism' and about 'the principle of the rights of nationalities' during the nineteenth century were confined to the European peoples and their branches, and did not include the Asian and African peoples. Because all the European thinkers used to claim that those peoples were not only 'backward', but were 'deprived of the ability for development and civilization' also. Thus, they did not deserve the rights which the European peoples deserved. Even the writers who were committed to the principle of 'the rights of nationalities' with the greatest commitment, and were enthusiastic about it with the greatest enthusiasm, did not take their views in that respect out beyond the sphere of the Europeans, and did not grant the like of those rights to the Asian and African peoples.

Practical 11.2 (Near-)synonym repetition and parallelism:
وبهذا الاسلوب البارز

Assignment

(i) Using the approach discussed and illustrated in sections 11.2 and 11.3, identify and analyze cases of (near-)synonym repetition (Section 7.2.1) and parallelism in the following ST.

(ii) Taking the fairly literal TT, which follows the ST, as your starting point, produce a more idiomatic TT, noting where and how you have reproduced, modified or eliminated ST parallelism in your TT.

Contextual information

The writer of this passage شوقي ضيف was a well-known literary critic (from Monteil 1960: 335). Note that Taha Hussein was blind and had to dictate the material he wrote rather than writing it down directly himself.

ST

وبهذا الاسلوب البارز الذي يمس القلوب ويثير العواطف بما فيه من سلاسة وعذوبة وصفاء وقدرة
على التصوير والتلوين، كتب طه حسين هذه الترجمة الذاتية «الايام»، كما كتب بقية قصصه وكتبه.
وقد تُرجمت الايام الى الانجليزية والفرنسية والروسية والصينية والعبرية.

ومن اهم ما يميز طه حسين في الايام وغير الايام: اسلوبه المتموج الزاخر بالنغم، فلا تستمع الى
كلام له، حتى تعرف بطوابعه المزينة في عباراته الملفوفة التي يأخذ بعضها برقاب بعض، في جرس
موسيقي بديع.

وكأنه يرى أن الادب الجدير بهذا الاسم، هو الذي يروع السمع كما يروع القلب في آن واحد،
وهو لذلك يوفّر لصوته كل جمال ممكن. ومن الغريب أنه لا يعدّل عبارة يمليها ولا يعدّ محاضرة قبل
إلقائها. فقد أصبح هذا الاسلوب جزءا من نفسه وعقله، فهو لا يملي ولا يحاضر الا به. وكثيرا ما تجد
فيه الالفاظ المكررة، وهو يعمد إلى ذلك عمدا، حتى يستتم ما يريد من إيقاعات وأنغام ينفذ بها الى
وجدان سامعه وقارئه.

Fairly literal TT

With this outstanding style which touches the hearts and moves the emotions
with what is in it of fluidity and sweetness and purity and the ability to paint
and colour, Taha Hussein wrote this interpretation of himself 'The Days' just
as he wrote the remainder of his stories and books. And 'The Days' has been
translated into English, French, Russian, Chinese, and Hebrew.

Among the most important of what distinguishes Taha Hussein in The Days
and other than The Days is his undulating style brimming with tunes, for you
do not listen to an utterance by him, until you know its decorated characteristics in wrapped up expressions each of which follows on in the footsteps of
the other in a marvellous musical tone.

It is as if he sees that the literature worthy of this name is that which appeals
to the hearing just as it appeals to the heart at one time, and he therefore provides his voice with all possible beauty. The strange thing is that he does not
alter an expression which he dictates and he does not prepare a lecture before
delivering it. This style has become part of his self and his intelligence, for
he does not dictate or lecture except by it. Frequently you find in it repeated
expressions, for he intends that intently, so that what he wants of rhythms and
tunes are completed with which he penetrates to the sentiment of his hearer
and his reader.

Practical 11.3 Parallelism: علمتني الأعوام ألا ابكي على عهد مضى

Assignment

(i) Discuss the strategic problems confronting the translator of the following text,
and outline your strategy for dealing with them, paying particular attention
to parallelism. You are to translate the text as part of a book titled *Mikhail
Naimy: Philosophical Writings*. While the English TT should give some
sense of the elegance of the ST, it is more important that the ST ideas are
retained and that these are not lost in a reproduction in the TT of aspects

of the ST parallelism that are alien to English style and that would deflect from comprehension of the TT.

(ii) Translate the text into English.

(iii) Explain the decisions of detail you made in producing your translation.

Contextual information

This passage is taken from النور والديجور (1958) (*Light and Darkness*), a philosophical work by the Lebanese novelist, essayist and poet ميخائيل نعيمة (1889–1988).

ST

علمتني الأعوام ألا ابكي على عهد مضى، ولا اضحك لعهد يأتي، وأن لا اعد خطواتي على رمال الزمان، فلا اندم على صبا تحجب وشباب تصرم، ولا اجزع من كهولة تفضي إلى شيخوخة وشيخوخة تنتهي إلى رمس، ورمس إن اتسع لرفاتي لن يتسع لكل ما فكرت واشتهيت وقلت وعملت. والذي فكرته واشتهيته وقلته وعملته هو بذاري أودعته ذمة الزمان، وأنا حريٌّ بأن استغله قبل أن يستغله سواي، وللزمان ذمة لا تخون .وعلمتني الأعوام أن الحياة زرع دائم وحصاد دائم، وأن من يزرع القطرب لا يجني القمح، ومن يغرس العوسج لا يحصد العنب. أما الزمان فلا يزرع ولا يغرس، ولا يحصد ولا يجني ولا هو يحصد البذار والغرس، ولكنه شاهد لا أكثر .وأما البذار فمنا وفينا، وكذلك الغرس منا وفينا، وأما الزارعون والغارسون، والحاصدون والجانون فنحن، والزمان براء من كل ما نعمل أو لا نعمل.

Practical 11.4 Parallelism and list restructuring: إن الرسول الكريم

Assignment

(i) Discuss the strategic problems confronting the translator of the following text, and outline your strategy for dealing with them, paying particular attention to parallelism and list restructuring (Section 7.3). You are to translate the text as part of a 'From the Arab Press' section of the English version of the Egyptian daily newspaper الأهرام (the English-language version of this has a certain degree of independence from official political pressure). The intended readership is mainly expatriate English speakers in Egypt, plus some other readers worldwide, who are likely to have a good knowledge of Middle Eastern culture and affairs.

(ii) Translate the text into English.

(iii) Explain the decisions of detail you made in producing your translation.

Contextual information

This passage is taken from the weekly Egyptian news magazine روز اليوسف (no. 3521, 4 December 1995). The article by عادل حمودة is titled لعبة الضفادع العقارب في عواصم الشرق الاوسط. The general theme of the article is the negative political effects of religious fundamentalism in the Middle East (text taken from Hetherington 1996: 34–35). This particular section deals with the behaviour of religious extremists.

ST

إن الرسول الكريم (صلعم) تنبأ في حديث شريف بأن اليهود سيتفرقون على ٧١ أو ٧٢ فرقة. وكذلك النصارى .. أما المسلمون فسيتفرقون على ٧٢ فرقة. والمجموع ٣١٤ أو ٣١٦ فرقة .. كل فرقة انقسمت إلى مجموعات .. كل مجموعة ترى أنها الوحيدة التي على صواب، وترى غيرها على ضلال .. وكل مجموعة يرى أتباعها أنهم أولياء الله، وجند الله، وأصفياء الله، وأصدقاء الله، والناطقون الرسميون باسم الله .. وما عداهم يعيشون في الحرام، والفساد، والجاهلية، والكفر، والإلحاد.

وبعضهم لين .. يميل إلى الحسنة .. ولكن السيادة الدينية – في زمن يختلط فيه البارود بالكتب المقدسة – تكون للأكثر تشدداً .. للأكثر تشنجاً، وتهورا، وتطرفا .. وللأكثر جرأة على القتل .. إن هؤلاء يقتلون باسم الله .. ويسلحون، ويفجرون، ويذبحون، ويغسلون العقول، ويكسرون العظام، ويحرمون الإبداع أيضا باسم الله!

لا هم استخدموا الدين للقضاء على الفقر ومتاعب الفقراء، ولا هم استخدموه من أجل الصفو والصفاء .. لا هم اعتبروه وسيلة لتحقيق العدالة الاجتماعية ولا هم وجدوا فيه علاجا للأمراض النفسية.

12 Sentential issues

12.1 The sentential level

We can use the lines from 'To Autumn' to show how different grammatical arrangements create different assumptions in the listener or reader in regard to the communicative purpose of an utterance. Keats's own lines –

> Season of mists and mellow fruitfulness,
> Close bosom-friend of the maturing sun; [. . .] –

are partly an address to autumn and partly an exclamation about it: the very structure of the utterance leads the listener/reader to expect an expression of wonderment and enthusiasm (as does the title, of course). A different grammatical arrangement, however, would most likely announce a different communicative purpose. For instance:

> Autumn is a season of mists and mellow fruitfulness.
> It is a close bosom-friend of the maturing sun.

This structure, despite the title, announces a more purely informative text – even though, in the event, phonic and lexical features do give the utterances something more than simply informative value. We can say that, in each version, the grammatical arrangement marks the utterances as having a particular communicative purpose, whatever overtones may turn out to be involved. When, as here, one looks at the *communicative purpose* of a given grammatical arrangement in its own right, one is looking at the utterance on the sentential level. On this level are considered sentences.

We define a sentence as a complete, self-contained and ready-made vehicle for communication: nothing needs to be added before it can be uttered and understood in concrete situations. The starter's one-word command 'Go!' is a sentence. So is 'No way!' as an expression of refusal or disbelief or 'Good' in response to confirmation that a room has a bath.

From a more theoretical perspective, there is a difference between a sentence in the full sense, as we are using it here, and a 'syntactic sentence' – that is, a collection of words arranged in an appropriate grammatical pattern, containing, for example, at least one main clause. This is evident in spoken language. Any spoken sentence has in addition to the words it contains a particular intonation pattern; in fact, it is virtually impossible to speak a sentence without some features of rhythm and stress, and, where these are artificially removed, as can be done with synthetic speech, the results are almost incomprehensible (indeed, even where such intonation features are not fully developed – as is sometimes the case with artificial speech on telephone answering services – the results are extremely odd).

That a sentence is more than a collection of words arranged in an appropriate grammatical pattern is also evident from the fact that in purely grammatical terms (as traditionally understood) 'They stopped the car at three-o-clock' and 'At three-o-clock they stopped the car' are identical (i.e. they both consist of a main clause 'They stopped the car', plus a subordinate element 'at three-o-clock'). They are clearly not, however, identical in terms of word order. Nor, as we shall see (Section 12.2.2, 12.2.2.2), are they identical in terms of the weighting they give to the bits of information conveyed. (Issues regarding the definition of a sentence are complex, and more detailed discussion of them here would go beyond the scope of this course. If you are interested in pursuing them, however, Dickins 2010b provides an account that develops the ideas discussed here.)

We should note here that, although this chapter deals with sentential issues in translation, it is often impossible both in translation and in linguistic analysis to consider one sentence in isolation from other surrounding sentences. Discussion at various points in the chapter will therefore sometimes go beyond the level of the single sentence, with the intention, however, of explicating features at the level of the individual sentence.

12.2   Textual variables on the sentential level

From the point of view of Arabic>English translation, there are three major non-syntactic features of the sentence, which we shall consider in turn in subsequent sections of this chapter. These are (i) prosodic features, such as intonation or stress; (ii) theme and rheme – that is, the presentation of information as more or less predictable typically through the choice of a particular sequential order of elements within the sentence; and (iii) foregrounding and backgrounding – that is, the presentation of information as more or less important for the overall development of the text.

12.2.1   *Prosodic features*

In spoken texts, several different sentences, marked for different purposes, can be created purely through intonation and stress – even though they comprise the same words in exactly the same order. Compare the following in English:

The salt.	[with falling intonation: *statement*]
The salt?	[with rising intonation: *question*]
The salt!	[with fall–rise intonation: *demand*]
The salt!	[with high, level intonation: *command*]

The same two words could be spoken in other ways to express encouragement (to pass the salt, etc.), warning (that the salt pot is about to fall, etc.) and so on.

As these examples suggest, the sentential level of spoken language is extremely rich, with fine shades of intonation distinguishing sentences with subtly different nuances. Stress can similarly be used in English to express different shades of meaning. English is able to stress words fairly freely in speech – for example, the neutral 'I know that man' versus '*I* know that man' versus 'I *know* that man' versus 'I know *that* man' versus 'I know that *man*'. Although stress is used in Arabic in this way, neither Standard Arabic nor the dialects exhibit the same freedom to shift stress within the sentence as English. To achieve similar effects, two other devices are available. First, Arabic can shift word order fairly freely – for example, ذلك الرجل أعرفه (or, more likely, الرجل أعرف). Second, it can make use of additional elements: 'I know *him*' could be rendered as أعرفه هو with the additional independent pronoun هو at the end of the sentence.

A lot of the features of the spoken sentential level simply disappear in written texts, because the sentential level in written language is relatively impoverished. Written English, of course, has punctuation marks. Most obviously, sentences are marked by a capital letter at the start of the first word and a full stop, question mark or exclamation mark at the end of the final word. These latter features identify the sentence in broad terms as a statement, question or order, etc. However, they do not allow for finer distinctions within these possibilities. Thus, it is not possible, for example, to distinguish in writing between 'The salt!', as a demand with fall–rise intonation, and 'The salt!', as a command with high, level intonation; nor between large numbers of other similar possibilities offered by the spoken language.

Of the remaining punctuation uses in English, some carry specific meaning and are obligatory where this meaning is intended. There is, for instance, a difference between 'My cousin who lives in Bristol visited us last week' and 'My cousin, who lives in Bristol, visited us last week'. In the first sentence, the relative clause 'who lives in Bristol' identifies which out of a number of possible cousins is intended. This is known as a defining (or restrictive) relative clause. In the second sentence, by contrast, the relative clause 'who lives in Bristol' merely provides further information about a cousin who is already assumed to be identified. This is known as a describing (or non-restrictive) relative clause.

Other punctuation uses in English are subject to greater variation, the comma being a case in point. Thus, in some contexts, there will be very little difference in meaning between 'Last week my cousin visited us' and 'Last week, my cousin visited us'. In other contexts, however, the two sentences will not only sound different but will also have a quite different communicative impact.

Punctuation in Arabic is even less systematic than punctuation in English. Traditionally, Arabic had no punctuation whatsoever; one still occasionally comes across modern books without punctuation. Conversely, modern editions of Classical Arabic texts, which originally had no punctuation, often have punctuation added. Even where punctuation exists, the conventions for Arabic are far less standardized than those of English. There is obviously no equivalent of Latin-script capital letters in Arabic. Modern Arabic texts do typically make use of full stops. However, the orthographic sentence in Arabic, defined as a stretch of text ending in a full stop (and preceded by another full stop, if the sentence is not text initial), is frequently much longer than the orthographic sentence in English. In English, the orthographic sentence typically corresponds directly to the spoken sentence. That is to say, if one were to read a written English sentence out loud, one would typically get a complete spoken sentence with a complete intonation pattern. By contrast, in Arabic, a single orthographic sentence fairly frequently does not correspond very happily to a single spoken sentence; read out loud, the single orthographic sentence would be likely to be split up into two or even more spoken sentences (i.e. with two or more complete intonation patterns, each of these patterns marking off a separate sentence).

Even where a single orthographic Arabic sentence can reasonably be regarded as corresponding to a single spoken Arabic sentence, Arabic sentences are often much longer than typical English ones, forcing the Arabic>English translator to find appropriate ways of adding additional sentence breaks in the TT. The frequent differences in length between Arabic and English sentences are one reason why discussion in this chapter must sometimes go beyond the level of the individual sentence.

Other punctuation markers in Arabic, such as the comma, are used even less systematically than the full stop. It is also worth noting the acceptability, even in formal Arabic, of multiple question marks or exclamation marks, or even a combination of question mark(s) and exclamation mark(s), where the writer wants to convey strong emphasis. Such usages in English are confined to informal writing.

Two other frequent punctuation usages of Arabic are also worth noting here, because they are rather different from those of English. The first is the heavy use of two dots in 'suspensive' contexts – that is, where the writer might have gone on to say something else and where the text can be regarded as potentially interrupted. These can be found in many places in the Arabic texts in this book; there are several examples in Practical 12.1, for example, at the end of this chapter. English also makes use of this device (sometimes called 'suspension points' or 'points of ellipsis'), though normally with three dots, rather than two, and normally where the suspensive element is unambiguous (i.e. where the sentence is clearly not complete). An example is 'I thought you were . . .', where the speaker/writer had originally intended to go on and complete the sentence by saying something further. Arabic double dots .. will be best translated into English by various things, depending on the context (e.g. a full stop or a dash).

The second common Arabic punctuation usage that is significantly different from English is that of round brackets or *parentheses* – that is, (and). In English, brackets are used for parenthetical information – that is, information that in principle could be removed without compromising the essential information conveyed or the grammatical structure of the text. An example of the use of round brackets in English is 'Ed Miliband (the leader of the Labour Party) resigned following his election defeat in 2015'. In Arabic, by contrast, round brackets, as well as other devices, such as « » and " ", are sometimes used to highlight key words. An example from the دستور سلطنة لهج (the Constitution of the Sultanate of Lahej, a

sultanate officially abolished in 1967) is the use of round brackets round الإسلام in
(دين السلطنة الرسمي (الإسلام) 'The official religion of the Sultanate is Islam'. In English, inverted commas, whether single or double, are used in this kind of context
to indicate that this is a usage that the writer does not accept (i.e. roughly 'this is
what some people say, but it is not a term with which I as the writer agree'). Thus,
if inverted commas were placed around 'Islam' in this example, giving "The official religion of the Sultanate is 'Islam'" or 'The official religion of the Sultanate is
"Islam"', this would indicate that the writer does not regard 'Islam' as the correct
term for this religion in English.

Parentheses are also used in Arabic to identify proper names when these are not
obvious in the context. An example from Practical 9.2 is وفي (مايفير) لندن, which
might be translated as 'and in Mayfair, London'. Here, using inverted commas in
English, as in 'and in "Mayfair", London' would indicate that 'Mayfair' is not the
real name of the area in question. For recent discussions of punctuation usages in
modern Arabic and in Arabic>English translation, see Khafaji (2001), Ghazala
(2004), and AlQinai (2008).

Apart from the use of punctuation, the only ways of conveying intonation and
stress in English writing are through typography. The most popular typographical
device is italics, but capitals or bold typeface are also sometimes used. None of
these devices is widely used in Arabic, and capitals do not exist. Sometimes, where
punctuation and typography cannot give the desired nuance, the writer or translator
has to fall back on adding explicit information about how the sentences are spoken,
as in 'she exclaimed in surprise', 'she said angrily' and so on.

12.2.2 *Theme and rheme*

The following is a brief account of the notions of theme and rheme with respect
to English and Arabic and is based on the ideas of several different authors and
approaches. For a fuller description of the major approaches to this topic, see
Baker (2011: 131–189). In relation to Arabic, cf. also Abdul-Raof (1998), Dickins
and Watson (1999: 337–351, 377–387), Dickins (2010b) and Al-Harthi (2011).

The basic idea behind theme and rheme is that sentences can be divided up into
some elements that provide at least relatively predictable information and others that provide at least relatively unpredictable information. The elements that
provide at least relatively predictable information are known as the theme, while
those elements that provide at least relatively unpredictable information are known
as the rheme. Consider the following from a text on Ayatollah Khomeini (from
Dickins and Watson 1999: 461):

> Ayatollah Khomeini was the son of a cleric. He was born in 1903 in the small
> town of Khomein in Isfahan province.

In the second sentence, the information given by 'He' is highly predictable,
because 'Ayatollah Khomeini' (to whom 'He' also refers) has been mentioned in
the previous sentence. 'He' accordingly identifies someone already known about in

the text and is the theme of this sentence. 'Was born in the small town of Khomein in Isfahan province', by contrast, is unpredictable; the information here is all new, and this element is accordingly the rheme.

The first sentence in this extract is somewhat more interesting. Let us imagine the situation in which 'Ayatollah Khomeini was the son of a cleric' was the first sentence of this text. In this case, we can see that neither the element 'Ayatollah Khomeini' nor the element 'was the son of a cleric' is known before the sentence, and therefore neither is absolutely predictable. In this case, however, we may say that the author chooses to treat 'Ayatollah Khomeini' as relatively predictable and therefore thematizes it (i.e. makes it theme). There are two reasons for doing this. First, it is fairly likely through their previous knowledge of the world that the readers of this text will know the name Ayatollah Khomeini but not know that he was the son of a cleric. Second, because the whole text is about Ayatollah Khomeini, we may say that the choice of 'Ayatollah Khomeini' as theme is justified by the subsequent development of the text – that is, looked at globally, 'Ayatollah Khomeini', or words such as 'He', when they refer to Ayatollah Khomeini, are going to be predictable elements throughout.

Both the sentences 'Ayatollah Khomeini was the son of a cleric' and 'He was born in 1903 in the small town of Khomein in Isfahan province' illustrate a general tendency, which is true of Arabic as well as English, for theme to precede rheme. This can be regarded as a 'natural' order in that it mirrors the order of things in the real world; when we are trying to work out something new, we start with what is known and proceed from there to what is not known.

12.2.2.1   *Sentence stress*

In spoken English and Arabic, theme and rheme can be related to notions of stress. If you read the sentence 'Ayatollah Khomeini was the son of a cleric' out loud, you will hear that the sentence stress falls on 'cleric'. The general tendency in both Arabic and English is for stress to fall on a word in the rheme.

This correlation between rheme and sentence stress can also be seen on the relatively rare occasions in English where rheme comes first in the sentence. Consider the following:

What happened to you?

(a) I got stung by a bee.
(b) A bee stung me.

Response (a) follows the standard theme-first, theme–rheme order, and the sentence stress falls on 'bee'. Response (b), however, has the reverse rheme–theme order; here again, however, sentence stress falls on 'bee'.

Where rheme precedes theme in English, as in 'A bee stung me', the sentence tends to carry a certain emotional charge. It would be perfectly possible – in fact, probably normal – to utter the sentence 'I got stung by a bee' in a matter-of-fact way. An utterance along the lines 'A bee stung me', however, is much more associated with annoyance or with some other strong emotion.

12.2.2.2   Emphatic preposing

It is important to distinguish between initial rhemes, which involve sentence stress, and preposed emphatic elements. Consider the following sentence:

> In the early sixties Ayatollah Khomeini led the movement against the Shah of Iran's 'White Revolution'.

This sentence is in fact the start of the next paragraph of the Ayatollah Khomeini text that we quoted from earlier. Here, the main sentence stress falls on 'Revolution' (i.e. the end of the rheme). There is, however, a secondary stress (signalled by a rising pitch), which falls on 'sixties'; such secondary stress can be termed 'phrasal stress' (or clausal stress in the case of a clause).

In this sentence, 'In the early sixties' is clearly not the main theme. It can be termed a 'preposed emphatic theme'. 'Preposed' with respect to English means 'placed before the subject'; in English, any element that is placed before the subject in a declarative sentence can be described as preposed. 'Emphatic' means that there is some sense of 'picking out' the element for a special purpose; here, the purpose is for linkage and contrast with several similarly preposed time phrases in subsequent sentences. Later sentences in the same paragraph, for example, begin 'Following an agreement between Iran and Iraq' and 'On 2 February 1979'.

Arabic, like English, makes use of preposed emphatic themes. In Arabic, however, anything that comes before the verb in a sentence that contains a verb may be a preposed emphatic theme. Thus, in sentences that have the word order subject-verb-(etc.), the subject may be emphatic (cf. Dickins and Watson 1999: 337–351). It would also appear that in sentences without a main verb, the subject is optionally emphatic. We shall consider further issues relating to sentences having the word order subject-verb-(etc.) in the following section.

12.2.2.3   Basic theme–rheme translation issues

In terms of Arabic>English translation, the distinction between thematic and rhematic information is most problematic where it proves difficult or impossible to reproduce roughly the same word order in English as in the original Arabic. If the word order of the original Arabic can be roughly maintained in the English, this will often reproduce the original theme–rheme structure, because English and Arabic both have a tendency to start with the most thematic element and end with the most rhematic element. This general principle is illustrated by the following:

وبنى هذا الجسر مهندسون مصريون
This bridge was built by Egyptian engineers

Here, the Arabic and English structures seem rather different; the Arabic is active, and the English is passive. However, the same basic order of ideas is maintained in both – 'bridge' first and 'engineers' next. The only difference here is that Arabic has the verb بُنِيَ right at the beginning, whereas the English 'was built' comes after the subject. In the case of English, however, it is in virtually all cases obligatory to have the verb after the subject in declarative sentences (in Arabic, the verb or the subject may come first). Therefore, word order in this respect is not alterable for theme–rheme considerations.

12.2.3   Foregrounding and backgrounding

The term 'subordinate' in 'subordinate clause' or 'subordinate element' may be said to indicate several things. From a grammatical point of view, a subordinate clause is subordinate in that it falls outside the main part of the sentence and can only occur together with this main part. From an informational point of view, a subordinate clause may be said to be informationally subordinate. This can be shown from the passage about Ayatollah Khomeini, which we briefly discussed in Section 12.2.2 (cf. Dickins and Watson 1999: 462):

> In the early sixties Ayatollah Khomeini led the movement against the Shah of Iran's 'White Revolution'. As a result, he was exiled in 1963, first to Turkey and then to the Islamic holy city of Najaf in Iraq. Following an agreement between Iraq and Iran he was expelled from Najaf and was forced to take up residence near Paris in the late seventies. On 2 February 1979, after a short stay in France, he returned to Tehran until after the Islamic revolution on 11 February 1979.

Notice how all the time phrases are subordinate, while the material carrying the main line of the story is in the main clauses. This is typical in English. Now compare the text with this alternative version, in which the time phrases are made into the subject of the main clause:

> The early sixties was a period of leadership for Ayatollah Khomeini against the Shah of Iran's 'White Revolution'. As a result, 1963 saw him exiled first to Turkey and then to the Islamic holy city of Najaf in Iraq. The period following an agreement between Iraq and Iran involved his expulsion from Najaf, and the late seventies forced him to take up residence near Paris. The 2nd of February 1979, which was preceded by a short stay in France, witnessed Khomeini's return to Tehran; 11 February 1979, the date of the Islamic revolution, marked the end of this period.

This version of the text is distinctly odd. One reason for this is that it consistently upgrades the time element from the subordinate, ancillary status it had in the actual text to a main status discoursally. While the ideas in the text tell us that it must be about Ayatollah Khomeini's life, the organization of these ideas suggests that the listed dates ought to be the topic of the text.

Subordinate elements are sometimes said to convey background information – that is, the kind of information that is not central to the overall topic of the text or section of text in question. Main clauses, by contrast, are said to convey **foreground information** – that is, information that is central to the overall topic. This situation is well illustrated by the Khomeini text.

The foregrounding–backgrounding distinction that is characteristic of subordination can be contrasted with the situation that obtains in cases of clausal coordination. Consider the following:

1   Disputes break out and people tend to blame one another.
2   When disputes break out, people tend to blame one another.

Without any context, example 1 seems odd because the information that 'disputes break out' is trivial. It is then coupled by the use of 'and' with the much more significant (i.e. worthy of foregrounding) information that people tend to blame one another. The implication of using 'and' to link these two pieces of information, however, is that they are of roughly equal significance to the overall topic of the text. There is a contradiction – or at least a tension – between the difference in the significance of the two pieces of information conveyed by the two clauses and the implication in the use of 'and' that these two pieces of information are of at least roughly equal significance.

This tension is resolved in example 2. 'When disputes break out' is here presented as relatively insignificant subordinate information, which simply provides background to the main point being made.

In saying that the two clauses connected by a coordinating conjunction such as 'and' are of roughly equal significance to the overall topic of the text or text section, we are not suggesting that one could reverse the order of the two clauses and retain the same meaning. Thus, there is a clear difference in meaning between 'Disputes break out and people tend to blame one other' and 'People tend to blame one other and disputes break out'. In the first case, the obvious interpretation of the sentence is that the disputes come first and lead to the blaming; in the second, the blaming comes first and leads to disputes.

Note also that 'Disputes break out and people tend to blame one another' is not *intrinsically* odd in English. All that is required to render it a perfectly reasonable utterance is a context in which 'Disputes break out' is made non-trivial by being linked to a specific time or place, as, for example, in the following: 'If the weather's bad or the order-book's not full, disputes break out and people tend to blame each other'.

12.2.4   *Interaction of theme–rheme and main–subordinate elements*

In the previous sections, we have looked independently at theme and rheme elements, as well as main and subordinate elements. Elements from these two pairs can come together in four possible ways:

Main theme	i.e. a theme that is a main clause or part of a main clause
Subordinate theme	i.e. a theme that is a subordinate element or part of a subordinate element

Main rheme	i.e. a rheme that is a main clause or part of a main clause
Subordinate rheme	i.e. a rheme that is a subordinate element or part of a subordinate element

We would expect these elements to express the following kinds of information:

Main theme	predictable, foreground information
Subordinate theme	predictable, background information
Main rheme	unpredictable, foreground information
Subordinate rheme	unpredictable, background information

We have already looked at some examples of main theme and subordinate theme in the text on Ayatollah Khomeini. In this text, the element that is most clearly both main and theme and hence predictable and foregrounded is 'Ayatollah Khomeini' in the first sentence and 'he' in every other sentence.

In the same text, the subordinate themes are typically initial temporal phrases: thus, 'In the early sixties', 'Following an agreement', 'On 2 February 1979, after a short stay in France'. As noted (Section 12.2.2.2), such initial non-subject themes are also emphatic.

Main rhemes in both English and Arabic seem to fulfil the expectation that they express information that is both unpredictable and significant to the overall topic of the text or section of text.

The most interesting category in both English and Arabic is subordinate rhemes. The expectation is that these should convey information that is both backgrounded and relatively unpredictable. In many cases, this expectation is fulfilled in both English and Arabic. A good example from English is the following (Leith 1983: 13; cited in Sekine 1996: 78):

> In short, the Roman empire witnessed a process known to sociolinguistics as *language shift*. The evidence for this is that Latin formed the base of French, Spanish, Italian, Portuguese, and Romanian {as they are spoken today}.

Here, 'as they are spoken today' is relatively unpredictable; or, at least, what predictability it has is entirely dependent on the previous mention of the languages concerned. At the same time, it is also background information; it is included only to make plain that what are being referred to are the contemporary versions of French, Spanish, Italian, Portuguese and Romanian, not earlier versions of the same languages. However, this would likely be the interpretation reached by the reader even without the inclusion of 'as they are spoken today'. This phrase, therefore, is of little importance informationally, and it is noteworthy that the text subsequently goes on to talk further about Latin rather than pursuing issues related to the modern Romance languages.

Sometimes, however, subordinate clauses in rheme position (i.e. towards the end of the phrase or sentence) convey foreground rather than background information.

This tendency seems more pronounced in Arabic than in English. Consider the following from زكريا تامر by النار والماء:

فتعالت ضحكات البنات {بينما انفجر غضب فواز}، فكف عن السير واستدار ووقف منفرج القدمين وواجه الفتيات الأربع بعينين حانقتين متحديتين.

A fairly literal translation of this would be:

> The girls' laughter rose, {while Fawaz's rage exploded}. He stopped walk-ing, turned around, stood feet apart, and stared at the four girls in anger and challenge.

This translation seems slightly odd for several reasons. The aspect of this oddity that concerns us here, however, is the phrase 'while Fawaz's anger exploded'. The fact that this is a subordinate clause coming after 'The girls' laughter rose', suggests that it should convey unpredictable but background information – and this is indeed what it does seem to convey. In the context, however, it would make better sense if the information conveyed were not only unpredictable but also fore-grounded. The reason for this is that Fawaz's explosion is an important feature of the text's development; as we can see from the following quoted lines, the text goes on immediately to describe Fawaz's behaviour as a result of his explosion of anger.

An actual translation of this section (St John 1999: 32) reads:

> When he heard the girls' laughter, {Fawaz exploded with rage}. He stopped, spun round, and stood, glaring furiously at the four young women.

Ignoring other differences between this TT and the more literal TT proposed earlier (as these are not relevant to the current discussion), we can see that the translator has reversed the subordination structure of the phrase فتعالت ضحكات البنات بينما انفجر غضب فواز. The main Arabic clause فتعالت ضحكات البنات has been converted into an English subor-dinate clause (with some other changes) 'When he heard the girls' laughter', while the subordinate clause انفجر غضب فواز has been converted into an English main clause (also with some other changes) 'Fawaz exploded with rage'. One effect of this is to foreground the information conveyed by 'Fawaz exploded with rage' and thus produce a more natural-sounding rendering than that of the more literal translation.

Reversal of the subordination structure is a fairly common strategy for dealing with cases in which rhematic subordinate clauses in Arabic convey foreground information. A second regular strategy is to translate the Arabic rhematic subor-dinate clause as a separate sentence in English. This strategy is illustrated by the following from Calderbank (1990: 23):

ولما كان الاقوياء بطبيعتهم لا يقبلون الطاعة العمياء للمرشد العام الإمام الشيخ حسن البنا بل ويقومون بمراجعته فيما يراه من أمور فإنه قد ألصق بهم صفة الخبث بل وعمد إلى إقصائهم عن الجماعة {بحيث} لم يبق حوله سوى الإخوان الذين من فرط ضعفهم لا يقدرون على الاختلاف مع الإمام {الأمر الذي} جعله يصفهم بالأمانه!!

This could be translated as follows:

> Since the strong by their very nature did not accept blind obedience to the
> Supreme Guide the venerable Hasan El Banna, and indeed, actively attempted
> to question some of his judgements, he termed them 'malicious', and went
> so far as to expel them from the Brotherhood. {As a result} the only remain-
> ing members of El Banna's inner circle were those whose extreme weakness
> meant that they were unable to oppose him. {These people} he called 'the
> trustworthy'.

Here, the two subordinate clauses introduced by بحيث and الأمر الذي in Arabic are
relayed by separate sentences in English.

12.2.5   Translation of Arabic coordinated clauses

Often, the translation into English of Arabic sentences involving the coordinating
conjunctions و and ف – and less commonly ثم – present no problem; و, for example,
is sometimes translatable as 'and'. Where it begins a sentence in Arabic, it will
typically have no correspondent in English; and where و occurs as a coordinating
conjunction in a long Arabic sentence, it may be appropriate in English to make
two sentences, otherwise omitting any equivalent of و.

Sometimes, however, Arabic coordinating conjunctions present more of a translation problem. Consider the following, which is taken from the start of the novel
عرس الزين by the Sudanese writer الطيب صالح (صالح n.d.: 11):

يولد الأطفال فيستقبلون الحياة بالصريخ، هذا هو المعروف ولكن يروى أن الزين، والعهدة على أمه
والنساء اللائي حضرن ولادتها، أول ما مس الارض، انفجر ضاحكاً.

This might be translated as:

> When children are born, they greet life with a scream; this is well known.
> However, according to his mother and the women who attended his birth, as
> soon as Zein came into the world he burst out laughing.

Here, Arabic uses the coordinating conjunction ف to link the two phrases يولد الأطفال
and يستقبلون الحياة بالصريخ. Because coordinating conjunctions typically present the
information given by the relevant clauses as equally foregrounded, one might
have expected the translation to read something like: 'Children are born, and they
greet life with a scream'. This, however, sounds somewhat odd in English, just as
a sentence 'Disputes break out, and people tend to blame one another' can sound
odd. The reason in both cases is that the structure accords too major a status to the
information given in the first clause (i.e. it makes the first clause too foregrounded).
Thus, in the case of this example, the notion that children are born is obvious.
(Indeed, one would probably only want to use this formulation in the TT if the
author were deliberately inviting the reader to re-examine the notion that children

are born and accord to it fresh significance. This is not the case here.) A more natural effect is achieved in the English by subordinating the phrase 'children are born' by introducing it with the subordinating conjunction 'When'.

Practical 12

Practical 12.1 Theme and rheme and mainness and subordination: لقد دفعت السعودية

Assignment

(i) Discuss the strategic decisions that you must take before starting detailed translation of the following text, and outline and justify the strategy you adopt. You are to translate the text as part of an 'From the Arab Press' section of the English version of the Egyptian daily newspaper الأهرام. The intended readership is mainly expatriate English speakers in Egypt, plus some other readers worldwide, who are likely to have a good knowledge of Middle Eastern culture and affairs.

(ii) Translate the text into English.

(iii) Explain the decisions of detail you made in producing your translation that are of relevance to theme–rheme issues and mainness–subordination issues.

(iv) Explain other decisions of detail you made in producing your translation.

Contextual information

This passage is taken from an article in the weekly Egyptian news magazine روز اليوسف (no. 3521, 4 December 1995). The article by عادل حمودة is titled لعبة الضفادع والعقارب في عواصم الشرق الاوسط. The general theme of the article is the negative political effects of religious fundamentalism in the Middle East (text taken from Hetherington 1996: 34–5).

ST

لقد دفعت السعودية في حرب الخليج ٥٥ مليارا من الدولارات، وبدلا من أنها كانت تسهر الليالي لمعرفة كيف تستثمر ١٨٠ مليار دولار – ودائعها في الغرب – أصبح سهر الليالي من أجل الديون المتراكمة وفوائدها التي وصلت الى ٧٠ مليار دولار.

وفي السعودية والخليج يقول الناس: قبل حرب الخليج كنا نحلم بزوجة يابانية ومرتب أمريكي، ومنزل ريفي انجليزي، وطباخ صيني .. ولكن بعد هذه الحرب لم يعد أمامنا سوى زوجة امريكية ومرتب صيني، ومنزل ياباني وطباخ انجليزي!

وعلى المستوى السياسي، نجحت المعارضة السعودية في استمالة بعض القيادات الدينية إلى جانبهم وضغطوا على الأسرة الحاكمة، وقدموا في يوليو ١٩٩٢ ما عرف بمذكرة «النصيحة» التي وقعها أكثر من ١٠٠ شخصية دينية، طالبوا الملك فهد فيها بإصلاحات «عميقة في النظام السياسي» .. وبمزيد من أسلمة مرافق الدولة ومؤسساتها (!!) وبالتخلص من التبعية السياسية للأمريكان، خصوم الله (!!) وبطرد قواتهم من البلاد .. وهي القوات التي رحلت عن عن من أوروبا – بعد سقوط الاتحاد

السوفيتي – وجاءت الى الخليج، ربما لتبقى نفس المدة التي بقيت فيها في أوروبا .. حوالى ٤٠ سنة
-سقوط الاتحاد السوفيتي – وجاءت الى الخليج، ربما لتبقى نفس المدة التي بقيت فيها في أوروبا ..
حوالى ٤٠ سنة.

Practical 12.2 Theme and rheme, mainness and subordination, coordination: وكأن القدر

Assignment

(i) Discuss the strategic decisions that you must take before starting detailed translation of the following text, and outline and justify the strategy you adopt.

(ii) Translate the text into English, paying particular attention to theme and rheme, mainness and subordination and coordination in the ST. The translation of this TT is to form part of a translation of several short stories by الطيب صالح for publication in a specialist 'African writers' series.

(iii) Explain the decisions of detail you made in producing your translation.

Contextual information

This extract is taken from a short story by the Sudanese writer الطيب صالح titled نخلة على الجدول (Montgomery 1994: 12–13/68–69). This section concerns a farmer, Sheikh Mahjoub, and his family. Sheikh Mahjoub is going through difficult times. His son Hassan left for Egypt from Sudan five years before this scene and has not been heard of since, and now Sheikh Mahjoub's farm seems to be failing. The word أبرَق (f. برَقاء) means 'piebald'. This is the form used in Sudanese Arabic; the more normal Standard Arabic form is أبْلَق. Note that the reader is already aware at this stage that Sheikh Mahjoub's entire flock has died. This text, however, involves the first mention of the death of the piebald ewe.

ST

وكأن القدر أراد أن ينسيهم كل شيء يربطهم بحسن، فرمى ما آخر ما في جعبته من سهام قاسية مسمومة
ظل يسددها منذ عامين، تباعاً وبدون توقف. وأصاب السهم الأخير النعجة «البرقاء» التي رباها حسن،
وجمع لها الحشيش وأشركها طعامه وأنامها في فراشه. ماتت وما عادت تثغو في بكرة الصباح حين
كان حسن يقفز نشيطاً خفيفاً من فراشه فيطعمها ويسقيها ويأخذها معه الى الساقية، ترعى وتمرح
وتتلف الزرع ريثما يفرغ هو من عمله. ماتت، وكذلك اجتاح المحل والقحط كل القطيع الذي رباه
شيخ محجوب.

Practical 12.3 Theme and rheme, mainness and subordination, coordination: حذرت تركيا من المضي قدما

Assignment

(i) Discuss the strategic decisions that you must take before starting detailed translation of the following text, and outline and justify the strategy you

adopt. You are to translate the text for the English version of the Al-Jazeera online news service.

(ii) Translate the text into English, paying particular attention to theme and rheme, mainness and subordination and coordination in the ST.

Contextual information

This text appeared on the Arabic Al-Jazeera website on 18 May 2010, following an agreement between Turkey and Iran that Turkey should enrich Iranian uranium in an attempt to solve the dispute between Iran and the West over Iran's uranium enrichment programme. Iran maintained that the purposes of the programme were peaceful, but the United States and some other Western countries claimed that Iran was attempting to develop a nuclear bomb and had imposed sanctions on Iran as a result.

ST

حذرت تركيا من المضي قدما في فرض عقوبات إضافية على إيران بعد الاتفاق الذي تم التوصل إليه بشأن مبادلة وقود نووي باليورانيوم الإيراني، في حين أظهرت الدول الغربية شكوكاً بشأن الاتفاق واعتبرت الولايات المتحدة أن احتمال فرض العقوبات ما زال قائما.

وقال وزير الخارجية التركي احمد داود أوغلو إن بلاده ستنسحب من الاتفاق في حال فرض عقوبات على إيران، معتبرا أن هذا الاتفاق يمثل أهم خطوة على طريق الحل السلمي لأزمة البرنامج النووي لإيران. وأكد أوغلو أن من حق إيران الحصول على التقنية النووية وفقًا للقوانين الدولية، لكنه طالبها في الوقت نفسه بسعي لكسب ثقة العالم والحديث مع الغرب بخطاب معتدل.

ويقضي الاتفاق الذي تم التوصل له أمس بين كل من إيران وتركيا والبرازيل بأن ترسل طهران الجزء الأكبر من اليورانيوم منخفض التخصيب إلى تركيا لتبادل به يورانيوم مخصبا إلى مستويات ملائمة للاستخدام في مفاعل خاص بالأبحاث الطبية في طهران.

13 Discourse and intertextual issues

13.1 Introduction

In the last chapter, we briefly discussed a grammatical rearrangement of the two lines from 'To Autumn':

> Autumn is a season of mists and mellow fruitfulness.
> It is a close bosom-friend of the maturing sun.

We saw that, on the sentential level, this arrangement marks the text as informative rather than as an expression of excitement. Now, part of this sentential effect derives from the pronoun 'It', which explicitly links the second sentence to the first as conveying additional information about autumn. Such linking of one sentence to another is the most significant feature found on the discourse level. (Note that the word 'discourse' has multiple meanings both within linguistics and beyond; for a discussion, see Coupland and Jaworski 2001: 134–148. In this book, we are using 'discourse' in only the specific sense of a level of language organization beyond that of the sentence.)

13.2 The discourse level

The textual variables considered on the discourse level are those that distinguish a **cohesive** and coherent textual flow from a random sequence of unrelated utterances. Strictly speaking, this level is concerned with intersentential relations (relations between sentences) and with relations between larger units, such as paragraphs, stanzas, chapters and so on. For our purposes, however, it is sometimes useful also to consider relations between *parts of* sentences on the discourse level (and particularly clauses), as if the parts were sentences in their own right. This is particularly important with respect to Arabic; as we have already seen (Section 12.2.1), Arabic sentences are often extremely long, and the lack of consistent punctuation in much modern Arabic writing (as well as its total lack in classical writing) also often makes it impossible to determine unambiguously where one sentence ends in Arabic and another begins. (For a very useful discussion of these and other issues relating to cohesion and translation, see Baker 2011: 190–239.)

Next, we shall consider some examples involving relations between parts of sentences rather than whole sentences. However, our main focus will be on intersentential issues, because these are what most clearly illustrate translation issues on the discourse level.

There is necessarily some overlap between the subject matter of Chapter 12 and the subject matter of this chapter. In practical terms, this does not matter. The crucial issue from the point of view of translation analysis is not that one assigns a particular feature to one of the two levels but rather that the overall theoretical framework allows for the feature in question to be dealt with somewhere.

13.2.1 *Cohesion and coherence*

It is useful to distinguish between two aspects of discourse: cohesion and coherence. Following Halliday and Hasan (1976), we define cohesion as the transparent linking of sentences (and larger sections of text) by explicit discourse connectives such as 'then', 'so', 'however' and so on. These act as signposts pointing out the thread of discourse running through the text. Additionally, features such as root repetition and lexical item repetition may have a cohesive function (as discussed in Section 10.2.3.2, 10.2.4.1), as may theme–rheme elements and main–subordinate elements (Chapter 12).

Coherence is a more difficult matter than cohesion, because, by definition, it is not explicitly marked in a text: it is a tacit, but discernible, thematic or emotional development running through the text. Consequently, all cohesive texts are coherent, but not all coherent texts are cohesive. We can illustrate the difference with a simple example:

> I was getting hungry. I went downstairs. I knew the kitchen was on the ground floor. I was pretty sure the kitchen must be on the ground floor. I didn't expect to find the kitchen so easily. I made myself a sandwich.

> I was getting hungry. *So* I went downstairs. *Well* . . . I knew the kitchen was on the ground floor. *I mean*, I was pretty sure *it* must be *there*. *Still*, I didn't expect to find *it* so easily. *Anyway*, I made myself a sandwich.

The first text is devoid of intersentential connectives. It is, however, coherent, thanks to the underlying chronological narrative structure. In the second text, a train of thought is restored by inserting connectives (shown in italics). These act as cohesion markers, setting up a transparent intersentential structure. Some of the cohesion markers link the sentences by explaining or commenting on the speaker's actions: 'So', 'I mean', 'Still', 'Anyway'. Others are instances of **grammatical anaphora** – that is, the replacement of previously used words and phrases by expressions referring back to them; here, the anaphoric elements are 'it' (replacing 'the kitchen') and 'there' (replacing 'on the ground floor').

As this example suggests, the sentential and discourse levels are by definition closely related. Many of the intersentential connectives also function on the sentential level; rather like sentence tags, they give each utterance a particular tone and tell the listener how to take it – 'So', 'Well', 'I mean', 'Still', 'Anyway'. Compare, for example, the two versions of the second sentence: 'I went downstairs' versus 'So I went downstairs'. These will almost certainly be spoken differently, because on the sentential level they have different functions: the first announces a new fact out of the blue, while in the second, 'So' marks the sentence as expressing a response to a situation. 'So' therefore has both a sentential and an intersentential function here.

Furthermore, many connectives can be used to join short sentences together to make longer ones. Conjunctions such as 'so', 'and' or 'but' are simple examples. This is another way in which intersentential and sentential functions are often close in practice, even though they are distinguishable in analysis. For instance, 'I was getting hungry, so I went downstairs' will likely have a different communicative impact from 'I was getting hungry. So I went downstairs'.

Similarly, rhetorical anaphora – that is, the repetition of a word or words in successive or closely associated clauses or phrases for a rhetorical purpose – can have a discourse function, even where it occurs within a single sentence. In the case of English, such lexical repetition normally has a rhetorical purpose. However, as we saw in Chapter 10, repetition of words, phrases and even roots in Arabic may have two other functions: (i) it may allow the writer to talk about closely related ideas, serving in this case much the same purpose as lexical variation does in English; (ii) it may serve a cohesive 'text-building' function in much the same way as connectives do. However, just like English, Arabic also uses lexical repetition for rhetorical purposes, the most obvious such purpose being to achieve a sense of emotional force.

Just as repetition is denser in Arabic than in English in non-rhetorical contexts, so we should expect it also to be denser in contexts where it is used for purposes of rhetorical anaphora. In this light, consider the following from a speech by جمال عبد الناصر titled كفاحنا للقومية العربية (Dickson 1999: 10–11). The full written text of this speech is available online at http://nasser.bibalex.org/Speeches/browser.aspx?SID=534. To listen to the recording, click on استمع لهذا الجزء in the top left-hand corner; the relevant section of the speech begins at 3 minutes, 17 seconds (3:17) and ends at 3 minutes, 52 seconds (3:52).

> إن القومية العربية ليست جمال عبد الناصر، وليست شكري القوتلي .. وليست زعيما من الزعماء، ولكنها أقوى من هذا كله، إنها أنتم أيها الشعب العربي .. أنتم أيها الإخوة .. أنتم أفراد لم التق بكم قبل اليوم لكني أرى في في كل عين من عيونكم .. أرى القومية العربية تنطلق وأرى الإيمان بالقومية العربية عميقاً، أرى هذا وأرى ان كل فرد منكم يؤمن بكل هذا إيمانا عميقا ..

In the following analysis of this text, we have placed items involving lexical repetition in curly brackets with superscript numbers to identify the different elements and their different occasions of use. (Thus [1] refers to إنَّ; [1.1] meaning that this is the first occurrence of إنَّ in this text, [1.2] means that this is the second occurrence of إنَّ in the text.)

> {[1.1]إن} {[2.1]القومية} {[3.1]العربية} {[4.1]ليست} جمال عبد الناصر، و{[4.2]ليست} شكري القوتلي .. و{[4.3]ليست} {[5.1]زعيما} من {[5.2]الزعماء}، ولكنها أقوى من هذا {[6.1]كله}، {[1.2]إنها}، {[7.1]أنتم} {[7.1]ايها}

الشعب {العربي^{3.2}} .. انتم {ايها^{7.2}} الاخوة .. انتم {أفراد^{8.1}} لم التق بكم قبل اليوم ولكني {أرى^{9.1}} في {كل^{6.2}} {عين^{10.1}} من {عيونكم^{10.2}} .. {أرى^{9.2}} {القومية^{2.2}} {العربية^{3.3}} تنطلق و {أرى^{9.3}} {الإيمان^{11.1}} بـ{القومية^{2.3}} {العربية^{3.4}} {عميقا^{12.1}}، {أرى^{9.4}} هذا و{أرى^{9.5}} ان {كل^{6.3}} {فرد^{8.2}} منكم يؤمن بـ{كل^{6.4}} هذا {ايمانا^{11.2}} {عميقاً^{12.2}} ..

The following is an attempt at an idiomatic translation:

> Arab nationalism is not Gamal Abd al-Nasser, it is not Shukri al-Quwatli, it is not any particular leader. It is stronger than all of this. It is you my friends, the Arab people. Before today, I had not even met you. However, in all your eyes I see the spirit of nationalism rising up, I see a deep belief in it. I see this; I see that every one of you is profoundly convinced.

The patterns of lexical item repetition in the Arabic ST and English TT compare as follows:

ST		TT
1	إنَّ: 2 occurrences	no correspondence: 0 occurrences
2	قومية: 3 occurrences	'nationalism': 2 occurrences
3	عربي: 4 occurrences	'Arab': 2 occurrences
4	ليست: 3 occurrences	'is not': 3 occurrences
5	زعيم/زعماء: 2 occurrences	['leader': 1 occurrence]
6	كل: 4 occurrences	'all': 2 occurrences [cf. also TT: 'every one': 1 occurrence]
7	أيها: 2 occurrences	no correspondence: 0 occurrences
8	فرد/أفراد: 2 occurrences	no correspondence: 0 occurrences [But cf. TT: 'every one']
9	أرى: 5 occurrences	'see': 4 occurrences
10	عين/عيون: 2 occurrences	['eyes': 1 occurrence]
11	إيمان: 2 occurrences	['belief': 1 occurrence; cf. root repetition with يؤمن] ['convinced': 1 occurrence]
12	عميق: 2 occurrences	['deep': 1 occurrence; 'profoundly': 1 occurrence]

These repetition patterns show that there are thirty-three instances of lexical repetition in the ST and thirteen in the TT. We included the English TT phrase 'is not' as a lexical item, as it corresponds to the Arabic lexical item ليست. It is worth spending time in class comparing repetition of two other sorts of features: phrase repetition and repetition of pronouns/possessive adjectives.

While lexical repetition is the most commonly used form of rhetorical anaphora in Arabic, as in the previous text, it is also possible to find root repetition used for rhetorical purposes. An example is the following, attributed to ابن خلدون, who is sometimes regarded as the founder of sociology:

المغلوب مولع بالاقتداء بالغالب

This has been translated (Stabler 1999: 17) as:

> the vanquished are always obsessed with imitating the vanquisher

Here, the translation reproduces something of the repetition of the ST, with its use of 'vanquished' and 'vanquisher'. This use of root repetition for rhetorical purposes is similar to rhetorical anaphora involving lexical items. It relies on the fact that not only is the root repeated, but the lexical items involved (in this case, مغلوب and غالب) have closely related meanings (here, they are antonyms).

Another area in which Arabic and English differ is in their use of discourse connectives. In many genres, Arabic sentences are typically longer than English sentences, and sentences and clauses in Arabic are typically connected either by one of the three basic connectives, و, ف, and ثم, or by the use of one of the simple secondary connectives, such as حيث, إذ, etc.

Particularly in Classical Arabic, و and ف are extremely common, as illustrated by the following extract from the المقدمة by ابن خلدون (example adapted from Holes 1995: 220):

{و}السبب في ذلك أنه قد عُرف {و}ثبت أن الواحد من البشر غير مستقل بتحصيل حاجاته في معاشه، {و}أنهم متعاونون جميعا في عمرانهم على ذلك، {و}الحاجة التي تحصل بتعاون طائفة منهم تشتد ضرورة الأكثر من عددهم أضعافا، {فـ}القوت من الحنطة مثلا لا يستقل الواحد بتحصيل حصته منه، {و}اذا انتدب لتحصيله الستة أو العشرة من حداد ونجار للآلات وقائم على البقر وإثارة الارض وحصاد السنبل وسائر مؤن الفلح، {و}توزعوا على تلك الاعمال أو اجتمعوا {و}حصل بعملهم ذلك مقدار من القوت، {فـ}إنه حينئذ قوت لاضعافهم مرات، {فـ}لاعمال بعد الاجتماع زائدة على حاجات العاملين وضروراتهم.

A published English translation of this by Franz Rosenthal (Ibn Khaldûn [1958] 1967]: vol. II, 271–272) reads as follows (we have placed relevant English connectives in curly brackets together with their ST equivalents):

> {Øو} The reason for this is that, as is well known {andو} well established, the individual human being cannot by himself obtain all the necessities of life. {Øو} All human beings must co-operate to that end in their civilization. {Butو} what is obtained through the co-operation of a group of human beings satisfies the need of a number many times greater (than themselves). {For instance ف}, no one, by himself, can obtain the share of the wheat he needs for food. {But و} when six or ten persons, including a smith and a carpenter to make the tools, and others who are in charge of the oxen, the plowing of the soil, the harvesting of the ripe grain, and all the other agricultural activities, {Øو} undertake to obtain their food {and} work toward that purpose either separately or collectively {and و} thus obtain through their labour a certain amount of food, {Ø ف} (that amount) will be food for a number of people many times their own. {Ø ف} The combined labour produces more than the needs and necessities of the workers.

Here, the ST makes use of connective و seven times and connective ف three times. The English omits any connective five times (omission being marked by Ø in the TT); these omissions correspond three times to ST و and twice to ST ف. و is translated twice by 'and' and twice by 'but'. ف is translated once by 'For example'.

A striking feature of this passage is the concessive use of و, which is translated twice by 'but' in the published English translation. Even in modern Arabic و, fairly frequently, and ف, rather less often, are best translated by a concessive. The following are two examples, with the relevant connectives placed in curly brackets in the Arabic original and English translation:

وفي نهاية الحوار غادرها {و}ظل يلوح اليها الى ان غاب عن المنطقة.

This has been translated (Brown 1996: 55) as:

After he had finished he left her, {although} he kept on waving until the grave was out of sight.

A second example is:

كان من المفترض أن تحدث الولادة في الربيع، {فـ}حدثت في الصيف ..

This might be translated (cf. Rolph 1995: 12) as:

The birth was supposed to take place in the spring, {but} it took place in the summer.

In some types of modern Arabic writing, the system of connectives is rather different from the Classical Arabic norm. Consider the following from a modern Arabic text on housing economics (from Holes 1995: 221). We have placed connectives in curly brackets.

{وعلاوة على ذلك فإن} صعوبات التخزين للمواد البنائية المصنعة تعتبر من الخصائص التي تنفرد فيها عن غيرها من المفردات الصناعية الأخرى. {ونظرا لـ}ما تتميز به منتجات هذه المواد من كبر الحجم {فإن} تكاليف التخزين لا بد من أن تكون باهظة، {كما أن} المستودعات سوف تضيق ذرعا بها {على الرغم من} توفر المساحات الواسعة لها. {وبناءً عليه فإن} السياسات الانتاجية السليمة هي التي تقوم بتصريف المنتجات أولاً باول {لكي} تتجنب مشاكل تجميد رؤوس الأموال المستثمرة فيها، {وأن} تغاير من سياساتها وفقاً للإنتاج الطلبي الذي يتم معرفته مسبقاً.

This might be translated as follows (we have placed the English connectives in curly brackets together with their ST equivalents):

{In addition وعلاوة على ذلك فإن}, the storing of ready-made building materials presents unique difficulties as compared with other manufactured units. {In view of ونظرا لـ} the large amounts of space taken up, {Ø فإن} storage costs are huge, {and أن كما} warehouses cannot cope, {despite على الرغم من} their relatively large size. {Accordingly وبناءً عليه فإن}, production policies need to be based on the selling of products as soon they are produced {in order to لكي} avoid the problem of tying up invested capital, {and وأن} to allow for production policy to be changed according to assessments of future consumer demand.

This text is typical of academic-oriented empirical writing in modern Arabic. The connectives used in modern Arabic academic-oriented writing are much more similar to those used in modern English argumentative writing than are the connectives used in comparable Classical Arabic writing. However, there are types of writing in modern Arabic in which the uses of connectives are typically rather different from those of English. A good example is written fictional narrative.

In English, unplanned narratives (storytelling) often make heavy use of 'and', as in the following example of a story spontaneously composed by a small child on the basis of a previous telling by an adult (from Hasan 1983: 189):

> There was once a little girl and a little boy and a dog. And the sailor was their daddy. And the little doggy was white. And they liked the little doggy. And they stroked it, and they fed it. And he ran away. And then the daddy had to go on a ship. And the children missed 'em. And they began to cry.

This kind of textual structure is quite easy to produce. All clauses are presented as fairly important (foregrounded) and therefore available for the future development of the text.

Unlike unplanned narratives, planned narratives in English, and particularly the narratives of written fiction, tend to make much greater use of subordination. In Arabic, by contrast, coordination is a typical feature of written fictional narratives as well as unplanned material (cf. also Section 12.2.5). In translating written fictional narrative material, therefore, it is often stylistically appropriate to convert coordinate structures in Arabic into subordinate structures in English. Consider the following from حقل البنفسج by زكريا تامر:

وتفاقمت أحزانه، وبدأت تسحقه ببطء وتشف، فنصحه صديق له بالذهاب الى ساحر [. . .]

This is translated (St John 1999: 6) as:

> As he became more and more depressed, slowly and thirstily she began to crush him until one of his friends urged him to go to a sorcerer [. . .]

Here, the Arabic has a series of coordinated clauses (beginning with وبدأت, وتفاقمت and فنصحه). The English reorganizes these around a single main clause (beginning 'slowly and thirstily'), with an initial subordinate clause (beginning 'As he became') and a final subordinate clause (beginning 'until one of his friends'). In this case, the change of subordination structure is partly to give the appropriate meaning in the English TT but also to produce a style that is generally acceptable in English.

In most modern Arab fiction, intersentential coordination – the use of و and ف in particular between sentences, as well as within sentences – is very common. It is worth noting, however, that several modern Arab novelists, as well as writers in other genres, use a rather English (and probably English-influenced) style where there are relatively few connectives between sentences or between major elements within sentences. A good example is the following extract from the novel الفيل الأزرق by أحمد مراد (2012: ٣٥), the opening few lines of which are reproduced here with Ø (zero) added at points where there is no coordinator but one might be expected:

تنبّهت حَواسي دفعة وَاحدة، Ø كنت رَاقداً على ظهري غارقاً في عَرقي حين استشعرت اللّهاث، Ø فتحت جفنيّ أسترق نظرة فوجدته عند باب الغُرفة واقفاً! كَلباً أسود فاحماً يَلهث كأنه رَكض شَهراً شَعره مُبعثر ولِسانه لَون الكَبد يقطر زَبَداً، Ø يحدق فيّ غَضَباً بعَينين مَحجريهما دم، Ø زمجر فارتفعت شَفته العُليا لتكشف عَن صفين من الحِراب المُدببة ونيّة في الانقِضاض، Øانتفضت هلعاً، Ø انتصب شعري وتعرقّت مَسامي، حاولت أن أثب أو أحتمي بشيء

The following is an attempted idiomatic translation, with Ø added wherever the Arabic ST has a zero:

> I came to my senses all at once. Ø I was lying on my back, drenched in sweat when I noticed the panting. Ø I opened my eyes to steal a glance, and saw it standing by the door. A jet black dog panting as if it had been running for a month, its fur scattered, and its tongue liver-red and dripping saliva. Ø It was staring at me angrily with bloodshot eyes. Ø It growled, curling up its lip to reveal two rows of sharpened spears and an intention to pounce. Ø I jumped up in fright, my hairs stood on end, and my pores began to sweat. Ø I tried to jump back or to seek shelter behind something.

The non-use of intersentential connectives in the TT here corresponds exactly to that of the ST, underlining how similar to English the non-use of connectives is in the ST.

Regardless of generic considerations, in many cases, Arabic connectives simply 'disappear' in the English TT or correspond to features of punctuation: حيث and إذ, for example, quite commonly signal the specific substantiation of a previous general claim and can be omitted in English or replaced by a semicolon, colon or dash. An example with حيث (from Dickins and Watson 1999: 312) is the following:

كانت محافظات الصعيد الثلاث [. . .] قد تحولت الى نيران مشتعلة، حيث تم احراق كنيسة وجامع [..]

This might be translated as:

> [. . .] the three provinces of Upper Egypt [. . .] had been transformed into a raging inferno: a church and a mosque had been burnt down.

For further discussion of إذا and حيث, see Dickins and Watson (1999: 309–315).

Other discourse markers that are often encountered in Arabic are إنَّ, and قد (with the perfect). These have specific functions in Arabic, some of which we encounter in this course (cf. also Dickins and Watson 1999: 419–428, 448–460; Dickins 2010b). They do not, however, normally have translation implications; that is to say, the very real subtleties of meaning that these discourse particles introduce into the Arabic ST do not need to be – and, normally at least, cannot be – reproduced in the English TT. A translator from Arabic to English, therefore, only occasionally needs to worry about إنَّ and قد.

A slightly more complicated case is presented by أما . . . . فـ . . . (e.g. أما هذا الرجل (فمشهور في مصر) (cf. Dickins and Watson 1999: 482–489). أما . . . . فـ . . . is sometimes glossed in Arabic>English dictionaries as meaning 'as for' (e.g. 'As for this man, he is famous in Egypt'). In fact, it relatively rarely translates idiomatically as 'as for'. Sometimes, like إنَّ and قد, it is best omitted from the English translation. Elsewhere, it will have quite different idiomatic translations, such as 'however', 'on the other hand', etc., as the three following examples show (relevant elements in the TT are placed in curly brackets).

The first is example is taken from the novel مدينة البغي by عيسى بشارة:

كانت اغصان الزيتون والنخيل قد يبست، اما الشجيرة البرية فكانت ما تزال تقاوم الموت.

This has been translated (Brown 1996: 55) as:

> The olive and palm branches were brittle; the wild bush, {however}, was still defying death.

The second example is taken from a magazine article on religious extremism and violence in the Middle East. The previous paragraph dealt with religious-oriented violence in Israel. The article also previously discussed an explosion in Saudi Arabia, to which the text now returns. This extract is from the beginning of a new paragraph:

أما حادث الانفجار في السعودية فيكشف عن ناحية أخرى [. . .]

This has been translated (Hetherington 1996: 26) as follows:

> {On the other hand}, an examination of the explosion in Saudi Arabia reveals a different aspect of the problem.

The third example is from an account of the British general election of 1997. Again, this is from a new paragraph in which the problems of the Labour Party in the 1980s are being contrasted with the success of the Conservatives under Margaret Thatcher:

أما حزب العمال فقد عانى من الانقسامات الداخلية

This has been translated (Conduit 1998: 21) as:

> The Labour Party, {meanwhile}, was riven by internal splits.

Languages also differ in their use of punctuation as a cohesion marker. It should be remembered that Arabic traditionally made no use of punctuation, and that even now punctuation is often used in Arabic in ways that seem rather arbitrary. Even the use of basic punctuation markers, such as full stops, can be highly idiosyncratic, particularly in literary writing.

13.2.1.1   *Sentence splitting*

Because sentences in Arabic tend to be longer than sentences in English, it is not infrequently necessary to split up one Arabic sentence into several English ones. The following is a good example:

فهذا أمر يحدث في أكثر من مكان، وقد رأينا صراعات من هذا النوع في هذه الدولة أو تلك، بل رأينا الحماقات التي يخلقها الشعور الديني المتعصب أو العرقي العنصري، ولكننا لم نشهد على الاطلاق هذا القدر من الشر والعنف الذي رأيناه في البوسنة والهرسك، ونشهده اليوم أضعافا مضاعفة في كوسوفو التي يسكنها تسعون في المائة من المسلمين ومن حقهم الطبيعي ان يطلبوا شيئا من الاستقلال الذاتي، وقد كان يهمهم هذا الاستقلال من قبل، ثم وافقوا على نوع متواضع من الحكم الذاتي في محادثات رامبوييه.

This could be translated (cf. Ives 1999: 12) as follows:

> Unfortunately such concerns are not unique to Kosovo though. We have seen struggles such as this in various countries, and have witnessed similar scenes of madness caused by religious fanaticism or extreme nationalism, but never on the scale which we saw in Bosnia. And yet, now we see it again, with redoubled force in Kosovo, whose population comprises some 90% Muslims, and whose natural right it is to demand some form of self-government. The Bosnians previously raised the issue of independence in the past, but eventually accepted a modest form of self-government at the Rambouillet talks.

Here, a single Arabic sentence is relayed by four English sentences.

13.2.1.2   *Textual restructuring*

Rather more tricky than sentence splitting is textual restructuring – that is, the reorganizing of chunks of textual material in the TT in order to make them read more cogently. Sentence splitting may be regarded as oriented towards cohesion in that it concerns the ways in which texts, in different languages, adopt different ways of linking material together. Textual restructuring, by contrast, is more oriented towards coherence; it concerns the ways in which languages typically organize their ideas differently from one another. Consider the following:

لقد اعتبرت السعودية الافكار القومية، والديمقراطية، والاشتراكية، والليبرالية افكارا مستوردة .. رجسا
من اعمال الشيطان .. فحاربتها ودعمت خصومها ووصفتها بالكفر [. . .]

This could be translated (cf. Hetherington 1996: 31) as:

> The Saudi state regarded nationalism, democracy, socialism and liberalism as imported ideas and thus evil works of Satan. It characterized them as godless ideologies, and fought against them by funding their opponents.

A more literal translation – for example, 'It fought against them, supported their opponents, and characterized them as godless ideologies' – seems odd in English, principally because it begins with the practical actions taken by the Saudis ('fought against them', 'supported their opponents') and then goes on to give the reason for these actions ('characterized them as godless ideologies'). It thus runs directly counter to the normal tendency in English, which is to start by describing principles (in this case, 'characterized them as godless ideologies') and then go on to describe the practical consequences of these principles ('fought against them by funding their opponents'). This is the order of the restructured TT. The restructured TT also reorganizes ودعمت خصومها حاربتها (literally, 'fought against them and supported their opponents') into the composite phrase 'fought against them by supporting their opponents', which provides what seems from the English point of view necessary substantiation of the claim that Saudi Arabia fought against nationalism, etc. It is important to stress that the fact that the TT reorganizes this material does not mean that the Arabic ST is illogical; from the Arabic point of view, it might be argued that the ST clause فحاربتها ودعمت خصومها ووصفتها بالكفر has cogency because it represents a build-up of increasingly strong responses – that is, Saudi Arabia not only fought these ideologies on its own behalf, it also went beyond this to actively support its opponents. Finally, and most strongly from an Islamic point of view, it characterized them as godless.

This kind of textual structuring is distinct from the kind of restructuring we saw at various points in Chapter 12 in that it is not a function of theme–rheme or main–subordinate considerations. Of course, in some cases, the kind of considerations we have looked at in this section may interact with other theme–rheme or main–subordinate considerations to produce changes in textual organization.

13.2.1.3　*Paragraphing*

Like punctuation, paragraphing can pose problems in Arabic>English translation. In English, there are some generic considerations involved in paragraphing; news reports tend to have very short paragraphs, sometimes only a single sentence; academic writing often makes use of extremely long paragraphs. However, in general, we may say that paragraphs typically cover a particular scene or episode within the overall set of scenes or episodes covered by the larger global text. In some cases, paragraphs begin with a so-called topic sentence – that is, a sentence that states the general topic of the paragraph. Thus, a publisher's blurb on the back cover of a book titled *The Sounds of the World's Languages* begins 'This book gives a description of all the known ways in which the sounds of the world's languages differ'.

In Arabic, similar conventions for paragraphing to those of English are followed by many writers. However, not infrequently, one comes across paragraphing in Arabic that clearly does not follow English-type conventions. Under such circumstances, the translator will normally expect to reparagraph the TT according to the conventions of English.

13.3   The intertextual level

We have just suggested that in order to determine the function of a textual variable on the discourse level, the translator must know whether it simply reflects SL conventions or whether it departs from them. But, of course, this is true of textual variables on any level. No text, and no part of any text, exists in total isolation from others. Even the most innovative of texts and turns of phrase form part of a whole body of speaking and writing by which their originality or unoriginality is measured. We shall give the term 'intertextual level' to the level of textual variables on which texts are viewed as bearing significant external relations to other texts in a given culture or cultures.

13.3.1   Genre membership

There are two main sorts of intertextual relations that particularly concern translators. The most common is that of genre membership (discussed in Chapter 6). As noted there, a traditional genre in the SL culture may not correspond precisely to a traditional genre in the TL culture. Even where there is a general generic correspondence, a play, for example, will or will not be typical of a certain sort of play in the SL culture; an instruction manual will or will not be typical of a certain sort of instruction manual and so on. Before translating an ST, then, the translator must judge how typical it is of its genre. If it is utterly typical of an established ST genre, it may be necessary to produce a similarly typical TT. This will be relatively straightforward in the case of, say, computer manuals. It can prove tricky where there is no TL genre corresponding to that of the ST.

A good example of a genre that is traditional in Arabic but that has no real correspondent in the English-speaking world is the مقامة. This form of writing was written in سجع, a term that is sometimes translated into English as 'rhymed prose' and that involved not only the standard monorhyme of Arabic poetry but also morphological repetition (Section 10.2.3) and other aspects of parallelism (Chapter 11) (cf. Hourani 1991: 52–53; Irwin 1999: 178–193).

The following text is from the start of المقامة الدمشقية by القاسم بن علي الحريري. Al-Hariri (1054–1122) was one of the best-known writers of مقامات. The TT is from Nicholson (1987: 119).

المقامة الدمشقية

حَكَى الْحَارِثُ بنُ هَمَّام قَالَ : شَخَصْتُ مِنَ العِرَاقِ إلى الغُوطَةِ . وَأَنَا ذُو جُرْدٍ مَرْبُوطَةٍ . وَجِدَةٍ مَغْبُوطَةٍ . يُلْهِينِي خُلُّ الذَّرْعِ . وَيَزْدَهِينِي حُفُولُ الضَّرْعِ . فَلَمَّا بَلَغْتُهَا بَعْدَ شِقِّ النَّفْسِ . وَإِنْضَاءِ العَنْسِ . أَلْفَيْتُهَا كَمَا تَصِفُهَا الأَلْسُنُ . وَفِيهَا مَا تَشْتَهِي الأَنْفُسُ وَتَلَذُّ الأَعْيُنُ . فَشَكَرْتُ يَدَ النَّوَى . وَجَرَيْتُ طَلَقًا مَعَ الهَوَى . وَطَفِقْتُ أَفُضُّ فِيهَا خُتُومَ الشَّهَوَاتِ . وَأَجْتَنِي قُطُوفَ اللَّذَّاتِ . إلى أَنْ شَرَعَ سَفَرٌ فِي الإِعْرَاقِ . وَقَدِ اسْتَفَقْتُ مِنَ الإِغْرَاقِ . فَعَادَنِي عِيدٌ مِنْ تَذْكَارِ الوَطَنِ . وَالحَنِينِ إلى العَطَنِ . فَقَوَّضْتُ خِيَامَ الغَيْبَةِ . وَأَسْرَجْتُ جَوَادَ الأَوْبَةِ .

The Makáma of Damascus

Al-Hárith son of Hammám related:

I went from 'Irák to Damascus with its green water-courses, in the day when I had troops of fine-bred horses and was the owner of coveted wealth and resources, free to divert myself, as I chose, and flown with the pride of him whose fullness overflows. When I reached the city after toil and teen on a camel travel-lean, I found it to be all that tongues recite and to contain soul's desire and eye's delight. So I thanked my journey and entered Pleasure's tourney and began there to break the seals of appetites that cloy and cull the clusters of joy, until a caravan for 'Irák was making ready – and by then my wild humour had become steady, so that I remembered my home and was not consoled, but pined for my fold – wherefore I struck the tents of absence and yearning and saddled the steed of returning.

The translator has chosen here to produce a TT that mirrors both the rhyme and the rhythm, and even the graphic presentation of the ST, reflecting the central importance of these features for the ST genre. As noted in Section 6.2, Irwin points out,

> There is nothing very like the *maqamat* genre in Western literature. The individual *maqamas* should not be read as short stories, as they are insufficiently and inconsistently plotted. Language and the display of language skills take precedence over story-telling in each of the episodes.
>
> (Irwin 1999: 179)

Given this, there is little choice for the translator but to convey at least some of the verbal art of the ST in his or her TT.

Readers will likely agree that Nicholson's translation of المقامة الدمشقية is something of a technical feat. Given the clear lack of correspondence of the TT to any established English genre, however, the TT is also clearly exotic. How highly readers rate this TT will depend at least in part on the extent to which they find it acceptable to reproduce an ST genre in a TT, where the TL has no such established genre.

The مقامة genre itself has effectively disappeared in modern Arabic, as has سجع in its pure form (cf. Beeston 1970: 113). It is, however, possible to find سجع-like material in modern literature, and even in some non-literary texts (cf. Dickins and Watson 1999: 548–549). An example that we saw in Section 9.1.1 was the following from the novel مدينة البغي by the Palestinian writer عيسى بشارة:

ولم يكن بوسعه أن يطغي نار العين بالإغضاء أو يخفي تكشيرة الناب بالإصغاء [. . .]

This has been translated (Brown 1996: 13) as:

It was not in his power to smother the fire in his heart with indifference or, by listening, to disguise his grimace.

As noted in Section 9.1.1, the translator chose here, with good reason, not to translate the Arabic rhyme into an English rhyme. There are occasions, however, where سجع-like material is acceptably translated into English rhyme. Consider the following from the historical novel أسد بابل by نواف حردان, which deals with the fall of Babylon in the sixth century BC. The novel adopts a somewhat archaic style in parts. This extract is from an initial introductory section lamenting the fall of Babylon:

كيف سقطت المدينة العظيمة الحصينة؟ ذات الأسوار المنيعة الشامخة .. والهياكل الشارخة والقصور الباذخة .. والجيوش الجرارة والبطولات الكرارة.

This has been translated (Morrey 2000: 8–10) as follows:

How could she fall, the Great Invulnerable City? With walls impregnably towering, temples divinely flowering, palaces proudly glowering, with armies vast and ferociously grave, heroes cunning and valiantly brave.

Much of the rhyme, parallelism and repetition of the Arabic ST is preserved in the English TT. However, this is only acceptable because of the archaic nature of the material and because the translator has chosen to translate this material in an archaizing manner reminiscent of the kind of rhyming used particularly in pre-modern plays. That is to say, although the ST is from a modern novel, the translator managed to find a TL generic model from outside the typical form of the modern novel, which makes this translation plausible.

Even where there is a more obviously close correspondence among genres in Arabic and English, there may be significant genre-related problems in translating between the two languages. Consider the following example of English>Arabic translation from Hemingway's novella *The Old Man and the Sea* (cited by Abdulla 1994: 69; the following discussion summarizes that of Abdulla). The original reads:

He was an old man who fished alone in a skiff in the Gulf Stream and he had gone eighty-four days now without taking a fish.

Abdulla compares two translations of this, which we can designate TT (a) and TT (b):

TT (a)

كان الرجل قد بلغ من العمر عتيا، ولكنه لا يزال رابضا في زورقه يطلب الصيد في الخليج «غولف ستريم» وقد عبرت به حتى الساعة أربعة وثمانون يوما لم يجد عليه البحر خلالها بشيء من الرزق.

TT (b)

كان رجلا عجوزا يصيد السمك وحده في قارب عريض القعر في تيار الخليج، وكان قد سلخ أربعين يوما من غير أن يفوز بسمكة واحدة

Abdulla notes that TT (a), which is by Salih Jawdat, a contemporary Arab Romantic poet, uses a much more poetic style than that of the simple and direct style of Hemingway's ST. Thus, for example, Jawdat employs the term عتيا ('decrepit'), echoing Zacharia in the Quran, who asks God how he can beget a son when he has grown decrepit from old age: سورة مريم, v. 8) قَد بَلَغْتُ مِنَ الكِبَرِ عِتِيًّا). Jawdat also adds an entire clause ولكنه لا يزال رابضا في زورقه) ('but he was still crouching alone in his boat'), which provides an element of sentimental suspense by likening the old man to an animal waiting for its prey. The general and abstract nature of the final TT phrase لم يجد عليه البحر خلالها بشيء من الرزق ('The sea has not endowed him with any sustenance') contrasts strongly with Hemingway's preference for the concrete (e.g. 'fish' rather than 'sustenance'). Jawdat thus presents Hemingway, who is well known for his objective, unadorned style, as a romantic writer prone to religious allusion, abstraction and verbal redundancy.

TT (b), which was done by the well-known Arabic–English lexicographer Munir Ba'albaki, provides a decidedly less romantic version than TT (a). In place of the Quranic عتيا, TT (b) uses the Standard Arabic term عجوزا ('old'), shifting later to the somewhat more respectful near-synonym شيخ. The only other element in Ba'albaki's translation that has somewhat Classical overtones is سلخ, which gives the sense of becoming weary through the passage of time (literally, 'take the skin off the body'). The remainder of the TT is in a very plain style that comes close to the ST, even in having the same number of words (37 words).

Abdalla concludes that the generally neutral (though somewhat inconsistent) style of TT (b) is closer to Hemingway than the consistently formal style of TT (a). TT (a), however, bridges generic differences by linking to the high tradition of Arabic narrative, which is much more alive today than the corresponding formal English style that Hemingway rejected (Abdulla 1994: 69–70).

13.3.2 *Quotation and allusion*

The second category of intertextual relations is that of quotation or allusion. A text may directly quote from another text. In such cases, the translator has to decide whether to borrow the standard TL translation of the quoted text. If it is very familiar in the TL culture, then there will have to be special reasons for departing from it. This is so, for example, in the case of من بعدنا الطوفان (cf. Practical 8.3), which is a quotation from Mme de Pompadour (mistress of the French king Louis XV), 'Après nous le déluge' ('After us the flood/deluge'), which is itself an allusion to the Biblical (and Quranic) Flood/Deluge. Similarly, another short story by يوسف إدريس titled شيء يجنن contains the phrase مثل فرنسي يقول فتش عن المرأة. Given that this saying is well known in English in its French form, one would likely translate this along the lines: '"Cherchez la femme", as the French saying puts it' – with an additional shift from indefinite (مثل فرنسي) in the ST to definite ('the French say-ing') in recognition of the fact that the proverb is well known in English (but not, apparently, in Arabic).

Sometimes, an ST quotation or allusion that is full of resonances for the SL reader would be completely lost on the TL reader. For example, the introduc-tion to طارق المهدوي's book الاخوان المسلمون على مذبح المناورة, having excoriated the Egyptian Muslim Brotherhood for its fruitless political manoeuvering over the past few decades, ends with the Quranic-type phrase ولعلهم لا يدركون 'And perhaps they know not'. This would be immediately picked up by an Arab reader (even an Egyptian Copt or other non-Muslim) but would be lost on the average British or American reader.

In such cases, the translator may either leave the quotation or allusion out alto-gether or simply translate it literally, or, if it has an important function in the ST, use some form of compensation. It all depends on what exactly the function is. In the case of the phrase ولعلهم لا يدركون, the translation 'And perhaps they know not', with its archaic 'Biblical' negative ('know not'), might be adequate to suggest to the English-speaking reader that this is a religious allusion, even if it is not neces-sarily clear to him or her what the allusion is to.

Particularly where ST intertextual features are more a matter of allusion than simple quotation, translation problems can become acute. An allusion is normally something deliberate, but we often see allusions where none were intended. An accidental allusion might be more accurately called an echo. When readers or listeners respond to intertextual features of this sort, they are real factors in the meaning and have an impact on the text. We know, for example, that Keats was not alluding to the 1960's pop-singer Donovan's 'They call me mellow yellow' in 'To Autumn'. What we do not know is whether Keats was alluding to Thomson's 'roving mists' or to Wordsworth's 'mellow Autumn charged with bounteous fruit'. But, for readers who do hear these possible echoes and allusions, they are part of the richness of Keats's lines.

Finally, it is as true on the intertextual level as on all other levels that the transla-tor must be careful to avoid accidentally introducing inappropriate features. For an example of how easily this can happen, consider again the phrase في العسر واليسر والمنشط والمكره, which formed part of the oath sworn to حسن البنا, the founder and leader of the Muslim Brotherhood by members of the Brotherhood (cf. Section 10.2.3.1). Given the pattern repetition in the ST, it is tempting to mark the formu-laic, ritualized tone by repeating the preposition 'in': 'in comfort and in adversity, in suffering and in joy'. Unfortunately, this might sound like an allusion to the marriage service in the Book of Common Prayer ('for better for worse, for richer for poorer, in sickness and in health') – a quite inappropriate intertext for a text on the Muslim Brotherhood! Luckily, this can be avoided by simply not repeating the 'in': 'in comfort and adversity, suffering and joy.'

A variation on genre membership is imitation, which may shade into parody. The following from Practical 11.4 provides a small-scale example. This extract is taken from a section of a magazine article dealing with extremist politico-religious groups in the Middle East:

[. . .] وكل مجموعة يرى أتباعها أنهم أولياء الله، وجند الله، وأصفياء الله، وأصدقاء الله، والناطقون الرسميون باسم الله [. . .]

This can be translated (cf. Hetherington 1996: 20) as:

The followers of each group see themselves as the companions of God, His chosen soldiers and friends – and His official spokesmen.

Most of this Arabic extract uses language that clearly belongs to a religious register (ولي, pl. أولياء is a traditional word for an Islamic 'saint'; جند 'army' is a word with strong Classical and Islamic overtones: cf. جيش, which is the more normal term for 'army' in modern Standard Arabic). By contrast, the phrase والناطقون الرسميون باسم . . . 'the official spokesmen for . . .' belongs specifically to the language of modern politics. The juxtaposition is used here to mock the pretensions of the extremist groups that the author is attacking.

Practical 13

Practical 13.1 The discourse level: cohesive-device revision of ولكن هذه الثمار السياسية *TT*

Assignment

Consider the following Arabic text and the English translation given after it. The English translation is in general fairly idiomatic. The connectives, however, are direct translations of the Arabic connectives. Your task is to produce a fully idiomatic English translation by replacing the connectives in the version of the English translation given here with more idiomatic ones, or, in some cases, with none at all. In certain cases, you will also need to make other changes to the English text, which follow on from changes made to the connectives. Connectives in the Arabic original and in the English translation to be edited have been placed in curly brackets { . . . } in order to make them easier to identify.

Contextual information

This passage is taken from الإخوان المسلمون على مذبح المناورة 'The Muslim Brothers on the Altar of Manoeuvre' (المهدوي 1986: 15). This is a fairly short book about the history of the Muslim Brotherhood in Egypt, written by المهدوي اسماعيل طارق. The author is a communist, and as might be expected, the book is very critical of the Muslim Brotherhood. As might also be expected, it is written in a highly polemical style; it not only employs some of the particular phraseology of Marxism and communism (الجماهير 'the masses', etc.), but it also makes extensive use of traditional Arabic persuasive rhetorical devices. The general argumentative nature of the text (i.e. the fact that it argues a particular case) is reflected in the widespread use in the text of connectives expressing logical relations (حيث, رغم, إذن, لذلك, etc.), as well as the more basic connectives, such as و and ف. The TT is adapted from Calderbank (1990).

ST

{ولكن} هذه الثمار السياسية كانت مخيبة للتوقعات الجماهيرية الشديدة التفاؤل التي صاحبت ثورة ١٩١٩ {فرغم} إعلان الاستقلال عام ١٩٢٢ {فإن} القوات المسلحة البريطانية استمرت ترابط على أرض الوطن {ولا سيما} في منطقة القنال {كما أن} المعتمد البريطاني استمر هو الحاكم الفعلي للبلاد {ورغم} إعلان الدستور الديمقراطي بما صاحبه من انتخابات برلمانية حرة {فإن} القوتين السياسيتين المتنازعتين على السلطة لم تلتزما بالديمقراطية إلا بالقدر الذي يضمن المزيد من النفوذ على حساب الآخرين!! {ف} حزب الوفد الوطني ما أن يصل إلى الحكم حتى يبطش بمعارضيه من الحزب الشيوعي المصري والحزب الوطني {حتى أن} سعد زغلول أصدر في مارس ١٩٢٤ قراراً بحل الحزب الشيوعي المصري وحرمانه من الوجود واعتقال كل قياداته وكوادره {و} على رأسهم محمود حسني العرابي زعيم الحزب وتحريم الانتماء إليه أو محاولة إحيائه من جديد {وفي الجهة المقابلة} {فإنه} ما أن يبدأ حزب الوفد في تثبيت أقدامه في الحكم حتى يطيح به تحالف القصر مع سلطات الاحتلال البريطاني من خلال انقلاب دستوري يحمل إلى الحكم أحزاب الأقلية التابعة لهذا التحالف {حتى أن} هذا التحالف أطاح بسعد زغلول بعد أقل من عشرة أشهر من الحكم {لـ} يضع بدلاً منه حكومة تتكون من حزبي الأحرار والاتحاد برئاسة أحمد زيور في نوفمبر ١٩٢٤ {وعليه فقد} استمر سيف الدكتاتورية مسلطاً على رقاب الجميع {مما} أصاب الجماهير المصرية بالإحباط الشديد تجاه النظام السياسي الجديد.

TT

{And but} these political gains failed to satisfy the high popular hopes which had greeted the revolution of 1919. {For despite} the declaration of Egyptian independence in 1922, {for that} British troops remained on Egyptian territory, {and especially} in the Canal Zone, {just as that} the British High Commissioner remained the de facto ruler of the country. {And despite} the proclamation of a democratic constitution and the subsequent holding of free elections, {for that} the two major factions in the struggle for power were only really committed to democracy to the degree that this guaranteed them even greater influence over other groups. {For}, as soon as the Wafd came to power, it launched an all-out attack on its rivals in the Communist and National Parties, {until that} Sa'ad Zaghloul decreed in 1924 the dissolution and delegalization of the Egyptian Communist Party, the arrest of its leadership and rank-and-file members ({and} notably the Party leader Mahmoud Husni El Arabi), and the outlawing of membership of the Party, as well as any attempt to reconstitute it. {On the opposite side} {for that} the Wafd, no sooner had it settled into office, than it was brought down by the alliance between the Palace and the colonial power, through a constitutional coup which brought into office the minority parties which were members of the coalition. {Until that} this alliance brought down Sa'ad Zaghloul after less than ten months in office, {in order to} establish in its stead a government consisting of the Liberal and Union Parties under the premiership of Ahmad Zayur in November 1924. {And thus} the shadow of dictatorship continued hanging over the entire population, {which} afflicted the Egyptian masses with a profound sense of disillusionment with the new political system.

Practical 13.2 The discourse level: من شارع الستين

Assignment

(i) Discuss the strategic decisions that you must take before starting detailed translation of the following text, and outline and justify the strategy you adopt. You are to translate this article for a pilot English-language version of العربي magazine aimed mainly at expatriate English speakers working in the Middle East.
(ii) Translate the text into English.
(iii) Explain the decisions of detail you made in producing your TT.

Contextual information

This Arabic article, titled صلابة حجر .. ورقة بشر – أكراد العراق .. الى اين, comes from a 2000 edition (no. 494) of the Kuwaiti magazine العربي, which is aimed at the general educated reader and covers cultural and scientific topics. The article concerns a visit to Iraqi Kurdistan made by two Kuwaiti journalists, during which they witnessed the destruction caused by war and Iraqi government repression in the region. This extract starts in the city of Arbil (text taken from Merchant 2000: 51–56).

ST

من شارع الستين الذي يسمّى بهذا الاسم نسبة الى عرضه، انطلقنا الى قلعة أربيل. من بعيد يقبع من مدخلها تمثال ضخم لابن المستوفي المؤرخ والوزير في عهد الملك مظفر الدين كوكبري والذي ألّف العديد من الكتب اهمها «تاريخ أربيل» الذي أصدره في أربعة مجلدات.

أفضى بنا الطريق الصاعد الى القلعة نحو الباب الرئيسي، الذي يرتفع بدوره عبر سلالم أسمنتية، ليصل إلى أحياء أخرى في ساحة القلعة بها العديد من المنازل الأثرية المسكونة، وشوارع يقف فيها البائعون الجائلون بعرباتهم الخشبية، ندخل مباشرة الى القلعة التي تخبرنا لوحة ضخمة مكتوبة باللغة العربية أن سبع حضارات مرت هنا، ففي المكان الذي وقفنا فيه والذي تحاول مديرية الآثار في كردستان بإمكانات متواضعة للغاية الحفاظ على عبق القيمة التاريخية والحضارية فيه، انطبعت آثار الغزاة والفاتحين، ترك بعضهم بصماته القوية، وفضل آخرون ايداع الدمار في ذاكرة التاريخ.

في طريق العودة المتجه من السليمانية إلى أربيل، ثم منها إلى دهوك وزاخو، فمعبر فيش خابور الحدودي كان ثمة سؤال يطرح نفسه بشدة بعد أن قضينا كل تلك الأيام في منطقة كان مجرد ذكر اسمها

يصيبنا بالرعب، والآن ها نحن نعود منها وقد اكتشفنا بأنفسنا حجم المبالغات التي أحاطت قضية الأكراد وأصابتها بتشويه لا مبرر له. كان السؤال هو «ما الذي سنكسبه نحن العرب عندما نخسر هؤلاء البشر احفاد الرجال العظام الذين ساهموا بشكل إيجابي في حضارتنا؟»

Practical 13.3 The discourse level: حظي الملف النووي الإيراني

Assignment

(i) Discuss the strategic decisions that you must take before starting detailed translation of the following text, and outline and justify the strategy you adopt. You are to translate this text for *Al-Ahram Weekly,* which is published in English in Egypt.

(ii) Translate the text into English.

(iii) Explain the decisions of detail you made in producing your TT.

Contextual information

This text is by خليل خوري, and was published on the independent الحوار المتمدن website (5 October 2010), which covers political topics (http://www.ahewar.org/debat/show.art.asp?aid=231042).

ST

حظي الملف النووي الإيراني بتغطية واسعة من جانب وسائل الإعلام المختلفة حيث لا يمر يوم دون أن تزودنا بمعلومات جديدة حول درجة تخصيب اليورانيوم في مفاعل بوشهر النووي وحول الفترة الزمنية الباقية لإنتاج القنبلة النووية الإسلامية. كذلك لا أظن أن ملفا سياسيا قد حظي باهتمام الإدارة الأميركية واحتل المرتبة الأولى في سلم أولويات سياستها الخارجية خلال العشر سنوات الماضية بمثل ما تم التركيز على هذا الملف اللهم إلا ملف «أسلحة الدمار الشامل الموجودة بحوزة الدكتاتور صدام حسين» الذي نفض الغبار عنه الرئيس السابق للولايات المتحدة الأميركية جورج بوش الابن واستند إليه للإطاحة بنظام صدام، ثم تبين فيما بعد أنها قصة مفبركة روجت لها الإدارة الأميركية وضخمتها بهدف توفير مبررات كافية لاحتلال العراق والسيطرة على ثرواتها الطبيعية. وكان محيرا ومثيرا للدهشة والاستغراب أن إدارة بوش لم تبدِ أي استعجال في ممارسة ضغوط فعالة على ملالي طهران تؤدي إلى تخليهم عن برنامجهم النووي خلافا لاستعجال بوش في توجيه ضربته العسكرية للعراق رغم تصريحاته المستمرة بأنه لم يسمح لإيران امتلاك قنبلة نووية لأن امتلاكها لهذا السلاح على حد زعمه لا يهدد الاستقرار والسلم العالمي فحسب بل يهدد أمن واستقرار إسرائيل وأصدقائه العرب في منطقة الخليج. وعندما انتهت ولايته واستلم مقاليد الإدارة في البيت الأبيض خلفه أوباما راجت في الأوساط السياسية والإعلامية تكهنات بأن الإدارة الجديدة ستكون أكثر حزما في التعاطي مع التحدي النووي الإيراني ولن يمضي وقت طويل حتى توجه ضربة عسكرية للمنشاءات النووية الإيرانية، ومما عزز من صحة هذه التكهنات أن قطعا من الأسطول الأميركي اخذت تحتشد في الخليج العربي فبالة السواحل الإيرانية فيما كانت الإدارة الأميركية تطلق تحذيرات بأنها لن تسكت طويلا وسترد على التحدي الإيراني باستخدام مختلف وسائل الضغط بما في ذلك الوسائل العسكرية، ومرة أخرى لم نلمس من جانب الإدارة أية جدية لردع ملالي إيران عن توجهاتهم النووية باستخدام الوسائل العسكرية بل رأيناها ومعها معظم الدول الكبرى تفرض عقوبات اقتصادية على إيران [. . .]

14 Metaphor

14.1 Introduction

In chapters 7 and 8 we looked at denotative and connotative meaning. In this chapter, we conclude our consideration of the semantic level of language by examining the translation of metaphor. Metaphor is typically used to describe something (whether concrete or abstract) more concisely, with greater emotional force and more often more exactly, than is possible in literal language. Compare even a cliché like 'UN slams China' with the more literal 'UN harshly criticizes China'. Of course, an original metaphor is likely to be more expressive than an unoriginal one. But it is also likely to be more imprecise, more open to interpretation – indeed, the expressive force of a metaphor often depends on this very imprecision. For instance, Shakespeare's '[Love] is the star to every wand'ring bark' expresses concisely and intensely the unmovableness and reliability of love in a shifting, uncertain and dangerous world. But why '*the* star' and not '*a* star'? Why a ship ('bark') and not, say, a walker or a desert caravan? The image of navigating the seas by the pole star is full of resonances that makes Shakespeare's metaphor less precise but much more expressive than 'UN slams China'.

Metaphor is only one of a number of what are traditionally known as figures of speech. Other figures of speech include synecdoche, metonymy (cf. Section 7.2.3), irony and simile. All are of interest in translation. However, metaphor is by far the most important, both because it is the most widespread, and because it poses the most challenging translation problems. According to Newmark, 'Whilst the central problem of translation is the overall choice of a translation method for a text, the most important particular problem is the translation of metaphor' (Newmark 1988: 104). Metaphor can give rise to difficulties in translation between any two languages, but where the languages concerned are as relatively different culturally and linguistically as English and Arabic, the difficulties are sometimes quite pronounced. For an introduction to the other figures of speech, see Abrams (1985). For further discussion of issues in metaphor translation, see Schäffner (2004) and Dickins (2005).

14.2 General definition of metaphor

Metaphor can be defined as a figure of speech in which a word or phrase is used in a non-basic sense, this non-basic sense suggesting a likeness or analogy with another more basic sense of the same word or phrase. Consider the first two senses of 'rat' given in the *Collins English Dictionary*: (i) 'any of numerous long-tailed murine rodents, esp. of the genus *Rattus,* that are similar to but larger than mice and are now distributed all over the world' and (ii) 'a person who deserts his friends or associates, esp. in times of trouble'. Here, each sense of 'rat' may be said to call to mind the other (although the first would in most contexts only weakly call to mind the second). That is to say, any use of 'rat' in a particular text has the potential to invoke a reflected meaning. However, 'rat' in the sense of 'a person who deserts his friends or associates' is a metaphor with respect to 'any of numerous long-tailed murine rodents'. By contrast, 'rat' in the sense of 'any of numerous long-tailed murine rodents' is not a metaphor with respect to 'a person who deserts his friends or associates'. This is because we perceive the sense of 'rat' 'any of numerous long-tailed murine rodents' as being more basic than the sense 'a person who deserts his friends or associates'. This is in line with a general perception of physical objects as more basic than non-physical attributes.

14.2.1   *Lexicalized metaphor and non-lexicalized metaphor*

From the point of view of translation, a useful basic distinction to make is that between **lexicalized metaphors** and **non-lexicalized metaphors**. What we mean by lexicalized metaphors are uses of language that are recognizably metaphorical but whose meaning in a particular language is relatively clearly fixed. 'Rat' in the sense 'a person who deserts his friends or associates' is an example. The fact that the meaning of 'rat' in this sense is relatively clearly fixed allows this meaning to be subjected to attempted dictionary definition. Accordingly, for practical purposes, we may say that lexicalized metaphors are metaphors whose meanings are given in dictionaries.

The other basic category of metaphor is what we are calling 'non-lexicalized metaphor'. In the case of non-lexicalized metaphor, the metaphorical meaning is not clearly fixed, but will vary from context to context, and has to be worked out by the reader on particular occasions. An example of a non-lexicalized metaphor is '[a] tree' in 'A man is a tree'. If this were uttered in a context in which the focus was on the distinction between the relatively small amount that is apparent or conscious about human personality and the relatively large amount that is hidden or unconscious, the reader might conclude that 'A man is a tree' is roughly equivalent to saying that 'A man is like a tree in that only a certain proportion is apparent (in the case of the tree: the trunk, branches and leaves) while much remains hidden (in the case of the tree: the extensive root system)'. If, however, 'A man is a tree' were uttered in the context of a description of the course of peoples' lives, the reader might conclude that what is meant is something more like 'A man is like a tree in that he grows up, develops, "bears fruit" like a tree, and then loses many of his attractive attributes (cf. the leaves), etc.'.

The example 'A man is a tree' raises the question of how non-lexicalized metaphor is to be analyzed in particular contexts. One approach that is useful for translation distinguishes between the following notions: topic, vehicle and grounds (e.g. Goatly 1997). The topic is the entity referred to; the vehicle is the notion to which this entity is being compared; and the grounds are the respect in which this comparison is being made. Consider the example 'Tom is a tree', in which '[a] tree' is the metaphorical element, and in a context in which we can take the intended meaning to be something like 'Tom is the type of person whose major psychological features remain hidden'. In this example, the topic is Tom; or, more precisely, it is the 'entity' to which the word 'Tom' here refers. The vehicle is '[a] tree' in its literal sense. The grounds are the respect to which Tom is like a tree – in this case, in the fact that major features of him are not apparent. From the point of view of this analysis, we might paraphrase 'Tom is a tree' as 'Tom *(topic)* is like a tree *(vehicle)* in that major psychological aspects of him are not apparent *(grounds)*'. Although it is a bit artificial to apply the notions of topic, vehicle and grounds to lexicalized metaphor, we will keep things simple by using the terms, where appropriate, in discussing both lexicalized and non-lexicalized metaphor.

The distinction between lexicalized and non-lexicalized metaphors is not always clear-cut. English speakers are likely to agree that the metaphorical sense of 'rat' that we have given is a lexicalized metaphor. They are also likely to agree that 'platypus' in English has no such fixed secondary sense and that, if it is used metaphorically, it is, in terms of the definition we have given, a non-lexicalized metaphor. They are likely to be less sure, however, about secondary senses of 'tiger', 'elephant' or 'ostrich' (cf. Leech 1981: 214–215). From the point of view of translation, the importance of the distinction between lexicalized and non-lexicalized metaphors is not that it should be absolutely true, but that it provides a reasonable way in the great majority of cases of distinguishing two major classes of metaphor, which, as we shall see, typically require rather different treatment in translation.

Note that both sorts of metaphor can consist of more than one word. Such metaphors are known as phrasal metaphors. Thus, '[Tom is] a tree whose leaves protect us all' is a non-lexicalized phrasal metaphor, and the idiom '[Tom] knows his onions' is a lexicalized phrasal metaphor. In principle, all lexicalized phrasal metaphors are idioms.

Simile can be treated in much the same way as metaphor. Thus, in 'Tom is like a shady tree', the simile element is 'like a shady tree', the topic is 'Tom', the vehicle is '[a] shady tree' and the grounds are that major aspects of him are not apparent.

14.2.1.1   *Categories of lexicalized metaphor*

It is useful to distinguish three types of lexicalized metaphors. (1) a *dead* metaphor is one which one does not normally even realize is a metaphor, as in the 'foot' of a mountain or 'run out' in 'time is running out'. (2) A *stock* metaphor is one that is widely used but where one normally realizes that it is a metaphor. The examples that Newmark gives are all idioms – for example, 'keep the pot boiling', 'throw a new light on' (cf. Newmark 1988: 108). However, the notion of stock metaphor can be extended to also include single-word metaphors, such as 'rat' ('person who deserts his friends or associate, etc.') or 'cold' ('Showing no warm or friendly feeling; the reverse of cordial, affectionate or friendly': *Oxford*

English Dictionary Online). (3) A *recent* metaphor is a 'metaphorical neologism', as in 'with it' (in the sense of 'fashionable'), hunting' (in the sense of 'recruitment') (cf. Newmark 1988: 111–112).

14.2.1.2 Categories of non-lexicalized metaphor

It is worth distinguishing two basic types of non-lexicalized metaphor. These are conventionalized metaphors and original metaphors.

Conventionalized metaphors are metaphors that are not lexicalized (and will not therefore be given in dictionaries) but do draw on either cultural or linguistic conventions. English, for example, makes use of a large number of lexicalized metaphors based on the general notion of argument as war (cf. Goatly 1997: 75) – for example, 'battle of wits', 'attack' or 'lash out' at an opponent, 'defend a position', 'counter-attack', 'bombard' with questions, 'win' an argument. If, in this kind of context, an English ST contains a phrase like 'he redeployed his troops', the reader will have little difficulty in interpreting it along the lines 'he refocused his argument' or 'he began to concentrate on another aspect of the debate'. Although 'redeploy [. . .] troops' is not a lexicalized metaphor in English, it is easy to interpret at least partly because of the generalized convention in English that arguments are described in terms of war and the existence of a large number of lexicalized metaphors along these lines.

There is also another more linguistically oriented form of conventionalized metaphor. This is what Newmark terms 'adapted' metaphor. An adapted metaphor is one in which a stock metaphor is slightly changed; an example is 'the ball is a little in their court' (Newmark 1988: 111). Here is an example we have already come across (Section 10.2.3.2):

> . . . فرفض البنا الاستجابة لهذا التكتل و{اشتبك} في عدة {اشتباكات} كلامية مع رفعت كانت تنتهي دومًا بالمزيد من المؤيدين لأحمد رفعت وإزاء سيطرة رفعت الكاملة على المركز العام للإخوان [. . .]

Proposed translation (Calderbank 1990: 27):

> El Banna refused to listen to the group and {crossed words} several times with Rifaat. These exchanges always ended up with more support for Rifaat and eventually, faced with Rifaat's complete control of the General Headquarters [. . .]

The phrase 'cross words', here, is an adapted metaphor that echoes the existing English phrase 'cross swords', meaning to clash with, particularly in debate or discussion.

Original metaphors are ones like 'Tom is a tree', quoted earlier. Because they are not simply relatable to existing linguistic or cultural conventions, original metaphors are difficult to interpret. More specifically, it is necessary to establish the grounds from the context, and, in many cases, these will be ambiguous.

14.2.2   The purposes of metaphor

Basing ourselves on Newmark, we can say that metaphor has two main purposes, a denotative-oriented purpose and a connotative-oriented purpose. (Newmark in fact uses different terminology; he calls these 'referential purpose' and 'pragmatic purpose', respectively.) The denotative-oriented purpose is 'to describe a mental process or state, a concept, a person, an object, a quality or action more comprehensively and concisely than is possible in literal or physical language' (Newmark 1988: 104). This analysis of the denotative-oriented purpose of metaphors is particularly appropriate in the case of lexicalized metaphors. Thus, if someone says, 'He lashed out at his opponent', this is a very concise way of saying that 'he burst into or resorted to verbal or physical attack' (cf. *Collins English Dictionary*). In the case of non-lexicalized metaphors, and original metaphors in particular, another denotative-oriented purpose is often foremost. This is the use of metaphor to express an open-ended denotative meaning or potential range of denotative meanings. This open-endedness of interpretation of original metaphors is a function of the fact that the grounds of a metaphor are often not defined precisely enough by the context to enable a reader to say exactly what the metaphor means.

The connotative-oriented purpose of metaphor 'is to appeal to the senses, to interest, to clarify "graphically", to please, to delight, to surprise' (Newmark 1988: 104): in short, metaphors tend to carry with them a strong emotional force. The reason metaphor is able to achieve these effects is a function of the fact that all metaphors except dead ones have a strong reflected meaning (Section 8.7), original metaphors typically having the strongest reflected meaning. Metaphorical usages are quite frequently extremely witty. Consider the following, from a football summary on British radio: 'Tottenham were a marshmallow of a team: sweet, expensive – and downright soft in the middle'. Here, the summarizer has made use of multiple metaphors to produce a memorable and entertaining turn of phrase.

14.2.3   Metaphorical force

On the basis of the previous account of metaphor, it is possible to draw up a scale of metaphorical force, as presented in Figure 14.1.

As this diagram shows, there is a typical correlation between non-lexicalized metaphors and metaphorical strength. Non-lexicalized metaphors tend to be more striking or forceful or vivid than lexicalized metaphors, at least partly because of the unpredictability of the meaning of non-lexicalized metaphors. However, the metaphorical force of conventionalized non-lexicalized metaphors is typically less than that of original metaphors. Thus, metaphors such as 'vultures are the sharks of the air' or 'my head is a balloon this morning' seem rather weak because it is fairly typical to use sharks as an example of rapacious animals, and there is a general convention in English that emptiness signifies lack of intelligence or understanding. Similarly, some non-lexicalized metaphors that were originally quite striking might be considered hackneyed now because of their frequent repetition. An example might be John Donne's 'No man is an island'.

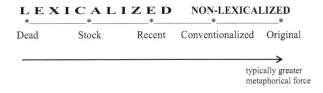

Figure 14.1 Metaphorical force.

Conversely, lexicalized metaphors tend towards the banal because of the defin-able and predictable nature of their meaning; often, lexicalized metaphors lose almost all their force and scarcely recall the more basic meaning of the word or phrase with respect to which they are metaphorical (i.e. they become dead meta-phors). Even such dead metaphors, however, can be 'debanalified' and rendered vivid. Normally, we would hardly think of 'sift' meaning 'examine minutely' as being a metaphor; 'He sifted the evidence' seems to have little metaphorical force and could be classified as a dead metaphor. As soon as we add 'through the fine mesh of his intellect' to give 'He sifted the evidence through the fine mesh of his intellect', however, the original metaphor 'fine sieve' 'resuscitates' and renders vivid the non-original metaphor 'sifted'.

14.3 Basic translation techniques for metaphor

The following procedures can be regarded as the most typical for translating the various categories of metaphors just discussed.

14.3.1 Dead metaphors

Because the metaphorical element in these is very weak, it can normally be ignored in the translation and some appropriate TL form sought. Sometimes, the obvious form will involve the same or virtually the same vehicle in the TT as in the ST. Thus, ارتفاع is the Standard Arabic word for 'rise' in the sense of a rise in prices. Some-times, the TT vehicle will appear in a slightly different form; so على يد versus 'at the hands of'. Sometimes, the TT will use a different metaphor from the ST; thus, عقرب الساعة versus 'hand' (of clock). Sometimes, the ST metaphor will be best translated by a non-metaphorical TT term; thus, لزم الفراش 'he took to his bed', قام من المرض 'he recovered from the illness'.

Where an ST dead metaphor is being translated by a TT metaphor, the transla-tor should bear in mind whether the TT metaphor is as dead as the ST: in some contexts, it would be inappropriate to use a metaphor with more metaphorical force than the ST one; in others, this may be acceptable or even desirable.

14.3.2 Stock metaphors

The following techniques are suggested for translating stock metaphors (cf. New-mark 1988: 108–111).

The stock SL metaphor can be retained as a stock metaphor having the same or nearly the same vehicle in the TL. This can be done provided the vehicle has comparable frequency and currency in the appropriate register in the TL as in the SL, as in the following (the metaphorical element in the ST and its equivalent in the TT in all the following examples are placed in curly brackets): لم يسبق لصابر [. . .] أن {استولت عليه} مثل هذه الافكار 'Never before had such thoughts {possessed} Saber' (Brown 1996: 34); وجدرانها {شاهدة على} جوعه وعطشه وبكائه ونشيجه 'its four walls had {witnessed} his hunger and thirst, his weeping and sobbing' (Brown 1996: 38).

The stock SL metaphor can be replaced with a stock TL metaphor having a different vehicle. This is appropriate where the vehicle in the SL and the TL have roughly equal frequency within the register in question. Examples of this are وتمكن من معرفة مكان منزلها، ثم أخذ فيما بعد {يحوم} حوله باستمرار [. . .] 'He managed to find out where she lived and began to {hang around} outside her house constantly [. . .]' (St John 1999: 5); [. . .] أن الصرب لم {يبرؤوا} من سموم التاريخ القديم 'that the Serbs have not been {cleansed} of the poisons of ancient history [. . .]' (Ives 1999: 14).

The SL metaphor can be converted to a TL simile. This technique works where, if translated literally into the SL, the TL metaphor appears too abrupt. An example is [. . .] الطرف الآخر من النهر بدا منكسرا {يكسوه} حزن ووجل 'the other side of the river appeared fractured {as if clothed in} fear and sadness' (Merchant 2000: 20), where كسا in the sense of covering is a stock metaphor in Arabic but not in English.

The metaphor can be reduced to grounds. This involves losing the metaphor altogether and the emotional effect associated with it. It may, however, be appropriate where other strategies are not acceptable for the TL. Examples are أيها {الإخوة} '{Friends}' (from the start of a speech) (Dickson 1999: 7); تململ صابر في سريره دون أن {يستبد بـ}ـه النعاس 'Saber fidgeted in his bed without {feeling} sleepy' (Brown 1996: 38); [. . .] عاش محمد أعواماً {مديدة} في مدينة صغيرة 'Mohammed had lived for {many} years in a small town' (St John 1999: 4).

Sometimes, it may be appropriate to introduce other features in the TT in order to compensate for the loss of emotional effect caused by the removal of the metaphor. An example is وليس من قبيل الصدفة ان نلاحظ أن العازفين والمغنين من الطلاب {يبلغون ذروة} الاحساس 'It is no coincidence that we see the student musicians and singers {demonstrate the utmost} sensitivity [. . .]' (Evans 1994: 16). Here, the translator has made use of a superlative form 'utmost', as well as the rather formal and elegant 'demonstrate', to achieve the same sort of emotional force as is relayed by the metaphor يبلغون ذروة in the ST (cf. the relative weakness of an alternative English formulation, such as 'display extreme sensitivity').

14.3.3 *Recent metaphors*

Where these are neologisms describing new objects or processes, equivalent TL technical terms can be sought out. This is less likely to be a problem translating into English than into Arabic, as the terms for such new objects and processes typically originate in English – and even original Arabic texts often make use of the English term (typically in Latin script) followed by a tentative translation.

'Buzz terms' present a slightly different problem. The formality of Standard Arabic means that such terms do not appear in and disappear from Arabic with the same speed as they do in English. One is therefore likely to reduce recent metaphors in translating into Arabic to stock metaphors or perhaps to grounds. In translating into English, recent metaphors could be used where general requirements of register make them appropriate.

14.3.4 Non-lexicalized (conventionalized and original) metaphors

The following techniques are suggested for translating conventionalized metaphors that fall under general cultural or linguistic patterns of metaphor organization in the SL.

The non-lexicalized SL metaphor can be retained as a non-lexicalized metaphor having the same or nearly the same vehicle in the TL. This is a fairly common technique with non-lexicalized metaphor. Examples are فمنذ أن كانت تضاء بأنوار القناديل [. . .] الخافتة قبل {غزو} الكهرباء 'ever since it had been lit by the light of subdued lamps – before the {invasion} of electricity' (Brown 1996: 38); {ولا القمر {يستدير بطنه في سمائنا بصورة طبيعية 'And the {belly} of the moon does not {grow round} in our sky naturally' (Rolph 1995: 13).

Sometimes, it is necessary to make other changes that do not essentially alter the metaphor but that render the context in which it occurs more acceptable in English. For example, {فيتشرد عبر المدينة و}قد تحول الى قط هزيل يموء مواءً حاداً 'He would roam across town, {an emaciated cat, mewing plaintively}' (St John 1999: 5–6). Here, the translator has omitted the وقد تحول الى 'changed/having changed into' element in the English translation; this would have rendered the English somewhat clumsy. The core of the metaphor, however, remains the same.

The non-lexicalized SL metaphor can be replaced with a non-lexicalized TL metaphor having a different vehicle. Sometimes, the TT vehicle does not work if transferred directly into the ST, but a non-lexicalized metaphor in the TT having a different vehicle does. An example is وما زال بعض الادب المعاصر يتذكر فترات الاثارة الدينية {والثارات المبيتة التي لم} تبرد نارها حتى الآن}. 'Some contemporary literature still refers to the period of religious tension and ensuing vengeance, {the flames of which have not yet died out}' (Ives 1999: 13). Here, the general metaphorical vehicle of fire is retained in the TT, reflecting the fact that it is conventional to use fire metaphors to describe anger and violence in both English and Arabic. However, the specific vehicle has been shifted from نار ('fire') and تبرد ('grew cold') in the ST to 'flames' and 'died out' in the TT.

Elsewhere, more subtle changes may be required. For example, وغادر محمد المسجد بينما كانت دماء شرايينه {أصواتاً تتوسل بلهفة، وتهتف ضارعة: يا الله}. 'Mohammed left the mosque, and as he did so, the blood in his veins became {a mass of imploring voices, calling out woefully: "Oh God"}' (St John 1999: 8). Here, the translator has somewhat strengthened the Arabic metaphor [. . .] أصواتاً 'voices' by using the phrase 'a mass of [. . .] voices'; he has also added the verb 'became'. Both of these changes have the effect of ensuring that the metaphor remains evident and comprehensible in the English translation, as it would not were a more direct translation adopted, such as 'Mohammed left the mosque, the blood in his veins imploring voices, calling out woefully: "Oh God".'

Sometimes, it is appropriate to replace the non-lexicalized ST metaphor with a stock TT metaphor. This is typically the case where the non-lexicalized ST metaphor is highly conventionalized and therefore does not have a particularly strong emotional impact. An example is والرواية المشهورة «جسر على نهر درينا» التي كتبها صربي فنان هو ايفو اندرتش، واظنه حصل بها على جائزة نوبل في سنة ١٩٦١، تكشف كوامن الكراهية في هذه البؤرة الملتهبة} ' 'The famous novel, *The Bridge on the Drina* written by the Serbian author Ivo Andric [. . .] reveals the deep-seated hatreds in this {flashpoint}' (Ives 1999: 13). Here, the Arabic metaphor البؤرة الملتهبة 'the flaming pit/abyss' is non-lexicalized but highly conventional in that fire metaphors are commonly used to describe violence, and pit metaphors are commonly used to describe extremely problematic situations. Accordingly, the stock phrase 'flashpoint' seems sufficient for the context. A similar example of a highly conventionalized but non-lexicalized metaphor translated as a stock metaphor is the following: {البركانية في هذه المنطقة [. . .] القلقة 'in this {explosive} and unhappy region [. . .]' (Ives 1999: 14). Here, if the Arabic البركانية 'volcanic' had been translated directly as 'volcanic', the reader might (initially at least) have thought it was simply a description of the geology of the area.

Occasionally, it will happen that a non-lexicalized metaphor in the ST corresponds more or less directly to a stock metaphor in the TT. In this case, it is likely to be appropriate to use the stock metaphor in the TT where the ST metaphor is conventionalized. Here is an example of a conventionalized non-lexicalized metaphor that is translated by a corresponding stock metaphor in English, with the addition of the topic: فتساقطت الضحايا من كافة المذاهب والملل . . . من مختلف الافكار والاعمار {الإعصار} إنه . . . من مختلف الاتجاهات والجنسيات . . . . 'Victims from all faiths and communities, from differing ideologies, generations, factions and nationalities have been caught up in this {whirlwind of violence}' (Hetherington 1996: 13). Here, the fact that إعصار is conventionalized (i.e. that violence is frequently talked about in terms of extreme weather conditions in Arabic) means that the English stock expression 'whirlwind of violence' is quite acceptable.

Where the ST metaphor is original in nature, translating by a stock metaphor in the TT will destroy the sense of originality and therefore lessen the emotional force. In this case, it may be more appropriate to translate it by a non-lexicalized metaphor in the TT having a different vehicle.

The SL metaphor can be converted to a simile. Converting an ST metaphor to a TT simile can be useful where it is appropriate to retain the ST vehicle (or a similar vehicle) but where the use of a metaphor in the TT would seem odd for some reason. An example is وكان محمد يشعر {بأنه جورب عتيق مهمل} 'making him feel {like an old discarded sock}' (St John 1999: 5). 'To feel like' is common usage in English; the more direct metaphorical 'making him feel that he was an old discarded sock' might seem somewhat strained and even comical. Consider also the following: وتلفت فيما حوله، فبدت لعينيه البيوت الترابية المتلاصقة بقايا {هيكل عظمي لحيوان قديم منقرض} 'He looked around at the grey contiguous houses, spread out before his eyes {like the skeleton of some ancient beast}' (St John 1999: 18). Here, the use of the simile allows the translator to integrate the phrase 'like the skeleton of some ancient beast' into the ST in a concise and elegant manner.

It is also possible, of course, for a simile in the ST to be translated as a metaphor in the TT. This is particularly common where the TT metaphor in question is a stock metaphor. An example is [. . .] {كالمسحور} فلحقها 'and he followed her, {enchanted}' (St John 1999: 5).

The metaphor can be reduced to grounds. This is most likely to happen where the ST metaphor is highly conventionalized and translation by a metaphor (of whatever kind) in the TT would sound clichéd. An example from a speech by جمال عبد الناصر is the following: {الشقيقة} أرحب بكم باسم شعب مصر العربي الذي يشعر نحو سوريا {بأنها قطعة من قلبها} 'Friends. I offer you a warm welcome to Egypt. The Arab people of Egypt feel {a strong affinity and deep affection} towards Syria' (Dickson 1999: 7). Here, the phrase قطعة من قلبها 'a piece of its heart' has been related to the grounds – that is, it is a piece of its heart by virtue of sharing a strong/close affinity and having deep affection. It is these grounds, rather than the metaphor, that figure in the translation; the metaphorical 'a piece of its heart' (or similar) would sound rather twee in English. (Note also the stock metaphor الشقيقة to describe another Arab country; this can be regarded as having been merged with قطعة من قلبها into the English TT version, 'a strong affinity and deep affection'.)

Here is a similar example: [. . .] {الشديد الحرارة} الايام الماضية بكل دفقها الدموي 'the past with all its {terrible} bloodshed [. . .]' (cf. Ives 1999: 14). Here, the direct equivalent of الشديد الحرارة 'extremely hot' does not collocate happily with دفقها الدموي 'its bloodshed' (or 'the shedding of its blood', etc.) and might appear comical in the context. The translator has accordingly chosen a non-metaphorical equivalent based on the grounds in which bloodshed can be 'hot' (such grounds being constructible along the lines that bloodshed is like extreme heat in that both are painful, difficult to bear, destructive of life, etc.).

A metaphorical element can be retained in the TT but with the addition of the grounds or the topic. As Newmark notes (1988: 110), this kind of approach is a compromise procedure that retains some of the emotive and cultural effect of the metaphor while also providing an explanation for readers who may not understand the original metaphor without further explanation.

Here is an example of the retention of a non-lexicalized (original) metaphor with addition of the topic: [. . .] أنثى {تبزغ فوق صحرائه} ولقد انتظر طويلا ان 'He had been waiting for a long time for a woman {to dawn over the desert of his life}' (St John 1999: 10). Here, a direct translation 'He had been waiting for a long time for a woman to dawn over his desert' might seem rather obscure to the English reader. The translator has accordingly added the phrase 'of his life', which specifies a topic for the word صحرائه '[his] desert' (i.e. it specifies what 'desert' refers to).

These examples, of course, are not an exhaustive list of all the methods that may be appropriate or acceptable for dealing with metaphor in Arabic>English translation, although it does cover a large proportion of cases. Particular circumstances, however, may give rise to the need for approaches quite different to the ones we have listed here.

14.4   Extended and mixed metaphors

One of the interesting stylistic features of metaphor is the tendency for a particular metaphorical image to be maintained over a fairly long stretch of text. By 'image' here, we mean a particular semantic field to which a series of vehicles belongs. Consider the following (Brown 1996: 36):

تراءت له مشاهد البؤس والخوف على شريط من الذكريات، فـ{اشتعل} فيه الحنين الى الهجرة، ولكن في اعماق قلبه {جمرة} تأبى {الانطفاء}، فهي كلما {ذوت} سرعان ما تعود الى {الاتّقاد} من جديد.

This can be translated fairly literally as follows:

> Scenes of wretchedness and fear presented themselves to him on a band of memories and the longing to emigrate {caught fire} in him. But in the depths of his heart an {ember} refused to {go out}; every time it {faded} it quickly {ignited} again.

In this case, the image of 'fire' is maintained both in the ST and in the TT. Metaphors that maintain the same general image in this way can be termed 'congruent metaphors'. Not all metaphors in a text are necessarily congruent. Metaphors that are not congruent with one another are often referred to as mixed metaphors. An example of a mixed metaphor is the following regarding the Maastricht Treaty promoting closer integration of the European Union: '[. . .] the Foreign Secretary, Douglas Hurd, said that what he called "trench warfare" against the treaty "had evaporated"' (BBC Radio 4 News, 18 May 1993). Another example of mixed metaphor is 'All the evidence must be sifted with acid tests'. Here, there is an incongruity between the image conjured up by 'sifted' and that conjured up by 'acid tests'. Compare in this regard the perfectly acceptable 'All the evidence must be subjected to acid tests'.

Where the metaphors in question are dead or stock metaphors, mixed metaphor is normally not particularly noticeable. So, 'the forces which make up the political spectrum' seems reasonably acceptable, despite the fact that the basic sense of 'spectrum' has to do with colour rather than (physical) force.

Accordingly, the use of mixed metaphors is not normally a significant problem in the translation of dead or stock metaphors, as is shown by the following extract from عرس الزين by the Sudanese author الطيب صالح (صالح n.d.: 11) and a possible English translation. Curly brackets and a following superscript number note metaphors and associated phenomena in both the ST and the TT.

ST

يولد الأطفال فـ{يستقبلون[1]} الحياة بالصريخ، هذا هو المعروف ولكن يروى ان الزين، والعهدة على امه والنساء اللائي حضرن ولادتها، اول ما {مس الارض[2]}، {انفجر[3]} ضاحكاً. وظل هكذا طول حياته. كبر وليس في فمه غير سنّين، واحدة في فكه الاعلى والاخرى في فكه الاسفل. وامه تقول ان فمه كان مليئاً بأسنان بيضاء {كاللؤلؤ[4]}. ولما كان في السادسة ذهبت به يوماً لزيارة قريبات لها، فمرا عند مغيب الشمس على خرابة يشاع انها {مسكونة[5]}. وفجأة {تسمر[6]} الزين مكانه وأخذ يرتجف

كمن به حمى، ثم صرخ. وبعدها {لزم⁷} الفراش اياماً. ولما {قام⁸} من مرضه كانت اسنانه جميعاً قد سقطت، الا واحدة في فكه الاعلى، واخرى في فكه الاسفل.

TT

When children are born, they {greet¹} life with a scream; this is well known. However, according to his mother and the women who attended his birth, as soon as Zein {came into the world²} he {burst out³} laughing. And this was how he remained his whole life. He grew up with only two teeth in his mouth, one in the upper jaw and one in the lower. His mother says that his mouth was once full of {pearly⁴} white teeth. Then one day, when he was six years old, she took him to visit some of her relatives. As the sun was setting, they passed by some ruins which were rumoured to be {haunted⁵}. Suddenly Zein became {fixed⁶} to the spot, and began to tremble as if he had a fever. Then he screamed. After that he {took to⁷} his bed for several days. When he {recovered⁸}, all his teeth had fallen out except one in his upper jaw and one in the lower.

There is no evident congruity in the metaphors used in this extract. However, the fact that none of the metaphors in the TT carry great metaphorical force means that there is also no sense of unacceptable mixed metaphor. The English TT, which makes use of a mixture of stock metaphors, dead metaphors and non-metaphors, similarly carries no sense of unacceptable mixing of metaphor.

This situation contrasts with cases, typically involving a high density of non-lexicalized metaphors, in which mixed metaphor (non-congruence) can present a considerable problem in translation. Consider the following (Brown 1996: 50):

[. . .] تمنى صابر لو أنه يستطيع ان {يفجر} هذا الصوت و{يفجر} معه {بركان} الحرية الذي {لا يصحو له جفن} و{لا تثور له ثائرة}.

TT

Saber wished that he could make this voice {burst forth} and that in turn the {volcano} of freedom would {erupt}, _____ nor had it {flared up in rage}.

Here, the ST metaphors are mostly non-lexicalized and closely congruent. The translator has relayed this congruence in the TT (although considerations of idiomaticness in the English have meant that she translated يفجر first in the context of 'voice' as 'burst forth' and subsequently in the context of 'volcano' as 'erupt'). A problem, however, is presented by the phrase لا يصحو له جفن, which we have omitted from the TT as presented here (the resulting gap being represented by a line). A possible translation of لا يصحو له جفن might be 'at which no one bats an eyelid', or perhaps more appropriately in this general context, 'at which no one had ever batted an eyelid'. However, the use of this particular idiomatic stock metaphor seems odd in this context, partly at least because the image (or vehicle) of batting an eyelid seems incongruent with the general image of volcanoes and fire. In order to avoid this incongruity, it might be appropriate in this case to opt for a relatively bland (though still metaphorical) translation of لا يصحو له جفن, such as 'which had never attracted anyone's attention' or 'which had never attracted a glance'. Together with further adjustments to sentence structure, this might yield a translation along the lines:

> Saber wished that he could make this voice {burst forth} and that in turn the {volcano} of freedom would {erupt}, which had never once {flared up in rage} nor even {attracted} people's attention.

14.5 Metaphor downtoning

Not infrequently, Arabic ST metaphors appear too strong or too dense for equivalent forms of English writing and there is some need to tone down the metaphors of the Arabic ST in the English TT.

Consider the following (St John 1999: 4), some aspects of which have been previously discussed in this chapter:

عاش محمد أعواماً {مديدة} في مدينة صغيرة {تقبع} {بذل} عند {أقدام} جبل شاهق {ترتطم} السحب بصخوره الصفراء.

> Mohammed had lived for {many} years in a small town. It {squatted} {insignificantly} at the {foot} of a towering mountain whose pale rocks {touched} the sky.

Here, of the five metaphors in the Arabic ST, three – مديدة, بذل, and ترتطم – have been toned down in the English, where they appear as the non-metaphorical 'many' (rather than 'extended', etc.), the stock metaphorical 'insignificantly' (rather than 'shamefully', etc.) and the stock metaphorical 'touched' (rather than 'crashed against'). The operative factor in this downtoning seems to be that this extract is taken from a relatively non-emotive section of the short story in question (in fact, it is the opening sentence). In such a context, more direct renderings of the ST metaphors into English would seem unacceptably emotive.

Another example of metaphor downtoning is provided by the following extract from a newspaper article by the Egyptian journalist مصطفى أمين from الشرق الاوسط 21 September 1982 (reproduced in transcription in Al-Jubouri 1984; extract previously discussed in relation to other issues in sections 6.1 and 11.4):

في استطاعة أي حزب أن ينجح إذا دافع عن قضية الحرية وحقوق الإنسان، إذا احتضن كل مظلوم، إذا قاوم الفساد، إذا ضرب الأمثلة في القدوة الصالحة، إذا حوّل الكلمات إلى افعال والوعود إلى حقائق. كل حزب يقف إلى جانب الشعب يقف الشعب إلى جانبه يحيط به عندما تُوجَّه إلى ظهره الخناجر وإلى صدره المدافع والسيوف.

Here is an attempted idiomatic translation of this text:

> For any political party to succeed, it must be prepared to stand up for freedom of expression and human rights, to protect the weak, to oppose corruption, to

set itself the highest standards, and to act according to these standards. Any party which supports and defends the people will find that it is supported and defended by the people.

As we saw earlier (Section 11.5), the English translation here involves considerable reduction of the parallelism of the Arabic ST. The TT also, however, involves extreme reduction of the metaphorical elements of the ST. Thus, احتضن is translated as the non-metaphorical 'protect'. More striking is the extended and complex metaphor كل حزب يقف إلى جانب الشعب يقف الشعب إلى جانبه يحيط به عندما تُوجَّه إلى ظهره الخناجر وإلى صدره المدافع والسيوف: literally, 'every party which stands beside the people, the people stand beside it, surrounding it when daggers are aimed at its back, and guns and swords at it chest'. This is translated as the non-metaphorical 'Any party which supports and defends the people will find that it is supported and defended by the people'. The only arguably metaphorical element in the English TT is 'stand up [for]', which is likely to be regarded as a dead metaphor, corresponding to the Arabic قاوم (which is even more of a dead metaphor, if it is to be regarded as metaphorical at all).

The metaphorical downtoning in the TT here, like the reduction in the degree of parallelism, reflects a general tendency for English to use less strongly emotive language than Arabic, particularly in texts that argue a strongly held belief.

Practical 14

Practical 14.1 Metaphor downtoning: ومنذ اللحظة

Assignment

Consider the following extract from a signed article titled السياسة الأمريكية تجاه فلسطين by أسعد عبد الرحمن, a Jordanian academic, from the Jordanian newspaper الرأي. The article was written after the end of the second Gulf War between Iraq and the American-led coalition following the Iraqi invasion of Kuwait in 1990. Metaphorical elements in the text have been placed within curly brackets with accompanying numbers in order to make their correspondents in the following English translation easier to trace.

The Arabic ST is followed by a fairly literal TT and then by a more idiomatic English TT. In both cases, correspondences to the Arabic metaphors are placed in curly brackets, the superscript numbering indicating which TT element(s) correspond to the original ST metaphors.

In what ways does the idiomatic TT tone down, fail to tone down or otherwise modify metaphorical elements in the ST? Are there any additional metaphorical elements introduced into the idiomatic TT that are not present in the ST?

ST

ومنذ اللحظة التي نطق فيها {المايسترو¹} الامريكي بذلك، تكاثرت الاقوال المماثلة والمشابهة من قبل كل {العازفين²} على {النغمة النشاز³}، سواء كانوا اولئك الذين {ينتظمون ضمن التخت الموسيقي⁴}

نفسه، او اولئك الذين {ينتظمون ضمن الكورس المواكب[5]}!!! ثم {تسارعت[6]} {الالحان النشاز[7]}، بل والاعمال {النشاز[8]}، الملاحقة! فلم يمض وقت طويل حتى بدأ العالم المشدوه يسمع تحرصات جديدة من الولايات المتحدة – يا رعاها الله!!! – قوامها المساواة، على صعيد هجومها التعسفي، بين منظمة التحرير الفلسطينية ورئيسها بحيث فقدت المنظمة في {بنك[9]} السياسة الامريكية الكثير من {رصيدها[10]}!!!

Fairly literal TT

Since the American {maestro[1]} first uttered that, similar and corresponding statements have proliferated on the part of the all the {players[2]} on the {discordant tune[3]}, whether they were those who {formed part of the orchestra[4]} itself, or those who {were part of the accompanying chorus[5]}!!! Then the {discordant melodies[7]} {became quicker[6]}, and indeed the subsequent/connected {discordant/recalcitrant[8]} actions. It was not long before the astonished world began to hear new fabrications from the United States – God preserve it! – whose basis, on the level of its arbitrary attack, was the equivalence between the PLO and its leader, such that the Organization had lost much of its {credit[9]} in the American political {bank[10]}.

Idiomatic TT

Since the Americans first {orchestrated[1]} this campaign, similarly {discordant notes have been struck[3]} by all the minor {players[2]}, whether they were actually {members of the alliance[4]} or merely {stood by applauding[5]} US actions. These {discordant voices[7]} have recently {reached a crescendo[6]} and have given rise to increasingly {violent actions[8]}. Now, a bewildered world has begun to hear new allegations from the glorious United States, whose abusive tones are directed not only against Arafat, but against the PLO in general, and which suggest that the PLO has {lost whatever credit[9,10]} it had with the Americans.

Practical 14.2 Metaphor: قال صابر مخاطبا نفسه

Assignment

(i) Discuss the strategic decisions that you must take before starting detailed translation of the following text, and outline and justify the strategy you adopt. You are to translate the text as part of a translation of the whole novel you are undertaking. This is to be published as one in a series of translations of modern Arabic novels. The intended readership comprises educated English speakers with a good general knowledge of English literature but no specialist knowledge of the Middle East.

(ii) Translate the text into English.

(iii) Explain the decisions of detail you made *in respect to metaphor* in producing your translation.

Contextual information

This extract is taken from the novel مدينة البغي by the Palestinian writer عيسى بشارة. The central character of the novel is a young journalist called صابر, who lives in the مدينة البغي of the title, which can be taken to be Jerusalem (or a fictional equivalent). صابر feels oppressed by the army that is blockading the city and that on one level can be understood as a reference to the occupying Israeli army. He also feels oppressed, however, by the fact that, where there should be harmony, respect and peace between people in the city, there is hatred and distrust. In this extract (from Brown 1996: 36), صابر is contemplating his predicament.

ST

قال صابر مخاطبا نفسه: «ما أصعبَ أن يشعرَ الإنسانُ بوطأة الحصار، بل ما أصعبَ أن يكون جلّادُه من دمهِ ولحمه» .. ثم شرع يستحضر الأحلام الكبيرةَ التي طالما شارك فقراء المدينة في رسمها وتلوينها، فبدت لهُ كالطيور المتساقطة برصاص الصيادين ..

تراءت له مشاهد البؤسِ والخوف على شريط من الذكريات، فاشتعل فيه الحنينُ الى الهجرة، ولكن في أعماقِ قلبه جمرةٌ تأبى الانطفاء، فهي كلما ذوَت سرعان ما تعود الى الاتّقادِ من جديد.

كان صابر نهباً للهواجس والأفكار، فغدت تتجاذبه المسافات القريبة والبعيدة على نحوٍ مُلح، وتحولت حجرته الضيقة الى مسرح يتّسع الى ما يجري في مدينة البغي حيثُ جعلَ منها خيالُهُ الجانح مزاراً يؤمُّه بشرٌ غير عاديين، يأتون كالطيف بدون استئذان ويغادرون كأنهم سحابةٌ حبلى بالمطر.

Practical 14.3 Metaphor: نهر المخلوقات البشرية

Assignment

(i) Discuss the strategic decisions that you must take before starting detailed translation of the following text, and outline and justify the strategy you adopt, paying particular attention to issues of metaphor in the ST. The translation is to be included in a collection of translations of short stories by the Syrian writer زكريا تامر aimed at a non-specialist English-speaking readership.

(ii) Translate the following text into English

(iii) Explain the decisions of detail you made in producing your translation.

Contextual information

The ST is from a short story titled الاغنية الزرقاء الخشنة by the Syrian author زكريا تامر.

ST

نهر المخلوقات البشرية تسكع طويلاً في الشوارع العريضة المغمورة بشمس نضرة، حيث المباني الحجرية تزهو بسكانها المصنوعين من قطن أبيض ناعم ضغط ضغطاً جيداً في قالب جيد. وتعرج النهر عبر الأزقة الضيقة وبين المنازل الطينية المكتظة بالوجوه الصفراء والأيدي الخشنة، وهناك امتزجت مياهه بالدم والدموع وبصديد جراح أبدية وعثر النهر في ختام رحلته على نقاط مبعثرة بمهارة، مختبئة في قاع المدينة، فصب فيها حثالته الباقية.

وإحدى هذه النقاط مقهى صغير قابع قبالة المعمل الذي طردت منه قبل أشهر لارتكابي خطأ أتلف آلة من آلاته، ورواد هذا المقهى عمال يشتغلون في المصانع القريبة وفلاحون وبائعون متجولون وسائقو سيارات وتراكتورات وعربات وحمالون وأناس بلا عمل – مثلي – يجلسون جميعاً باسترخاء، يحتسون الشاي على مهل، ويثرثرون دون أن يكون بينهم أي معرفة سابقة.

وصاحب المقهى أبو أحمد رجل هرم، طويل القامة، عريض الكتفين، شاربه كث يضفي مسحة من القسوة على وجهه المملوء بالتجاعيد، وهو جد فخور بمقهاه وقد قال لي منذ أيام: «أبي كان فقيراً، لم يترك لي شيئاً عندما مات، هذا المقهى ملكته بعد تعب وجوع وغربة. لكي يكون الإنسان سعيداً، يجب أن يكون له شيء ما .. ملكه ويخصه وحده.»

15 Language variety

Register, sociolect and dialect

15.1 Basic principles

In this chapter, we look at an elusive, but important, aspect of meaning: characteristics in the way the message is formulated that reveal information about the speaker or writer. We shall call this 'speaker-related information'. For simplicity's sake, we shall apply the terms 'speaker' and 'listener' to spoken and written texts alike.

In this chapter, we will look at five kinds of speaker-related information: **tonal register**, **social register**, **sociolect**, dialect and **temporal variety**. Tonal and social register both fall under the more general category of register, while sociolect, dialect and temporal variety fall under a more general category that could be called 'sublanguage'. The relationship between these can be represented as in Figure 15.1.

There are two broad categories of speaker-related information that can be revealed through the manner, or style, in which the message is formulated. The first comprises things that speakers intend to reveal, notably the effect they want their utterances to

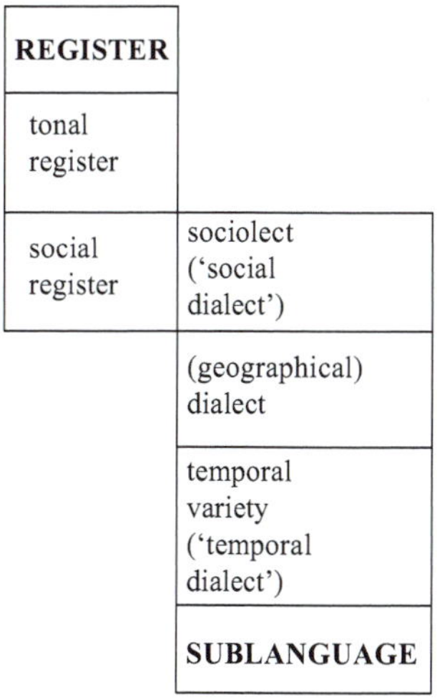

REGISTER	
tonal register	
social register	sociolect ('social dialect')
	(geographical) dialect
	temporal variety ('temporal dialect')
	SUBLANGUAGE

Figure 15.1 Types of speaker-related information.

have on the listener. The second comprises things that they do not necessarily intend to reveal, notably the social stereotypes they appear to belong to, as well as their regional and class affiliations. Any or all of these things can occur together, but, in analyzing style, it is useful to keep them as clearly distinct as possible, because it helps the translator to pin down what features are textually important.

15.2 Register

'Register' is a term used in so many different ways that it can be positively misleading. It is possible to isolate at least four theoretically distinct types of register that might be used in the analytic description of language (Hervey 1992). For our purposes, however, these fall into two types of register that it is methodologically useful for translators to distinguish.

15.2.1 Tonal register

The first is what we shall call 'tonal register'. This is the feature of linguistic expression that carries affective meaning, which we examined in Section 8.4. That is, it is *the tone that the speaker takes* – vulgar, familiar, polite, formal, etc. The affective meaning of a feature of tonal register is conveyed by a more or less deliberate *choice* of one out of a range of expressions capable of conveying a given literal message – compare, for example, الرجاء الصمت as opposed to اسكت or اخرس or in English 'Would you mind being quiet' or 'Silence please' as opposed to 'Shut up!'. As these examples suggest, the effect of tonal registers on listeners is something for which speakers can be held responsible, in so far as they are deliberately being obscene, polite, etc.

In handling tonal register, it is clearly important for the translator to accurately assess where the ST expression comes on the SL 'politeness scale' and to render it with an expression as close as possible to a corresponding TL degree of politeness. But it is not enough just to have a repertoire of expressions capable of injecting various affective meanings into a given literal message. Equally important is the *situation* in which the expression is used: different sorts of social transactions – preaching in a mosque or in a church, defending a client in court, selling a car to a male customer, etc. – all imply different tonal registers. Thus, at the start of a political speech in Arabic, the phrase وبهذه المناسبة اريد ان اقول is more likely to be translated by the relatively formal cliché 'I would like to take this opportunity to say [. . .]' than the less formal 'On this occasion I want to say [. . .]' (Dickson 1999: 12).

A case in which tonal register presents a more complex translation problem is the following, from a rather 'gushing' account of a visit to Morocco by a journalist from العربي magazine (Boothby 1996: 101): فلا نقول وداعا يا عذوبة المغرب بل . . . . إلى اللقاء 'And so we do not say "adieu" to Morocco but "au revoir"'. Here, the use of the Frenchisms in the English translation conveys the rather ornate and mannered nature of the original.

A further complication is presented by the fact that the source culture and the target culture may have different expectations regarding the appropriate tonal register(s) for a given situation. As the example أديني كيلو رز (Section 8.4) showed, it is as important to be aware of cultural differences as of situation.

15.2.2 Social register

A social register is a particular style from which the listener confidently infers what social stereotype the speaker belongs to. Of course, a stereotype by definition excludes individual idiosyncrasies of people belonging to the stereotype; but, however unfortunate this may be, we do tend to organize our interactions with other people on the basis of social stereotypes. These stereotypes cover the whole spectrum of social experience. They range from broad value-judgemental labels, such as 'pompous', 'down-to-earth', 'boring', etc., to increasingly specific stereotypical personality types, such as 'the henpecked husband', 'the macho football fan', 'the middle-aged *Guardian*-reading academic', etc. In so far as each of these stereotypes has a characteristic style of language use, this style is what we mean by social register. One important way in which social register differs from tonal register, therefore, is that the speaker typically does not intentionally reveal the speaker-related information. Social register carries information about such things as the speaker's educational background, social persona (i.e. a social role the person is used to fulfilling), occupation and professional standing and so on.

A social register is, in other words, a style that is conventionally seen as appropriate to both a type of person and a type of situation. This is one reason why a given genre, or text type (Chapter 6), requires a specific style and often a specific jargon. Selecting the appropriate style and jargon is to a great extent a matter of fulfilling expectations with regard to social register: selecting a wrong social register risks undermining the speaker's social persona as a credible authority on the subject.

Clearly, in translating an ST that has speaking characters in it, or whose author uses social register for self-projection, a major concern is constructing an appropriate TL register. In purely informative texts, this is relatively straightforward, the main problem being to find the conventional TL style for the genre. The more journalistic or literary the ST, however, the greater the importance of characterization and therefore of social persona. When the translator is operating between closely related cultures – such as two Western European cultures, for example – it is sometimes possible to match social stereotypes reasonably closely – football fans, perhaps, or guests at an aristocratic ball, or university students. However, when the cultures are more distant from each other – for example, British culture and Egyptian culture – matters become more problematic. It is, for example, difficult to say what would be the British 'equivalent' of a peasant from southern Egypt or of a populist Islamic preacher, just as one could hardly imagine the Egyptian equivalent of a New Age 'guru'.

Social and tonal register are not always fully distinguishable, for two reasons. First, it is not always clear whether a style of expression reflects social stereotyping or the speaker's intentions towards the listener. For some speakers, an utterance 'I am not prepared to put up with further prevarication' might be a reflection of their social status; certain highly educated older people in particular tend to have a consistently formal social register. For many other speakers, however, this style of language would be a function of tonal register; it is a form of language that they would only use when they were deliberately adopting a tone of formality and authority.

Second, characteristics of particular social registers often include features of tonal register. 'The boys done well' said by a football manager to a television interviewer after a winning match not only reflects a social persona of the manager as 'down-to-earth' and 'straight-speaking' but is also an instance of a tonal register in which the manager presents himself as an authoritative but kindly father figure.

In the case of Standard Arabic, it is easier to identify tonal register than it is to identify social register. The intrinsic formality of Standard Arabic makes it difficult to establish clear links between the kind of language used and social stereotypes. In translating Standard Arabic into English, however, this does not mean that social register should necessarily be ignored. In order to achieve a form of English that is contextually acceptable, it may be necessary to impose a social register on the translation, even where there is no obvious social register in the ST.

In cases where it is impossible to disentangle tonal and social register without lengthy analysis, it is acceptable for translation purposes simply to use 'register' as a cover term.

15.3   Sociolect

We turn now to three language varieties that might be termed 'sublanguages', because they can, for some people, constitute a complete language (i.e. the only language variety they ever use). These are sociolect, dialect ('geographical dialect') and temporal variety ('temporal dialect').

Whereas a social register belongs to a fairly narrowly stereotyped social persona, a sociolect is defined in terms of sociological notions of class. A sociolect is a language variety typical of one of the broad groupings that together constitute the 'class structure' of a society. Examples of major sociolects in the UK are those labelled 'urban working class', 'white collar', etc. However, mixed sociolectal/regional designations are often more helpful in recognizing language variants than purely sociological ones – for example, 'Leith urban working class' or 'Bermondsey urban working class'. Further complications arise from the often marked differences in the speech of men and women.

Despite these reservations, sociolectal features can convey important speaker-related information. If they are salient features of the ST, the translator cannot ignore them when deciding on a strategy. The first crucial factor to consider is what their function is in the ST. So, for example, translating an eyewitness account of a crime for Interpol, one would very likely decide to subordinate sociolect to getting the facts clear. On the other hand, if sociolect is not incidental, one might need to find a way of showing this in the TT.

Even in such cases, however, the translator has to weigh several questions in forming a strategy: What is the function of the ST sociolect(s)? What is the purpose of the TT? Would it not be safest to produce a TT in a bland 'educated middle class' sociolect? If the strategy is to incorporate some TL sociolectal features corresponding to those in the ST, the requirements are similar to those involved in choosing social register: it has to be decided what sociolects are the most appropriate, and there must be no inconsistencies in TT sociolect (assuming there are none in the ST sociolects).

The inherent formality of Standard Arabic means that Standard Arabic cannot really be said to have different sociolects. Like English, however, colloquial Arabic does have sociolects. This means that, in translating from Arabic to English, one only needs to worry about sociolect in the ST if the ST is written wholly or partly in colloquial Arabic. However, as with social register, it may sometimes be necessary to impose a sociolect on the TT in order to achieve a form of English that is contextually acceptable. Where different colloquial Arabic sociolects are related to education, these will tend to fit into one of the three levels of عامية, as described in Section 15.5.1.

15.4 Dialect

The fourth type of speaker-related information that can be inferred from style concerns what part of the country speakers are from – where they grew up, where they live and so on. This inference is based on dialect (sometimes called 'geographical dialect'), a language variety with features of accent, lexis, syntax and sentence formation characteristic of a given region.

Marginally at least, both standard varieties of English and Standard Arabic can be said to have dialect forms. Thus, even in formal writing in Scotland, 'outwith' is the standard equivalent of English 'outside', American 'diaper' is the equivalent of British 'nappy', etc. In Standard Arabic, the word for 'training' is تكوين (calqued on French 'formation') in North Africa but تدريب elsewhere. Similarly, in Morocco, the normal Standard Arabic form for 'noon' is زوال while in most Arab countries it is ظهر. Neologisms are also frequently subject to regional variation within the Arab world, as different forms are proposed in different countries. Thus, 'mobile phone' was originally referred to as جَوَّال in Saudi Arabia, نَقَّال in Kuwait and سَيَّار in the Emirates, as well as تلفون محمول (or هاتف محمول) and موبايل, this last being a cultural borrowing that is in general use.

In the Arab world, most dialects fit into the definition of dialect given in this section; they are language varieties characteristic of a given region. There are also dialectal varieties of Arabic, however, that do not fit this definition – tribal dialects where the tribe in question does not inhabit a discrete region and where it may live together with speakers of other dialects in the same region. Tribal dialects do, of course, have a regional element; there are areas that are the home regions of particular tribes and others that are not. A tribe, however, is also a socially defined entity. Accordingly, tribal dialects in the Arab world are partially geographical – that is, they are partially dialects as the term 'dialect' was defined at the beginning of this section, and they are partially sociological (i.e. they also have a sociolectal aspect).

15.5 Temporal variety

In addition to socially based language varieties – sociolects – and geographically based language varieties – dialects (as well as socially and geographically based language varieties as in the case of many tribal dialects of Arabic) – languages also have what we can call 'temporal varieties' (sometimes called 'temporal dialects'), reflecting the fact that the pronunciation, spelling, lexis, morphology, syntax and semantics, etc. of any language change over time. We can see this in English: the language of Shakespeare is different from modern English, but even that of nineteenth-century novelists is different from that of modern novelists. Very few people in Britain now say 'five-and-twenty past four' – though this is the older form; almost everyone now uses the more modern form 'twenty-five past four'.

Arabic is a language with a very long and unbroken written tradition. The language of pre-Islamic poetry is generally agreed in some sense to be the same Arabic language as is used in contemporary newspapers, despite the fact that pre-Islamic Arabic has many linguistic features that are no longer found in modern Arabic. This is partly a social and cultural matter: it is how Arabs view the situation. But more importantly, it reflects the fact that the commonalities between pre-Islamic Arabic and 'Modern Standard' Arabic, particularly in terms of grammar, are so great that the two can be happily regarded as temporal varieties of the same language.

In the case of English, by contrast, while we might regard the language of Shakespeare and contemporary English as varieties of the same language, the language used by Chaucer (who lived two hundred years before Shakespeare), known as Middle English, is better regarded as a different language to contemporary English. The grammatical, lexical and other differences between Middle English and contemporary English are so great that a modern English speaker can only really understand Middle English if he or she makes a special study of it.

Temporal issues are potentially relevant to the translation of any pre-modern Arabic text into English. In some cases, one is unlikely to want to translate a pre-modern text, even one that has obviously archaic features, into a form of English that includes non-contemporary features. Thus, a translation of the universal history كتاب تاريخ الرسل والملوك (839–923) محمد بن جرير الطبري by the classical Islamic writer (Tabari's *Annals*) is likely to be better translated using contemporary English, there being no obvious reason for introducing non-contemporary English into the TT.

In the case of Quran translation, by contrast, translators have opted for different styles, some of which include features of non-contemporary temporal varieties. Consider the following, verse 5 of سورة الضحى:

ولسوف يعطيك ربك فترضى

This has been translated by different Quran translators (Pickthall 1930; Yusuf Ali 1938; Arberry 1964; Shakir 1983; Sarwar 1981; Al-Hilali and Khan 1997; and Saheeh International 1997) as follows:

> *Saheeh International:* And your Lord is going to give you, and you will be satisfied.

Pickthall: And verily thy Lord will give unto thee so that thou wilt be content.

Yusuf Ali: And soon will thy Guardian-Lord give thee (that wherewith) thou shalt be well-pleased.

Shakir: And soon will your Lord give you so that you shall be well pleased.

Muhammad Sarwar: Your Lord will soon grant you sufficient favors to please you.

Al-Hilali and Khan: And verily, your Lord will give you (all i.e. good) so that you shall be well-pleased.

Arberry: Thy Lord shall give thee, and thou shalt be satisfied.

The only TTs that do not make use of archaic elements are Saheeh International and Muhammad Sarwar. For example, Pickthall, Yusuf Ali and Arberry make use of the archaic second-person singular pronouns 'thy', 'thee' and 'thou'. Pickthall and Al-Hilali and Khan use the archaic 'verily'. Yusuf Ali and Shakir make use of the archaic verb inversion after 'soon' ('soon will').

The use of archaic forms in Quran translation clearly reflects the language of earlier Bible translations, such as the King James Version (though when this was first published in the seventeenth century, the language was not particularly archaic). It thus seems to be motivated by a desire to produce an English translation in an appropriately 'religious' register. Just as more recent Bible translations into English have abandoned archaic elements, so more recent Quran translations (e.g. Saheeh International 1997) adopt a more contemporary style of language.

Sometimes modern texts incorporate archaic elements. An example that we have already seen in Section 13.3.2 is the use by the Egyptian communist طارق المهدوي in his book ولعلهم لا يدركون of the Quranic-type phrase الاخوان المسلمون على مذبح المناورة to pour scorn on the Muslim Brotherhood, translated by Calderbank (1990) as 'And perhaps they know not', where the archaic negative 'know not' is used to suggest a religious association of the phrase, even if English-speaking readers may not be fully aware of its quasi-Quranic nature.

15.5.1 Diglossia

In many European languages, some speakers have as their own dialect the so-called standard language. Technically, a standard language can be defined as a language variety that 'cut[s] across regional differences, providing a unified means of communication and thus an institutionalized norm that can be used in the mass-media, in teaching the language to foreigners and so on' (Crystal 2008: 450). In English, most educated speakers share a standard language, albeit with some regional influence, especially in the area of pronunciation.

Arabic differs from English in that the standard language – Standard Arabic – is not the native language of any speakers; that is to say, nobody is brought up speaking Standard Arabic. Rather, everyone starts out learning the dialect (عامية) of the area in which they live, and if they go on to achieve literacy, they subsequently learn Standard Arabic (فصحى) in an educational environment.

The language situation of Arabic is sometimes referred to as one of **diglossia**. Diglossia can be defined as a situation where two very different varieties of a language co-occur throughout a community of speakers, each having a distinct range of social functions. These varieties are felt to be alternatives by native speakers and usually have special names. It is customary to talk in terms of a high variety and a low variety, corresponding broadly to a difference in formality; the high variety is learnt in school and tends to be used in religious contexts, on radio programmes, in serious literature, formal lectures, etc. Accordingly, it has greater social prestige. The low variety, by contrast, is used in family conversations and other relatively informal settings.

Within the basic diglossic distinction between Standard Arabic and colloquial Arabic, it is possible to make further distinctions. It has been proposed by the Egyptian linguist El-Said Badawi (Badawi and Hinds 1986: viii–ix) that, within Standard Arabic, one can distinguish between what he terms (i) فصحى التراث 'Standard Arabic of the classical heritage' and (ii) فصحى العصر 'contemporary Standard Arabic'. The former is specifically the linguistic vehicle of the legacy of Islamic high culture and religion, whilst the latter is used to deal with modern culture and technology. In Egypt, which is the focus of Badawi's account, فصحى التراث is little different from the classical descriptions of فصحى, as might be expected in what is now in effect a liturgical language. فصحى العصر, on the other hand, exhibits features that contrast with the usual classical conventions – particularly, Badawi suggests, a marked preference for sentences beginning with a noun rather than a verb. When spoken, فصحى العصر shows other departures (phonic, morphological and syntactic) from the norms of فصحى التراث, most of which reflect forms found in Egypt colloquial Arabic.

Badawi believes that three levels of colloquial Arabic can usefully be distinguished in Egypt: (i) عامية الاميين 'colloquial Arabic of the illiterate'; (ii) عامية المتنورين 'colloquial Arabic of the "enlightened" (i.e. literate)'; and (iii) عامية المثقفين 'colloquial Arabic of the highly educated'. The mother tongue of any Egyptian child is always either عامية المتنورين or عامية الاميين, depending normally on whether the child comes from a literate or illiterate background. If the child then goes to school, he or she learns and begins to function either in فصحى العصر (in secular schools) or فصحى التراث (within the religious system). Mastery of the third, acquired, level of عامية المثقفين is restricted to a small percentage of the population. This level of colloquial Arabic is in effect the spoken counterpart of the written فصحى العصر and is used only in formal contexts between highly educated people or the would-be highly educated. Elsewhere, their language is normally عامية المتنورين, although some may also initially have been speakers of عامية الأميين.

The situation in other Arab countries is typically analogous to that in Egypt, the most important exceptions being the countries of the Maghreb – Tunisia, Algeria and Morocco – where French is widely spoken in addition to Arabic (and in some areas Berber).

It is possible that a translator will be called upon to translate material in an Arabic dialect; films, plays and television soaps are all typically written (and performed) in dialect; informal interviews are also likely to be highly dialectal. In such cases, there are three potential main problems.

First, it has to be decided how important the dialect features of the ST are to its overall effect. In the case of an informal Arabic interview, for example, one is likely to want to put the TT into informal but not obviously dialectal English. In the case of literary works, however (e.g. where some speakers' speech is represented in a specific marked dialect), the translation might also justifiably represent this in a dialect form.

Second, if dialect does have a function in the ST, an essential strategic decision is whether and why to use TL dialectal features. There are very obvious dangers in using TL dialect. It is likely to be a fairly arbitrary matter which – if any – TL dialects correspond to the ST ones. An English TL dialect is also likely to sound ridiculous on the lips of a Sudanese farmer, or a Moroccan labourer or a Lebanese society hostess. In many cases, dropping ST dialect features is likely not to incur very damaging translation loss. If it does, but there seems no reasonable way of using dialect in the TT, the important ST effects produced by dialect must likely be rendered through compensation. One technique is to make occasional additions (e.g. '[. . .] she said in a thick Tangiers accent').

Sometimes, if ST dialectal features are closely associated with other features of language variety, it is possible to use TL sociolect or register to compensate for the loss of connotations carried by the ST dialect(s).

A final, drastic possibility is wholesale cultural transplantation. This is the exception rather than the rule. It is generally only done with literary works, for commercial reasons. It often requires such extreme adaptation that it can barely be described as translation, however brilliant the TT may be.

The third problem is one that applies to sociolect and register as well: once a decision is taken to use TL dialect, it must be accurate, and it must be consistent. Many literary TTs in particular are sabotaged by weaknesses in the translator's grasp of language variety. Among the many skills a translator has to have is that of pastiche.

15.6   Code-switching

It must also be borne in mind that many people are adept at switching between language varieties, and even between languages. This is known as **code-switching**. Code-switching in Arabic may be between one of the three levels of عامية or two levels of فصحى (adopting Badawi's classification) or between a form of عامية and a form of فصحى. Speakers may switch codes relatively unconsciously, particularly in a formal situation (such as a radio or television interview), and start out speaking فصحى, or a form of Arabic close to فصحى, but gradually drift into a form of Arabic more obviously like عامية, because they find it impossible to maintain their flow of speech using فصحى.

Language users may also make use of code-switching more consciously for social camouflage, to match their social persona to the particular situation they are in. Or they may use it for storytelling purposes, imitating the various characters in their story. Or they may use it for satirical purposes, sprinkling the text with expressions from different registers, sociolects or dialects. In this respect, consider the following from an article in the well-known Kuwaiti cultural magazine العربي about Muslims in America (Pennington 1999: 16):

وهكذا «فالمستقبل لنا» كما يقول الدكتور مهدي، المتكلم في مجلس الشؤون الاسلامية في امريكا،
وهو المتفائل الاكبر في أمريكا، فعندما كان العرب والمسلمون يقولون له «مش ممكن!» كان يرد على
المتخاذلين «بالعمل والصبر كل شيء ممكن» [. . .]

As the spokesman for the Council of Islamic Affairs in America and America's greatest optimist, Dr Mahdi, puts it, 'The future belongs to us'. When Arabs and Muslims used to tell him, 'That's impossible', his reply to these weak-willed characters was 'With work and patience all things are possible'.

Here, the use of the colloquial مش ممكن is particularly striking. As might be expected from a text of this kind, the entire article is otherwise written in Standard Arabic. And although the colloquial مش ممكن represents what people may actually have said, and literally states that something is impossible, it does more than this. The use of the dialectal form also connotes an attitude of unconsidered negativeness – that is, this was the kind of throwaway response Dr Mahdi got from people, an answer not even worth expressing in 'proper' (i.e. Standard) Arabic. By contrast, Dr Mahdi's attitude بالعمل والصبر كل شيء ممكن is expressed in rather elegant Standard Arabic, highlighting his dignified, considered and confident view of the problem.

Because code-switching is a definite strategic device, translators must be prepared to convey in the TT the effects it has in the ST. In doing this, of course, they are subject to the requirements and caveats that we have outlined in discussing register, sociolect and dialect. Thus, in the previous example, the translator has not attempted to put مش ممكن into a rather obviously implausible 'equivalent' English dialect form and has equally avoided a more colloquial English form than 'That's impossible', such as 'No way'. There is, however, a degree of compensation for the use of the relatively neutral 'That's impossible' in the translation of بالعمل والصبر كل شيء ممكن. Although 'With work and patience all things are possible' is a fairly direct translation of the Arabic, it also has a rather formal and even poetic feel to it in English (notably more so than a more workaday translation, such as 'Nothing's impossible if one works/you work hard', which might be more normal in many contexts). This maintains at least some stylistic contrast with the previous 'That's impossible' in the English TT and creates a similar effect to that produced by the juxtaposition of colloquial and Standard direct speech in the Arabic.

Code-switching is also fairly common in political speeches. It was a particularly prominent feature of the speeches of the late Egyptian leader جمال عبد الناصر; indeed, عبد الناصر is often said to have been the first political leader to have made wide use of colloquial Arabic in his speeches. Consider the following, which is taken from a speech delivered at Port Said on Victory Day, 23 December 1957 (cited in Holes 1993: 43; the following analysis is based on that of Holes). This was one year after Egypt's nationalization of the Suez Canal and the subsequent confrontation between Britain, France and Israel on the one hand and Egypt on the other. Following Egypt's nationalization of the Suez Canal, Israel occupied Egypt up to the Canal under the terms of a secret agreement with Britain and France, and Britain and France then occupied the Canal Zone under the pretext of protecting the Canal. This 'tripartite aggression' was foiled by American insistence that Britain, France and Israel withdraw. The outcome was perceived in the Arab world as a great victory for Egypt, and عبد الناصر became a central figure in Arab politics and the non-aligned movement of Third-World states. The full written text of this speech is available online at http://www.nasser.org/Speeches/browser.aspx?SID=569&lang=ar. To listen to the recording, click on استمع لهذا الجزء in the top left-hand corner; the relevant section of the speech begins at 55 minutes, 43 seconds (43:55) and ends at 65 minutes, 92 seconds (92:65).

Colloquial elements in this text have been placed within curly brackets to make them easier to identify. The symbol ﻗ is also used exceptionally here to indicate a *hamza* in Egyptian colloquial Arabic, which derives from a ق in Classical Arabic. Where ث is pronounced as س, this is transcribed as ﺙ. Where ذ is pronounced as ز, this is transcribed as ﺫ. Except where marked in the text, final case and mood endings are not pronounced in the original speech.

إن مصر أيها الإخوة رغمَ ما قاسيناه، إن {إحنا بنتّبع سياسِية} عدم الانحياز، سيا{سِ}ـة الحياد الايجابي {علشان} نكبّر معسكر {إلـ}سلام لأن العالم إذا انقسم الى معسكرين وأصبحت دول {إلـ}ـعالم منقسمة جز{ء} منها مع هـ{ﺫ}ا المعسكر وجز{ء} مع المعسكر الآخر، لا بد أن تقوم حرب ولا بد أن تقاسي البشرية الأهوال .. {إلنهاردا} حينما ننادي بالحياد {إلا}يجابي وحينما ننادي بعدم الانحياز، إنما نعمل على كسر حِدّة التوتر [. . .] وإنما نعمل على تـ{ﺛ}ـبيت {إلـ}سلام وعلى تدعيم {إلـ}سلام .. {إلنهاردا} يا اخواني {نبصّ} للماضي بانتصاراته .. {نبصّ} للماضي بمعاركه .. {نبصّ} للماضي {بتاعنا} بشهدائه .. {نبصّ} للاعلام {بتاعتنا اللي} رفعناها بالنصر {ونفْتِكِر الاعلام بتاعتنا اللي} ضُرّجت بالدماء ونتّجه الى المستقبل ونعمل ونبني من أجل {إلـ}سلام، نعمل ونبني من أجلِ خلق وطن متحرر قوي ..

A fairly literal translation of this (Holes 1993: 43), with English elements corresponding to major colloquial features of the ST in curly brackets, is as follows:

Egypt, brother Egyptians, despite what we have suffered – {we are pursuing the policy} of non-alignment, the policy of positive neutrality {so that} we increase the size of the peace camp, because if the world is divided into two camps, one group in one camp and one in the other, there is bound to be war, and humanity is bound to suffer its horrors . . . {Today}, when we call for positive neutrality, and when we call for non-alignment, we are simply working towards reducing the sharpness of tension [. . .], and working towards stabilizing and supporting peace . . . {Today}, my brothers, {we look} to the past with its victories, {we look} to the past with its battles, {we look} to the past of ours with its martyrs, {we look . . . to the flags of ours} which we held aloft in victory and {we remember those flags of ours which} were soaked in blood, and go forward to the future to work and build for the sake of peace, to work and build to create a strong, liberated homeland.

Some of the colloquial uses in this text – and particularly those that have not been marked up in the English TT – may be thought of as incidental, in the sense that they give the text a slight colloquial flavour without fully removing it from the realm of Standard Arabic into the realm of colloquial Arabic. Obvious examples are those deviations from Standard Arabic that involve only a slight change in pronunciation. More interesting from a stylistic point of view are cases in which unambiguously colloquial forms are used (i.e. cases where the word itself is part of colloquial Egyptian rather than part of Standard Arabic). Cases in point are احنا 'we', بنتّبع '[we] follow' (with the colloquial prefix بـ), النهاردا 'today' (twice), نبصّ 'we look' (four times), بتاعنا/بتاعتنا 'of us/our' (three times) and اللي (twice). This text in some respects deals with quite general and even abstract issues (e.g. لأن العالم إذا انقسم الى معسكرين وأصبحت دول الـعالم منقسمة جزءٍ منها مع هذّا المعسكر وجزءٍ مع المعسكر الآخر، لا بد أن تقوم حرب ولا بـد أن تـقاسي البشرية الأهوال). However, where the unambiguously colloquial elements are used, they tend to be much less abstract, to deal with the here and now (e.g. النهاردا 'today') and to introduce a sense of intimacy and solidarity between the speaker and the audience by making use of the notion of 'us' (e.g. احنا 'we', نبصّ 'we look', بتاعنا 'our').

From the point of view of producing a more idiomatic translation than the one just given, this presents something of a challenge. Clearly, it would not be appropriate to render the Arabic colloquial forms into English dialectal forms. It might, however, be possible to compensate in kind and in place in various ways. For example, النهاردا حينما ننادي بالحياد الإيجابي وحينما ننادي لعدم الانحياز might be translated along the lines 'Today, my friends, when we advocate positive neutrality, and non-alignment' with the addition of 'my friends' in the English to compensate for the loss of 'solidarity' in the use of the word 'today'. An alternative might be 'Today, when we in Egypt advocate positive neutrality and non-alignment' or 'Today, when we Egyptians . . . '. In other circumstances, other techniques might be possible; in yet others, it might be better to accept the translation loss without attempting any form of compensation.

15.7 Representations of speech in written Arabic

The examples بالعمل والصبر كل شيء ممكن and مش ممكن, which were discussed in Section 15.6, illustrate two approaches to the representation of spontaneous speech in written Arabic. The first is to relay speech as it was actually said, or, in the case of fiction, as it might have been said. The second is to 'convert' the actual or imagined colloquial Arabic into Standard Arabic.

One type of writing in which spontaneous speech is regularly represented is modern fiction. Some writers make regular use of colloquial Arabic in representing direct speech. The following is from the short story عرس الزين by the Sudanese writer الطيب صالح (n.d.: 5). (This will also be the ST for Practical 15.3.) Here, the colloquial elements are in a rural Sudanese dialect of an area on the Nile north of Khartoum. Because most readers are unlikely to be familiar with this dialect, we have provided English glosses for the dialect forms (marked with a superscript in the ST) in notes at the end of the ST.

قالت حليمة لبائعة اللبن لآمنة – وقد جاءت كعادتها قبل شروق الشمس – وهي تكيل لها لبناً بقرش:

«سمعت الخبر؟ الزين مو داير يعرّس».[1]

وكاد الوعاء يسقط من يدي آمنة. واستغلت حليمة انشغالها بالنيا فغشتها اللبن.

كان فناء المدرسة «الوسطى» ساكناً خاوياً وقت الضحى، فقد أوى التلاميذ إلى فصولهم. وبدا من بعيد صبي يهرول لاهث النفس، وقد وضع طرف ردائه تحت إبطه حتى وقف أمام باب «السنة الثانية» وكانت حصة الناظر.

«يا ولد يا حمار. ايه أخَّرك؟»[2]

ولمع المكر في عيني الطريفي:

«يا أفندي سمعت الخبر؟»[3]

«خبر بتاع ايه يا ولد يا بهيم؟»[4]

ولم يزعزع غضب الناظر من رباطة جأش الصبي، فقال وهو يكتم ضحكته:

«الزين ماش يعقدو له بعد باكر».[5]

وسقط حنك الناظر من الدهشة ونجا الطريفي.

Notes on colloquial forms in ST

1 الزين مو داير يعرّس 'Doesn't Zein want to get married?': مو = negative particle, داير = 'wanting', '[he] wants'.

2 «يا ولد يا حمار. ايه أخَّرك؟» 'Boy, donkey, what has made you late?': ايه = 'what'.

3 «يا افندي سمعت الخبر؟» 'Sir, did you hear the news?': افندي = 'Sir'.

4 «خبر بتاع ايه يا ولد يا بهيم؟» 'News of what, boy, dumb animal?': بتاع = 'of', بهيم = 'dumb animal'.

5 «الزين ماش يعقدو له بعد باكر» 'Zein, they're going to make the wedding contract for him the day after tomorrow': ماش = '[they are] going to', يعقدو = 'they make the wedding contract', باكر = 'tomorrow', بعد باكر = 'the day after tomorrow'.

The following, by contrast, illustrates the use of Standard Arabic for representing spontaneous speech. This extract is taken from the novel قلب الليل by نجيب محفوظ (n.d.: 3). (It will also be the ST for Practical 15.4.) The elements that we will further discuss next are placed in curly brackets.

قلت وأنا اتفحصه باهتمام ومودة :

- {إني} أتذكرك جيدا.

انحنى قليلا فوق مكتبي وأحدّ بصره نحو الغائم . وضح لي من القرب ضعف بصره، نظرته المتسولة، ومحاولته المرهقة لالتقاط المنظور، وقال بصوت خشن عالي النبرة يتجاهل قصر المسافة بين وجهينا وصغر حجم الحجرة الغارقة في الهدوء:

- حقا !؟ .. لم {تعد} ذاكرتي {أهلا لـ}لثقة، ثم {أن} بصري ضعيف..

- ولكن أيام خان جعفر لا يمكن أن تنسى ..

- مرحبا، إذن فأنت من {أهل} ذلك الحي!

قدمت نفسي داعيا إياه إلى الجلوس وأنا أقول :

- لم نكن من جيل واحد ولكن {ثمة} أشياء لا تنسى .

فجلس وهو يقول :

- ولكني أعتقد أنني تغيرت {تغيرا كليا} وأن الزمن وضع على وجهي قناعا قبيحا {من صنعه هو لا من صنع والدي} !

وقدم نفسه بفخر دون حاجة إلى ذلك قائلا :

- الراوي، جعفر الراوي، جعفر ابراهيم سيد الراوي ..

In this extract, not only is the dialogue relayed in Standard Arabic but also in a form of Standard Arabic that is quite formal and clearly distinct from colloquial Arabic. The writer chooses to use {إني} أتذكرك جيدا instead of أتذكرك جيدا or even أنا تغيرتُ {تغيرا}, both of which would be closer to the colloquial. Similarly, أتذكرك جيدا {كلياً, with its use of the absolute accusative (cf. root repetition; Section 10.2.3.2) and ولكن {ثمة} أشياء لا تنسى, are markedly formal usages (cf. the less formal ولكن هناك أشياء لا تنسى). Even {من صنعه هو لا من صنع والدي}. as is the word order in the phrase usages such as {لم {تعد}, {أهلا لـ}, {أن {ثم and {أهل} (in the way in which it is used here) seem chosen to distance the forms of this extract from those of colloquial speech.

Some writers choose in their representation of speech to avoid both colloquial Arabic and a markedly non-colloquial form of Standard Arabic. There are two ways in which this can be done. The first is to make use of a form of Arabic that obeys all the grammatical rules of the Standard language but that avoids words, phrases and grammatical usages that are markedly in contrast with those of colloquial Arabic. The result is a form of Arabic that has a colloquial feel without being colloquial. This approach was adopted by the playwright توفيق الحكيم, amongst others.

The second technique is to adopt a form of writing that makes various concessions to colloquial Arabic, either by using a certain number of colloquial words and phrases or by the sporadic adoption of colloquial and non-Standard grammatical forms. Consider the following from a book of jokes titled نوادر جحا relating to the Middle Eastern folk character Juha and written by يوسف سعد (n.d.: 10). (This will also be the ST for Practical 15.5.) Elements of relevance to the current discussion have been placed in curly brackets.

قابل أحد الفلاحين جحا وسار معه إلى أن وصل منزله وقال لجحا:
هل لك أن تسلفني حمارك اليوم فقط لأنقل عليه بعض السباخ؟
جحا: {هو} أنت لا تعرف؟
الفلاح: {أعرف ماذا}؟
جحا: في الواقع أن حماري مات {من} شهرين.
الفلاح: بعد أن سمع نهيق حمار جحا – {يعني} الحمار لا زال حياً يا جحا ولم يمت!
جحا: {يعني} تكذبني وتصدق الحمار!

Here, the form هو in the phrase هو أنت لا تعرف؟ 'Don't you know' is used, not pronominally as in Standard Arabic but as an 'interrogative particle signalling surprise or mild disbelief' (Badawi and Hinds 1986: 918) as in Egyptian Arabic. Similarly, أعرف ماذا adopts the word order of Egyptian Arabic أعرف أيه 'I know what' rather than the grammatically correct Standard Arabic ماذا أعرف. Finally, the use of يعني in the sense of 'You mean to say that' (etc.) is typical of Egyptian colloquial Arabic.

As might be expected, texts that make use of specifically colloquial elements also tend to make use of Standard Arabic forms that are compatible with the colloquial. In this example, for instance, the writer has used the phrase من شهرين, which is acceptable in both Standard and colloquial Arabic, avoiding the form منذ شهرين, which is only used in the Standard language.

It is also possible to find occasions where writers make use of forms that are not, strictly speaking, Standard Arabic in narration or other contexts where speech is not being represented. An example is the use of colloquial Arabic forms by يوسف إدريس in the first paragraph of the ST in Practical 4.3. This is reproduced here for convenience:

وحين كان يسترد أنفاسه لاحت له فكرة اللوكاندة، ولكنه نبذها في الحال فهم اثنان، وزبيدة حرمه، وخطرة، والحسبة فيها بالراحة خمسون ستون قرشا، والحكاية على الله.

Here, the colloquial Arabic elements الحكاية على الله, بالراحة, حسبة, حرمه, etc. (cf. Practical 4.3 for the meaning of these) are used within a general context of Standard Arabic vocabulary and sentence structure. The result is a combination of intimacy, as though the reader is being made privy to the thoughts of الشبراوي, as well as emotional distance, in that the authoritative third-person 'Standard Arabic' voice of the author is still present.

From a translation point of view, the various approaches to the representation of spoken colloquial in written Arabic present several problems. In most cases, the translator is unlikely to want to render dialect by dialect for reasons discussed in Section 15.5.1, although it would seem sensible to render forms that are dialectal or at least reminiscent of dialect in Arabic into fairly colloquial forms in English. In the case of the extract from يوسف إدريس, which we have just looked at, it would seem very difficult to find any technique for relaying in a TT the effect produced by the incorporation of colloquial Arabic forms in a Standard Arabic framework.

Interesting problems also arise in cases where the writer uses Standard Arabic to represent spoken Arabic and particularly where the form of Standard Arabic chosen is fairly distant from the colloquial. Here, the context may be decisive. Consider the following, which has already been discussed in Section 5.2 (Montgomery 1994: 21):

«يفتح الله»

« عشرون جنيها يا رجل، تحل منها ما عليك من دين، وتصلح بها حالك . وغدا العيد، وأنت لم تشتر بعد كبش الضحية ! وأقسم لو لا أنني أريد مساعدتك، فإن هذه النخلة لا تساوي عشرة جنيهات » .

TT

'No deal!'

'Look here my man, with twenty pounds you could settle your debts and make your life a lot easier. The Eid festival is tomorrow and you haven't even bought a sacrificial lamb yet. As I would not ordinarily pay more than ten pounds for a date palm like this, I would like to think that I am being of some assistance to you.'

As noted in Chapter 5, the use of slightly stilted formal English here is motivated by the rather formal nature of the Arabic and by the fact that the rest of the Arabic dialogue in the story is in colloquial.

Elsewhere, the informality of the situation itself may in effect rule out anything but a highly informal translation in English. This is the case with regard to the extract from النار والماء in Practical 2.2.

In other cases, however, the situation is not so clear. This is partly because the choice of colloquial or Standard Arabic or something in between to represent speech in written Arabic is, to a degree, at least a matter of personal preference on the part of the writer. Some writers, such as نجيب محفوظ, have consistently refused to make use of colloquial Arabic in their works (نجيب محفوظ has described the use of col-loquial as a 'disease'; Somekh 1991: 27). By contrast, يوسف إدريس uses colloquial Arabic to represent speech in some of his books but not in others – and it is not always evident that there is a reason behind the choice (cf. Holes 1995: 303–309).

Given this, the safest technique is likely to translate most Arabic representations of spoken language into contextually normal – and, in most cases, informal – TL forms in English. The exception is where a representation of spoken language in Arabic is so obviously formal and distant from spoken colloquial Arabic that the writer is clearly using this distance for stylistic effect. In such a case, it might be reasonable to use a similarly formal register in the English TT.

Practical 15

Practical 15.1 Tonal register: سيادة الأخ العزيز

Assignment

(i) Discuss the strategic decisions that you must take before starting detailed translation of the following text, and outline and justify the strategy you adopt.

(ii) Translate the text into English, paying particular attention to features of tonal register in the ST. The TT is to be included in a semi-academic book titled *The Road to War in the Gulf,* and you should take it that the TT audience will also be people with an academic interest in the subject (and therefore some specialist knowledge).

(iii) Explain the decisions of detail you made in producing your translation, paying particular attention to elements of formality and politeness in the ST and the TT.

Contextual information

This text is the start of an open letter written by the late King Hussein of Jordan in 1990 to the Iraqi leader Saddam Hussein after the Iraqi invasion of Kuwait but before the second Gulf War (between the American-led coalition and Iraq). In this letter, King Hussein is attempting to put himself forward as a possible mediator in the dispute. As subsequent parts of the letter make plain, King Hussein's general position is that, although Iraq may have had legitimate grievances against Kuwait, the invasion was unacceptable, and Iraqi troops must first withdraw from Kuwait before these can be addressed.

ST

سيادة الأخ العزيز الرئيس صدام حسين حفظه الله ورعاه

تحية المودة والأخوّة، عربية هاشمية أبعث بها إليك وبعد

فقد عدت لتوّي من لقاء الرباط الذي دعاني اليه جلالة الملك الحسن الثاني، مثلما دعا اليه فخامة الرئيس الشاذلي بن جديد، وقد كان موضوع اللقاء البحث في أزمة الخليج التي أصبحت أزمة الأمة العربية منذ تفجرها في الثاني من آب الماضي حين احتلت القوات العراقية الكويت وبدأ مسلسل الانزلاق نحو المظلم المجهول، وما رافقه من قلق لا ينتهي، بل يزداد حدة مع كل يوم وساعة ونحن نرى أن ما تمكنت أمتنا من تحقيقه في نضالها منذ مطلع هذا القرن، مهدد بالزوال أو الاندثار. ويحدث ذلك بعد فترة انتهاء الحرب الباردة، وفي الوقت الذي يعيش العالم فيه مرحلة انبثاق حقبة جديدة، تتشكل فيها ملامح نظام عالمي جديد، وتوضع للعبة الدولية فيه قواعد وقوانين تختلف عما عهدنا في الحقبة التي انحسرت ثم غربت.

Practical 15.2 Code-switching: الاشتراكية زي ما قال الميثاق

Assignment

(i) Discuss the strategic decisions that you must take before starting detailed translation of the following text, and outline and justify the strategy you adopt. Consider in particular where and why colloquial Arabic is being used in the text and the possible implications for translation. You are to translate the text for a work titled *The Language of Ideology,* which presents speeches by several modern political leaders and discusses the ideologies behind them.

(ii) Identify all elements in the ST that are in colloquial Egyptian Arabic.

(iii) Translate the text into idiomatic English.

(iv) Explain the decisions of detail you made in producing your TT.

Contextual information

This text is part of a speech by the former Egyptian leader جمال عبد الناصر delivered on 22 February 1964, Unity Day: الحرية السياسية والحرية الاجتماعية (from Holes 1993: 41–42). This speech has no particular historical significance, although it was made at a time when Nasser and Nasserism were at the height of their popularity, and socialism was a powerful political idea in the Arab world.

The full written text of this speech is available online at http://www.nasser. org/Speeches/browser.aspx?SID=1070&lang=ar. To listen to the recording, click on الجزء (جزء ١) استمع لهذا الجزء in the top left-hand corner; the relevant section of the speech begins at 43 minutes, 57 seconds (43:57) and ends at 47 minutes, 11 seconds (47:11).

Note that as in the case of the speech by عبد الناصر discussed in Section 15.6, in this passage, the symbol ڤ is used exceptionally to indicate a hamza in Egyptian colloquial Arabic, which derives from a ق in Classical Arabic. Where ث is pronounced as س, this is transcribed as ﺚ. Where ذ is pronounced as ز, this is transcribed as ﺬ. No attempt is made to mark vowel length reduction in Egyptian Arabic – for example, *waahid + a* (ة + واحد) > *wahda* (وحدة) 'one (f.)', although, where it differs from Standard Arabic, the colloquial vowelling is marked (in this case colloquial واخدة as opposed to Standard واجدة).

ST

. . . الاشتراكية زي ما قال الميثاق، هي الترجمة الصحيحة لكون الثورة عملاً تقدميّا . . . الاشتراكية يعني ايه؟ الاشتراكية ككلمة معناها إقامة مجتمع الكفاية والعدل .. إقامة مجتمع تكافؤ الفرص . . . إقامة مجتمع الانتاج وإقامة مجتمع الخدمات . . . الاشتراكية يعني ايه؟ نقُول اشتراكية كِلْمة واخدة بس . . . معناها تحرير الإنسان من الاستغلال الاقتصادي ومن الاستغلال الاجتماعي . . . الديمقراطية . . . الديمقراطية معناها تأكيد سيادة الشعب ووضع السلطة كلها في يد الشعب . . . وتكريسها لتحقيق أهداف الشعب . . . الديمقراطية هي الحرية السياسية والاشتراكية هي الحرية الاجتماعية . . . الكلام دا قلناه قبِل كدا، الكلام دا جا في الميثاق . . . ولا يمكن الفصل بين الديمقراطية والاشتراكية بأي حال من الأحوال . . . بدونُهم أو بدون واخدة منهم لا يمكن للحرية أن تتحقق . . . كأنّنا عندنا تجربة واضْحة . . . من قبل الثورة واجهة الديمقراطية المزيّفة لم تكن بأي حال تمثّل إلا ديمقراطية الرجعية . . . الديمقراطية إللي كانت موجودة قبل الثورة، لما كانت الرجعية تسيطر على اقتصاد البلاد وثروة البلاد، وكانت هي صاحبة النفوذ، وكانت الرجعية هي صاحبة الامتيازات، كانت ديمقراطية مزيّفة وكانوا بيقُولوا انّو فيه حرية سياسية أو فيه ديمقراطية سياسية .. ولكن الاستغلال والإقطاع ورأس المال المستغلّ قضى على كِلْمة الديمقراطية إللي قالوها . . . وعلشان كدا إحنا بنقُول . . . لا يمكن في أي حال أن يقال أن هناك حرية إلاّ إذا توفّرت الديمقراطية السياسية مع الديمقراطية الاجتماعية.

Practical 15.3 Representation of speech in written Arabic: قالت حليمة بائعة اللبن

Assignment

(i) Discuss the strategic decisions that you must take before starting detailed translation of the extract from the short story عرس الزين by the Sudanese writer الطيب صالح (n.d.: 5) discussed in Section 15.7 and beginning قالت حليمة بائعة اللبن. Outline and justify the strategy you adopt. You are to translate the text as part of a new English translation of the novel. Your intended readership is educated English speakers with only a general knowledge of the Arab world.

(ii) Translate the text into English.

(iii) Explain the main decisions of detail you made in producing your TT, paying special attention to issues of the translation of direct speech.

Contextual information

صالح (عرس الزين n.d.: 33) is a well-known novel by the contemporary Sudanese writer الطيب صالح. الزين himself is a kind of wise fool whose character has religious overtones. This extract is taken from the very start of the novel. الطُّرَيْفي (or, in

Sudanese Arabic, الطَّرَيِفِي) is the name of a schoolboy. ناظِر is an old word for 'headmaster'.

Practical 15.4 Representation of speech in written Arabic: قلت وأنا اتفحصه باهتمام ومودة

Assignment

(i) Discuss the strategic decisions that you must take before starting detailed translation of the extract from the novel قلب الليل by the Egyptian writer نجيب محفوظ (n.d.: 3) discussed in Section 15.7 and beginning قلت وأنا اتفحصه باهتمام ومودة. Outline and justify the strategy you adopt. You are to translate the text as part of a new English translation of the novel. Your intended readership is educated English speakers with only a general knowledge of the Arab world.

(ii) Translate the text into English.

(iii) Explain the main decisions of detail you made in producing your TT, paying special attention to issues of the translation of direct speech.

Contextual information

This extract is taken from the very start of the novel. The central character of the story is جعفر ابراهيم سيد الراوي, who we later learn has lost his family, position in society and fortune following his marriage to a Bedouin girl for love.

Practical 15.5 Representation of speech in written Arabic: قابل أحد الفلاحين جحا

(i) Discuss the strategic decisions that you must take before starting detailed translation of the joke from the book of Juha jokes titled نوادر جحا by يوسف سعد (n.d.: 10) discussed in Section 15.7 and beginning قابل أحد الفلاحين جحا. Outline and justify the strategy you adopt. You are to translate the text as part of a complete English translation of the book. Your intended readership is educated English speakers with only a general knowledge of the Arab world.

(ii) Translate the text into English.

(iii) Explain the main decisions of detail you made in producing your TT, paying special attention to issues of the translation of direct speech.

Contextual information

Juha is a fictitious character, whose humorous anecdotes – often with a moral, or even spiritual, element – are told throughout the Middle East.

16 Introduction to technical translation

16. 1   Introduction

All texts can be characterized in terms of genre. Therefore, there is no a priori reason for giving special attention to any one genre rather than any other. However, because most language students are not trained in a technical specialism, they are often in awe of more or less 'technical' texts. This is why we are devoting a whole chapter to the main translation issues they raise.

The term 'technical' is not confined to natural science and technology – though it is fairly frequently used as a shorthand term for 'natural scientific and technological'. Any specialist field has its own technical terms and its own genre-marking characteristics: a look at a hobbies magazine, a review of the rock scene or the city pages and the sports section of the paper is enough to confirm this. Texts in these and any other specialized fields are properly speaking 'technical' texts. In this and the following chapters, we will examine four major types of technical texts: medical texts (this chapter), botanical texts (Chapter 17), constitutional texts (Chapter 18) and Islamic finance texts (Chapter 19).

16.1.1   *Cultural commonality versus cultural non-commonality*

It is useful to make a basic distinction between two types of technical texts: culturally common technical texts (i.e. those technical texts whose basic notions are shared by both the SL culture and the TL culture) and culturally non-common technical texts (i.e. those technical texts whose basic notions are not shared by both the SL culture and the TL culture; cf. also cultural transposition, Chapter 4). It is, of course, possible to find texts that fall somewhere between these two types; the distinction is, however, useful for practical purposes.

Examples of culturally common texts are natural scientific and mathematical texts; these involve notions that are (or are considered to be) universal and therefore properly speaking independent of particular cultures. Another example of a culturally common text would be a text detailing the rules of football (soccer). The notions involved here are common to both the English-speaking world and the Arab world; although not universal in the sense that mathematics and the natural sciences are taken to be universal, they are culturally shared.

The main problems that arise in translating culturally common technical texts are likely to relate to technical terms, although there may also be difficulties relating to genre. Quite a lot of translation takes place between European languages in the natural sciences and associated technical areas. Although English has become the predominant global language in these areas, enough is still written in French, German, Spanish and other European languages to make this an area in which professional translators can specialize. In Arabic, on the other hand, one is unlikely to come across primary research in the natural sciences and fairly unlikely to come across highly technical technological material. It is much more likely that the professional translator will be called upon to translate government documents and other official material from Arabic to English, which, while not technical in the full sense, contain enough technical material to require specialist knowledge on the translator's part.

Good examples of culturally non-common texts, where the basic notions are not shared between the SL and the TL cultures, are texts in the traditional Islamic disciplines, such as exegesis – whether Quranic (تفسير) or poetic (شرح), Islamic Jurisprudence (فقه) and traditional Arabic grammar (نحو) and rhetoric (بلاغة). Another example is texts in the modern discipline of Islamic finance (Chapter 19), which draws centrally on Islamic Jurisprudence. A professional translator is not likely to be asked to translate texts on traditional Arabic grammar (although some academics do so). He or she is also relatively unlikely to be asked to translate texts in Islamic Jurisprudence, although there is a market for such translation amongst non-Arabic-speaking Muslims, and there exist several organizations in Britain, the United States and elsewhere devoted to promoting such translation. With the rapid growth of Islamic banks over the past few years, however, it is quite likely that Islamic finance will become an area in which specialized translators are in demand.

As is shown by the examples of the three types of lexical problem discussed next in Section 16.2, access to up-to-date specialist dictionaries and databanks is essential for technical translators working in scientific and technological fields. Of course, even the most recent materials will, by definition, lag slightly behind innovations and new coinages, because all scientific and technological fields are constantly developing. In any case, even the best reference material does not always give a single, unambiguous synonym for a particular technical term. This means that the normal caveats concerning use of dictionaries apply also to technical translation but in particularly acute form. That is, translators can only select the appropriate TL term from those offered by the dictionary if they have a firm grasp both of the textual context and of the wider technical context. The problem is not lessened, of course, by the fact that some of the context may remain obscure until the correct sense of the ST terms has been defined! We will consider now three types of lexical problems and two types of conceptual problems that can make technical texts difficult to translate.

16.2 Lexical problems in technical translation

By definition, technical texts tend to be relatively inaccessible to the non-specialist reader. There are both lexical and conceptual reasons for this inaccessibility. Lexical problems arise from the use of the following three types of ST terms:

1 Technical terms that are totally unfamiliar to the lay translator, because they are only used in technical contexts;

2   Technical terms that are familiar to the translator because they are also used in non-technical contexts but look as if they are being used in some technically specialized way in the ST;

3   Technical terms that are familiar to the translator because they are also used in non-technical contexts but do not obviously look as if they are being used in some technically specialized way in the ST.

All three of these lexical reasons can be illustrated from the following text, which is taken from a Syrian medical textbook, with following English translation (adapted from Al-Muhammad 1993: 205–209). Relevant lexical items have been placed in curly brackets; the superscript number before the closing bracket refers to the type of problem (1–3), as previously identified, and the symbol ø is used to indicate translation by omission.

ST

الاختبارات الجلدية

وهي ضرورية ومفيدة لدراسة وكشف بعض الإصابات الجلدية {الأرجية¹}. يلجأ الى هذه الاختبارات لتعيين وتحديد المواد {المحسسة¹} أو الضارة، كما هي الحال في أكزيما {التماسّ²} وخاصة {المهنية²} وفي {الشرّى¹} {المعاند¹} وفي {الأرج¹} الغذائي أو الدوائي وفي حالات {التحسس¹} بـ{الجراثيم³} و{الفطور²} و{الخميرات²} ومفرزاتها.

التفاعلات الجلدية

وهي قائمة على اختبار {تحسس²} خلايا طبقات الجلد كلها. {البشروية¹} و{الأدمية¹} (خلايا {مالبيكي¹} و{خلايا الأدمة³} و{المادة الاساسية²}).

طريقة التطبيق

يُنظَّف الجلد {بالأثير³} ويُنشَّف {يُخدَش³} بـ{نصيلة¹} التلقيح «{فاكسينوستيل¹}» شريطة ألا ينزف. ثم توضع المادة المراد اختبارها فوق {الخدش³} (كما هي الحال في لقاح الجدري) ويفضَّل أن يُجرى قريبًا من هذا {الخدش³} {شاهد²} خال من المادة المراد اختبارها. وتُقرأ النتيجة بعد ٢٤ أو ٤٨ ساعة.

TT

Skin tests

These tests are necessary for the study and investigation of some {allergic¹} skin reactions. They are conducted in order to specify and diagnose the {allergenic¹} or harmful substances, as for example in the case of {contact²} eczema, especially {occupational²}, in {chronic²} {urticaria¹}, and in food or drug {allergies¹}, or in {sensitivities¹} to {bacteria³}, {fungi²}, or {yeasts²} and their products.

Cutaneous reactions

These reactions are built on the {sensitivity[1]} of all skin layers, i.e. both {epidermal[1]} and {dermal[1]} layers ({Malpighian[1] cells}, and {intradermal cells[3]} and the {basal cell layer[2]}).

Methodology

First the skin is cleaned with {spirit[3]} and dried, then a {scratch[3]} is made using a {ø[1]} {vaccinostyle[1]} so that no bleeding is caused. Then, the substance which is to be tested is applied to the {scratch[3]} (as in a smallpox vaccination). Simultaneously, a {control[2]} test should be carried out close to the area of the {scratch[3]}. The result is read after 24 or 48 hours.

There are a fair number of Type 1 lexical problems in the ST. Examples are:

ST	TT	Additional notes
الأرجية	allergic	
المحسسة	allergenic	
الشرّى	urticaria	
المعاند	chronic	
الأرج	allergies	
التحسس	sensitivity	
البشروية	epidermal	Wehr gives بَشَرة as meaning 'outer skin, epidermis; cuticle; skin; complexion'; a translator might, therefore, be able to guess that بشروي is a technical term for 'epidermal' in this context.
الأدمية	dermal	Although أدمي is not given by Wehr, أدَم and أدَمة are given in the sense of 'skin'. The reference is to the layers that constitute the dermis (skin) itself. The *Oxford Arabic Dictionary* gives أدَمة as 'dermis'.
مالبكي	Malpighian	A specialist term that can only be discovered from specialist sources.
نصيلة	Ø	The phrase نصيلة التلقيح is used as a gloss, meaning the same as 'vaccinostyle'. نصيلة is not given in Wehr or in the *Oxford Arabic Dictionary*.
فاكسينوستيل	vaccinostyle	

Examples of Type 2 lexical problems are the following:

ST	TT	Additional notes
التماسّ	contact	Wehr gives تَماسّ as meaning '(mutual) contact'; 'contact eczema' is a technical term for eczema

		contracted through contact with certain substances (e.g. nickel, rubber).
المهنية	occupational	Wehr gives مهني as meaning 'professional, vocational'; while not strictly a technical term, 'occupational' seems a more appropriate adjective to apply to eczema contracted in a work environment.
الفطور	fungi	Both 'fungi' and 'mushrooms' are given by Wehr as translations of فِطْر. (Wehr does not, in fact, list the plural form فطور, but the translator could likely guess this.) The translator would need to be aware, however, that the hyperonym 'fungi' is intended here rather than the hyponym 'mushrooms'.
الخميرات	enzymes	'Leaven; ferment; barm, yeast; enzyme' are all given by Wehr as translations of خميرة. (Wehr does not, in fact, list the plural form خميرات, but the translator could likely guess this). The translator would need to be aware that 'yeasts' is intended here rather than 'enzymes', for example.
المادة الأساسية	basal cell layer	'Basal cell layer' is a technical term to denote the deepest cell layer of the dermis.
شاهد	control	Both Wehr and the *Oxford Arabic Dictionary* list شاهد in its standard non-technical sense of 'witness' but not in the technical sense of 'control' (in an experiment). Cf. also خال من المادة المراد اختبارها, subsumed under sense of 'control test'.

Type 3 lexical problems are the most dangerous, because the translator can easily fail to recognize the term as a technical one and mistakenly render it in its ordinary sense. The following terms, all found in Wehr, are used here in a technical sense that is not immediately apparent in the context:

ST	*TT*	*Additional note*
الجراثيم	bacteria	'Bacteria' is a technical term; 'germs' is an imprecise lay term.
خلايا الأدمة	intradermal cells	The gloss for أدمة given in Wehr, 'skin', could well mislead the translator here into thinking the term أدمة is being used in a standard non-technical way. The *Oxford Arabic Dictionary*, however, gives أدمة in the sense of 'dermis'. (The astute

		translator could also perhaps have guessed that this is a technical usage from the use of الأدمية as contrasted with البشروية earlier in the same sentence.)
الأثير	spirit	Wehr gives أثير to mean 'ether'.
يُخدَش	scratch	Wehr gives خدش as meaning 'scratch, scratch mark; graze, abrasion'. The term is used here in the sense of 'scratch', a specific technique used in vaccination and skin tests.
الخدش	scratch	See previous note.

16.3 Conceptual problems in technical translation

Conceptual problems in technical translation arise from ignorance of underlying knowledge taken for granted by experts but not understood by non-specialists and not explicit in the ST. Here are three examples from the Syrian medical text:

الاختبارات الجلدية	skin tests	The standard term in English is 'skin tests'. A form such as 'cutaneous tests' conveys the sense in English but is not the normal form used; it would suggest a translator who is not sure of the field.
الأرج الغذائي	food allergy	Wehr gives غذائي as meaning 'alimental, alimentary, nutritional, nutritious, nutritive'. A form such as 'nutritional allergy' is at best ambiguous but would certainly suggest a non-specialist translator.
[الأرج] الدوائي	drug [allergy]	Wehr gives دوائي as meaning 'medicinal, medicative, curative' (دواء is listed as meaning 'remedy, medicament, medication, medicine, drug'). 'Medicinal/curative allergy' amounts to a contradiction in terms and implies a translator ignorant of the field.

As illustrated by this example, conceptual problems in technical translation may arise from ignorance of underlying knowledge taken for granted by experts but not understood by non-specialists and not explicit in the ST. We may term this a Type 1 conceptual problem. However, conceptual problems may also arise from ignorance of what might be called the 'logic' of a discipline – methods of argumentation, the development of relations between concepts. We may term this a Type 2 conceptual problem.

Conceptual problems are particularly well illustrated by culturally non-common texts, although they can also be evident in culturally common texts. Consider the following text by the person considered to be the father of traditional Arabic grammar, سيبويه (1975, vol. 1: 34). Here, سيبويه discusses the use of the word order verb-object-subject in Arabic, taking as an example sentence ضَرَبَ زيداً عبدُ الله as opposed to the more normal verb-subject-object word order, as illustrated by ضَرَبَ عبدُ اللهِ زيداً, which he has just discussed:

ST

فإن قَدَّمتَ المفعول وأخَّرتَ الفاعل جرى اللفظ كما جرى في الأول وذلك قولك «ضرب زيداً عبدُ الله»، لأنك إنما أردتَ به مؤخراً ما أردتَ به مقدماً ولم تُرِد أن تُشغِل بأول منه وإن كان مؤخراً باللفظ [. . .] كأنهم إنما يُقدِّمون الذي بيانه أهمّ لهم وهم ببيانه أعنى [. . .]

It is worth giving a fairly literal translation of this text first, in order to make the Arabic material, which is quite difficult to follow, more comprehensible.

Fairly literal TT

If you prepose the object and postpose the subject, the utterance will be the same as in the first example; this is your saying, ضرب زيداً عبدُ الله, because you only intend by having it postposed what you intended by having it preposed. You did not intend to cause government in something which came first, even if it is postposed in the utterance. [. . .] It is as if they prepose that whose presentation is more important to them and what they are more concerned to present.

A more idiomatic translation of this, which attempts to respect some of the conventions of academic writing in English is as follows:

Idiomatic TT

If the direct object is preposed and the subject postposed – i.e. when the form ضرب زيداً عبدُ الله is used – the utterance will be essentially the same as in the previous example (i.e. ضَرَبَ عبدُ اللهِ زيداً). This is because the denotative meaning of an utterance containing a postposed subject is the same as that of an utterance containing a preposed subject; it is not intended that the verb should govern something which comes before the subject, even if the subject is postposed in the utterance. [. . .] Rather, it seems to be the case that the Bedouin Arabs prepose the element whose presentation is more important to them and which they are more concerned to focus on.

This text contains several cases of Type 1 conceptual problems (i.e. those that arise from ignorance of underlying knowledge taken for granted by experts but not understood by non-specialists and not explicit in the ST). The following are examples:

(i) In traditional Arabic grammar, different word orders (cf. Chapter 12) are described in terms of 'movement' of elements. Thus, in a word order verb-object-subject, the object is said to be 'preposed' (مقدم) and the object 'postposed' (مؤخر), as compared to what is regarded as a more basic word order, verb-subject-object. Even in this more basic verb-subject-object word order, however, one can talk about the subject being preposed (as in the phrase ما أردت به مقدماً in this text).

(ii) The word لفظ, which is given in Wehr as 'sound-group, phonetic complex; expression; term; word; wording' (etc.), has here a technical sense that seems to comprise not only the forms of the words in question, including, in particular, the case endings that the subject and object take, but also the denotative meaning (Chapter 7).

(iii) The phrase ما أردت به in this context must be taken to refer to denotative meaning rather than the kind of meaning that has to do with predictability of information, theme and rheme, etc. (Section 12.2.2).

(iv) The verb تُشغل is being used here to refer to the notion of 'government'. In traditional Arabic grammar, verbs are said to govern nouns; that is to say, nouns – and particularly direct objects – have the case endings they have (in the case of direct objects normally (لَ-) because of the 'government' or 'working' (إشغال) of the verb.

This text is also rendered extremely difficult to translate by the pervasiveness of Type 2 conceptual examples (those involving the 'logic' of the discipline – methods of argumentation, the development of relations between concepts). The following are examples of these:

(i) The entire argument is based on the notion of the reader as listener (قدّمتَ, أخّرتَ, لأنك, etc.). This directness was well motivated in an oral context in which a scholar directly addressed his students, as was the case in Classical Arabic culture. However, such a direct address to the reader is atypical of modern academic writing; if an attempt is made to render this text into a style that is at least reminiscent of such modern writing, a more impersonal style (involving such things as widespread use of the passive) is required (cf. Section 16.5).

(ii) Classical Arabic often made rather vague use of pronouns and other items whose reference could only be deduced from consideration of elements within the wider text. English tends to be more specific. Thus, the phrase في الاول has been translated in the idiomatic TT as 'in the previous example (i.e. ضَرَبَ عبدُ اللهِ زيداً)' – with the original Arabic phrase included in brackets. Similarly, in the phrase ما أردت به, the idiomatic TT makes explicit that the pronoun suffix ـه refers to a postposed subject by using the noun phrase 'postposed subject'. Finally, in the Arabic ST, كأنهم refers back to a fairly distant reference to العرب, which, in the case of Arabic grammatical writing, normally means the Bedouin Arabs who had retained the older, 'purer' forms of Arabic and were therefore felt to be the most reliable sources for correct

Arabic forms. In the English translation, the noun phrase 'The Bedouin Arabs' has been used in contrast to the Arabic pronominal هم.

As these examples show, conceptual problems are the most intractable of all those that face the technical translator. Non-specialists are always likely to reach a conceptual impasse from which no amount of attention to syntax or vocabulary can rescue them. In that case, they have only two options: to learn the concepts of the field in which they wish to translate or to work in close consultation with experts. In practice, trainee translators generally do both of these, quickly becoming experts themselves with the help of specialist supervisors. The best qualification for a technical translator is perhaps a combined technical and foreign language degree. However, not even people with that kind of qualification can expect to keep abreast of all the latest research – for instance, in a natural science – while at the same time earning their livings as translators, and they will sooner or later come up against problems that can only be solved by consulting other experts or, where possible, the author of the ST.

16.4   Legality and accuracy

These remarks about the need for consultation are not to be taken lightly. They raise the important question of the responsibility – and perhaps the legal liability – of the translator. There is a difference here between literary translation and technical translation. It is not that literary translators are not held responsible for their work, but the implications of mistranslation are generally less serious for them than for technical translators, where one mistake could cause financial damage or loss of life and limb. This is another respect in which technical translation is exemplary, bringing out extremely clearly a golden rule that is in fact essential to all translation: never be too proud or embarrassed to ask for help or advice.

The spectre of legal liability is a reminder that even the minutest error of detail on any level of textual variables is typically magnified in a technical text. A good example is the danger of confusing closely similar technical names in chemistry. Consider how similar are some of the prefixes and suffixes that can be attached to the root 'sulph' and how many possible permutations of them there are, as shown in Figure 16.1.

```
per-                          -ate
bi-                           -ide
de-        {  sulph  }        -ite
hypo-                         -onate
hydro-
```

Figure 16.1 Prefix and suffix permutations for 'sulph'.

The slightest error in affixation here will be a major factual error, whereas, in non-technical language, affixation may sometimes be a matter of style. For instance, there is generally little difference in practice between 'disbelieving' and 'unbelieving' or between 'inexcusable' and 'unexcusable', while 'dissociate' and 'disassociate' are synonyms of each other. In literary texts, the choice between affixes can often be based on euphony or style. But with technical terms in specialist texts of any kind, that temptation must be resisted absolutely.

Some parts of technical texts may be formulated in mathematical symbols. These normally need minimal effort in translation, although they cannot always be literally transcribed. Careful attention must be paid to any differences between SL and TL conventions. For example, where English has a decimal point in figures, Arabic has a comma.

The technical translator's paramount concerns, then, are accuracy of and conformity with the requirements of genre. In so far as the requirements of genre imply style, register is also important: the wrong tonal register may alienate the reader and undermine confidence in the TT; the wrong social register may misrepresent a social persona that the ST author has been at pains to project.

The relationship between accuracy and style is not always straightforward, however. If an ST is badly written or ungrammatical, should these infelicities be reflected in the TT, or should they be ironed out? This is a general and controversial issue. In our view, translators are not in principle responsible for 'improving' defective STs. However, this is sometimes necessary with technical texts (as indeed with any purely informative text), because the crucial thing is factual accuracy. If there is any potentially misleading or dangerous ambiguity or obscurity in the ST, there is every reason to keep it out of the TT – if necessary, after consultation with the author or an expert.

16.5   Generic features of English technical texts

Before embarking on the Practical, it will be useful to sharpen awareness of technical genres by noting some of the characteristics of technical texts in English. We shall take as an example text a British medical text on bacillary dysentery (Al-Muhammad 1993: 181–182).

Bacillary dysentery

The bacilli belong to the genus *Shigella* of which there are three main pathogenic groups, *dysenteriae, flexneri*, and *sonnei*, the first two having numerous serotypes. In Britain the majority of cases of bacillary dysentery are caused by *Shigella sonnei* although in recent years there has been a significant increase in imported infections caused by *Sh. flexneri* whereas sonnei dysentery has decreased.

Epidemiology

Bacillary dysentery is endemic all over the world. It occurs in epidemic form wherever there is a crowded population with poor sanitation, and thus has been a constant accompaniment of wars and natural catastrophes.

Spread may occur by contaminated food or flies but contact through unwashed hands after defecation is by far the most important factor. Hence the modern provision of hand basins, disposable towels and hot air driers goes a long way towards the prevention of the faecal-oral spread of disease.

Outbreaks occur in mental hospitals, residential schools and other closed institutions. The disease is notifiable in Britain.

Pathology

There is inflammation of the large bowel which may involve the lower part of the small intestine.

Sigmoidoscopy shows that the mucosa is red and swollen, the submucous veins are obscured and the mucopus is seen on the surface. Bleeding points appear readily at the touch of the endoscope. Ulcers may form.

Clinical features

There is great variety in severity. Sonne infections may be so mild as to escape detection and the patient remains ambulant with a few loose stools and perhaps a little colic. Flexner infections are usually more severe while those due to dysenteriae may be fulminating and cause death within 48 hours. In a moderately severe illness, the patient complains of diarrhoea, colicky abdominal pain and tenesmus.

The stools are usually small, and after the first few evacuations, contain blood and purulent exudate with little faecal material. There is frequently fever, with dehydration and weakness if the diarrhoea persists.

On examination there will be tenderness over the colon more easily elicited in the left iliac fossa. In sonne infection the patient may develop a febrile illness and diarrhoea may be mild or even absent; there is usually some headache and muscular aching. Arthritis or iritis may occasionally complicate bacillary dysentery as in Reiter's disease. Diagnosis depends on culture of faeces.

The following are typical features of technical texts in English:

1   The language is usually informative. Thus, although the *Bacillary Dysentery* text deals with a rather nasty and potentially fatal disease, there is little in it that expresses the emotional feelings of the writer towards the disease. As Pinchuk notes, 'the controlled language of science is manipulated in the direction of insipidity and colourlessness' (Pinchuk 1977: 165). Perhaps the only phrase in the text with some emotional charge is 'a constant accompaniment of wars and natural catastrophes' in section 2. Here, an emotional effect is achieved – whether deliberately or not – by the rhythm of the phrase as well as alliteration and assonance.

2   An impersonal style is used. Accordingly, the following features are likely to be encountered:

a The subjects of sentences are likely to be abstract. Thus, in section 2 of the *Bacillary Dysentery* text, the subjects of the sentences are 'Bacillary dysentery', 'It' (used to refer back to 'Bacillary dysentery' in sentence 1), 'Spread', 'the modern provision', 'Outbreaks', 'The disease'.

b The passive is likely to be extensively used. Thus, in section 1 of *Bacillary Dysentery,* we find 'are caused by' and 'caused by'. In section 3, we find 'is seen' and 'are obscured'. There are also many examples of verbs that are passive-like in *Bacillary Dysentery* in that their subjects are not the agents (or 'doers') of an action, as is typical of subjects of active verbs in English. Examples in section 1 are 'belong to', 'has been'; in section 2, 'occur(s)' (three times); in section 3, 'involve', 'appear', 'may form'. In accounts of experiments or research programmes, the passive is used extensively. The use of passive or passive-like verbs focuses attention on the effect or result rather than on the person performing the action.

3 Where texts involve procedures performed by human beings in particular, formulations of cause and effect are normal, reflecting the importance of the logic and development of such texts. Cause-and-effect formulations may include connectives such as 'consequently', 'hence' and 'thus', verbs such as 'cause', 'determine' and 'result in' and the use of 'by + -ing' to signal method. There are some examples in the *Bacillary Dysentery* text: in section 1, 'caused by', 'are caused by'; in section 2, 'thus', 'hence'; and in section 4, 'due to', 'cause'. However, in general, *Bacillary Dysentery* follows a pattern more typical of purely descriptive technical texts, in which sentences begin with subjects, and relations between sentences are often not marked by any connectives. As a rule, technical translation into English requires economy of language, precision and clarity, as well as clear use of standard cohesion markers, such as 'moreover', 'likewise', 'however', etc.

4 Nominalization is common. There are numerous examples in the *Bacillary Dysentery* text, including, in section 1, '[a significant] increase' (contrast the use of 'decreased' later in the same section), and in section 2, 'population', 'accompaniment', 'spread', 'provision', 'Outbreaks'. As Pinchuk notes, 'The nominalized style is easier to write and its impersonality avoids commitment to tense, unlike the conversational style' (Pinchuk 1977: 165).

5 Compound nouns are also a feature of many technical texts. Examples in the *Bacillary Dysentery* text include, in section 1, 'sonnei dysentery'; in section 2, 'hand basins', 'hot air driers' (cf. also 'oral-faecal spread'); in section 3, 'bleeding points'; and, in section 4, 'Sonne infections'.

16.6 Information sources

Pinchuk (1977: 246–251) points out that, before embarking on a translation, it is important to ascertain whether the work has already been translated. He provides a list of organizations that have registers of available translations, including Aslib (The Association of Special Libraries and Information Bureaux; see http://www.aslib.com/

index.htm). Internet searches are also useful for checking for very recent translations. Of course, technical translation, like translation in any genre, requires familiarity with ST and TL material of a similar type to serve as a source of information and as a stylistic model. Translators may well need some time to find the information (e.g. concepts or lexis) they are seeking. Useful sources of information include monographs, abstracting and indexing journals, encyclopedias, standards and trade journals, theses and dissertations. Most of these are likely now available online.

Some organizations, such as the European Union, keep databanks containing centrally agreed translations of technical expressions. These are continually added to, and translators are expected to conform to the agreed renderings in the interests of organization-wide consistency and clarity. The most important European Union databank is Inter-Active Terminology for Europe with terms in twenty-five languages. The Latvian-based consortium databank, EuroTermBank, covers thirty-three languages, while the government of Canada has a databank called Termium Plus (four languages). None of these databanks include Arabic terms, although the terminology may still be of use for Arabic translators for comparative purposes. Databanks giving Arabic terms include the Saudi BASIM databank (البنك العربي السعودي للمصطلحات; see http://basm.kacst.edu.sa), with terms in Arabic, English, French and German, and the بنك المصطلحات الموحدة of the Arab League's Educational, Cultural and Scientific Organization (المنظمة العربية للتربية والثقافة والعلوم), see http://www.arabization.org.ma/الرئيسية.aspx, with terms in Arabic, French and English. For a more detailed discussion of this area, see Cragie, Higgins, Hervey and Gambarotta (2016; Chapter 18).

As noted in Section 1.5, before the invention of the Internet, the checking of specialist sources in paper form would involve visiting academic libraries and spending a long time going through the indices and relevant sections of specialist books and articles. Now, the Internet makes vast amounts of technical information very rapidly available. The fundamental issue, then, becomes not the information itself but how to identify which sources of information about a particular technical topic are reliable and which are not.

In general, academic articles, particularly those published in reputable academic journals, are likely to provide more reliable – though perhaps less easily understood – information than popular accounts. Many academic articles are directly available online, even when they were originally published in a separate journal.

There are ranking lists for academic journals, such as the Harzing Journal Quality List (http://www.harzing.com/jql.htm). All journals on this list can be presumed to be reliable scholarly sources, although there are certainly many academic journals that do not figure in these lists but that are also scientifically respectable.

Online journals with strange-sounding names that do not represent clearly established branches of science, such as *NeuroQuantology: An Interdisciplinary Journal of Neuroscience and Quantum Physics,* are generally better avoided. Regardless of the scholarly virtues (or otherwise) of such sources, the ideas they present are non-mainstream and therefore unlikely to be of relevance to any translation in which the ST falls within mainstream science.

A word about Wikipedia is in order, as this is often the first port of call for people seeking general information from the Internet (and often appears as the first 'hit' on an Internet search). Although Wikipedia must be treated with a degree of caution, it is a generally reliable source for scientific topics, and, in some areas, such as computer science, it is a source for disseminating the most recent research information – making it more up to date than anything but the most current articles and books. By contrast, in any areas to do with politics and business interests, Wikipedia is much less reliable. In these areas, so-called conflict-of-interest editing regularly occurs, where particular businesses, governments or lobby groups remove information that they regard as damaging to themselves and that they do not want to appear. Wikipedia itself has a page titled 'Conflict-of-interest editing on Wikipedia' (https://en.wikipedia.org/wiki/Conflict-of-interest_editing_on_Wikipedia), which details some of the most prominent cases of such editing.

An examination of technical translations reveals that, apart from the lexical, conceptual and stylistic problems outlined in this chapter, technical translation is not essentially different from most other sorts of prose translation: as long as specialist help can be called on, there is no reason why anyone should not confidently tackle technical translation in any field. For a more detailed introduction to scientific and technical translation, see Byrne (2012), and for medical translation see Montalt and González-Davies (2007).

Practical 16

Practical 16.1 Translation of technical terms:
وذلك خلال الفترة ١٩٩٣ – ٢٠٠٠

Assignment

(i) Discuss the strategic decisions that you must take before starting detailed translation of the following text, and outline and justify the strategy you adopt. You are to translate this article for a pilot English-language version of العربي magazine aimed mainly at expatriate English speakers working in the Middle East.

(ii) Translate the text into English.

(iii) Explain the decisions of detail you made in producing your TT, especially those relating to technical questions.

Contextual information

The article, written by امين حامد مشعل and titled مستقبل الارض, comes from a 1993 edition (no. 418) of the Kuwaiti magazine العربي, which is aimed at the general educated reader and covers cultural and scientific topics. This is not a piece of technical translation. However, the text contains some technical and semi-technical environmental terms and therefore provides practice in dealing with lexical problems related to technical translation.

The Arabic text begins in mid-sentence. It is talking about an environmental programme drawn up at the 1992 earth summit in Rio de Janeiro in Brazil, designed to involve local communities in sustainable development. Begin your

translation with a new sentence, starting 'This programme is designed to run
[. . .]'. The phrase على أن, which begins the second clause on line 1 of the text,
has the sense 'although', 'however'. The text is taken from Evans (1996: 13).

ST

[. . .] وذلك خلال الفترة ١٩٩٣ – ٢٠٠٠، على أن يمتد هذا البرنامج بعد ذلك للقرن الواحد والعشرين.
ولذلك فقد اشتهرت تسميته بـ«جدول أعمال ٢١» أو «أجندة ٢١»، وهي عبارة عن خطة عمل تقع
في ٨٠٠ صفحة للخطوات المطلوبة عملها تجاه المشاكل البيئية والتنموية الملحة التي تواجه الأرض،
والتي تشمل على سبيل المثال ظاهرة تزايد الدفء العالمي، وإزالة الغابات، واضمحلال طبقة الاوزون
فضلا عن مشاكل الفقر والتنمية في العالم. وكان من أهداف المؤتمر وضع حلول لهذه المشاكل
والعمل على حماية وإدارة الموارد الطبيعية للأرض، وصون التنوع البيولوجي بها، وتشجيع استعمال
التكنولوجيا البيولوجية التي لا تضر بالبيئة [. . .]

Practical 16.2 Semi-technical translation: المادة المظلمة

Assignment

(i) Consider the strategic problems confronting the translator of the following text, and outline your own strategy for dealing with them. You are to
translate this article for a pilot English-language version of العربي magazine
aimed mainly at expatriate English speakers working in the Middle East.

(ii) Translate the text into English.

(iii) Explain the decisions of detail you made in producing your TT, especially
those relating to technical questions.

Contextual information

This Arabic article comes from the June 1994 edition of the Kuwait magazine
العربي, which is aimed at the general educated reader and covers cultural and scientific topics. Properly speaking, therefore, this is not a piece of technical translation
but rather what is sometimes termed 'popular scientific writing'. The text does,
however, contain some technical concepts and therefore provides practice in some
of the problems typical of technical translation.

Included after the Arabic text are several footnotes covering technical terms
and concepts that you will not be expected to be find in a typical Arabic>English
dictionary (such as Hans Wehr).

ST

المادة المظلمة[1]
لغز الكون

بقلم: رءوف وصفي

تختلف المادة المظلمة عن أي شيء نعرفه أو حتى نتخيله، وتحتاج لفهم جديد تماما لكل مكونات
الكون، ولسبر كنه أسرارها تبنى الفلكيون وغيرهم من العلماء كثيرا من الأساليب لحل لغز

المادة المظلمة و هم يجمعون الأدلة ويفحصونها ويستخدمون قدراتهم على الاستنتاج للتوصل إلى حل مقبول.

من المعروف أن الكون يتكون من وحدات أساسية هي المجرات التي تعرف بأنها تجمع هائل من النجوم والسدم والكواكب والأجرام الفضائية الأخرى والغازات الكونية، تتخللها مجالات كهربية ومغناطيسية جبارة، وخارج مجرتنا «الطريق اللبني» توجد آلاف الملايين «بلايين» المجرات الأخرى، وهي ليست موزعة بانتظام في الفضاء وإنما توجد في حشود قد تتضمن آلاف المجرات ويطلق عليها العناقيد المجرية.[2]

وأول دليل على وجود المادة المظلمة جاء من ملاحظات لعناقيد المجرات[2]، ففي عام ١٩٣٣ قاس الفيزيائي الفلكي السويسري «فيرتز زويكي»[3] حركة المجرات في العنقود المجري «الذؤابة»[4] وتبين له أن المجرات الفردية تتحرك بسرعات كبيرة جدا، بحيث لا[5] تظل المجرات متجاورة لفترة طويلة من الزمن، ولا بد أن تؤدي حركة كل مجرة في العنقود إلى ابتعاد أجزاء المجموعة عن بعضها البعض، إلا أن عملية الرصد الفلكي تؤكد أن العنقود المجري لا يزال متماسكا كوحدة واحدة.

Notes on technical terms and notions appearing in ST

1   المادة المظلمة: 'dark matter'.

2   عنقود المجرات, عنقود مجري: A distinction is made in astronomy between galaxy clusters and galactic clusters. Galaxy clusters are clusters of galaxies (i.e. clusters consisting of galaxies), and it this that seems to be meant in the Arabic both by العناقيد المجرية and by عناقيد المجرات (para. 3, sentence 1). Galactic clusters are a type of star cluster. Galactic star clusters – or open star clusters – contrast with globular star clusters. Open star clusters are much less compact than globular star clusters and are concentrated towards the plane of the galaxy – hence their alternative name 'galactic clusters'.

3   فريتز زويكي: 'Fritz Zwicky'.

4   الذؤابة: 'Coma' (from Greek, lit. = 'wisp of hair'; cf. under ذؤابة in Hans Wehr).

5   In respect of the section:

لا تظل المجرات متجاورة لفترة طويلة من الزمن، ولا بد أن تؤدي حركة كل مجرة في العنقود إلى ابتعاد أجزاء المجموعة عن بعضها البعض، إلا أن عملية الرصد الفلكي تؤكد أن العنقود المجري لا يزال متماسكا كوحدة واحدة

consider the following from an article about dark matter titled *The Dark Side of the Universe* (Economist Magazine, 23 June 1990):

The idea that most of the universe is invisible follows from the strange behaviour of the parts that are not. Galaxies, for example, spin too fast. If they were nothing more than the shining whirlpools of stars seen from earth, they would not be heavy enough to hold themselves together; centrifugal force would tear them apart. Since they are not falling apart, they must be heavier than they look. Some hidden mass must provide enough gravitational attraction to hold them together. Similar arguments apply to the arrangement of the galaxies. Their clustering can only be explained if the weight of a cluster is more than that of the bright galaxies it contains.

Practical 16.3 Technical translation: الزحار العصوي

Assignment

(i) Discuss the strategic decisions that you must take before starting detailed translation of the following text, and outline and justify the strategy you adopt. You are to translate the text for English-speaking doctors who are working on a development project in Syria that involves practical in-service training of Syrian health workers. The Syrian health workers have studied the ST as part of their training, and the English doctors require an English translation in order to help them assess what the health workers know.

(ii) Translate the text into English.

(iii) Explain the decisions of detail you made in producing your TT, concentrating on those relating to technical questions; you should also write brief notes on any expressions whose translation you are unsure of, explaining what the problem is.

(iv) After class discussion of the exercise, discuss the differences between your TT and that of an expert, which will be given to you by your tutor.

Contextual information

This text is taken from a medical textbook used at the University of Damascus (from Al-Muhammad 1993: 233–235). You may find it useful to refer to the text titled *Bacillary Dysentery* in Section 16.5.

ST

الزحار العصوي

مرض إنتاني يمتاز تشريحيا بالتهاب الأمعاء الغليظة يسببه عُصَيَّات من نوع «شيغلا» وتدخل الى الجسم بالطريق المعدي المعوي بواسطة الطعام والماء والأصابع الملوثة. وتنطرح الجراثيم بعدد وافر أثناء الدور الحاد للمرض مع البراز السائل. وقد يكون ذلك خلال دور النقاهة وحتى بعد شفاء المريض تماماً وقد يظهر الزحار بشكل وبائي حيث يتجمع الناس وتنعدم الشروط الصحية والنظافة. وتساعد شروط الطقس الحار في البلاد الاستوائية على انتشار المرض بواسطة الذباب.

الصفحة السريرية

آلام بطنية شديدة، ترفع حروري، زحير، ويظهر الاسهال خلال بضع ساعات من بدء المرض، ويكون البراز سائلاً بادئ الامر إلا أنه يصبح مائياً بسرعة، ويترافق بموادّ مخاطية وقيحية، وفي بعض الأحيان يكون مُدمَى. وقد يشتدّ الاسهال ويتكرّر ليحوي فقط مواد مخاطية دموية تسمى بـ«القشع الزحاري». وتسوء الحالة العامة إذا ما استمر الاسهال، وللمرض حالات خفيفة وشديدة. يتم التشخيص بفحص البراز، وتنظير المستقيم الذي يوضّح وجود وَذُمة والتهاب في المستقيم مع تقرحات واسعة متقطعة إنما سطحية.

17 Technical translation

Botanical texts

17.1 Introduction

English has become the global language of science. According to Montgomery (2013), more than three-quarters of scientific papers today globally are published in English – and, in some fields, it is more than 90%. The Arab world is also weak in scientific research, accounting for only 1.4% of global scientific papers, according to the UNESCO Science Report 2010 (http://unesdoc.unesco.org/images/0018/001899/189958e.pdf). Given the paucity of contemporary original natural science texts written in Arabic, there is very little translation of this type from Arabic to English. There is some translation into English of Classical Arabic scientific texts, but this is largely aimed at an academic audience interested in the history of science or the history of Arab and Islamic culture rather than at natural science researchers. There is also a certain amount of translation of natural science research articles and textbooks from English into Arabic – with some publishers, such as the Beirut-based الدار العربية للعلوم (http://www.aspbooks.com/index.aspx), specializing in this area.

There is some translation of popular science from English to Arabic – that is, scientific material presented in such a way that it is accessible to the intelligent and relatively well-informed non-specialist reader (an example is the text in Practical 16.2). An example is مجلة العلوم, published by the Kuwait Foundation for the Advancement of Sciences, which is a translation of the well-known popular science magazine *Scientific American.*

There are some areas in which original scientific material is written in Arabic. These include botanical writing, particularly where this relates to trees and plants found in the local (national) environment. King Saud University in Saudi Arabia, for example, publishes some botanical material in Arabic, and there are several specialist journals, such as مجلة وقاية النبات العربية (*Arab Journal of Plant Protection*), that publish entirely in Arabic.

17.2 Translating Arabic botanical texts

In this section, we will look at major scientific and technical issues in translating botanical texts from Arabic to English by considering the translation of an Arabic ST published online by جامعة أم القرى (Umm Al-Qura University) in Saudi Arabia

titled العشر (http://uqu.edu.sa/page/ar/126031). The brief is to produce a translation for a book titled *Wild Plants of Saudi Arabia*. This is to be a scholarly work
that is also accessible to the intelligent general reader. For ease of presentation,
we will look at each of the paragraphs making up the ST in turn, followed first
by a proposed TT and then by notes, to illustrate some of the scientific and other
technically oriented issues involved in the translation of each paragraph. Words
and phrases that are commented on are noted in curly brackets in both the ST and
the TT, followed by a superscript number that is reused in the following discussion in the notes. The entire ST is reproduced in Practical 17.1 at the end of this
chapter, which focuses on translation problems in this ST that are not of a scientific
or technical nature but that are relevant to wider issues involved in the translation
of botanical texts.

Before we start, it is worth recalling the three types of lexical problems identified in Section 16.2 in relation to terms found in technical texts, which we will refer
to where appropriate in subsequent discussion in this section. These are:

1   Technical terms that are totally unfamiliar to the lay translator, because they
    are only used in technical contexts;
2   Technical terms that are familiar to the translator because they are also used
    in non-technical contexts but look as if they are being used in some techni-
    cally specialized way in the ST;
3   Technical terms that are familiar to the translator because they are also used
    in non-technical contexts but do not obviously look as if they are being used
    in some technically specialized way in the ST.

ST – paragraph 1

{العشر}[1] أحد النباتات المشهورة في المملكة وهو نبات {شجيري}[2] {معمر}[3] {دائم الخضرة}[4]
يصل ارتفاعه إلى خمسة أمتار. أفرع النبات {متخشبة}[5] هشة، لحاؤها {اسفنجي}[6]، الأوراق كبيرة،
{لحمية}[7] ذات لون أخضر مزرق ليس لها {عنق}[8]. تحتوي جميع أجزاء النبات عصارة لبنية غزيرة.
الأزهار مخضرة من الداخل بنفسجية من الخارج وتوجد على مدار العام.

TT – paragraph 1

{Apple of Sodom}[1] is one of the best-known plants of Saudi Arabia. It is a
{perennial}[3] {dendritic}[2] {evergreen}[4] shrub, which reaches five metres in
height. The branches are {woody}[5] and brittle, and it has a {spongy}[6] bark.
Apple of Sodom has large, grey-green {succulent}[7] leaves without {petioles}[8].
All parts of the plant contain a thick milky sap. The flowers are greenish in the
middle, and purple on the outside and grow throughout the year.

Notes to paragraph 1

1   Because عشر is the standard, everyday word for a specific plant, عشر is not a
    technical term in Arabic. However, there is a need to find out precisely what
    the technical equivalent is in English. This is made quite easy here, because

the Latin botanical or scientific name '*Calotropis procera*' is, in fact, given in Latin script in paragraph 2 of the ST (for the ST of paragraph 2, see the following section). There is a slight difference between a botanical name and a scientific name. A botanical name is a formal scientific name conforming to the International Code of Botanical Nomenclature for algae, fungi, and plants (see Simpson 2010: 12). It is standard for the first word only of a botanical (or scientific name) to be capitalized and for all words to be italicized. It is standard for technical botanical texts in Arabic to include the botanical name in Latin script, so this can be taken as a starting point for translating most texts of this kind into English. In this case, we know that the botanical term for the عشر is '*Calotropis procera*'. The string "Calotropis procera" (in double inverted commas to specify a complete phrase rather than just the two words in close proximity) yields about 150,000 hits on Google (as of 2 July 2015). The first listed hit is the Wikipedia article (as is standard for many technical terms). In fact, Wikipedia is a good place to start to get a sense in English of the topic in hand.

In translating عشر, it would be possible to use the botanical name '*Calotropis procera*' (though this would require some adjustment to the TT in paragraph 2, where, as noted, the ST has the term '*Calotropis procera*' in Latin script). Assuming we do not do this, it seems sensible to look for a preferred common name. According to both the online Encyclopedia of Life (http://eol.org/pages/11196010/names/common_names) and the online Invasive Species Compendium (http://www.cabi.org/isc/datasheet/16848), the preferred common name is 'Apple of Sodom'. We have accordingly used this name in our TT.

2 شجيري presents a Type 2 lexical problem ('Technical terms that are familiar to the translator because they are also used in non-technical contexts but look as if they are being used in some technically specialized way in the ST'). It could simply mean 'bushy' or even 'woody' (and these are certainly possible translations in this context). However, شجيري also has the more specific technical sense 'dendritic' (meaning 'Of a branching form; arborescent, tree-like': *Oxford English Dictionary Online*), which seems more appropriate here given the technical context. (It is also worth noting that شجري is a technical equivalent of English 'arboreal'.)

3 مُعَمَّر also presents a Type 2 lexical problem. It can simply be the passive participle of the verb عَمَّر 'to populate, make inhabited; build a house' (*Oxford Arabic Dictionary*), but this does not fit in this context. Nor does the somewhat more technical sense 'senior (in sport)' given in Hans Wehr. The *Oxford Arabic Dictionary* also, however, gives 'perennial', which is the standard technical equivalent for معمر, when applied to plants; cf. 'Sodom apple [= Apple of Sodom] is a roundish, perennial shrub' (http://www. herbiguide.com.au/Descriptions/hg_AppleofSodom.htm). 'Perennial' is technically defined as 'Of plants, their roots, etc.: remaining alive for a number of years; *spec.* designating a herbaceous plant that dies down above ground and sends up fresh growth every year': *Oxford English Dictionary Online*.

4   دائم الخضرة has a standard English technical equivalent 'evergreen' and is itself originally a calque (Section 4.3) on the English 'evergreen'. This is technically a Type 2 lexical problem, because دائم الخضرة could have other senses in Arabic apart from the technical or semi-technical botanical sense 'evergreen'.

5   متخشب has the non-technical senses 'rigid' and 'turned to wood'. Here, متخشب seems to be appropriately translated by the semi-technical 'woody'. 'Woody' is found in several online descriptions of *Calotropis procera* – for example, '*Calotropis procera* is a woody perennial' (http://www.gardeningknowhow. com/ornamental/shrubs/calotropis/calotropis-procera.htm). This is a Type 2 lexical problem.

6   While اسفنجي might look as though it is being used in a technical sense here, the use of 'spongy' on several websites describing *Calotropis procera* indicates that the word is being used in a non-technical sense. 'Spongy bark' is relatively rare in English (with 5,280 hits on Google; 17 June 2015). However, the apparent alternative 'corky bark', while more common (84,100 hits on Google; 17 June 2015), is the name of a disease. The term 'cork-like bark' is, however, found (http://www.gardeningknowhow.com/ornamental/shrubs/ calotropis/calotropis-procera.htm) and is a possible alternative translation here.

7   لحمي, although derived simply from the basic word لحم 'meat' by the addition of the *nisba*-suffix ي, is a Type 1 technical term ('Technical terms that are totally unfamiliar to the lay translator, because they are only used in technical contexts'), because the word لحمي does not have a non-technical sense in Arabic. The forms 'succulent leaves' and 'fleshy leaves' are both used (the latter is more common and less technical).

8   There are two apparent possible translations for Arabic عنق, 'pedicel' or 'petiole'. These are defined as follows: '*Pedicel*: A small stalk or stalklike structure in a plant; spec. (a) the filament of a stamen (obs.); (b) each of the stalks that immediately bear the flowers in a branching inflorescence (now the usual sense); (c) a peduncle (main stalk) of a flower or fruit, esp. if short or slender; (d) the stalk of an algal antheridium or fungal spore. *Petiole*: The stalk by which a leaf is attached to the stem of a plant. Also: the stalk of a leaflet': *Oxford English Dictionary Online*. The leaves of the Apple of Sodom in fact have extremely short petioles, as can be verified by reference to several websites. The difference between a pedicel and a petiole is that a pedicel is a stalk bearing a single flower or spore-producing body within a cluster, while a petiole is the stalk of a leaf, attaching the blade to the stem. Here, what seems to be meant is a petiole. This is a Type 2 technical problem, because عنق is a word that has non-technical senses – the most basic being 'neck' – but is being used here in a technical sense.

ST – paragraph 2

الثمار {جرابية}١ تقع في أزواج، اسفنجية كبيرة تشبه المنقة، لونها أخضر باهت، البذور بيضاء يكسوها شعر حريري أبيض ناعم جداً وهذه عبارة عن ألياف حريرية طويلة ولامعة [. . .]. الموطن الأصلي

لنبات العشر: المملكة العربية السعودية وجميع البلدان الصحراوية والهند وأفغانستان وباكستان وأغلب المناطق الرملية. نادراً ما يوجد على الكثبان الساحلية ويفضل الأماكن الجافة التي يصيبها قليل من المطر وقد يموت إذا روي بكثرة أو إذا ما تجمعت مياه الأمطار في مواقع نموه. يعرف العشر بعدة {أسماء شعبية}[2] مثل الخيسفوج، الأشخر، الوهط، عشار، كرنكا، برمباك، برنبخ. ويعرف علمياً باسم Calotropis Procera: الجزء المستخدم من نبات العشر: القشور، الأوراق، الأزهار، العصاء اللبنية.

TT – paragraph 2

The fruit is {kidney-shaped}[1]. It grows in pairs, and is large, spongy, similar in shape to a mango and light green. The seeds are white and covered in tufts of very soft white, silky hairs, made up of long, shiny, silky fibres [. . .]. Apple of Sodom is native to Saudi Arabia, India, Pakistan, desert areas generally and most sandy environments. It is occasionally found on coastal dunes. It favours arid areas with low rainfall. It may die if it receives too much water, or if rainwater collects where it is growing. Apple of Sodom is known by several {names}[2] in Arabic, including *khaysafuj*, *ashkhar*, *wahat*, *ushar*, *karanka*, *barmabak*, and *barnabakh*. Its scientific name is *Calotropis Procera*. The parts of the plant which are used are the bark, the leaves, the flowers, and the milky sap.

Notes to paragraph 2

1 جرابية Several online sources describe the fruit of *Calotropis procera* as 'kidney-shaped' (e.g. https://tropicalfloweringzone.wordpress.com/2013/03/30/a-follow-up-on-the-calotropis-procera-tree/). There seems to be no online evidence that a more literal translation, such as 'pouch-shaped' or 'sack-shaped', is appropriate. Given that 'kidney-shaped' is a general, rather than a technical, designation, this does not really fall under types 1–3 technical problems identified in Section 16.2 (reproduced earlier).

2 اسم شعبي translates most standardly as 'common name' (as opposed to 'botanical name', e.g. http://www.motherherbs.com/calotropis-procera.html, or 'scientific name', e.g. http://www.cabi.org/isc/datasheet/16848). Here, it is necessary in the TT to add 'in Arabic' (or similar) to make plain that these are not common names of *Calotropis procera* in English (or some other language). One could accordingly translate عدة أسماء شعبية as 'several common names in Arabic'. However, the fact that these are non-botanical (non-scientific) names is obvious from the context. We have therefore removed mention of 'common' in our TT. The identification of the fact that شعبي is being used here in the technical sense 'common' (as opposed to its non-technical sense 'popular', etc.) is a Type 2 problem.

ST – paragraph 3

المحتويات الكيميائية لنبات العشر: يحتوي على {جلوكوزيدات قلبية من أهمها عشرين، عشرايدين، كالولزوباجنين، كلاكتين، ومدارين، وجيجانتين}[1] [. . .].

TT – paragraph 3

The chemical constituents of apple of Sodom include {cardiac glycosides, the most important of which are uscharin, uscharidin, calotropagenin and calactin, as well as mudarin, and gigantin}[1] [. . .]

Notes to paragraph 3

1   The TT chemical terms 'cardiac glycosides' (for جلوكوزيدات قلبية), 'uscharin' (for عشرين), 'uscharidin' (for عشرايدين), 'calotropagenin' (for كالولزوباجنين), 'calactin' (for كلاكتين), 'mudarin' (for مدارين) and 'gigantin' (for جيجانتين) can all be found in online chemical descriptions of *Calotropis procera*.

ST – paragraph 4

لقد استعمل العشر من مئات السنين في المداوة حيث ورد ذكر نبات العشر (الأشخر) في الطب المصري القديم فقد ورد في {قرطاس "هيرست"}[1] الطبي وصفة تتعلق بالأوعية الدموية يدخل فيها الأشخر وهي مكونة من أشخر + دوم + دقيق قمح بحيث يطحن الجميع ويوضع على المكان المصاب.

TT – paragraph 4

Apple of Sodom has been used medicinally for many hundreds of years. The name of the plant *ushar* (or *ashkhar*) is found in Ancient Egyptian medical texts. In the {Hearst Papyrus}[1], there is a prescription relating to blood vessels, which uses Apple of Sodom. This involves mixing Apple of Sodom with the fruit of the doum palm and wheat-flour. The mixture is ground up, and placed on the affected spot.

Notes to paragraph 4

1   For the term 'Hearst papyrus', see https://en.wikipedia.org/wiki/Hearst_papyrus. Here, the use of inverted commas, in "هيرست", tells us that هيرست is a proper name (cf. Section 12.2.1), and we may guess that it is the name of a person. Even given this, however, it is sometimes difficult to identify proper names of this type in Latin script. It is not immediately possible to know whether the original Latin-script name is 'Hearst', 'Hirst', 'Hurst' or something else. Indeed, it is not possible to be sure whether this is an English name at all, or a name from another European, or non-European, language. It may therefore be necessary to work through a lot of different possible names using an Internet search in order to come up with the right one.
    In this case, a clue is provided by the fact that قرطاس here must mean 'papyrus' and not, for instance, 'sheet of paper'; the ancient Egyptians did not have paper (which was invented in China in the third century BC and only reached the Middle East in the eighth century AD). Accordingly, we can be confident that قرطاس "هيرست" must be something like 'the Hirst/Hurst/Hearst papyrus'. The Internet itself can provide further help. Thus, a Google search

for "Hirst papyrus" (using double inverted commas) yields the automatic response 'Did you mean: "*Hearst* papyrus"', directing the translator to the correct form, even though he or she has put in the wrong one.

Identifying Latin-script names from Arabic-script versions is not a technical problem in the sense defined in Section 16.2 (and earlier in this section), but it is a serious and recurrent difficulty in the translation of scientific STs.

ST – paragraph 5

ويستعمل مسحوق الأوراق المحروقة مخلوطة مع العسل لعلاج {الربو الشعبي}¹ و{السعال المنتج للبلغم}² .ويقول {ملير}³ إن العصارة اللبنية توضع على رؤوس الدمامل فتفجرها. كما تستخدم لعلاج الأمراض الجلدية.

TT- paragraph 5

A powder made of burnt Apple of Sodom flowers mixed with honey is used to treat {asthma}¹ and {chesty coughs}². According to {Miller}³, the milky sap is applied to the heads of boils, causing them to burst. Apple of Sodom is also used to treat skin diseases.

Notes to paragraph 5

1   It is important to know that the word شعبي here is in fact شُعَبي 'bronchial' and not شَعْبي 'popular' or 'common' (as a technical term; the sense it has in paragraph 2). This can be checked by the fact that there is no such disease as 'common asthma' in English but there is 'bronchial asthma'. This is commonly referred to 'asthma', the term we have used in the TT (http://www.healthline.com/health/asthma-bronchial-asthma). The translation of الربو الشعبي here is, properly speaking, a Type 1 technical problem (given that ربو has only a technical sense 'asthma' and that شُعَبي has only a technical sense 'bronchial'). However, the fact that شعبي could also be read as شَعْبي makes this partly a de facto Type 2 lexical problem – as we need to know that this form شعبي is not شَعْبي being used in its non-technical sense of 'popular, common'.

2   'Chesty cough' is a fairly common term for a cough that brings up phlegm (http://www.nhsdirect.wales.nhs.uk/encyclopaedia/c/article/cough/). Some doctors also use the phrase 'productive cough'. Another alternative that is sometimes used is 'mucus cough', although a more accurate translation of السعال المنتج للبلغم would be 'phlegm-producing cough', which is also found. السعال المنتج للبلغم could hardly have a non-technical interpretation, making this a Type 1 lexical problem.

3   The same fundamental problems that applied to "هيرست" also apply to ملير (in this latter case, no double inverted commas are used, so the reader or translator is not even explicitly alerted that this is a proper name). The same basic technique can be used to identify ملير in Latin script as was used to identify هيرست: an Internet search that combines a guess about the

unidentified element with an accompanying identified element. In the case of ملير, we already know that this has to do with *Calotropis procera*. We can therefore make an Internet search containing the term '*Calotropis procera*' together with a guess about the Latin-script equivalent of ملير. In the case of ملير, the process might take quite a long time, because one would expect 'Miller' in English to be transliterated as ميلر (rather than ملير) in Arabic. Further investigation reveals that this is a reference to *Plants of Dhofar, The Southern Region of Oman: Traditional, Economic, and Medicinal Uses* by Anthony G. Miller, Miranda Morris and Susanna Stuart-Smith (1988).

A translation that would be truer to the original source than 'According to Miller' would, of course, be 'According to Miller, Morris and Stuart-Smith'. One might even add a more explicit reference to the book, as well as to the page on which the information is found – for example, 'According to Miller, Morris and Stuart-Smith in their book *Plants of Dhofar, The Southern Region of Oman: Traditional, Economic, and Medicinal Uses* (1988, p. 42)'. What Miller, Morris and Stuart-Smith actually say is, 'The latex was applied around the pointed head of boils, or around infected wounds to draw the pus' (Miller, Morris and Stuart-Smith 1988: 42).

Practical 17

Practical 17.1 Botanical translation: العشر

Assignment

Consider again the translation of the text العشر, key technical terms in which were discussed in Section 17.2, immediately preceding. We have provided the ST and a TT for this practical. In the TT, we have put in curly brackets followed by a super-script number words and phrases posing translation problems that are not, strictly speaking, of a technical nature. For each of these words and phrases, (i) where online information is a plausible source for the chosen translation, identify appropriate online sources for the translation chosen; (ii) identify possible alternative transla-tions, whether available from online or other sources; (iii) assess the reasonableness of the translation of the particular word or phrase given in the TT as opposed to that of other possible translations. Thus, the appropriateness of the translation element [6] ذات لون أخضر مزرق as 'grey-green' can be ascertained from the online source http://www.arkive.org/sodoms-apple-milkweed/calotropis-procera/, though there are also other online sources giving other possible translations, which you should also iden-tify. In contrast, there are no obvious online sources for element [2] (i.e. the translation of في as 'of'). You should, however, be able to think of at least one other possible translation here and assess the relative merits of the alternatives.

ST

العشر أحد النباتات {المشهورة}[1] {في}[2] المملكة وهو نبات شجيري معمر دائم الخضرة {يصل ارتفاعه إلى خمسة أمتار}[3]. أفرع النبات متخشبة هشة، {لحاؤها اسفنجي}[4]، {Ø}[5] الأوراق كبيرة،

لحمية {ذات لون أخضر مزرق}⁶ ليس لها عنق. تحتوي جميع أجزاء النبات {عصارة لبنية}⁷ غزيرة. الأزهار مخضرة من الداخل {بنفسجية}⁸ {من الخارج}⁹ و{توجد على مدار العام}¹⁰.

الثمار جرابية {تقع في أزواج}¹¹، {إسفنجية}¹² كبيرة {تشبه}¹³ المنقة، لونها {أخضر باهت}¹⁴، البذور بيضاء يكسوها {Ø}¹⁵ {شعر}¹⁷ حريري أبيض {ناعم}¹⁶ جداً وهذه عبارة عن ألياف حريرية طويلة ولامعة. [. . .] {الموطن الأصلي}¹⁸ لنبات العشر: {المملكة العربية السعودية وجميع البلدان الصحراوية والهند وأفغانستان وباكستان وأغلب المناطق الرملية}¹⁹. نادراً ما يوجد على الكثبان الساحلية و{يفضل}²⁰ {الأماكن}²² {الجافة}²¹ {التي يصيبها قليل من المطر}²³ وقد يموت إذا {روي بكثرة}²⁴ أو إذا ما تجمعت مياه الأمطار في مواقع نموه. يعرف العشر بعدة {أسماء شعبية مثل الخيسفوج، الأشخر، الوهط، عشار، كرنكا، برمباك، برنبخ}²⁵. و{يعرف علمياً باسم}²⁶ :Calotropis Procera. {الجزء}²⁷ المستخدم من نبات العشر: {القشور}²⁸، الأوراق، الأزهار، {العصارة اللبنية}²⁹.

{المحتويات الكيميائية لنبات العشر: {يحتوي}³⁰ على جلوكوزيدات قلبية من أهمها عشرين، عشرايدين، كالولزوباجينين، كلاكتين، {و}³¹مدارين، وجيجانتين [. . .].

لقد استعمل العشر من {مئات السنين}³² في المداواة حيث ورد ذكر نبات العشر (الأشخر) {في الطب المصري القديم}³³ فقد ورد في قرطاس ''هيرست'' الطبي وصفة تتعلق بالأوعية الدموية يدخل فيها الأشخر وهي مكونة من {أشخر + دوم + دقيق قمح}³⁴ بحيث يطحن الجميع و{يوضع}³⁵ على {المكان المصاب}³⁶.

[. . .]

ويستعمل مسحوق الأوراق المحروقة مخلوطة مع العسل لعلاج الربو الشعبي والسعال المنتج للبلغم. {ويقول ملير}³⁷ إن العصارة اللبنية توضع على رؤوس {الدمامل}³⁸ {فتفجرها}³⁹. كما تستخدم لعلاج {الأمراض}⁴⁰ الجلدية.

TT

Apple of Sodom is one of the {best-known}[1] plants {of}[2] Saudi Arabia. It is a perennial dendritic evergreen shrub, which {reaches five metres in height}[3]. The branches are woody and brittle, and {it has a spongy}[4] bark. {Apple of Sodom}[5] has large, {grey-green}[6] succulent leaves without petioles. All parts of the plant contain a thick {milky sap}[7]. The flowers are greenish in the middle, and {purple}[8] {on the outside}[9] and {grow throughout the year}[10].

The fruit is kidney-shaped. {It grows in pairs,}[11] and is large, {spongy}[12], {similar in shape}[13] to a mango and {pale green}.[14] The seeds are white and covered in {tufts of }[15] very {soft}[16] white, silky {hairs},[17] made up of long, shiny, silky fibres [. . .]. Apple of Sodom is {native to}[18] {Saudi Arabia, India, Pakistan, desert areas generally and most sandy environments}[19]. It is occasionally found on coastal dunes. {It favours}[20] {arid}[21] {areas}[22] {with low rainfall}[23]. It may die if it {receives too much water}[24], or if rainwater collects where it is growing. Apple of Sodom is known by several names {in Arabic, including *khaysafuj*, *ashkhar*, *wahat*, *ushar*, *karanka*, *barmabak*, and *barnabakh*}[25]. Its {scientific name}[26] is *Calotropis procera*. {The parts}[27] of the plant which are used are the {skin of the fruit}[28], the leaves, the flowers, and the {milky sap}[29].

The chemical constituents of apple of Sodom {include}[30] cardiac glycosides, the most important of which are uscharin, uscharidin, calotropagenin and calactin, {as well as}[31] mudarin, and gigantin [. . .]

Apple of Sodom has been used medicinally {for many hundreds of years. [32]} The name of the plant *ushar* (or *ashkhar*) is {found in Ancient Egyptian medical texts}[33]. In the Hearst Papyrus, there is a prescription relating to blood vessels, which uses Apple of Sodom. This involves mixing {Apple of Sodom with the fruit of the doum palm and wheat-flour}[34]. The mixture is ground up, and {placed on}[35] the {affected spot}[36].

[. . .]

A powder made of burnt Apple of Sodom flowers mixed with honey is used to treat asthma and chesty coughs. {According to Miller}[37], the milky sap is applied to the heads of {boils}[38], {causing them to burst}[39]. Apple of Sodom is also used to treat skin {diseases}[40].

Practical 17.2 Botanical translation: الأرطة

Assignment

(i) Consider the strategic problems confronting the translator of the following text, and outline your own strategy for dealing with them. You are to translate this article for a book titled *Wild Plants of Saudi Arabia*. This is to be a scholarly work that is also accessible to the intelligent general reader.

(ii) Translate the text into English.

(iii) Explain the decisions of detail you made in producing your TT, especially those relating to technical questions.

Contextual information

This Arabic article comes from an online article about الأرطة on the website of جامعة آل المجمعة (Majmaah University) in Saudi Arabia: http://faculty.mu.edu.sa/ gselem/%D8%A7%D9%84%D8%A3%D8%B1%D8%B7%D9%80%D9%80% D8%A9.

ST

الأرطـة

الأرطة أحد نباتات البيئة السعودية المشهورة ولها استعمالات شعبية وتدخل في عدة مستحضرات شعبية وأثبتت الدراسات العلمية تأثيراتها ضد البكتيريا وبعض الديدان المستوطنة. للأرطة عدة أسماء شعبية مثل العبل أو عبلي وارطي وارطا ورمو ورسمة وتيب. وتعرف الارطة علميا باسم Calligonum comosum من فصيلة الحماضيات.

ما هي الأرطة؟

هي نبات شجيري يتراوح ارتفاعه ما بين متر إلى ثلاثة أمتار تقريبا. أوراقه قليلة ويبدو شكل النبات خشبيا نظرا لقلة أوراقه. للنبات ازهار زاهية جميلة المنظر ذات لون أحمر وردي. ثمرة النبات مفلطحة ومغطاة بزوائد متفرعة. الموطن الأصلي للأرطة المملكة العربية السعودية وتتركز في شمال الحجاز وشرق نجد.

المحتويات الكيميائية لنبات الأرطه:

تحتوي جميع أجزاء نبات الأرطة على فلافوينيدات وقلويدات واستيرولات وتربينات ثلاثية وانثراكينونات ومواد عفصية وكومارينات وقد فصل قسم العقاقير بكلية الصيدلة عدة مركبات فلافونيدية [. . .]، كما يحتوي النبات على مواد صابونينيه ونبات الأرطة يعطي كميات كبيرة من المواد العفصية خلال شهر مايو واكتوبر [. . .] يسيل من نبات الأرطة سائل لزج يتجمع تحت النبات على هيئة مادة تشبه الدبس أو العسل ذي لون بني إلى قرمزي ويقوم الناس بجمعة واستعماله كعلاج للكحة.

الاستعمالات:

لقد عرفت استعمالات الارطة الدوائية منذ أزمنة طويلة حيث استعملها قدماء المصريين منذ نحو 4000 سنة في علاج الأمراض حيث ورد ذكر ثمار نبات الأرطة في وصفة طبية في "قرطاس هيرست" لعلاج الرعشة في أي عضو وذلك بطبخه مع غيره من الأعشاب ليعطي مرهماً تدهن به الأعضاء المريضة. وفي دولة الامارات حيث يكثر هذا النبات يقوم المواطنون بفرم الأفرع الطرفية الغضة للنبات ويضعونها مع الأرز أو تخلط مع اللبن أو تطبخ مع السمك والأرز ليزين رائحته. كما تدق الأفرع الغضة مع قليل من الماء ويشرب لعلاج المعدة.

Practical 17.3 Botanical translation: الرجلة

Assignment

(i) Consider the strategic problems confronting the translator of the following text, and outline your own strategy for dealing with them. You are to translate this article for a book titled *Wild Plants of Saudi Arabia*. This is to be a scholarly work that is also accessible to the intelligent general reader.

(ii) Translate the text into English.

(iii) Explain the decisions of detail you made in producing your TT, especially those relating to technical questions.

Contextual information

This Arabic article comes from an online article about رجلة in English 'purslane' or 'common purslane' in the Saudi الرياض newspaper: http://www.alriyadh. com/430423.

ST

الرجلة تشفي من المشكلات البولية والهضمية

للرجلة تأثير فعال في علاج الديدان الشعبية

الرجلة عشب حولي منها ما هو منتصب ومنها ما هو منبسط، ويصل ارتفاعها إلى حوالي 30 سم، ساقها وأفرعها ملساء ذات لون مخضر إلى محمر عصيرية رخوة، أوراقها بيضية مقلوبة مستديرة القمة، الأزهار صغيرة صفراء اللون جالسة بدون أعناق تتفتح في الصباح ثم تنغلق غالباً قبل منتصف النهار.

تعرف الرجلة بعدة أسماء، ففي بلاد الشام تعرف بالبقلة والفرحين والفرحينة وفي مصر بالرجلة وأصلها من البربرية، كما تشتهر باسم البقلة الحمقاء وسميت بهذا الاسم لأنها تنبث في مجاري الأودية

والمياه، وفي بعض دول الخليج تعرف بالبقلة المباركة ورشاد، وتعرف الرجلة أو البقلة الحمقاء علمياً باسم portulaca oleracea.

الموطن الأصلي أوروبا وآسيا وتزرع حالياً في استراليا والصين كما تنبت عفوياً في جميع المناطق دون استثناء، وتفضل مجاري الوديان حيث تغطي مساحات شاسعة في مواسم الأمطار وتكثر في المزارع المهملة وعلى حواف القنوات وجوانب الطرقات. تستعمل الأجزاء الهوائية من الرجلة.

المحتويات الكيميائية

تحتوي الرجلة على قلويدات وفلافونيدات وكومارينات وجلوكوزيدات قلبية وانثراكينونية، كما تحتوي على حامض الهيدروسيانيك وزيت ثابت، كما أن الرجلة غنية جداً بالكالسيوم والحديد وفيتامين أ، ب، ج وحمض الأكساليك ونترات البوتاسيوم وكلوريدات البوتاسيوم وكبريتات البوتاسيوم.

الاستعمالات

لقد اعتبرت الرجلة منذ القدم أنها من أفضل النباتات الطبية فقد قال عنها ابن البيطار أن فيها قبضاً يسيراً وتبرد تبريداً شديداً لمن يجد لهيباً وتوقداً، متى وضعت على فم معدته، وإذا أكلت أو شربت فعلت ذلك، وهي تشفي الضرس بتلميسها، وبسبب قبضها فهي موافقة لمن به قرحة الأمعاء وللنساء اللواتي يعرض لهن النزيف، ومن ينفث الدم وعصارتها أقوى في هذا الموضوع، وهي باردة مطفئة للعطش، تبرد البدن وترطبه وتنفع لمحرورين في البلدان الحارة، ومن يجعلها في فراشه لم ير حلماً، وإذا شويت وأكلت قطعت الاسهال، وتقطع العطش المتولد من الحرارة في المعدة والقلب والكلى، وتنفع من حرق النار مطبوخة ونيئة إذا تضمد بها.

18 Technical translation

Constitutional texts

18.1 Definition

By a constitution we mean an agreed set of principles and rules by which an organization is run. Constitutional texts are thus a subtype of legal or quasi-legal text and include all kinds of constitutions, ranging from those of international organizations and states to those of sports and social clubs. They also include communiques, statements, etc. that have the general form of constitutions, as described next. Constitutional texts therefore offer an accessible introduction to some of the more general problems of legal translation. (For a general introduction to legal translation, see Alcarez and Hughes 2002, and for official documents, of which constitutions are a subtype, see Asensio 2003. For a more detailed discussion of Arabic>English legal translation, see El-Farahaty 2015.)

18.2 General structure

Typical constitutional texts can be divided into two parts: an optional preamble followed by the main text.

18.2.1 Preamble

The preamble does not form part of the constitution as such and therefore does not have the same legal status as the constitution itself. However, it presents the rationale for and/or situation of the proclamation of the constitution. The normal Arabic translation of 'Preamble' is المقدمة. It is common in English to have a preamble without a title line 'Preamble'. The Constitution of the United States, for example, begins 'WE THE PEOPLE OF THE UNITED STATES, IN ORDER TO FORM A MORE PERFECT UNION [. . .]'. The Constitution of India, by contrast, uses the title 'PREAMBLE' followed by the opening statement, '*We, the People of India*, having solemnly resolved to constitute India into a *Sovereign Democratic Republic* [. . .]'.

Preambles often begin with a first-person plural subject 'We' followed by a parenthetical statement of who is making the constitution. The United States constitution, for example, has as its preamble:

WE THE PEOPLE OF THE UNITED STATES, IN ORDER TO FORM A MORE PERFECT UNION, ESTABLISH JUSTICE, INSURE DOMESTIC TRANQUILITY, PROVIDE FOR THE COMMON DEFENSE, PROMOTE THE GENERAL WELFARE, AND SECURE THE BLESSINGS OF LIB-ERTY TO OURSELVES AND OUR POSTERITY, DO ORDAIN AND ESTABLISH THIS CONSTITUTION FOR THE UNITED STATES OF AMERICA.

The preamble to the Indian Constitution is as follows:

We, the People of India, having solemnly resolved to constitute India into a *Sovereign Democratic Republic* and to secure to all its citizens:

Justice, social, economic and political;
Liberty of thought, expression, belief, faith and worship;
Equality of status and opportunity;
and to promote among them all
Fraternity assuring the dignity of the individual and the unity of the Nation;
In our Constituent Assembly this twenty-sixth day of November, 1949, do *hereby Adopt, Enact and Give to Ourselves this Constitution.*

The Jordanian Constitution is introduced by the following (which is perhaps techni-cally not to be regarded as a preamble, having rather the form of a royal decree com-manding the putting into effect of the constitution: this is known in Arabic as a ديباجة):

نحن طلال الاول ملك المملكة الاردنية الهاشمية
بمقتضى المادة الخامسة والعشرين من الدستور وبناء
على ما قرره مجلسا الاعيان والنواب نصدق على
الدستور المعدل الآتي ونأمر بإصداره

The English translation of this reads:

We Talal the First
King of the Hashemite Kingdom of Jordan
In accordance with Article 25 of the Constitution,
and in pursuance of the resolution of
the Senate and House of Deputies,
do hereby give my assent to
this revised Constitution
and command that it be put into effect

All three of these texts employ several devices that are typical of preambles. The main verb, plus other elements dependent on the main verb, are placed at the end of the preamble, while the middle section of the preamble consists of subordinate phrases (in some cases, subordinate clauses). Preambles typically involve forms of structural parallelism.

Thus, in the American constitution, there is a series of verb–object (or verb–prepositional phrase) pairs in which the object is further defined (in most cases, by an adjective, and, in one case, by a genitive 'of'-phrase): (i) 'form a more perfect union'; (ii) 'insure domestic tranquility'; (iii) 'provide for the common defense'; (iv) 'promote the general welfare'; (v) 'secure the blessings of liberty'.

Arabic preambles may also contain subordinate phrases, such as the phrases بمقتضى المادة الخامسة والعشرين من الدستور وبناء على ما قرره مجلسا الاعيان والنواب in the Jordanian example. Arabic materials of this kind may also contain combinations of subordinate clauses and complete sentences. The following is from a preamble to a Christian–Muslim summit in Lebanon at the start of the Lebanese civil war:

كان من عناية الله على لبنان وعلى ابنائه ان وفق رؤساء الطوائف اللبنانية بعقد الاجتماع الاول من اجتماعاتهم في جلستين، الصباحية في بكركي والمسائية في دار الفتوة الاسلامية.

{وقد تدارسوا المآسي الرهيبة} التي تسود البلاد والاخطار التي تهدد وحدتها واستقلالها وسلامة أبنائها وتعرض سلامة البلدان العربية الشقيقة والقضية الفلسطينية للخطر الكبير.

{ولاحظوا ان هذه المآسي} بدأت تأخذ في صورة متزايدة طابعا طائفيا فتحصل اعتداءات اثيمة على الابرياء وتجاوزات على الكنائس والمساجد وعلى رجال الدين باسم الدين والدين منها براء. ومن هنا فإن الخطر بات يهدد كيان لبنان وطابعه الحضاري المميز.

{وبعد البحث المسؤول في هذه الاوضاع} عقدوا العزم على متابعة اجتماعاتهم المشتركة في سائر بيوت الطوائف اللبنانية ووضعوا مخطط عمل وشكلوا هيئة للمتابعة واصدروا في نهاية اليوم الاول البيان الاتي:

As the material put in curly brackets indicates, the Arabic text utilizes a combination of main verbs (main clauses) and subordinate phrases to pick out the main points of importance in this 'preamble' section. The following are the start of main clauses: وقد تدارسوا المآسي الرهيبة (paragraph 2); ولاحظوا ان هذه المآسي (paragraph 3). The final paragraph, by contrast, begins with a subordinate phrase: وبعد البحث المسؤول في هذه الاوضاع (paragraph 4).

Here is a possible English translation of this extract:

> Through God's providential concern for Lebanon and its people, the leaders of the Lebanese confessional groups have been led to hold the first of their meetings in two sessions, a morning session in Bakirki and an afternoon session in the Islamic Dar Al-Futuwwa.
>
> {Having given careful consideration to the tragic events} which have befallen the country, and the dangers which not only jeopardize its unity and independence, and the well-being of its citizens, but also pose a grave threat to other Arab states and to the Palestinian cause:
>
> {Having noted that these events} have started to become increasingly sectarian in nature, that outrages have been perpetrated against innocent people, and that sacrilegious attacks have been carried out in the name of religion against churches and mosques and men of religion, thus threatening Lebanon's political structure and its unique cultural constitution:
>
> {Having discussed this situation in a responsible manner}, and {having determined to pursue their joint meetings in the centres of the various

Lebanese confessional groups}, they do hereby draw up a plan of action and establish a monitoring committee, and at the end of their first day of meetings, issue the following statement:

The English translation involves greater use of parallel subordinate clauses than the Arabic original. The main verb phrase beginning paragraph 2 in the Arabic وقد تدارسوا المآسي الرهيبة is transferred into the English subordinate phrase 'Having given careful consideration to the tragic events' (paragraph 2). The main verb phrase beginning paragraph 3 in the Arabic ولاحظوا ان هذه المآسي is transferred into the English subordinate phrase 'Having noted that these events' (paragraph 3). The Arabic subordinate phrase beginning paragraph 4 وبعد البحث المسؤول is retained as a subordinate phrase 'Having discussed this situation in a responsible manner' (paragraph 4). However, the subsequent Arabic main verb phrase وعقدوا العزم على متابعة اجتماعاتهم المشتركة (paragraph 4) is also converted in the English translation into a subordinate phrase 'having determined to pursue their joint meetings', with the result that the verb of the main clause does not occur in the English translation until 'they do hereby draw up a plan of action' – that is, the translation of the Arabic ووضعوا مخطط عمل (paragraph 4). That is to say, from the second paragraph onwards, everything before this in the English translation is some part of a subordinate clause; and the second to fourth paragraphs of the translation constitute three parallel subordinate clauses (with further forms of parallelism within each).

As the previous example suggests, it seems more necessary in English than in Arabic to maintain a structure in preambles either of the type:

1   SUBJECT – SUBORDINATE ELEMENTS – MAIN CLAUSE (as exemplified in the American Constitution)

or of the type:

2   SUBORDINATE ELEMENTS – MAIN CLAUSE (as exemplified in the English translation of بيان القمة المسيحية الاسلامية)

Arabic texts may have a preamble that involves a series of subordinate elements followed by a main clause. A good example is the following, which is the beginning of a proclamation issued by عزيز الاحدب, the Commander of the Beirut Region and 'Provisional Military Ruler' of Lebanon on 11 March 1976:

{انقاذا لوحدة الجيش واعادة اللحمة الى العسكريين} و{انقاذا للوضع المتدهور في البلاد}.
و{لما كانت تحذيراتي قد ذهبت ادراج الرياح}، {وحفاظا على المصلحة اللبنانية العليا} و{اعادة اللحمة الى الشعب اللبناني الكريم}، و{بوحي من ضميري واصالتي العسكرية}، و{انطلاقا من مسؤوليتي امام الله والتاريخ} اقرر ما يأتي :

Here, each of the phrases in curly brackets is a subordinate (adverbial) phrase (only one of which, لما كانت تحذيراتي قد ذهبت ادراج الرياح, is a clause). This is followed at the end by the main verb اقرر, with its object ما يأتي.

It is also common, however, to find Arabic preambles that involve repeated use of complete sentences, frequently introduced by the emphatic particles قد (or لقد) followed by a perfect verb or إنّ followed by a noun or pronoun. In such cases, the translator would almost certainly be forced to adopt a style in which the preamble consisted of several separate sentences, despite the typical preference for preambles in English to consist of a single sentence with numerous parallel subordinate clauses.

18.2.2 *Main text*

18.2.2.1 *Subdivisions*

The main text may be broken up into subdivisions. The largest subdivision is that of the 'Part'. This typically corresponds in Arabic to باب. In the Lebanese Constitution, for example, the Arabic الباب الأول – أحكام اساسية is translated into English as 'PART I – FUNDAMENTAL PROVISIONS'. Within each part, there may be several Chapters; 'chapter' in English corresponds to فصل in Arabic. The Lebanese Constitution has as its first chapter within its first part الفصل الأول – في الدولة وأراضيها. This is translated into English as 'CHAPTER I – THE STATE AND ITS TERRITORY'. The basic unit of the main text is the Article. The first article of the Jordanian Constitution reads as follows:

المادة ١ – المملكة العربية الاردنية الهاشمية دولة عربية مستقلة ذات سيادة ملكها لا يتجزأ ولا ينزل عن شيء منها، والشعب الاردني جزء من الامة العربية ونظام الحكم فيها نيابي ملكي وراثي.

This is translated into English as:

1　The Hashemite Kingdom of Jordan is an independent Arab State. It is indivisible and no part of it may be ceded. The people of Jordan form part of the Arab nation. The form of Government shall be parliamentary with hereditary monarchy.

It is usual, as in this example, for the articles to be introduced as المادة ١ – (etc.). In English-language constitutions, however, the word 'Article' does not always appear, and the number of the article is followed by a full stop.

It is possible for articles themselves to have subclauses. These may also be introduced by numbers, as in the following example from the Jordanian Constitution:

المادة ٩ ـ ١ـ لا يجوز ابعاد اردني من ديار المملكة.
٢ ـ لا يجوز أن يحظر على اردني الاقامة في جهة ما ولا ان يلزم بالاقامة في مكان معين الا في الاحوال المبينة في القانون.

This is translated into English as:

9　(i)　No Jordanian shall be exiled from the territory of the Kingdom.
　　(ii)　No Jordanian shall be prevented from residing at any place, or be compelled to reside in any specified place, except in the circumstances prescribed by law.

As this example shows, 'secondary' numbers in Arabic are typically translated into English as Roman numerals in round brackets (each of these numbers refers to what is known technically as a 'paragraph' in English, فقرة in Arabic).

Articles in Arabic may also contain further subclauses in addition to those labelled with numbers. The following is an example from the Jordanian Constitution:

المادة ٢٣ - ١ -   العمل حق لجميع المواطنين وعلى الدولة ان توفره
للاردنيين بتوجيه الاقتصاد الوطني والنهوض به .

٢ -   تحمي الدولة العمل وتضع له تشريعا يقوم على المبادئ الآتية:

أ - اعطاء العامل أجراً يتناسب مع كمية عمله وكيفيته.

ب - تحديد ساعات العمل الاسبوعية ومنح العمال أيام راحة اسبوعية وسنوية
مع الأجر .

This is translated into English as:

23. (i)   It is the right of every citizen to work, and the State shall provide opportunities to work to all citizens by directing the national economy and raising its standard.

(ii)   The State shall protect labour and enact a legislation therefore based on the following principles: –

(a)   Every workman shall receive wages commensurate with the quantity and quality of his work.

(b)   The number of hours of work per week shall be limited. Workmen shall be given weekly and annual days of rest with wages.

As this example shows, further subclauses in Arabic, labelled - أ, - ب etc., are typically translated into English as (a), (b), etc.

18.2.2.2   *Salient linguistic features of the main text*

In Arabic, the standard verb tense in constitutions is the imperfect. The normal verb form in English, however, is 'shall + verb'. In the previous extract from the Jordanian Constitution, the phrase تحمي الدولة العمل is translated as 'The State shall protect labour'. In fact, this principle is not always consistently applied. In the extract from the Jordanian Constitution, the Arabic العمل حق لجميع المواطنين is translated into English as 'It is the right of every citizen to work'.

In general, the use of the present tense in English suggests a description of what 'has always been', while the use of 'shall + verb' can suggest a change of state. Accordingly, where stress is to be laid on the fixed and unchangeable nature of things, the present tense may also be used – for example, 'Kuwait is a fully sovereign Arab State' (rather than 'Kuwait shall be a fully sovereign state'). Note also that the phrase لا يجوز is typically translated into English as 'shall not'. An example from Article 9 of the Jordanian Constitution, already quoted earlier, is لا يجوز ابعاد اردني من ديار المملكة. This is translated into English as 'No Jordanian shall be exiled from the territory of the Kingdom.' The word يجوز on its own in the positive, however, is typically translated as 'may'. Article 15 (iv) of the Jordanian Constitution reads as follows:

يجوز في حالة اعلان الاحكام العرفية أو الطوارئ ان يفرض القانون على الصحف والنشرات والمؤلفات والاذاعة رقابة محدودة في الامور التي تتصل بالسلامة العامة وأغراض الدفاع الوطني .

This is translated into English as:

> In the event of the declaration of martial law or a state of emergency, a limited censorship on newspapers, pamphlets, books and broadcasts in matters affecting public safety or national defence may be imposed by law.

18.3   Concluding remarks

Not all material that is 'constitutional' in a general sense will fit neatly into the patterns just outlined. While translators should respect the general conventions of constitutions in translating them, they must also be sensitive to cases where the text in question does not fit entirely into the standard format of constitutions, and they must be prepared to give themselves sufficient freedom to deal effectively with translation problems that arise.

At the same time, it must be borne in mind that constitutional materials are a form of legal material. The translator must therefore ensure that the information is conveyed accurately and unambiguously from one language to the other. Accordingly, there may be occasions where it is necessary to sacrifice naturalness in the translation for the sake of retaining the details of the meaning. At the level of individual words, for example, this means that different terms having similar but distinct meanings in the ST must be translated by different terms in the TT. Thus, if the ST uses both خلاف and نزاع, it would normally be necessary to translate these by different English terms, even though considerations of TL idiomaticness might suggest that خلاف and نزاع both be translated by a single term, such as 'dispute'.

Practical 18

Practical 18.1 Constitutional translation:
مشروع دستور جديد للجمهورية اللبنانية

Assignment

(i) Discuss the strategic decisions that you must take before starting detailed translation of the following text, and outline and justify the strategy you adopt. You are to translate the text for a Lebanese political group that intends to use it as an official translation when dealing with the English-speaking world.

(ii) Translate the text into English.

(iii) Outline the decisions of detail you made in producing your translation.

Contextual information

This proposed constitution was drawn up in the 1970s by عصام نعمان, a lawyer and lecturer in constitutional law at the Lebanese University (نعمان 1979: 141–142). The text bears an interesting resemblance to the Indian Constitution discussed in this chapter. Where it is possible, make use of words and phrases that appear in the Indian Constitution in order to translate elements.

ST

مشروع
دستور جديد للجمهورية اللبنانية

مقدمة

نحن الشعب اللبناني،
وقد صممنا على أن نجعل من لبنان جمهورية علمانية ديمقراطية ذات سيادة، وعلى أن نكفل لجميع المواطنين :
حرية الفكر والتعبير والعقيدة والدين والعبادة، وعدالة اجتماعية واقتصادية وسياسية، ومساواة أمام القانون وفي المراكز والفرص،
وعلى أن ننمي بينهم جميعا أواصر المحبة والاخاء ضمانا لكرامة الفرد ووحدة الوطن والشعب،
وعلى أن نشارك أشقاءنا العرب آمامهم وآمالهم انطلاقا من وحدة التاريخ والمصير،
وعلى أن نتابع مقيمين ومغتربين، دورنا الحضاري في نشر المعرفة وتعزيز قيم الحرية والعدالة والسلام،
نعلن ونمنح أنفسنا هذا الدستور.

الباب الاول
المقومات الأساسية

المادة ١ – لبنان جمهورية عربية علمانية ديمقراطية ذات وحدة لا تتجزأ وسيادة تامة.
المادة ٢ – حدود الدولة هي تلك المعترف بها دوليا المبينة في الدستور اللبناني الصادر في الأول من ايلول سنة ١٩٢٦.
المادة ٣ – عاصمة الدولة مدينة بيروت.
المادة ٤ – لغة الدولة هي اللغة العربية.
المادة ٥ – علم الدولة أحمر فابيض فاحمر أقسامها أفقية، تتوسط الأرزة الخضراء القسم الابيض المساوي حجم القسمين الأحمرين معا.

Practical 18.2 Constitutional translation: دستور دولة الكويت

Assignment

(i) Discuss the strategic decisions that you must take before starting detailed translation of the following text, and outline and justify the strategy you adopt. You are to translate the extracts from the Kuwaiti constitution for use by the Kuwaiti government for official, legal purposes in dealing with the English-speaking world.

(ii) Translate the text into English.

(iii) Outline the decisions of detail you made in producing your translation.

Contextual information

All the material here is reproduced directly from the Kuwaiti constitution.

ST

دستور دولة الكويت
بسم الله الرحمن الرحيم

نحن عبد الله السالم الصباح أمير الكويت

رغبة في استكمال أسباب الحكم الديمقراطي لوطننا العزيز،

وإيمانا بدور هذا الوطن في ركب القومية العربية وخدمة السلام العالمي والحضارة الانسانية،

[. . .]

وبناء على ما قرره المجلس التأسيسي،

صدقنا على هذا الدستور وأصدرناه:

الباب الأول
الدولة ونظام الحكم

(مادة ١)

الكويت دولة عربية ذات سيادة تامة، ولا يجوز النزول عن سيادتها أو التخلي عن أي جزء من أراضيها.

وشعب الكويت جزء من الامة العربية.

[. . .]

(مادة ٤)

الكويت امارة وراثية في ذرية المغفور له مبارك الصباح.

ويعين ولي العهد خلال سنة على الاكثر من تولية الأمير، ويكون تعيينه بأمر أميري بناء على تزكية الأمير ومبايعة من مجلس الأمة تتم، في جلسة خاصة، بموافقة أغلبية الاعضاء الذين يتألف منهم المجلس.

وفي حالة عدم التعيين على النحو السابق يزكي الأمير لولاية العهد ثلاثة على الأقل من الذرية المذكورة فيبايع المجلس أحدهم وليا للعهد.

ويشترط في ولي العهد أن يكون رشيدا عاقلا وابنا شرعيا لأبوين مسلمين.

[. . .]

(مادة ٥)

يبين القانون علم الدولة وشعارها وشاراتها وأوسمتها ونشيدها الوطني.

(مادة ٦)

نظام الحكم في الكويت ديمقراطي، السيادة فيه للامة مصدر السلطة جميعا، وتكون ممارسة السيادة على الوجه المبين في هذا الدستور .

Practical 18.3 Constitutional translation:
مقتطفات من ميثاق جامعة الدول العربية

Assignment

(i) Discuss the strategic decisions that you must take before starting detailed translation of the following text, and outline and justify the strategy you adopt. You are to translate the text on behalf of the League of Arab States for legal purposes in dealing with the English-speaking world.

(ii) Translate the text into English.

(iii) Outline the decisions of detail you made in producing your translation.

Contextual information

All the material here is reproduced directly from the Charter of the League of Arab States (ميثاق جامعة الدول العربية).

ST

١ – لا يجوز الالتجاء إلى القوة لفض نزاع بين دولتين أو أكثر من دول الجامعة العربية فإذا نشب بينهما خلاف لا يتعلق باستقلال الدولة أو سيادتها أو سلامة أراضيها ولجأ المتنازعون إلى المجلس لفض هذا الخلاف كان قراره عندئذ نافذا ملزما

٢ – يتوسط المجلس في الخلاف الذي يخشى منه وقوع حرب بين دولة من دول الجامعة وبين أية دولة أخرى من دول الجامعة أو غيرها للتوفيق بينهما وتصدر قرارات التحكيم والقرارات الخاصة بالتوسط بأغلبية الآراء

٣ – إذا وقع اعتداء من دولة على دولة من أعضاء الجامعة أو خشي وقوعه فللدولة المعتدى عليها أو المهددة بالاعتداء أن تطلب دعوة المجلس للانعقاد فورا ويقرر المجلس التدابير اللازمة لدفع هذا الاعتداء ويصدر القرار بالإجماع فإذا كان الاعتداء من إحدى دول الجامعة لا يدخل في حساب الإجماع رأي الدولة المعتدية

٤ – ما يقرره المجلس بالإجماع يكون ملزما لجميع الدول المشتركة في الجامعة، وما يقرره المجلس بالأكثرية يكون ملزما لمن يقبله

19 Technical translation

Islamic finance texts

19.1 Introduction

Gait and Worthington (2007: 4) define Islamic finance as a financial service implemented to comply with Islamic Law (Shariah). According to Al-Saleem,

> Islamic finance can be considered as a system of finance that is bound by religious laws that prevent the taking of interest payments. At the same time, joint ventures in which the funder and the borrower share profits and risks are acceptable.
>
> (Al-Saleem 2013: 17)

Islamic finance is a rapidly growing area of activity. It has been estimated that, globally, the Islamic finance industry was worth $2 trillion at the end of 2014 and that it will be worth $4 trillion by 2020. Islamic finance operates not only in Muslim societies but is also well established in the West; in 2009, Shariah-compliant (Islamic) mortgages in Britain were said to be worth around £1.4 billion. The value of Shariah-compliant bonds (صُكوك, sg. صَك) issued on the London stock exchange already listed on the London market exceeds $34bn (£21bn) over the past five years, with more than 50 bonds quoted by the London Stock Exchange. Because of its global nature, and because the language of much of the world's banking is English, there is a significant amount of translation of Islamic finance material from Arabic to English.

19.2 Fundamentals of Islamic finance

Islamic Law or Shariah (الشريعة الإسلامية), as understood in Sunni Islam, has several sources: Quran (القرآن), Sunna (السنة) (the most important element of which is Hadith الحديث),*ijma'* (الإجماع), *qiyas* (القياس) and *ijtihad* (الاجتهاد) – to which is sometimes added *urf* (العرف) 'traditional, customary practice'. The Quran is regarded in Islam as the literal Word of God and is therefore the primary source of Islamic Law. Sunna (السنة) is the Prophet's habitual practice and behaviour, particularly the statements of the Prophet, the Hadith (الحديث), as recorded in various authoritative Hadith collections. *Ijma'* (الإجماع) is unanimity among Muslim scholars upon specific issues. *Qiyas* (القياس), 'analogy', is the use of deduction to reach an opinion in a case not mentioned in the Quran or Sunna by comparing it with other issues referred to in the Quran and Sunna. *Ijtihad* (الاجتهاد) is a jurist's judgment relating to the applicability of certain Shariah rules to issues not mentioned in the Quran or Sunna (cf. Gait and Worthington 2007: 4–8). Islamic legal judgements are called *fatwas* (فتوى), and the qualified scholar who delivers them is a *mufti* (مفتٍ). Fundamental issues involving Islamic finance are thus determined through *fatwas*. In this chapter, we will look particularly at the translation of *fatwas* relating to Islamic finance.

19.3 Cultural commonality and non-commonality in Islamic finance

There is a high degree of cultural non-commonality (Section 16.1.1) between Islamic and Western notions of Islamic finance. This extends to basic notions, such as مضاربة. According to the Institute of Islamic Banking and Insurance Glossary (http://www.islamic-banking.com/glossary_M.aspx), مضاربة is:

> An investment partnership with profit-loss-sharing implications. One or more partners as investors (Rab al Mal [رب المال]) provide 100% of the capital to an entrepreneur (the partner who provides entrepreneurship and management known as Mudarib [مضارب]) to undertake a business activity. Profit is shared between the partners on a pre-agreed ratio, any loss is borne only by the investing partner(s) alone. For the Mudarib the loss is the share of the expected income for the efforts put into the business activity. The investors have no right to interfere in the management of the business but can specify conditions that would ensure better management of the capital money. In this way Mudarabah [مضاربة] is sometimes referred to as a sleeping partnership. As a financing mode, an Islamic bank can provide capital to a customer for a business activity. The customer provides the expertise, labour and management; profits are shared between the bank and the customer according to predetermined ratio while financial losses are borne by the bank and the bank risks losing the capital invested with the customer which justifies the bank's claim to a share of the business profit. Islamic banks also apply the concept of Mudarabah to pay a return on customer deposits held in investment account. The Bank becomes wholly responsible and liable in the management and investment the customer deposits and utilises the funds as business capital by the bank, the bank will have the right to manage the funds as it thinks fit in permissible activities that it considers are profitable and share the profit on the basis of the agreement made between the bank and the customer.

Although مضاربة has features in common with Western financial contracts, it does not exactly correspond to anything in Western finance.

The cultural non-commonality between Islamic financial notions and Western financial notions is most obvious in pre-modern texts. Consider the following from

بر هان الدين علي بن أبي بكر ,الهداية: شرح بداية المبتدي ,الهداية, known more commonly as الهداية by أبي بكر علي بن الدين بر هان
المرغيناني (1135–1197). This is the standard work of فقه (Islamic Jurisprudence) used in the Hanafi *madhhab* (المذهب الحنفي), the 'Law School', which is predominant among Sunni Muslims from Egypt and Turkey eastwards as far as Bangladesh (المرغيناني 2000: 104, vol:1).

ST

(ومن كان عليه دين يحيط بماله فلا زكاة عليه) وقال الشافعي رحمه الله: تجب لتحقق السبب، وهو ملك نصاب تام. ولنا أنه مشغول بحاجته الأصلية فاعتبر معدوماً كالماء المستحق بالعطش وثياب البذلة والمهنة [. . .].

This has been translated by Nyazee (2006: 249–250) as follows:

TT

If a person has a debt that covers his entire wealth, there is no obligation of *zakāt* on him. Al-Shāfi'ī (God bless him) said that it is imposed due to the realisation of the cause, which is the ownership of the complete *niṣāb*. We maintain that the wealth stands engaged through his primary need (of repayment to the creditor) and is, therefore, deemed to be non-existent like water for quenching thirst (for the rule of *tayammum*) and clothes required to provide service and meet professional commitments.

Some of the strangeness of the TT arises from cultural non-commonality – Islamic concepts that have no real near-equivalent in Western-based English-speaking cultures. In the case of *zakāt* for زكاة and *niṣāb* for نصاب, the translator has used cultural borrowing (Section 4.5) to deal with this. At another point, there is an addition of cultural borrowing in the TT, *tayammum,* that does not occur in the ST. Finally, there is one case of simple cultural transplantation, 'God bless him' for رحمه الله.

There are other features of the TT that make it rather non-idiomatic, as illustrated by the translation of يحيط بماله as 'that covers his entire wealth', of فلا زكاة عليه as 'there is no obligation of *zakāt* on him' and of تجب لتحقق السبب as 'it is imposed due to the realisation of the cause', to take three examples from the start of the ST. These do not, strictly speaking, reflect cultural differences between Arabic and English; they have to do with the style of the ST, which, like many pre-modern Arabic texts, is quite distant from the style of modern English and is significantly different also from the typical style, and even grammar, of modern Standard Arabic. Thus, for example, the third-person feminine singular form تجب hardly occurs in modern Standard Arabic: the masculine form يجب has become almost universal, even when the subject as here (زكاة) is feminine.

Some of this stylistic unidiomaticness could be fairly easily eliminated. Thus, the first TT sentence 'If a person has a debt that covers his entire wealth, there is no obligation of *zakāt* on him' might be recast more idiomatically as 'No-one whose debts are greater than their wealth is obliged to pay *zakāt*'. In other cases, the style of Classical Arabic is likely to prove much more resistant to recasting into idiomatic English.

There is, however, a further reason why the translator of this text might want the TT to be fairly literal – and by unavoidable extension therefore somewhat unidiomatic. An Arabic Islamic legal text (of which Islamic finance texts are a type) really only has authority in its original Arabic version. An English translation of such a text is not a replacement to be used instead of the original but only a guide to the original. Therefore, specialist readers might well use the English TT as a means of better understanding the ST. In this case, a TT that remains fairly literal, and whose elements therefore can be easily individually related back to corresponding elements in the ST, is more useful (provided it adequately conveys the meaning of the ST) than a TT that is very idiomatic but where it is not easy to see which specific element of the TT corresponds to which specific element of the ST.

The ancillary nature of translations of Islamic finance texts is also evident in the retention by the translator of Arabic technical terms as cultural borrowings – *zakāt* and *niṣāb* in this TT (as well as the introduction of a term not found in the ST: *tayammum*). Here, the translator also makes use of a consistent transliteration system (Section 4.7) – for example, using *ā* for ﺍ, and *ṣ* for ﺻ, thus allowing the reader to unambiguously 'reconstruct' the original Arabic forms.

Other authors on Islamic finance, whether writing originally in English or translating from Arabic, are not so consistent. Thus, the definition of مضاربة, which we quoted earlier from the Institute of Islamic Banking and Insurance Glossary, uses 'Rab al Mal' for رب المال, 'Mudarib' for مضارب and 'Mudarabah' for مضاربة. It thus makes no distinction between cases of short *a* (as in رب and the second and third *a* in مضاربة) and long *ā* (as in مضارب, مال and the first 'a' in مضاربة). Nor does it distinguish between doubled 'b' (i.e. 'b' with a *shadda*), as in رب, and single 'b' (i.e. 'b' without a *shadda*), as in مضارب and مضاربة. Finally, it transcribes the ض in مضارب and مضاربة as 'd', which is used elsewhere in the Glossary to transcribe د.

Whichever technique is adopted, strict transliteration or looser transcription, two points should be borne in mind. First, it is the norm in Islamic finance translation to use transcription (cultural borrowing) of some kind for terms that are specific to Islamic finance. Translators do not attempt to use approximate Western equivalents for culturally specific Islamic finance terms, as these would almost certainly mislead the reader in understanding precisely what is meant. There are issues regarding which notions are specific to Islamic finance and which are not. The words دين and مال have been translated by Nyazee previously as 'debt' and 'wealth', respectively. Closer investigation is likely to reveal, however, that what are technically meant by دين and مال in Islamic finance are slightly different to what are technically meant by 'debt' and 'wealth' in British law, for example. A degree of tolerance of marginal difference is, however, necessary in order to produce a translation that is not overloaded with cultural borrowings and therefore very difficult for anyone but the most specialist reader to understand.

The second point to be borne in mind is that technical Islamic finance terms, like technical terms generally, should be translated consistently. If a translator uses a transliteration *muḍārib* on one occasion in a particular TT to translate مضارب, he or she should not use *mudarib* on another.

19.4 Modern Islamic finance texts

Modern Islamic finance texts pose far fewer problems, whether cultural or stylistic, in translation into English than do Classical ones. There are several reasons for this.

Culturally, modern Islamic financial writing his heavily influenced by Western financial concepts and practices. As Bello, Yasin, Hassan and Bin (2015: 36) note, 'There are many aspects of conventional banking that have been applied in Islamic banking particularly in the area of deposit and investment'. While areas of cultural non-commonality remain, the 'Westernization' of Islamic finance means that many concepts are held in common with Western ones (having been taken over from the West), and, as a corollary, the overall density of culturally non-common concepts is reduced. While in a Classical Arabic Islamic finance text, the translator into English might have to deal with many culturally non-common concepts on every page, in a modern Arabic text, there are likely to be relatively few culturally non-common concepts, embedded in an overall text, where major concepts are culturally shared with those of the West.

Stylistically, modern Arabic has in most genres also been extensively influenced by Western languages. Given the cultural influence of Western financial notions on Islamic finance, it is not surprising that modern Islamic finance texts have also been influenced stylistically by modern Western finance writing. Consider the following modern *fatwa* (فتوى) from the *Fatawa of the Kuwait Finance House, Question 143, pp. 142–143,* recorded and translated by Yusuf Talal Delorenzo in his *Compendium of Legal Opinions on the Operation of Islamic Banks* (1997: 13):

تضاف ثمن البضاعة المبيعة بالمرابحة المصاريف المنضبطة التي جرى بها العرف وتزيد في قيمة البضاعة وتتصل بها مباشرة. أما مرتبات الموظفين والكتبة والمراجعين فلا تضاف لأنها من تمام عملية الشراء التي بها يستحق الربح الاصلي. وأما بالنسبة للمخلصين بالجمارك فإن كانوا من خارج موظفي البنك فيضاف فقط ما يدفع عادة على تخليص السيارة ذاتها، ولا يضاف مرتب الموظف المخلص.

This has been translated by Delorenzo as:

Expenses which may lawfully be added to the price of goods sold by the bank by means of murabahah include only those which are regularly incurred in accordance with customary practice, those which add value to the goods, and those which are incurred directly. The salaries of bank employees, however, are not to be added as they are a part of the (purchasing process and the) services offered by the bank in exchange for its right to make a profit. With respect to customs clearance, if those who undertake this work are not bank employees (but agents), then whatever is paid to them may be added to the price of the goods. If they are bank employees, however, their salaries may not be added; though the expenses they incur while clearing the goods may be added.

The only terms in this text that are not culturally shared between Arabic (Islamic) and Western cultures are مرابحة, translated by cultural borrowing as 'murabahah', and عرف, sometimes accepted as one of the sources of Islamic law (as noted in Section 19.2), and translated as 'customary practice'.

Practical 19

Practical 19.1 Classical Islamic finance: وإن كان ماله أكثر من دينه

Assignment

(i) Consider the strategic problems confronting the translator of the following text, and outline your own strategy for dealing with them. You are to translate this text as part of a new translation of الهداية by المرغيناني (cf. Section 19.3) aimed at Muslims living in the West with a general interest in Islamic law but only a basic knowledge of Arabic.
(ii) Translate the text into English.
(iii) Explain the decisions of detail you made in producing your TT, especially those relating to technical questions.

Contextual information

This Arabic text is from المرغيناني (2000: 104, vol: 1) and follows on immediately from the extract discussed in Section 19.3 (beginning ومن كان عليه دين and ending وثياب البذلة والمهنة).

ST

(وإن كان ماله أكثر من دينه زكى الفاضل إذا بلغ نصاباً) لفراغة عن الحاجة، والمراد به دين له مطالب من جهة العباد حتى لا يمنع دين النذر والكفارة، ودين الزكاة مانع حال بقاء النصاب، لأنه ينقص به النصاب، وكذا بعد الاستهلاك، خلافا لزفر فيهما ولأبي يوسف رحمه الله في الثاني على ما روى عنه لأن له مطالباً وهو الامام في السوائم ونائبة في أموال التجارة فإن الملاك نوّابه.

Practical 19.2 Modern Islamic finance: بالنسبة لبيع المرابحة

Assignment

(i) Consider the strategic problems confronting the translator of the following text, and outline your own strategy for dealing with them. You are to translate this text as part of a new translation of fatawa (fatwas) of the Kuwait Finance House.
(ii) Translate the text into English.
(iii) Explain the decisions of detail you made in producing your TT, especially those relating to technical questions.

Contextual information

This text is taken from *The Fatawa of the Kuwait Finance House: Question no. 97, pp. 102–13* (reproduced in Delorenzo 1997: 31).

ST

بالنسبة لبيع المرابحة إما أن يكون الاتفاق على سعر الشراء فلا يجوز إضاقة مصاريف مطلقاً، وإما ان يكون على الثمن مضافاً إليه التكلفة المبينة في العقد، فحينئذ يضاف إليها نسبة الربح المتفق عليه، وأما بعد الاتفاق إذا جدت مصاريف فتؤخذ هذه المصاريف فقط دون إضاقة ربح، وذلك بعد الإشارة في العقد إلى تحميله المصاريف المستجدة.

Practical 19.3 Modern Islamic finance: الاشتغال بشركة المقاولات

Assignment

(i) Consider the strategic problems confronting the translator of the following text, and outline your own strategy for dealing with them. You are to translate this text as part of a new translation of online fatwas issued by the Saudi-based الرئاسة العامة للبحوث العلمية والإفتاء.

(ii) Translate the text into English.

(iii) Explain the decisions of detail you made in producing your TT, especially those relating to technical questions.

Contextual information

This text is taken from the website of the Saudi-based الرئاسة العامة للبحوث العلمية والإفتاء: http://www.alifta.net/fatawa/fatawaDetails.aspx?View=Page&PageID=9300&PageNo=1&BookID=3 (reproduced in Al-Saleem 2013: 125).

ST

الاشتغال بشركة المقاولات التي تتعامل بالرشوة، فترشي المسئولين عند المناقصات مثلا ليتم لها إرساء المناقصة عليها، والتي تتعامل أيضا مع البنوك معاملات ربوية من أجل مقاولات الشركة ـ الاشتغال بهذه الشركة وأمثالها فيه تعاون على الإثم [. . .] والعدوان، بتقييد المعاملات الربوية، أو نقلها، أو التعقيب عليها، وقبض ما فيها أو إقباضه، إلى غير ذلك مما يتعلق بالربا والرشوة، والتعاون في ذلك حرام ؛ لقوله تعالى: (وَتَعَاوَنُوا عَلَى الْبِرِّ وَالتَّقْوَى وَلَا تَعَاوَنُوا عَلَى الْإِثْمِ وَالْعُدْوَانِ وَاتَّقُوا اللَّهَ إِنَّ اللَّهَ شَدِيدُ الْعِقَابِ) ولما صح عن الرسول صلى الله عليه وسلم أنه (لعن آكل الربا وموكله وكاتبه وشاهديه، وقال : هم في الإثم سواء) . رواه مسلم، وعلى ذلك لا يجوز أخذه المرتب ولا النسبة المعينة على توليه التعقيب على معاملات ربوية، واستخلاص مبالغها، وينبغي له أن يبحث عن عمل آخر ليس فيه مباشرة لمحرم ولا إعانة عليه، اتقاء لما حرم الله، وحرصا على الكسب الطيب.

20 Consumer-oriented texts

20.1 Introduction

We have stressed that all texts, including translations, are produced for a purpose. The purpose of the TT is always a major factor to be taken into account in deciding a strategy. This truth is particularly clear in translating what can broadly be classed as consumer-oriented texts. This, together with the fact that many translators earn their livings with these sorts of text, is why we are giving them a chapter to themselves.

By 'consumer-oriented texts', we mean texts that either try to persuade the public to buy something, or tell purchasers how to use what they have bought, or advise on commodities that might be bought or courses of action that might be taken. This range of texts most obviously includes advertisements, but it also includes things like tourist brochures, public notices, information leaflets, user manuals, consumer or hobby magazines, recipe books, CD booklets and so on – even a lot of propaganda can be classified under this heading. (For a general discussion of this area of translation, see Torresi 2010.)

20.2 Tourist material

A good example of the problems involved in translating consumer-oriented texts is provided by tourist material. In fact, there are often quite clear differences between tourist material in English and that in Arabic.

20.2.1 English-language tourist material

Here for class discussion is an excerpt from a British tourist brochure advertising the Costa Blanca in Spain. Typical features worth discussing are register, the choice of adjectives and adverbs and sentence structure.

> Sunshine, bright lights and superb sandy beaches, blue-green seas, orange groves and picturesque villages, mountains, old fortresses and starry evenings – all part of the Costa Blanca's charm.

The weather is exceptional. In spring it's warm and sunny and the colours of citrus fruits, flowers and blossom splash the countryside. In summer it's gloriously hot and in autumn the balmy days merge slowly into one another. This is perhaps why the Costa Blanca has become so incredibly popular with holidaymakers.

20.2.2 *Arabic tourist material*

Compare the English text with the following extract from a tourist brochure, along with an English translation, both published by the Yemeni General Authority of Tourism (title of Arabic version: الجوف – مارب – شبوة, and of English version: *Al-Jouf – Marib – Shabwa*) (Republic of Yemen, General Authority of Tourism 1997: 2, 3):

ST

الزائر العزيز

لقد كرست هذه النشرة السياحية للتعريف بثلاث محافظات يمنية تقع جميعها في إطار النطاق الصحراوي الواقع في الزاوية الداخلية بين المرتفعات اليمنية الغربية والجنوبية المعروفة تاريخياً بمفازة صيهد واليوم رملة السبعتين.

وهو موطن الحضارات اليمنية القديمة التي بدأ ازدهارها منذ مطلع الألف الأول قبل الميلاد على ضفاف الوديان.

يسود هذا النطاق مناخ قاري حار جاف صيفاً بارد شتاءً.

كما يسود بعض اطرافها مظاهر الحياة البدوية. وفي هذا الجزء من الجمهورية اليمنية تقوم العديد من الشركات باعمال التنقيب وانتاج النفط الذي سوف تسهم عائداته في تنمية البلاد ورفع مستوى معيشة السكان ان شاء الله.

TT

Dear Visitor,

This touristic publication is devoted to introduce to you three Yemeni provinces, which are all situated in the geographical scope, lying in the inner angle of the coastal mountain ranges of Yemen, which was called by mediaeval Arab geographers as the 'Sayhad desert and today as Ramlat al-Sabaatain'.

It is the abode of the Ancient Yemeni Civilizations which started to flourish since the beginning of the first millennium BC, along the banks of the valleys. The tropical climate prevails this area, i.e., it is hot and dry in summer but cold in winter.

Some parts of it are dominated by nomadic life. In this part of the Republic of Yemen, many companies carry out drilling works and oil production, which by the will of Allah, will contribute to the development of the country and the upgrading of the standard of living.

This English translation suffers from several linguistic and stylistic problems; here is a more idiomatic version:

Revised TT

Dear Visitor,

This tourist brochure aims to introduce you to three Yemeni provinces all of which lie within the inland desert region between the southern and western Yemeni highlands. This area was known historically as the Say-had Desert and today is called Ramlat al-Sabaatain.

This is the home of the ancient civilizations of Yemen which flourished at the beginning of the first millennium BC on the banks of the river valleys. The region enjoys a continental climate – hot and dry in summer, and cold in winter.

In some areas the local people follow a Bedouin life-style. In this part of the Republic of Yemen, a number of companies are engaged in oil-drilling and oil-production. It is to be hoped that the revenues from these activities will contribute to the development of the country and the raising of living standards.

The revised English translation deals with most of the obvious problems in the official English translation. However, the general style is rather formal for a tourist brochure. Even the opening words, 'Dear Visitor', while not impossible in a British tourist brochure, seem a little out of place; they perhaps suggest an official notice from a hotel to its clients rather than a text that will entice visitors to explore.

Similarly, the start of the first main paragraph, 'This tourist brochure aims to introduce you to [. . .]' is more reminiscent of the initial 'Abstract' section of an academic article (e.g. 'This paper deals with several current problems in plant morphology [. . .]') than of an English-language tourist publication.

In the second paragraph, the second sentence 'The region enjoys a continental climate – hot and dry in summer, and cold in winter' is almost technical in tone compared with the description of the weather in the *Costa Blanca* text.

Closely related to the generally formal tone of the Arabic brochure is its rather academic subject matter. British tourist brochures do sometimes contain historical information – 'This is the home of the ancient civilizations of Yemen [. . .]' might not be out of place in a British tourist brochure. However, it is less likely that a British tourist brochure would devote significant space to oil exploration and production and the implications of these for national development, as is done in the third and final paragraph here.

The use of the phrase ان شاء الله at the end of the paragraph also raises an interesting cultural issue. The official English translation contains the exotic 'by the will of Allah', a form of expression that seems quite alien to the genre of the tourist brochure in English. Accordingly, this has been rendered as 'It is to be hoped that' in the idiomatic English version – with, of course, a significant translation loss, as it presumably involves a clear distortion of the original intention of the writer of the ST. This example is a reminder of how important it is for the translator to consider carefully the central feature of cultural differences between the SL public and the TL public.

20.3 Cultural stereotyping

Different cultures, then, value different things and have different taboos. In addition, there is also evidence that different cultures stereotype consumers differently. There may be a tendency in American advertising, for example, to hector or hustle or patronize the consumer more than in some European cultures; and Japanese advertisements are well known for taking an indirect, and, in many cases, quite surreal, approach to the products they are trying to sell.

In this light, consider the following announcement for a photography competition, from *Golden Falcon*/الصقر الذهبي, the inflight magazine of Gulf Air (Karkouti 2000: 38, 41). This appears in both the English and Arabic versions of the magazine. Judging from the fact that the author is named as Jo Mapp in the English version, the English version appears to be the ST and the Arabic the TT. The two texts should be compared and discussed in class. Something to concentrate on particularly is the differences in tone between the texts and how these differences are created.

Competition
It's your shot
Your assignment

by Picture Editor Jo Mapp

Have you ever looked at a photograph taken in a magazine and thought to yourself 'I could do that'? Well here's your chance. We want you to send us a photograph taken by yourself – a photograph that you think would be worthy of publishing in *Golden Falcon* or featuring on the front cover. And, when our judges have selected the best entry, that's exactly what we will do – publish it in the magazine or feature it on the cover. Simply read the guidelines set out by our photography expert – and get shooting.

We would like the photograph you send to have some kind of relevance to the theme of travel and tourism.

مسابقة أفضل صورة

إنها فرصتك .. لا تفوتها. هل تشعر بأن لديك موهبة في التصوير الفوتغرافي .. هل سبق ورأيت صورة في إحدى المجلات وقلت لنفسك: نعم أستطيع التقاط مثلها. إذن، ها نحن نتيح لك فرصة لاختبار موهبتك التي قد تكون البداية في انطلاقك كمصور صحفي محترف .. وما عليك إلا أن تلتقط صورة تستحق أن تنشر في أحد أعداد «الصقر الذهبي»، أو ربما تجد طريقها للنشر على الغلاف. بعد إرسال الصور إلينا وانتهاء لجنة التحكيم من فرزها سيتم نشر الصور الفائزة.

ولكن تريث قليلا قبل أن تنطلق لالتقاط الصور إذ نرجو منك أن تقرأ التوجيهات أدناه التي أعدها مدير التصوير في مؤسستنا:

١ – يجب أن يكون موضوع الصورة له علاقة مباشرة بالسياحة والسفر.

In part, the reformulations in the Arabic TT reflect the nature of Standard Arabic. Because of diglossia (Section 15.5.1) and the contrast with colloquial Arabic, Standard Arabic can be regarded as an intrinsically formal language. The conventions of usage in Arabic require that a written announcement of a photography competition in a magazine be made in Standard Arabic. Thus, an Arabic text of this nature is bound to be more formal than an English text written in a fairly intimate style.

Over and above differences related to diglossia, however, there are clear culturally related differences between the ST and the TT. The tendency towards greater distance between writer and reader, with the writer adopting at times a markedly authoritative tone, seems to reflect a general cultural preference in Arabic and is not a direct or inevitable result of diglossia.

There are other ways in which consumer-oriented texts may vary among cultures. For instance, certain sorts of consumers may be treated differently in different cultures: in one culture the average consumer of a certain type of product may, for example, be regarded as having more specialist knowledge than the average consumer of the same type of product in another culture. An example of this is found in a later part of the photo-competition text we have just been discussing. The English ST has four guidelines (of which we have reproduced only the first in our version, beginning 'We would like the photo you send [. . .]'). The third one of these reads: 'If you are aiming to feature your photograph on the cover then it needs to fit the A4 format of the magazine'. This guideline is simply omitted from the Arabic TT; the most likely reason for this seems to be that although A4 paper is used in some parts of the Middle East, the typical Arab reader is felt to be less knowledgeable in this area than the typical English reader and is not expected to know what A4 paper is. Therefore, the guideline (in this specific form at least) is not worth putting into the Arabic TT.

20.4   Genre mixing in consumer-oriented texts

Material within a given genre may also vary culturally in other ways. Take the average recipe book. On the face of things, this may seem to belong to the category of empirical genres, for it appears to classify cooking techniques in a descriptively systematic manner, to offer factual and objective accounts of the contents and appearances of dishes, as well as of their preparation. In itself, this almost makes recipe books sound like scientific texts. But this does not account for several features, in English at least, of recipe books; the fact that they are rarely written in a technically and scientifically neutral style; the fact that their use of tonal style is often calculated to draw the reader into a comfortable, possibly flattering, relationship; the fact that they have a transparently helpful organization, beyond what could be expected of the most indulgent scientific textbook; and the fact that recipe books are often lavishly illustrated with glossy pictures. Such features indicate a consumer-oriented purpose in recipe books that contain them and are well worth looking out for when translating certain kinds of 'commercial' ST. Even if not directly consumer oriented to the sale of particular foodstuffs, most recipe books are, at the very least, specimens of a hybrid genre characterized by the dual purpose of description and persuasion.

Choosing a register for a consumer-oriented TT can be problematic in itself. For instance, there may be little in common among the groups of consumers aimed at by the ST and the TT, respectively. In any case, any TL genre selected as a prototype for the TT is likely to provide specimens in widely divergent styles and registers, leaving the translator with several possible models: the decisive question is that of the purpose and audience of the TT.

Practical 20

Practical 20.1 Translation of consumer-oriented texts:
ان كانت مدينة فاس تفخر

Assignment

Read the following extract from an article in *Golden Falcon* الصقر الذهبي (Karkouti 2000: 42–43), the inflight magazine of Gulf Air, together with its Arabic translation, which appears in the same magazine. The article, which is designed to interest readers in the touristic virtues of Morocco, is titled 'Discover Morocco with Gulf Air' in the English ST and حلقوا مع «طيران الخليج» لاكتشاف المغرب in the Arabic TT. The extract is taken from a section that deals with Fez.

Using the same general procedure for detailing differences as you used for discussing the photo-competition text in Section 20.3:

(i) Identify the places where the TT differs significantly from the ST.
(ii) Comment on the differences, accounting for them – where possible – in terms of the following categories:

   (a) *tone* (tonal register)
   (b) *culture* (especially identification with cultural heritage in contemporary Arab culture)
   (c) *religion* (i.e. religious sensibilities)
   (d) *sensitivity* (i.e. avoidance of sensitive or taboo subjects other than religion)

Some examples of changes may fit more than one category. Where they do, you may mark them as belonging to two or more categories. You may feel that other categories can be added to those listed under (ii); feel free to add these. You may also find changes that do not fit easily into any category. If you do, list these as uncategorized.

ST

Fez has a lot to be proud of. It is the place where the great 14th-century historian and traveller Ibn Khaldoun lived and its centrepiece is the grand Karaouine mosque, reputedly one of the world's oldest universities. The city has built on these venerable origins by organizing a series of festivals throughout the year. Music, painting and cooking become the focus of scholarly debates, conferences and informal discussions about the place of artistry in the modern world. There's a terrific enthusiasm for the subjects and those curious to know more about Fez and its heritage travel from around the globe crossing the usual boundaries that keep people apart.

These special cultural programmes take place in the warren of tiled courtyards and narrow alleyways that make up the heart and the head of this fascinating city. Heart and head because Fez is both a sort of forerunner of Oxford and Cambridge, the centre where intellectual rigour and scientific endeavour was pioneered and then fostered, but also its heart for it is here that Moulay Idriss founder and patron saint of Fez (and also founder of Morocco's first royal dynasty) is buried and pilgrims from all over Morocco come to his shrine. Additionally there are over 3,000 mosques and *medrasas* or religious schools within its dark, maze-like streets.

TT

ان كانت مدينة فاس تفخر بأشياء تميز تاريخها وحضارتها، فإنها تفخر على وجه الخصوص بعلاقتها بالمؤرخ وعالم الاجتماع العربي الشهير، صاحب «المقدمة» ابن خلدون، كما انها تفخر بكونها موطن جامعة القرويين، اقدم الجامعات في العالم. وتكاد مدينة فاس تعيش على امتداد العام حالة احتفال مفتوح، إذ تشهد أيامها المتعاقبة، وفصولها المختلفة احتفالات ومهرجانات متنوعة، منها ما يخص الازياء، والموسيقى، والفنون الشعبية، وحتى فنون الطبخ، وفي فاس ما يكفي من الحضارة العريقة والثقافة الرفيعة، اللتين تجذبان الزوار والراغبين في معرفة تراثها وحضارتها من كل بقاع العالم، ومن شتى الاجناس والاعراق والاديان. وعادة ما تنظّم في المدينة لقاءات ثقافية، تعقد في افنية يزين جدرانها زخارف من السيراميك «الزليج»، تحكي بعضاً من تاريخ البلاد وتعكس وجها من هويتها. وتبحث هذه الندوات والملتقيات مختلف المواضيع العلمية والادبية والفنية والاجتماعية. وتجمع مدينة فاس بين كونها مقصدا لطلاب العلم والثقافة، تماماً كما هي مدينتا كامبريدج واكسفورد في بريطانيا، وكونها مقصدا روحيا، إذ يحج الناس الى مقام المولى ادريس مؤسس مدينة فاس، متوسلين البركات، وطالبين الشفاعة. وعلاوة على ذلك تزخر فاس بأكثر من 3000 مسجد ومدرسة للتعليم الاساسي والديني [. . .]

Practical 20.2 Translation of consumer-oriented texts: مرحبا بكم في تونس

Assignment

(i) Discuss the strategic problems confronting the translator of the following text, and outline your own strategy for dealing with them.
(ii) Translate the text into English.
(iii) Explain the decisions of detail you made in producing your translation.

Contextual information

This text is taken from the website http://www.tourisme.gov.tn/index. php?id=92&L=1. This is run by the Tunisian government and is intended to attract

Arab tourists to Tunisia. You have been asked to produce an English-language version aimed principally at potential tourists from Britain and Ireland but also at other English-speaking countries, such as Canada, the United States, Australia and New Zealand, as well as English speakers from mainland Europe.

ST

مرحبا بكم في تونس

مرحبا بكم حيث الشمس ساطعة والسماء زرقاء، ويمكنكم الإطلاع على المعالم الأثرية الفريدة والمتميزة، والتقاليد الأصيلة، والمناظر الخلابة من صحراء رملية وشواطئ ذهبية وجبال رائعة واكتشاف الكثير من المناطق السياحية الجميلة.

إكتشف تونس

متجهة نحو إيطاليا وضاربة جذورها في أعماق الصحراء، تمثّل تونس بحقّ حلقة الوصل بين أوروبا وإفريقيا، وقد أثّرت وتأثّرت بالحضارات العريقة التي قامت في المنطقة، فقد كانت قلب الحضارة القرطاجية، التي لا تزال بعض تقاليدها الشعبيّة حاضرة إلى اليوم، وكانت أيضا مقاطعة رومانية متميّزة. ولا تزال لوحات فسيفسائية كبيرة ورائعة شاهدة على ذلك.

البحر والشمس والترفيه

الرمل الأبيض الصافي، ونسمات البحر العليلة، من مميزات شواطئ البلاد التونسية. وعلى كامل الشريط الساحلي تمتدّ سلسلة من الفنادق المصنفة، الكثير منها شيد حديثا ومنها ما تمّ إعادة ترميمه، ليتلاءم مع أذواق ومتطلبات كافة السياح، ويستمد الطابع المعماري الفندقي التونسي خصوصياته من الطبيعة، حيث الجنان المزدهرة وحدائق الياسمين.

للسياحة العائلية مكانة خاصة

للأطفال هنا مكانة خاصة، فالكلّ أعدّ للطفل من الظروف ما يجعله يقضي عطلة تجمع بين الترفيه والإفادة. الصغار منهم سينعمون باللعب على الشواطئ ذات الرمال الذهبية الصافية، ويجدون أيضا في الفنادق مسابح خاصّة بهم، ونواد للرسم وصناعة الفخّار وغير ذلك من الأشغال اليدويّة.

Practical 20.3 Translation of consumer-oriented texts: جزيرة جربة – جرجيس

Assignment

  (i) Discuss the strategic problems confronting the translator of the following text, and outline your own strategy for dealing with them.
 (ii) Translate the text into English.
(iii) Explain the decisions of detail you made in producing your translation.

Contextual information

Like the ST in Practical 20.2, this text is taken from the website http://www.tour isme.gov.tn/index.php?id=108&L=1. This is run by the Tunisian government and is intended to attract Arab tourists to Tunisia. You have been asked to produce an English-language version aimed principally at potential tourists from Britain and Ireland but also at other English-speaking countries, such as Canada, the United States, Australia and New Zealand, as well as English speakers from mainland Europe.

ST

جزيرة جربة – جرجيس

تقع جربة في قلب البحر الأبيض المتوسّط، وقد استطاعت هذه الجزيرة على مدى التاريخ أن تسحر سكانها وزائريها بطقسها الرائع وأجوائها الجميلة. تمتلك الجزيرة شواطئ من الرمل الناعم، تحيط بها أشجار النخيل الباسقة.

وقد أصبحت جزيرة جربة بفضل مطارها الدولي أحدَ أهمِّ المقاصد السياحية في المتوسط، لما تزخر به من فنادق فخمة وبنية سياحية متطوّرة. ومنذ بضع سنوات، انطلقت في الجزيرة عديد المراكز للمعالجة بمياه البحر وهي تقدم خدمات طبية متميزة، يزيد عددها عن 15 مركزًا.

يربط طريق يعود إلى العصر الروماني جزيرة جربة بجرجيس. هذه المدينة الواقعة في قلب غابات النخيل تتميّز بمحطّة سياحيّة هامّة وهي شهيرة بشواطئها الذهبيّة. دون أن ننسى الحفاوة المتميزة وما تزخر به من معمار أصيل.

جربة جزيرة الأحلام: المشاهد الطبيعية والأفق الجميل، المناخ اللطيف وشواطئ الرمل الناعم الأبيض، والمعمار المتفرّد، المكوّن من المنازل المكعّبة والقباب البيضاء.

هذه الجزيرة عبق التاريخ يعود إلى آلاف السنين، لتكون منطقة جربة-جرجيس عبارة عن تحيّة للجمال والبهاء. "أوليس" بذاته انبهر بسحر المكان وهذا الجمال. ولا يزال هذا السحر له مفعول خاص لدى الزائرين الذين ينبهرون بالجمال، فيفتقدون الإرادة، كما كان حال "أوليس" ومن معه.

هذه الجزيرة الواحة، لا تزال فرادتها في المتوسّط تجلب السيّاح وتسحرهم._

عديد المعالم في جزيرة جربة لا تزال شاهداً على ماضي هذه الجزيرة العريق وتاريخها الحافل، مثل البرج الكبير وبرج القسطل . . .

الزائر سينبهر بمساجد هذه الجزيرة ذات المعمار المتميّز، التي مثّلت أيضًا منابر لمقاومة الغزاة. في قلب الجزيرة تقع الحارة الكبيرة والحارة الصغيرة، كدلالة على الوجود اليهودي في الجزيرة.

بيعة الغريبة:

الطائفة اليهودية تعيش في جزيرة جربة منذ القدم في تناغم كامل مع باقي السكّان. تملك بيعتها أحد أهمّ النصوص التوراتيّة في العالم، وهي أيضًا مزارًا لليهود أصيلي المغرب العربي.

البرج الكبير (برج غازي مصطفى):

تعود هذه القلعة المهيبة إلى القرن الخامس عشر، وقد صد على أسوارها القرصان درغوث هجمات الأسبان سنة 1560.

21 Summary and conclusion

The only conclusion necessary to *Thinking Arabic Translation* is a summing up of what the translator is supposed to be thinking *about*. The first thing to remember is that, whatever revision or editing the TT has undergone, it is the translator who is ultimately responsible for it. 'Thinking' translation implies a clear-sighted acceptance of this responsibility, but it also implies reducing the element of chance in how the TT will be received. If responsibility entails making decisions, applying the method presented in this book will enable the translator to make them intelligently and imaginatively enough to be confident of what the overall impact of the TT will be. This is why we have stressed throughout the course the need for a clearly formulated initial strategy and for clearly formulated decisions of detail rationally linked to the strategy.

One thing we hope to have shown is that no strategy can be assumed a priori. Formulating an appropriate strategy means assessing the salient features of a particular ST and of the particular circumstances in which it is to be translated. The crucial question then is: How do I decide which features are salient? What we have tried to do is equip the student translator with a way of answering this question, whatever the nature of the ST. For our purposes, the salient features of a text can be said to be its most *relevant* ones, those that have significant expressive function. Devising a strategy means prioritizing the cultural, formal, semantic, stylistic and genre-related properties of the ST according to two things: their relative textual relevance and the amount of attention they should receive in translation. The aim is to deal with translation loss in as rational and systematic a way as possible. This implies being prepared, if necessary, to lose features that have relatively little textual relevance in a given ST (e.g. alliteration in a technical text on mining), sacrificing less relevant textual details to more relevant ones. And, of course, it implies using compensation to restore features of high textual relevance that cannot be more directly rendered (e.g. a play on words in a literary text).

'Textual relevance' is thus a qualitative measure of how far particular properties of a text are responsible for its overall impact. Textually relevant features are those that stand out as making the text what it is. Because it is the translator who decides what is textually relevant, the decision is inescapably subjective but not necessarily damagingly so. A fairly objective test of textual relevance is to imagine that a particular textual feature is omitted from the text and to assess what difference this would make to the overall impact of the text. If the answer is 'little or none', the property in question has little textual relevance. But if omitting it would imply a loss in either the genre representative or the individual character of the text, then it has high textual relevance.

Developing a translation strategy by assessing textual relevance in an ST entails scanning the text for every *kind* of feature that might be relevant to producing an appropriate TT. For this scanning to be effective, it is vital to have in mind a systematic set of questions to ask of the ST. These questions correspond to the checklist of kinds of textual features introduced in the schema of textual matrices at the end of the Introduction to this book. The successive chapters of *Thinking Arabic Translation* tackle the sorts of translation issues lying behind the questions that need to be asked of texts. The idea is that the translator learns to ask the questions systematically, one after the other. As students working through the book will have found, it only takes a bit of practice to be able to do this very quickly and efficiently.

Some comments are called for on aspects of the relation between the schema of textual matrices and the book you have read. First, the 'cultural' matrix is different in focus from the others. Unlike the others, it does not list types of features that may *in themselves* be salient in the ST before the translator starts forming a strategy. Corresponding to Chapter 4, it lists types of features whose relevance can only be decided when the translator starts to form a strategy. That is, it draws attention to features that force the translator to choose between source-culture and target-culture elements. As such, it invites the translator to assess how far the culture specificity of ST features is textually relevant – this is why we have included it in the schema of textual matrices.

The other matrices are more straightforward reminders of what sorts of thing to look for when asking what the relevant features of a text are. Chapter 6, corresponding to the genre matrix, gives a set of parameters to apply in identifying textual genre preparatory to translation. Chapters 7, 8 and 14 correspond to the semantic matrix, introducing translation issues raised by the denotative, connotative and metaphorical properties of texts. Chapters 9–10 and 12–13 correspond to the formal matrix; the translation issues addressed here are the ones most typically raised by formal features of the texts. Chapter 11 corresponds to both the semantic and the formal matrices. Chapter 15 corresponds to the varietal matrix; the questions to ask here concern language variety and its translation implications. Chapters 16–20 then give a brief sample of the many subgenres from which professional translators will normally choose their specialities.

Some vital topics in this book do not figure as such in the schema of matrices. This is because they either apply universally from top to bottom of the schema or concern a translation operation, not a textual feature. Grammatical transposition, for example, is introduced in Chapter 2 but is of central relevance in every chapter and every practical. There is a case to be made for including it in the cultural matrix, but it is so pervasive that it is not useful to identify it as a discrete element in the matrix.

Another absolutely crucial topic is revising. Although this involves subtle analyses, which ultimately require consideration of all the matrices, it is introduced very early in the course, in Chapter 3, because it is a vital stage in the translation process and figures in several chapters and practicals. Similarly, compensation, introduced in Chapter 5, applies everywhere. More than anything else, successful compensation exemplifies the combination of imagination and rigour that is the mark of a good translator. However, even though compensation very often involves cultural and/or grammatical transposition, it is a translation operation, not a textual feature.

One preeminent translation issue is neither a textual feature nor a translation operation. This is the translation brief – why the text is being translated, on whose behalf and for what audience. As we suggest in Chapter 6, it is useful, for practical translation needs, to see the communicative purpose of a text as very closely linked with its genre. Genre, of course, *is* a textual feature and as such figures at the head of the schema at the end of the Introduction. The reason why it is placed at the top is precisely that it shares a prime importance with communicative purpose: the translation *process* will result in a translation *product,* a text having specific textual features and produced in order to meet a communicative demand. This demand, formulated by the work provider, is the translation brief. As the brief is neither a process nor a textual feature, it does not have a chapter to itself. But it has decisive importance, and that is why we have everywhere stressed its role as a parameter in assessing the relevance of ST and TT textual features, and why, in practicals, you have been asked to produce your TTs as if in response to a specific commission.

It should be remembered that the schema of matrices can be used to analyze any text, not just an ST. It can be applied to draft TTs, their features being systematically compared with those of the ST so as to see which details will be acceptable in the final version. Published TTs can also be evaluated in the same way. But whatever the text that is analyzed by this method, never forget that the watchword is *thinking* translation. This course encourages a methodical approach based on reasoned analysis of textual features and the translation problems they pose. But 'methodical' is not synonymous with 'mechanical' or 'automatic'. As we said in the Introduction, good translators know what they are doing: for thinking translation, there has to be a thinker, an individual person using flair and rigour to take creative, responsible decisions.

To sum up, then, we have tried to do two things in this course. First, to help you ask and answer the strategic questions we listed in Section 1.1: What is the message content of this particular ST? What are its salient linguistic features? What are its principal effects? What genre does it belong to, and what audience is it aimed at? What are the functions and intended audience of my translation? What are the implications of these factors? If a choice has to be made among them, which ones should be given priority? And second, to help you use intelligent, creative techniques for the translation operation, the battle with the problems of syntax, lexis, etc. that has to be fought in translating particular expressions in their particular contexts.

Finally, having completed the course, you may wish to find out about becoming a professional translator. Books giving advice for aspiring and practising translators include Jenner and Jenner (2010), Samuellson-Brown (2010) and McKay (2011). A nice summary is provided in Cragie, Higgins, Hervey and Gambarotta

(2016; chapters 17 and 19). A good place to find companies that offer in-house training and posts in Britain is the Institute of Translating and Interpreting's *ITI Bulletin,* published every two months. The *ITI Bulletin* offers membership, gained by examination and experience, which is valuable if you are thinking about progressing to freelance work. An equally valuable qualification is the Diploma in Translation of the Chartered Institute of Linguists; the examination for this is held every November, and several institutions offer preparatory courses for it, whether on site or by distance learning. For details of the services provided by these bodies, and the categories of membership they offer, you can visit their websites:

> Institute of Translation and Interpreting: www.ITI.org.uk
> Chartered Institute of Linguists: https://www.ciol.org.uk/

In the United States, several organizations offer certification and training in translation. These include:

> American Translators Association: www.atanet.org

The Wikipedia article 'List of translators and interpreters associations' includes information about associations in most English-speaking countries as well as Jordan in the Arab world:

> https://en.wikipedia.org/wiki/List_of_translators_and_interpreters_associations

If you decide that you do want a career in translation, remember that you must be enthusiastic and determined. Freelancing in particular can be precarious to begin with. Workflow is usually erratic, at least until you become established and have several work providers. But once you are established, you will be unlikely to want to return to a routine job, as the independence of freelancing makes for an interesting, varied and stimulating occupation. May the loss be with you!

Glossary

This glossary contains a list of all key terms used in the book, which are high-lighted in the main text in bold when they first occur. Immediately following each term, the glossary also includes a reference to the chapter or section in which the term is most fully discussed.

addition   see **translation by addition**.

affective meaning   (Section 8.4) a type of **connotative meaning**, affective meaning is the emotive effect worked on the addressee by using one particular **linguistic expression** rather than others that might have been used to express the same literal message.

alliteration   (Section 9.1.1) the recurrence of the same sound or sound cluster at the beginning of two or more words occurring near or next to one another; not to be confused with **onomatopoeia**.

allusive meaning   (Section 8.5) a type of **connotative meaning**; in a given **linguistic expression**, allusive meaning consists of invoking the meaning of an entire saying or quotation in which that expression figures. NB If a saying or quotation appears in full, then that is a case of *citation* (e.g. 'The darling buds of May are just beautiful this year'); *allusion* occurs when only part of the saying or quotation is used but that part evokes the meaning of the entire saying or quotation (e.g. 'Brrr . . . No darling buds yet awhile, I'm afraid').

anaphora   see **grammatical anaphora** and **rhetorical anaphora**.

associative meaning   (Section 8.3) the **connotative meaning** of a **linguistic expression** that takes the form of attributing to the referent certain stereo-typically expected properties culturally or linguistically associated with that referent.

associative repetition   (Section 7.2.3) **semantic repetition** involving at least two or more elements, one of which is a basic element, and the other, or others, of which are associated with that element. An example is المنهج التجريبي ومزاياه, translated literally as 'the experimental method, and its features' but more idiomatically as 'the features of the experimental method'.

assonance   (Section 9.1.1) the recurrence of a sound or sound cluster within words occurring near or next to one another; not to be confused with **onomatopoeia**.

attitudinal meaning   (Section 8.2) the **connnotative meaning** of a **linguistic expression** that takes the form of implicitly conveying a commonly held attitude or value judgement in respect to the referent of the expression.

background information   see backgrounding.

backgrounding   (Section 12.2.3) the conveying in a sentence of background information (i.e. information that is not central to the overall topic of a particular section of **text**). Background information is normally conveyed through the use of subordinate clauses.

back-translation   (Section 2.2.1) translation of a **TT** back into the **SL**; the resulting text will almost certainly not be identical to the original **ST**.

calque   (Section 4.3) a form of **cultural transposition** whereby a **TT** expression is closely modelled on the grammatical structure of the corresponding **ST** expression; a calque is like a moment of **exoticism**, although exoticism proper is a feature of whole texts or sections of texts. NB Calque is different from **cultural borrowing**, which imports the ST expression verbatim into the TT.

code-switching   (Section 15.6) the alternating use of two or more recognizably different language variants (varieties of the same language, or different languages) within the same **text**.

cognitive meaning   see **denotative meaning**.

coherence (adj. **coherent)**   (Section 13.2.1) the tacit, yet intellectually discernible, thematic or affective development that characterizes a **text** as distinct from a random sequence of unrelated sentences.

cohesion (adj. **cohesive)**   (Section 13.2.1) the explicit and transparent linking of sentences and larger sections of **text** by the use of overt linguistic devices, such as conjunctions or **grammatical anaphora**, that act as 'signposts' for the **coherence** of the text.

collocation   (Section 8.6) occurrence of one word in close proximity to another.

collocative meaning   (Section 8.6) the **connotative meaning** lent to a **linguistic expression** by the meaning of some other expression with which it frequently collocates (e.g. 'intercourse' almost invariably acquires a **connotation** of 'sex' from the common **collocation** of 'sexual intercourse'). Collocative meaning is thus the 'echo' of expressions that partner a given expression in commonly used phrases.

communicative translation   (Section 2.1.4, Section 4.6) a mode of **free translation** whereby **ST** expressions are replaced with their contextually/situationally appropriate cultural equivalents in the **TL** (i.e. the **TL** uses situationally apt target culture equivalents in preference to **literal translation**).

compensation   (Chapter 5) a technique of reducing **translation loss**; where any conventional translation, however **literal** or **free**, would entail an unacceptable translation loss, this loss is mitigated by deliberately introducing a less acceptable one, important **ST** effects being approximated in the **TT** through means other than those used in the ST. NB Unlike an unavoidable standard **grammatical transposition**, for example, compensation is not forced on the translator by the constraints of **TL** structure – it is a free, conscious, careful, *ad-hoc* choice.

compensation by splitting (Section 5.2) **compensation** that involves dividing up a feature carried in a relatively shorter stretch of the **ST** and spreading it over a relatively longer stretch of the **TT**; an *ad-hoc* choice, not a grammatical constraint.

compensation in kind (Section 5.2) **compensation** that involves using a different kind of textual effect in the **TT** from the one used in the corresponding part of the **ST**; an *ad-hoc* choice, not a grammatical constraint; most compensation is compensation in kind, whatever other features it has.

compensation in place (Section 5.2) **compensation** that involves a **TT** textual effect occurring at a different place, relative to the other features in the TT context, from the corresponding textual effect in the **ST** context; an *ad-hoc* choice, not a grammatical constraint.

connective (Section 13.2.1) an expression that links two sentences together (or, by extension, that links two clauses together) by making plain the relationship between those two sentences (or clauses).

connotation see **connotative meaning**.

connotative meaning (or connotation) (Chapter 8) the implicit overtones that a **linguistic expression** carries over and above its **denotative meaning**. NB The *overall meaning* of an expression is a compound of its denotative meaning plus these overtones and its contextual nuances.

cultural borrowing (Section 4.5) taking over an **SL** expression verbatim from the **ST** into the **TT**; the borrowed term may remain unaltered in form or it may undergo some degree of **transliteration**. NB Cultural borrowing differs from **calque** and **exoticism**, which do not use the **ST** expression verbatim but adapt it into the **TL**, however minimally.

cultural transplantation (Section 4.4) the highest degree of **cultural transposition** involving the wholesale deletion of source-culture details mentioned in the **ST** and their replacement with target-culture details in the **TT**.

cultural transposition (Chapter 4) any departure from **literal translation** that involves replacing **SL**-specific features with **TL**-specific features, thereby to some extent reducing the foreignness of the **TT**.

decisions of detail (Section 1.1) translation decisions taken in respect to specific problems of **lexis, syntax,** etc.; decisions of detail are taken in the light of previous **strategic decisions**, although they may well in their turn lead the translator to refine the original **strategy**.

denotative meaning (Chapter 7) the conventional range of referential meaning attributed to a **linguistic expression**. NB The *overall meaning* of an expression in context is compounded by this denotative meaning plus any **connotative meanings** and contextual nuances of the expression.

dialect (Section 15.4) a language variety with non-standard features of accent, vocabulary, **syntax** and **sentence** formation characteristic of the regional provenance of its users.

diglossia (Section 15.5.1) a situation where two very different varieties of a language co-occur throughout a community of speakers, each having a distinct range of social functions. The co-existence of Standard Arabic (فصحى) and colloquial Arabic (عامية) is an example of diglossia.

discourse level   (Section 13.2) the level of **textual variables** on which whole **texts** or sections of text are considered as **coherent** or **cohesive** entities.

editing   (Section 3.3) the final 'polishing' of a **TT**, following **revision**, and focusing on matching TT style and presentation to the expectations of the target readership.

exegetic translation   (Section 1.3) a style of translation in which the **TT** expresses and comments on additional details that are not explicitly conveyed in the **ST** (i.e. the TT is an explication, and usually an expansion, of the contents of the ST).

exoticism   (Section 4.2) the lowest degree of **cultural transposition**, importing linguistic and cultural features wholesale from the **ST** into the **TT** with minimal adaptation; exoticism generally involves multiple **calques**. NB Exoticism is different from **cultural borrowing**, which does not adapt ST material into the **TL** but quotes it verbatim.

foreground information   see **foregrounding**.

foregrounding   (Section 12.2.3) the conveying in a **sentence** of foreground information (i.e. information that is central to the overall topic of a particular section of **text**). Foreground information is normally conveyed through the use of main clauses.

free translation   (Section 2.1.3) a style of translation in which there is only a global correspondence between units of the **ST** and units of the **TT** – for example, a rough **sentence**-to-**sentence** correspondence, or an even looser correspondence in terms of even larger sections of **text**.

generalization   see **generalizing translation**.

generalizing translation (or generalization)   (Section 7.1.3) rendering an **ST** expression by a **TL hyperonym** (e.g. translating خال as 'uncle'). The **denotative meaning** of the **TT** expression is wider and less specific than that of the corresponding ST expression (i.e. a generalizing translation omits detail that is explicitly present in the **denotative meaning** of the ST expression).

genre (or text type)   (Chapter 6) a category to which, in a given culture, a given **text** is seen to belong and within which it is seen to share a type of communicative purpose with other texts – that is, the text is seen to be more or less typical of the genre.

gist translation   (Section 1.3) a style of translation in which the **TT** expresses only the gist of the **ST** (i.e. the TT is at the same time a synopsis of the ST).

grammatical anaphora   (Section 13.2.1) the replacement of previously used **linguistic expressions** by simpler and less specific expressions (such as pronouns) having the same contextual referent (e.g. 'I dropped the bottle, and *it* broke').

grammatical level   (Section 10.2) the level of **textual variables** on which are considered words, the decomposition of inflected, derived and compound words into their **morphological** constituent parts and the **syntactic** arrangement of words into phrases and **sentences**.

grammatical transposition   (Section 2.1.2) translating an **ST** expression having a given grammatical structure by a **TT** expression having a different grammatical structure containing different parts of speech in a different arrangement.

hyperonym or **superordinate** (Section 7.1.2) a linguistic expression whose **denotative meaning** includes, but is wider and less specific than, the range of denotative meaning of another expression (e.g. 'vehicle' is a hyperonym of 'car').

hyperonym-hyponym repetition (Section 7.2.2) repetition involving a **hyperonym** and a **hyponym**. An example is والباعة والمتجولون, translated literally as 'sellers and barrow-men' but more idiomatically as 'shopkeepers and barrow-men'.

hyperonymy-hyponymy (Section 7.1.2) the semantic relationship between a **hyperonym** and a **hyponym**; a lesser degree of semantic equivalence than **synonymy**.

hyponym (Section 7.1.2) a **linguistic expression** whose **denotative meaning** is included in, but is narrower and more specific than, the range of denotative meaning of another expression (e.g. 'lorry' is a hyponym of 'vehicle').

idiom (Section 2.1.5) a fixed expression whose meaning cannot be deduced from the **denotative meanings** of the words that constitute it (e.g. 'office politics is a *can of worms*', 'that's not my *cup of tea*', 'she's so *stuck up*').

idiomatic (Section 2.1.5) an idiomatic expression is one that is unremarkable, 'natural', 'normal' and completely acceptable in a given language. NB 'Idiomatic' is not synonymous with **idiomizing**.

ↄ **idiomizing translation** (Section 2.1.5) a relatively **free translation** that respects the **ST** message content but typically uses **TL idioms** or phonic and rhythmic patterns to give an easy read, even if this means sacrificing some semantic details or nuances of tone. NB 'Idiomizing' is not synonymous with **idiomatic**.

interlinear translation (Section 2.1.1) a style of translation in which the **TT** provides a literal rendering for each successive meaningful unit of the **ST** (including affixes) and arranges these units in the order of their occurrence in the ST, regardless of the conventional grammatical order of units in the **TL**.

intersemiotic translation (Section 1.2) translating from one semiotic system (i.e. system for communication) into another.

intertextual level (Section 13.3) the level of **textual variables** on which **texts** are considered as bearing significant external relationships to other texts (e.g. by allusion or imitation, or by virtue of **genre** membership).

intralingual translation (Section 1.3) the re-expression of a message conveyed in a particular form of words in a given language by means of another form of words in the same language.

lexical see **lexis**.

lexical item repetition (Section 10.2.4.1) repetition of the same lexical item (word) in close proximity.

lexicalized metaphor (Section 14.2.1) a metaphor whose meaning is relatively fixed and can therefore be given a dictionary definition.

lexis (adj. **lexical**) (Section 10.2.1) the totality of the words in a given language.

linguistic expression (Section 2.1.5) a self-contained and meaningful item in a given language, such as a word, a phrase or a **sentence**.

literal meaning see **denotative meaning**.

literal translation   (Section 2.1.2) an **SL**-oriented, word-for-word style of translation in which the **denotative meaning** of all words in the **ST** is taken as if straight from the dictionary, but the conventions of **TL** grammar are respected.

metaphor   (Chapter 14) a figure of speech in which two things (or ideas or emotions) are likened to each other by being fused together into a new, non-denotative compound (e.g. 'the army is a rampart against invasion', 'the red, red rose of my love', 'he blew a fuse'); metaphor is thus different from *simile*, in which the two things are compared but not fused together (e.g. 'the army is like a rampart against invasion', 'my love is like a red, red rose', 'it was as if he were an electrical installation with a fuse that blew').

morphology (adj. **morphological**)   (Section 10.2) the branch of grammar that concerns the arrangement of basic grammatical elements, *morphemes,* into words.

(near-)synonym repetition   see **synonym and near-synonym repetition**.

near-synonymy   (Section 7.1.5) a case of **hyperonymy-hyponymy** or semantic overlap that comes close to being **synonymy**.

non-lexicalized metaphor   (Section 14.2.1) a metaphor whose range of potential meanings is not definable and cannot therefore be given a dictionary definition.

omission   see **translation by omission**.

onomatopoeia   (Section 9.1.2) a word whose phonic form imitates a sound; not to be confused with **alliteration** or **assonance**.

parallelism   (Chapter 11) the use of at least two phrases whose **denotative meaning**, grammar and possibly phonic features are closely related to one another.

partial overlap   see **partially overlapping translation**.

partially overlapping translation (or partial overlap)   (Section 7.1.4) rendering an **ST** expression by a **TL** expression whose range of **denotative meanings** overlaps only partially with that of the ST expression (e.g. translating أستاذة as 'lecturer') – that is, the denotative meaning of the **TT** expression both *adds* some detail not explicit in the denotative meaning of the ST expression (she works in a university, not in a school) and *omits* some other detail that *is* explicit in the denotative meaning of the ST expression (she is female); partially overlapping translation thus simultaneously combines elements of **generalizing translation** and **particularizing translation**.

particularization   see **particularizing translation**.

particularizing translation (or particularization)   (Section 7.1.3) rendering an **ST** expression by a **TL hyponym** (e.g. translating ساعة as 'watch'). The **denotative meaning** of the TT expression is narrower and more specific than that of the corresponding ST expression (i.e. a particularizing translation adds detail to the TT that is not explicitly expressed in the ST).

pattern repetition   (Section 10.2.3.1) the repetition of the same pattern (فَعَل, فاعِل, مَفْعُول, فُعْل, مَفْعَلة, etc.) in two or more words in close proximity, as in أفكار وأحلام 'thoughts and dreams'.

phonic/graphic level   (Section 9.1) the level of **textual variables** on which is considered the patterned organization of sound segments (phonemes) in speech or of letters (graphemes) in writing.

phrase repetition   (Section 10.2.4.2) repetition of the same phrase in close proximity.

polysemy   (Section 7.1) a situation in which a lexical item has a range of different and distinct meanings or senses (e.g. *plain* = (i) 'clear', (ii) 'unadorned', (iii) 'tract of flat country'). A large proportion of a language's vocabulary is polysemic (or polysemous).

propositional meaning   see **denotative meaning**.

prosodic level   (Section 9.2) the level of **textual variables** on which are considered 'metrically' patterned stretches of speech within which syllables have varying degrees of *prominence* (e.g. through stress and vowel differentiation), varying degrees of *pace* (e.g. through length and tempo) and varying qualities of *pitch*.

reflected meaning   (Section 8.7) the **connotative meaning** given to a **linguistic expression** by the fact either that the form used calls to mind another **denotative meaning** of the same word or phrase (in which case reflected meaning is a function of **polysemy**) or another denotative meaning of another word or phrase that is the same or similar in form (in which case reflected meaning is a function of *homonymy*, or near-homonymy) – that is, reflected meaning is the 'echo' of another denotative meaning whose form sounds or is spelt the same or nearly the same as the form in question.

register   see **social register** and **tonal register**.

rephrasing   (Section 1.3) the exact rendering of the message content of a given **ST** in a **TT** that is radically different in form but that *neither* adds details that are *not* explicitly conveyed by the ST *nor* omits details that *are* explicitly conveyed in it; perfect rephrasing is rarely achieved.

revision   (Section 3.2) checking a **TT** against the **ST**; compare **editing**.

rheme   see **theme**.

rhetorical anaphora   (Section 13.2.1) the repetition for rhetorical effect of a word or words at the beginning of successive or closely associated clauses or phrases.

rhyme   (Section 9.1.1) rhyme occurs when, in two or more words, the last stressed vowel and all of the sounds that follow it are identical and in the same order.

root repetition   (Section 10.2.3.2) repetition of the same root in two or more words in close proximity, as in أطماع الطامعين.

semantic distancing   (Section 7.2.1) relaying both elements of an ST phrase involving **synonyms** or near-synonyms by different words in the TL but choosing TL words whose meanings are more obviously distinct than those of their ST counterparts. An example is 'astonishes and alarms' in the translation of يدهشه ويذهله as 'it astonishes and alarms him'.

semantic field   (Section 7.3) an area of meaning that is recognized as being fairly discrete (e.g. the semantic field of terms describing agricultural machinery).

semantic repetition   (Section 7.2) repetition of meaning, most basically involving the use of two (or more) **synonyms** or near-synonyms (see **synonym and near-synonym repetition**), but by extension involving **hyperonym-hyponym** repetition and **associative repetition**.

sentence   (Section 12.1) a complete, self-contained linguistic unit capable of acting as a vehicle for communication; over and above the basic grammatical units that it contains, a sentence must have sense-conferring properties of intonation or punctuation in English (although in Arabic some writing is without punctuation). It may in addition contain features of word order etc. that contribute to the overall meaning, or 'force', of the sentence.

sentential level   (Section 12.1) the level of **textual variables** on which **sentences** are considered.

SL   see **source language**.

social register   (Section 15.2.2) a style of speaking/writing from which relatively detailed stereotypical information about the social identity of the speaker/ writer can be inferred.

sociolect   (Section 15.3) a language variety with features of accent, vocabulary, **syntax** and **sentence** formation characteristic of the class and other social affiliations of it users.

source language (or **SL**)   (Section 1.1) the language in which the **ST** is expressed.

source text (or **ST**)   (Section 1.1) the **text** requiring translation.

ST   see **source text**.

strategic decisions   (Section 1.1) the initial decisions that constitute the translator's **strategy**; strategic decisions are taken, in the light of the nature of the **ST** and the requirements of the **TT**, as to which ST properties should have priority in translation; **decisions of detail** are taken in the light of these strategic decisions.

strategy   (Section 1.1) the translator's overall 'game plan', consisting of decisions taken before starting to translate in detail – for example, whether and when to give **denotative meaning** a higher priority than style, to address a lay readership or a specialist one, to maximize or minimize foreignness in the **TT**, to use formal language or slang, prose or verse, etc.

suffix repetition   (Section 10.2.3.3) repetition of the same suffix at the end of words in close proximity. An example is the repetition of ـات in أرض النبوءات والرسالات والخرافات والمخابرات.

superordinate   see **hyperonym**.

synonym   (Section 7.1.1) a **linguistic expression** that has exactly the same range of **denotative meaning** as one of more other linguistic expressions.

synonym and near-synonym repetition (also termed **(near-)synonym repetition**)   (Section 7.2.1) repetition of meaning involving two (or more) **synonyms** or near-synonyms. This is used in Arabic for emphasis and other purposes.

synonymy   (Section 7.1.1) the semantic relationship between **synonyms**; synonymy is the highest degree of semantic equivalence.

syntax   (adj. **syntactic**) (Section 10.2) the branch of grammar that concerns the arrangement of words into phrases and – with the addition of features of intonation, punctuation and word order – into **sentences**.

target language (or **TL**)   (Section 1.1) the language into which the **ST** is to be translated.

target text   (or **TT**) (Section 1.1) the **text** that is a translation of the **ST**.

temporal variety   (Section 15.5) a language variety defined by its standard use at a particular time period (e.g. Victorian English).

text   (Section 1.1) any stretch of speech or writing produced in a given language (or mixture of languages – cf. **code-switching**) and assumed to make a **coherent** whole on the **discourse level**.

text type   see **genre**.

textual variables   (Introduction) all of the demonstrable features contained in a **text** and that could, in another text, have been different (i.e. each textual variable constitutes a genuine *option* in the text).

theme (and rheme)   (Section 12.2.2) the organization of phrases and **sentences**, mainly through word ordering, into elements that have greater or lesser degrees of predictability.

TL   see **target language**.

tonal register   (Section 15.2.1) a style of speaking/writing adopted as a means of conveying an affective attitude of the speaker/writer to the addressee. The **connotative meaning** of a feature of tonal register is an **affective meaning**, conveyed by the choice of one out of a range of expressions capable of conveying a particular literal message (e.g. 'Excuse me, please' versus 'Shift your butt').

translation by addition   (Section 2.2.2.2) the addition to the **TT** of something that does not occur in the **ST**.

translation by omission   (Section 2.2.2.1) the omission from the **TT** of something that occurs in the **ST**.

translation loss   (Section 2.2.1) any feature of incomplete replication of the **ST** in the **TT**; translation loss is therefore not limited to the omission of ST features in the TT; where the TT has features not present in the ST, the addition of these also counts as translation loss. In any given TT, translation loss is inevitable on most levels of **textual variables** and likely on all. NB The translation losses in the TT are only significant in so far as they prevent the successful implementation of the translator's **strategy** for the TT.

transliteration   (Section 4.7) the use of **TL** spelling conventions for the written representation of **SL** expressions.

TT   see **target text**.

References

English-language references

Abdulla, A.K. 1994. 'The translation of style', in de Beaugrande, R., Shunnaq, A., and Heliel, M.H. (eds.). *Language, Discourse and Translation in the West and Middle East.* Amsterdam: John Benjamins. Pp. 65–72.

Abdul-Raof, H. 1998. *Subject, Theme and Agent in Modern Standard Arabic.* Surrey: Curzon Press.

Abrams, M.H. 1985. *A Glossary of Literary Terms.* 6th edn. Fort Worth and London: Harcourt Brace Jovanovich.

Alcarez, E. and Hughes, B. 2002. *Legal Translation Explained.* London and New York: Routledge.

Al-Harthi, N. 2011. *Argumentative Text Structures in English and Arabic.* PhD thesis: University of Salford.

Al-Hilali, T. and Khan, M.M. 1997. *Interpretation of the Meanings of the Noble Quran in the English Language.* Riyadh: مكتبة الدار.

Al-Jubouri, A. 1984. 'The role of repetition in Arabic argumentative discourse', in Swales, H. and Mustafa, H. (eds.). *English for Specific Purposes in the Arab World.* Aston: University of Aston Language Studies Unit. Pp. 99–117.

Allen, R. 2000. *An Introduction to Arabic Literature.* Cambridge: Cambridge University Press.

Al-Muhammad, M. 1993. *Patterns of Cohesion in Medical Textbook Discourse in Arabic and English.* PhD thesis: University of Surrey.

Al-Saleem, K.O. 2013. *The Translation of Financial Terms between English and Arabic with Particular Reference to Islamic Banking.* PhD thesis: University of Salford.

AlQinai, J. 2008. 'Mediating punctuation in English Arabic translation'. *Journal of Applied Linguistics* 5:1. Pp. 5–29.

Anderson, A. and Avery, C. 1995. 'Checking comes in from the cold', *ITI Bulletin*, February 1995.

Anderson, V. 1972. *The Brownie Cookbook.* London: Hodder & Stoughton.

Arberry, A.J. 1964. *The Koran Interpreted.* Oxford: Oxford University Press.

Asensio, R.M. 2003. *Translating Official Documents.* London and New York: Routledge.

Badawi, E. and Hinds, M.J. 1986. *A Dictionary of Egyptian Arabic.* Beirut: Librairie du Liban.

Baker, M. 2011. *In Other Words.* 2nd edn. London and New York: Routledge.

Bauer, L. 2003. *Introducing Linguistic Morphology.* Edinburgh: Edinburgh University Press.

Beeston, A.F.L. 1970. *The Arabic Language Today*. London: Hutchinson.

Beeston, A.F.L. 1974. 'Parallelism in Arabic prose'. *Journal of Arabic Literature* 5. Pp. 134–146.

Bello, S.A.A., Yasin, N.M., Hassan, R.B., and Bin, Z.K.M.Y. 2015. 'Al-'urf and its applicability in Islamic deposit products'. *Journal of Economics, Finance and Management* 1:2. Pp. 35–42.

Boothby, D. 1996. *Translation of Magazine Article on Tourism in Morocco*. BA translation project: University of Durham.

Brown, C. 1996. *Translation of Extracts from* مدينة البغي *by* عيسى بشارة. BA translation project: University of Durham.

Byrne, J. 2012. *Scientific and Technical Translation Explained*. London and New York: Routledge.

Calderbank, T. 1990. *Translation Strategies for an Arabic Political Argumentative Text*. Unpublished MA dissertation: University of Salford.

Conduit, N. 1998. *Translation of* الانتخابات البريطانية (from العالم magazine, May 1997). BA translation project: University of Durham.

Coupland, N. and Jaworski, A. 2001. 'Discourse', in Cobley, R. (ed.). *The Routledge Companion to Linguistics and Semiotics*. London and New York: Routledge. Pp. 134–148.

Cragie, S., Higgins, I., Hervey, S.G.J., and Gambarotta, P. 2016. *Thinking Italian Translation*. 2nd edn. Routledge: London and New York.

Cruse, D.A. 1986. *Lexical Semantics*. Cambridge: Cambridge University Press.

Crystal, D. 2008. *A Dictionary of Linguistics and Phonetics*. 5th edn. Oxford: Blackwell.

Delorenzo, Y.T. 1997. *A Compendium of Legal Opinions on the Operation of Islamic Banks*. London: Institute of Islamic Banking and Insurance.

Dickins, J. 2005. 'Two models for metaphor translation'. *Target* 17:2. Amsterdam: John Benjamins. Pp. 227–273.

Dickins, J. 2010a. 'List restructuring in Arabic/English translation'. *Babel* 56:5. Pp. 341–362.

Dickins, J. 2010b. 'Junction in English and Arabic: Syntactic, discoursal and denotative features'. *Journal of Pragmatics* 42:4. Pp. 1076–1136.

Dickins, J. 2012. 'The translation of culturally specific items', in Littlejohn, A. and Mehta, S.R. (eds.). *Language Studies: Stretching the Boundaries*. Cambridge: Cambridge Scholars Press. Pp. 43–60.

Dickins, J. 2014. 'Associative meaning and scalar implicature: A linguistic-semiotic account'. *Linguistica Online*: http://www.phil.muni.cz/linguistica/art/dickins/dic-003.pdf.

Dickins, J. and Watson, J.C.E. 1999. *Standard Arabic: An Advanced Course*. Cambridge: Cambridge University Press.

Dickson, J. 1999. *Translation of Three Speeches by* جمال عبد الناصر (n.d. In قال الرئيس. Cairo: دار الهلال). BA translation project: University of Durham.

Egyptian General Petroleum Corporation (الهيئة المصرية العامة للبترول). October 1999. *Petroleum*. Cairo: Egyptian General Petroleum Corporation.

Elewa, A. 2004. *Collocation and Synonymy in Classical Arabic: A Corpus-Based Study*. PhD thesis: University of Manchester Institute of Science and Technology.

El-Farahaty, H. 2015. *Arabic-English-Arabic Legal Translation*. London and New York: Routledge.

El-Serafi, I. 1994. *Translation of* عبد الرحمن زكي ابراهيم السكان .. عقبة ام مورد *by* (from العربي magazine, no. 420, November 1993). BA translation project: University of Durham.

Enríquez Raído, V. 2014. *Translation and Web Searching*. London and New York: Routledge.

Evans, J. 1996. *Translation of* مستقبل الأرض *by* امين حامد مشعل (from العربي magazine, no. 418, September 1993). BA translation project: University of Durham.

Evans, P. 1994. *Translation of* معهد الدراسات النغمية ومستقبل الموسيقى العراقية *by* قاسم حسين (n.d. In المؤسسة العربية للدراسات والنشر :Beirut. دراسات في الموسيقى العراقية). BA translation project: University of Durham.

Flacke, M. 1999. *Translation of* معيار استعادة مصر . . . مجابهة العدو الصهيوني *by* إنعام رعد (from شؤون فلسطينية magazine, no. 127, 1982). BA translation project: University of Durham.

Foreman, D. 1996. *Translation of* السيد ومراته في مصر *by* بيرم التونسي. BA translation project: University of Durham.

Gait, A.H. and Worthington, A.C. 2007. *A Primer on Islamic Finance: Definitions, Sources, Principles and Methods*. Wollongong: University of Wollongong.

Geeraerts, D. 1988. 'Where does prototypicality come from?' in Rudzka-Ostyn B. (ed.). *Topics in Cognitive Grammar.* (Current Issues in Linguistic Theory, 50). Amsterdam: John Benjamins. Pp. 207–229.

Gentzler, E. 2001. *Contemporary Translation Theories*. Bristol: Multilingual Matters.

Ghazala, H. 2004. 'Stylistic-semantic and grammatical functions of punctuation in English-Arabic translation'. *Babel* 50:3. Pp. 230–245.

Goatly, A. 1997. *The Language of Metaphors*. London: Routledge.

Graham, J.D. 1983. 'Checking, revision and editing', in C. Picken (ed.). *The Translator's Handbook*. London: Aslib. Pp. 99–105.

Gully, A. 1996. 'The discourse of Arabic advertising: Preliminary investigations'. *Journal of Arabic and Islamic Studies* 1:1. Pp. 1–49.

Halliday, M.A.K. and Hasan, R. 1976. *Cohesion in English*. London: Longman.

Hasan, R. 1983. 'Coherence and cohesive harmony', in Flood, J. (ed.). *Understanding Reading Comprehension*. Delaware: International Reading Association. Pp. 181–219.

Hatim, B. 1997. *Communication across Cultures: Translation Theory and Text Linguistics*. Exeter: University of Exeter Press.

Hatim, B. and Mason, I. 1990. *Discourse and the Translator*. London: Longman.

Hatim, B. and Mason, I. 1997. *The Translator as Communicator*. London: Longman.

Hermans, T. 1999. *Translation in Systems: Descriptive and Systemic Approaches Explained*. Manchester: St. Jerome Publishing.

Hervey, S.G.J. 1992. 'Registering registers'. *Lingua* 86. Pp. 189–206.

Hervey, S.G.J. and Higgins, I. 1992. *Thinking Translation: A Course in Translation Method: French to English*. London: Routledge.

Hetherington, M. 1996. *Translation of* لعبة الضفادع والعقارب في الاوسط عواصم الشرق *by* عادل حمودة (from روز اليوسف magazine, no. 3521, 1995). BA translation project: University of Durham.

Hitti, Y.K. and Al-Khatib, A. 1989. *Hitti's New Medical Dictionary*. Beirut: Librairie du Liban.

Holes, C. 1993. 'The uses of variation: A study of the political speeches of Gamal Abd Al-Nasir', in Eid, M. and Holes, C. (eds.). *Perspectives on Arabic Linguistics V.* Current Issues in Linguistic Theory, 101. Amsterdam: John Benjamins. 13–45.

Holes, C. 1995. *Modern Arabic: Structures, Functions and Varieties*. London and New York: Longman.

Hollander, J. 1981. *Rhyme's Reason: A Guide to English Verse*. New Haven and London: Yale University Press.

Holmes, J.S. 1988. *Translated!* Amsterdam: Rodopi.

Hourani, A. 1991. *A History of the Arab Peoples*. London: Faber and Faber.

Humphrys, S. 1999. *Translation of Extract from* العسكر والحكم في البلدان العربية by فؤاد اسحاق الخوري (1990. Beirut: Al-Saqi Books). BA translation project: University of Durham.

Ibn Khaldûn. [1958] 1967. *The Muqaddima: An Introduction to History* (3 vols.), Rosenthal, F. (trans.). (Bollingen Series XLIII). Princeton: Princeton University Press.

Irwin, R. 1999. *Night and Horses and the Desert: The Penguin Anthology of Classical Arabic Literature*. Harmondsworth: Penguin Books.

Ives, S. 1999. *Translation of* «الفصح» غارات حلف الاطلسي ستستمر اسابيع ولن تتوقف خلال *and* مدينة الموت (from الشرق الاوسط 2 April 1999). BA translation project: University of Durham.

Jakobson, R. 1971. *Selected Writings* (vol. II). The Hague: Mouton.

Jawad, H. 2007. 'Paraphrase, parallelism and chiasmus in literary Arabic: Norms and translation strategies'. *Babel* 50:3. Pp. 230–245.

Jawad, H. 2009. 'Repetition in literary Arabic: Foregrounding, backgrounding, and translation strategies'. *Meta* 54:4. Pp. 753–769.

Jenner, J. and Jenner, D. 2010. *The Entrepreneurial Linguist: The Business-School Approach to Freelance Translation*. Las Vegas: EL Press.

Johnson-Davies, D. [1968] 1985. *The Wedding of Zein*. Washington, DC: Three Continents Press.

Johnstone, B. 1991. *Repetition in Arabic: Paradigms, Syntagms and the Ecology of Language*. Amsterdam: John Benjamins.

Jones, L. 1999. *Translation of* الحاج رئيسا للكتائب بفارق ٧ أصوات (from النهار newspaper, 2 March 1999). BA translation project: University of Durham.

Karkouti, M. (ed.). September 2000. *Golden Falcon*/الصقر الذهبي (Inflight magazine of Gulf Air). Bahrain: Gulf Air Publicity and Promotions Dept.

Keats, J. 1958. *The Poetical Works of John Keats*, Garrod, H.W. (ed.). 2nd edn. London and New York: Longman.

Khafaji, R. 2001. 'Punctuation marks in original Arabic texts'. *Journal of Arabic Linguistics* 40. Pp. 7–24.

Khayat, M.H. and Anuti, J. 1983. *The Unified Medical Dictionary: English–Arabic–French*. Switzerland: Medlevant AG.

Koller, W. 1995. 'The concept of equivalence and the object of translation studies'. *Target* 7:2. Pp. 191–222.

Lane, A. 1994. *Translation of Extracts from* البخلاء by الجاحظ. BA translation project: University of Durham.

Lanham, R.A. 1991. *A Handlist of Rhetorical Terms*. 2nd edn. Berkley and Los Angeles: University of California Press.

Lee, D.Y.W. 2001. 'Genres, registers, text types, domains, and styles: Clarifying the concepts and navigating a path through the BNC jungle'. *Language Learning and Technology* 5:3. Pp. 37–72.

Leech, G. 1981. *Semantics*. Harmondsworth: Pelican Books.

Leith, D. 1983. *A Social History of English*. London: Routledge, Kegan and Paul.

McKay, C. 2011. *How to Succeed as a Freelance Translator*. Denver: Two Rat Press.

Merchant, A. 2000. *Translation of* صلابة حجر .. ورقة بشر ـ أكراد العراق .. الى اين (from العربي magazine, no. 494, March 2000). BA translation project: University of Durham.

Miller, A.G., Morris, M., and Stuart-Smith, S. 1988. *Plants of Dhofar, the Southern Region of Oman: Traditional, Economic, and Medicinal Uses*. Muscat: Diwan of the Royal Court of Oman.

Montalt, V. and González-Davies, M. 2007. *Medical Translation Step by Step*. London and New York: Routledge.

Monteil, V. 1960. *L'arabe Moderne*. Paris: Klincksieck.

Montgomery, A. 1994. *Translation of* نخلة على الجدول *by* الطيب صالح (1953. Beirut: دار العودة). BA translation project: University of Durham.

Montgomery, S. 2013. *Does Science Need a Global Language? English and the Future of Research*. Chicago: University of Chicago Press.

Morrey, D. 2000. *Translation of Extracts from* اسد بابل *by* نواف حردان. BA translation project: University of Durham.

Mossop, B. 2014. *Revising and Editing for Translators*. London and New York: Routledge.

Munday, J. 2016. *Introducing Translation Studies: Theories and Applications*. 4th edn. London and New York: Routledge.

Neubert, A. and Shreve, G.M. 1992. *Translation as Text*. Kent, OH: The Kent State University Press.

Newmark, P. 1981. *Approaches to Translation*. Oxford: Pergamon.

Newmark, P. 1988. *A Textbook of Translation*. New York: Prentice Hall International.

Nicholson, R.A. 1987. *Translations of Eastern Poetry and Prose*. London: Curzon Press; New Jersey: Humanities Press.

Nida, E. 1964. *Toward a Science of Translating*. Leiden: Brill.

Nyazee, I.A.K. 2006. *Al-Hidayah: A Classical Manual of Hanafi Law*. Bristol: Amal Press.

Pennington, S. 1999. *Translation of* المسلمون في أمريكا وتأثيرهم في المستقبل *by* الحاج داود الحاوي (from العربي magazine, no. 470, January 1998). BA translation project: University of Durham.

Pickthall, M.M.W. 1930. *The Meaning of the Glorious Qur'an*. London: Allen and Unwin.

Pinchuk, I. 1977. *Scientific and Technical Translation*. London: Andre Deutsch.

Pym, A. 2009. *Exploring Translation Theories*. London and New York: Routledge.

Qutbuddin, T. 2008. 'Khuṭba: The evolution of early Arabic oration', in Gruendler B. (ed.). *Classical Arabic Humanities in Their Own Terms*. Leiden: Brill. Pp. 176–273.

Ravin, Y. and Leacock, C. 2001. *Polysemy: Theoretical and Computational Approaches*. Oxford: Oxford University Press.

Reiss, K. [1977] 1989. 'Text-types, translation types and translation assessment', in Chesterman, A. (ed.). *Readings in Translation Theory*. Helsinki: Finn Lectura. Pp. 160–171.

Republic of Yemen, Ministry of Culture and Tourism. 1997. Arabic version: الجوف - مارب - شبوة; English Version: *Al-Jouf–Marib–Shabwa*. Sana'a: General Authority of Tourism.

Republic of Yemen, Ministry of Culture and Tourism. N.d. جزيرة السعادة .. سقطرى / *Socotra: the Island of Happiness*. Sana'a: General Authority of Tourism.

Roden, C. 1970. *A Book of Middle Eastern Food*. Harmondsworth: Penguin Books.

Rodwell, J.M. 1909. *The Koran*. London: Dent.

Rolph, D. 1995. *Translation of* الى بيروت الانثى مع حبي *by* نزار قباني (In الاعمال الشعرية الكاملة, vol II. 1981. Beirut: منشورات نزار قباني). BA translation project: University of Durham.

Saheeh International. 1997. *The Qur'an: Arabic Text with Corresponding English Meanings*. Jeddah: Abul-Qasim Publishing House.

Samuellson-Brown, G. 2010. *A Practical Guide for Translators*. 5th edn. Clevedon, Bristol, PA, Adelaide, SA: Multilingual Matters.

Sarwar, S.M. 1981. *The Holy Qur'an*. Elmhurst: Islamic Seminary.

Schäffner, C. 2004. 'Metaphor and translation: Some implications of a cognitive approach'. *Journal of Pragmatics* 36. Pp. 1253–1269.

Sekine, F. 1996. *Clause Combining in Contextual Grammar in English*. PhD thesis: University of Birmingham.

Shakir, M.H. 1983. *The Holy Qur'an*. New York: Tahrike Tarsile Qur'an.

Simpson, M.G. 2010. *Plant Systematics*. Amsterdam: Elsevier.

Snell-Hornby, M. 1988. *Translation Studies: An Integrated Approach*. Amsterdam: John Benjamins.

Somekh, S. 1991. *Genre and Language in Modern Arabic Literature*. Wiesbaden: Otto Harrassowitz.

Sperber, D. and Wilson, D. 1986. *Relevance: Communication and Cognition*. Oxford: Blackwell.

Stabler, H. 1999. *Translation of* تعريب التعليم في نهايات القرن العشرين *by* الشراح احمد يعقوب (from العربي magazine, no. 483, February 1999). BA translation project: University of Durham.

St John, J. 1999. *Translation of* حقل البنفسج *and* النار والماء *by* تامر زكريا (1973. In الحرائق دمشق. Damascus: الانوار دار). BA translation project: University of Durham.

Stoetzer, W. 1998. 'Prosody', in Meissner, J.M. and Starkey, P. (eds.). *Encyclopedia of Arabic Literature* (2 vols.). London: Routledge. Pp. 619–622.

Taylor, J.R. 1989. *Linguistic Categorization: Prototypes in Linguistic Theory*. Oxford: Clarendon.

Torresi, I. 2010. *Translating Promotional and Advertising Texts*. London and New York: Routledge.

Toury, G. 1980. *In Search of a Theory of Translation*. Tel Aviv: The Porter Institute for Poetics and Semiotics.

Toury, G. 1995. *Descriptive Translation Studies and Beyond*. Amsterdam: John Benjamins.

Tunnicliffe, S. 1994. *Translation of* الخيول *and* المرأة وتلك الرجل ذلك *by* عبد الربيعي مجيد الرحمن (1976). Tunis. BA translation project: University of Durham.

Turner, C. 1997. *The Quran: A New Interpretation*. Richmond: Curzon.

van Gelder, G.J. 2000. 'Some brave attempts at generic classification in premodern Arabic literature', in Roest, B. and de Varennes, F. (eds.). *Aspects of Genre of and Type in Pre-Modern Literary Cultures*. Groningen: Styx. Pp. 15–28.

Versteegh, K. 2009. 'Sound symbolism', in Versteegh, K., Eid, M., Elgibali, A., Woidich, M., and Zaborski, A. (eds.). *Encyclopedia of Arabic Language and Linguistics* (vol. 4). London: Routledge. Pp. 282–290.

Wehr, H. 1974. *A Dictionary of Modern Written Arabic*, Cowan, J.M. (ed.). 3rd edn. Beirut: Librairie du Liban.

Yusuf Ali, A. 1938. *The Holy Qur'an: Translation and Commentary*. Lahore: Sh. Muhammad Ashraf Publishers.

Arabic-language references

ادريس, يوسف. 1954. مشوار (short story), in ليالي أرخص (collection). Cairo: مصر مكتبة.

ادريس, يوسف. 1971. الرحلة (short story), in لحم من بيت (collection). Cairo: مصر مكتبة.

ادريس, يوسف. N.d.a. شيخة الشيخ (short story), in الدنيا آخر (collection). Cairo: مصر مكتبة.

ادريس, يوسف. N.d.b. السماء من طبلية (short story), in شرف حادثة (collection). Cairo: مصر مكتبة.

N.d. Hamamat: الخليج مطبعة. ٢٤ طريقة إعداد .. تونسية أكلات.

الأسد, الدين ناصر. 1997. والآخر نحن. Amman: والنشر للدراسات العربية المؤسسة.

Amman. العهد على .. الأردن. 12 December 1988. الرأي (newspaper).

London. البريطانية الانتخابات. May 1997. العالم (magazine).

الغتيت, علي محمد. 1974. السياسية والزعامة العبقرية. Cairo: الشعب دار.

الشرق دار. 2010. Beirut. والإعلام اللغة في المنجد.

المرغيناني, بكر أبي بن علي الدين برهان. 2000. المبتدي بداية شرح: الهداية. Lebanon:لبنان العالمية الكتب دار.

المهدوي, اسماعيل طارق. 1986. المناورة مذبح على المسلمون الاخوان. Beirut: آزال دار.

امين, مصطفى. 21 September 1982. فكرة, in الأوسط الشرق (newspaper). London.

تامر, زكريا. 1973. حقل البنفسج and النار والماء (short stories), in دمشق الحرائق (collection). Damascus: دار الانوار.

حردان, نواف. 1997. أسد بابل. Beirut: بيسان للنشر والتوزيع.

حسن, يوسف فضل. 1986. الشلوخ. Khartoum: Khartoum University Press.

حمودة, عادل. لعبة الضفادع والعقارب في عواصم الشرق الاوسط. 4 December 1995, in روز اليوسف (magazine), no. 3521. Cairo.

خوري, فؤاد اسحاق. 1990. الحكم والعسكر في البلدان العربية. London: Al-Saqi Books.

سيبويه, عمر بن عثمان. 1988. الكتاب, ed. by عبد السلام هارون. Beirut: عالم الكتب.

الطيب, صالح. N.d. عرس الزين. Beirut: دار العودة.

الطيب, صالح. 1953. نخلة على جدول. Beirut: دار العودة.

عبد الرحمن, أسعد. 1990. السياسة الأمريكية تجاه فلسطين, in الرأي (newspaper). Amman.

عبد الناصر, جمال. N.d. كفاحنا للقومية العربية (speech), in قال الرئيس. Cairo: دار الهلال.

قباني, نزار. 1981. الأعمال الشعرية الكاملة. Beirut: منشورات نزار قباني.

قطب, سيد. 1990. معالم في الطريق. Cairo and Beirut: دار الشروق.

محفوظ, نجيب. N.d. الأعمال الكاملة (vol. 7) (الجزء السابع). Beirut: المكتبة العلمية الجديدة.

مراد, أحمد. 2012. الفيل الأزرق. Cairo: دار الشروق.

مشعل, امين حامد. 1993. مستقبل الارض, in العربي (magazine), no. 418. Kuwait.

مطر, فؤاد. 1984. (5 .vols) سقوط الإمبراطورية اللبنانية. Beirut: دار القضايا.

منصور, أنيس. 1964. حفنة تراب (short story), in بقايا كل شيء (collection). Cairo: دار الشروق.

نعمان, عصام. 1979. إلى أين يسير لبنان. Beirut: دار الطليعة للطباعة والنشر.

نعيمة, ميخائيل. 1958. النور والديجور. Beirut: مؤسسة نوفل.

Index

Arabic